DUMBARTON OAKS
MEDIEVAL LIBRARY

Jan M. Ziolkowski, General Editor

ACCOUNTS OF MEDIEVAL

CONSTANTINOPLE

DOML 24

Accounts of
Medieval
Constantinople

The *Patria*

Translated by

ALBRECHT BERGER

DUMBARTON OAKS
MEDIEVAL LIBRARY

HARVARD UNIVERSITY PRESS
CAMBRIDGE, MASSACHUSETTS
LONDON, ENGLAND
2013

Library of Congress Cataloging-in-Publication Data
Accounts of medieval Constantinople : the Patria / translated by Albrecht
Berger.
    pages cm. — (Dumbarton Oaks medieval library ; 24)
    English and Greek in parallel text on facing pages.
    Includes bibliographical references and index.
    ISBN 978-0-674-72481-5 (alk. paper)
    1. Istanbul (Turkey) — History — To 1453. 2. Greeks — Turkey — Istanbul —
History. I. Berger, Albrecht, 1957– translator. II. Scriptores originum
Constantinopolitanarum. III. Scriptores originum
Constantinopolitanarum. English.
    DR729.S4413 2013
    939′.8618 — dc23   2013005027

Contents

Introduction

The four books now usually called the *Patria* of Constantinople are a collection of short notes and anecdotes about the statues and buildings of the city. The compilation also includes a historical introduction, which begins with the legendary origins of the city of Byzantion[1] in the seventh century BCE and ends with the refoundation of the city by Constantine the Great in the fourth century CE. In its present form the *Patria* was compiled in the late tenth century, but it contains large amounts of older material, which date between the sixth and ninth centuries.

THE LITERARY GENRE OF *PATRIA* IN ANTIQUITY

The word *Patria* means "history of a native place" or "local history." In fact, this designation fits only the first book, which contains the legendary history of Byzantion and the earliest years of Constantinople.[2]

The genre of local history, that is, the history of individual cities and countries as opposed to universal history, existed already in the Hellenistic period. At that time local histories of cities, such as Athens, became popular, and following the campaigns of Alexander the Great in 334–323 BCE, numerous works were written about the newly acces-

sible regions in the Middle East. Known by their titles, but lost to us are, among others, the works of Teukros of Kyzikos and Alexander of Miletos, both authors of the first century BCE; their works included texts about many cities and regions in the eastern Mediterranean and beyond.

When the Roman Empire gained control over the Near East and Egypt in the first century BCE, the production of local histories began to decrease, but still continued to the second century CE, with works on Egypt, the Parthians, and the Jews, the most famous of them being the *Jewish War* and the *Jewish Antiquities* of Flavius Josephus. At the same time, in a continuing tradition from Hellenistic times, cities and regions of the Orient tried to establish a connection to Greek culture by fitting their own history into the context of Greek history. One popular way to achieve this was to claim that a Greek hero such as Perseus or Herakles founded a city.[3]

It is not until the fourth century CE that the name *Patria* was given to such more or less legendary histories. But of all the works mentioned by later sources—such as the *Bibliotheke* of patriarch Photios in the ninth century, and the *Souda,* a Byzantine dictionary, in the tenth—only one has come down to us, and that is Hesychios's *Patria* of Byzantion.

HESYCHIOS OF MILETOS

Hesychios of Miletos, surnamed Illoustrios, lived in Constantinople in the sixth century CE, during the reign of Justinian (527–565).[4] Of the works attributed to him by the ninth-century patriarch Photios in codex 69 of his *Bibliotheke,* only fragments have survived, the longest of them be-

ing his *Patria* of Byzantion, a history from the earliest begin-
nings of the city down to the time of Constantine the Great,
which probably formed an excursus in his World History at
the beginning of its sixth and last book.[5] These *Patria* of
Byzantion have been completely integrated into Book 1 of
the *Patria* of Constantinople.

Although Hesychios's account is full of allusions to ancient Greek mythology and shows no sign that its author
was a Christian, his religious affiliation is still disputed.

THE *PARASTASEIS SYNTOMOI CHRONIKAI*

A collection of notes on the buildings and monuments of
Constantinople can first be found in the so-called *Parastaseis syntomoi chronikai* ("brief historical notes"),[6] a text
apparently composed by a number of anonymous authors
throughout the eighth century, beginning in the reign of Justinian II (685–695, 705–711).[7] It consists of eighty-nine chapters of very different lengths, ranging from short dictionary-
like entries to lengthy stories and anecdotes.

The *Parastaseis* is written in an awkward and often ellipti-
cal style, which makes its interpretation rather difficult. As
discussed below, most of it later passed into Book 2 of the
tenth-century *Patria,* either directly or through an inter-
mediary source. The obvious smoothing and omissions in
the text, which were made during the process of excerpting,
strongly suggest that the *Parastaseis* did not have, in its original form, a linguistically more refined shape, and that its de-
plorable present state cannot be ascribed to errors of the
later tradition.[8]

The *Parastaseis* is mainly concerned with the interpretation of the works of ancient Greek and Roman sculpture

that were still on display in Constantinople in the eighth century. Instead of finding detailed and objective descriptions of these statues, however, we are confronted with anecdotal and fantastic narratives about them, sometimes also with allegorical interpretations. Given that under the influence of Christianity the style and subject matter of art had changed fundamentally since the founding era of Constantinople, it is understandable that the naturalistic marble and bronze statues, which were often larger than life and dressed in ancient costumes or even nude, must have made a strange and threatening impression on the inhabitants of the city, at least on those without a traditional education. Obviously these statues represented pagans or pagan gods, and since the ancient polytheistic religion was now considered as idol worship that also included magical practices, it was often believed that the statues were enchanted, that is, that they were imbued with a protective spell or an apocalyptic prophecy, or that they were animated and therefore—in most such cases—dangerous.[9] Although this perception can occasionally be found already in the sixth century, for instance in the chronicle of John Malalas, it is only in the *Parastaseis* that it has been systematically expanded and become the object of a whole literary work.

Recently, Benjamin Anderson has argued that the *Parastaseis* represents the endeavor of a group of bureaucrats from old Constantinopolitan families who claimed that they alone were able to understand the real meaning of the statues of Constantinople, thus forming a sort of xenophobic opposition to ambitious newcomers to the imperial service.[10]

The *Parastaseis* is, in many respects, a very odd work.

Among its oddities are, on the one hand, a strange interest in the pagan emperors shortly before Constantine, such as Carus (282–283) and Numerian (283–284), and a surprising lack of interest in the person of Justinian (527–565), on the other, as the Nika Riot in 532 and the emperor's subsequent building activities are ignored altogether.

THE *DIEGESIS* ABOUT THE CONSTRUCTION OF HAGIA SOPHIA

Another "patriographic" text in the wider sense of the word is the *Diegesis* (narrative) about the construction of Hagia Sophia in the age of Justinian I (532–565).[11] In this story, truth and legend are so closely intertwined that they can hardly be separated from each other. Some of the persons appearing are historical, others are obviously invented, and the history of the construction is described in a completely legendary way.

The date of composition of the *Diegesis* is still disputed. Certain parts of it may go back to a time shortly after the church was built, for a number of historical persons, such as the *magistros* and treasurer Strategios, the *quaestor* Basilides, and the prefect Theodoros (correctly Theodotos), were unknown in later times. In the form known to us today, however, the text cannot predate the late ninth century.[12]

THE *PATRIA* OF CONSTANTINOPLE

These three texts, i.e., the *Patria* of Hesychios of Miletos, the *Parastaseis,* and the *Diegesis,* were finally joined in the late tenth century, together with various other materials, in the

work today known as the *Patria* of Constantinople, and
which is translated here.[13]

This *Patria* of Constantinople in four books is apparently
the work of a single, anonymous author. This is apparent
from various cross-references between its different parts,
including a number of time calculations in Books 2, 3, and 4,
which do not originate from an older source and are mostly
calculated according to a uniform system, in which the foundation of Constantinople is set in the twelfth year of Constantine's reign, 317, instead of the traditional date of 324,
and for every emperor only one fixed date is used.[14] Two of
these calculations have "today" as their end point,[15] which
leads us to the year 989/90 for the completion of the work.

Book 1 includes, in its first part, the complete text of Hesychios's *Patria,* with the history of the city of Byzantion from
its foundation by the legendary king Byzas to the new foundation under Constantine.[16] At the end of this part, some
new chapters are added about the alleged building activities
of the emperor Severus[17] and about the churches built by
Constantine.[18]

The second part of Book 1 is a greatly expanded paraphrase of Hesychios's short final chapters, in which Constantine's refounding of the city is described.[19] Here, several
new legends are introduced that actually emerged long after
the time of Hesychios and were still unknown to the *Parastaseis,* including that twelve persons helped Constantine
when he built his city and that he forced twelve noblemen
or senators to come with him from Rome and settle in his

new town. In addition, the legendary figure of the chamberlain Euphratas, who allegedly converted Constantine to Christianity, is introduced here. The only other source in which both this person and Constantine's otherwise unknown war against the Persians are mentioned is a contemporaneous hagiographical *Life of Constantine,*[20] where it is also claimed that a church of the Mother of God was founded by Euphratas near the square called Leomakellon.[21] Obviously a church surnamed "of Euphratas" actually existed in Constantinople, but as its founder was unknown in later times, a fictitious Life was composed that made him Constantine's counselor, with the intention to glorify his foundation.

Some names and events mentioned in this second part of Book 1 clearly allude to political events of the tenth century, such as the insurrection of Constantine Doukas in 913 and Emperor John I Tzimiskes's campaigns against the Bulgarians in 971.[22]

Book 2, perhaps originally entitled "On Statues,"[23] consists of 110 entries, of which more than half are taken from the *Parastaseis.* This happened in two different ways: on the one hand, from a version of the *Parastaseis* that was very similar to the text of its only surviving manuscript, and on the other, via an intermediate source,[24] which contained, in addition to the excerpts from the *Parastaseis,* excerpts about words beginning with the letter *alpha.* These excerpts are taken from the works of the sixth-century author John Lydos and have—with one exception—nothing to do with

Constantinople, but they are nevertheless included in Book 2, of which they form 15 percent. As a result, only about a third of Book 2 has been excerpted from other sources[25] or was written by the editor himself.

In the newly added entries, a great number of events and persons are mentioned that can be dated after the probable time of origin of the *Parastaseis:* the Russians played a larger role in the consciousness of the Byzantines only after their failed attack on Constantinople in 860 (chap. 47); the ninth-century emperors Michael I Rhangabe (811–813) and Theophilos (829–842) appear on the stage, as well as the chamberlain Basil, a well-known political figure in the second half of the tenth century who was finally overthrown in 985, just a few years before the *Patria* was composed.[26]

A continuous topographic order cannot be discerned in Book 2; only chapters 41–58, which are taken from the *Parastaseis,* follow the path of the main street (Mese) from the city center to the Golden Gate.

Two manuscripts of the *Patria* also contain, as an appendix to Book 2, a short synopsis of the Ecumenical Councils, which is here included in the translation for the sake of completeness.

Book 3 bears the title "On Buildings" and consists of 215 entries, which are, however, mostly shorter than those in Book 2.[27] In contrast to Book 2, there is no use of an older main source such as the *Parastaseis.* Persons and events of the ninth and tenth centuries therefore appear here much more often: the iconoclast emperors Leo III (717–741) and Constantine V (741–775) are mentioned several times and vilified

polemically; Emperor Theophilos (829–842) and his son, Michael III (842–867), play a major role, as do Michael's murderer and successor Basil I (867–886) and Basil's son Leo VI (886–912), while Romanos I Lekapenos (920–944) is mentioned only twice. The emperors of the redactor's own time, Constantine VII Porphyrogennetos (944–959), John I Tzimiskes (969–976), and Basil II (976–1025), appear only in a sort of appendix at the end of the book.

The first twenty chapters of the book constitute a list of alleged or real buildings of Constantine. In chapters 21–29a, 30–39a, 40–75, and 86–99, four topographically arranged sightseeing routes follow, with a number of dispersed entries in between. The second part of the book is formed by entries in no particular order, including lists of palaces, city gates, monasteries within and outside of Constantinople, and so forth.

It seems that the author or redactor of 989/90 compiled his entries here and in the new parts of Book 2 from a number of chronicles, including older collections of excerpts and other sources, many of which cannot be identified today. He also seems to have invented many anecdotes himself, for the simple reason that no usable information could be found in his sources. Often the stories told have nothing to do with the buildings to which they have been attached, as in the case of the brilliant anecdote about the righteous emperor Theophilos and the church To Karabitzin in 3.28. Some narratives that explain the name of a building are based on paretymology using an intentionally distorted form of the name, as in the cases of the Tetrapylon and the Mesomphalon in 2.54 and 55. Also, people are frequently associated with places by the claim that their house

had been in that location, and sometimes buildings are even presented as resulting from a conversion of a house, such as the church of the Mother of God of Eugenios in 3.21, the homes for old people of Artabasdos and Isidoros in 3.63 and 121, and the bath of Germanos in 3.141.

Book 4, finally, consists of the *Diegesis* about the construction of Hagia Sophia, which has been shortened by the omission of some chapters[28] but expanded again at the end by some additional chapters. These include an anecdote about the alleged architect of the church, Ignatios, and one about the church of the Apostles, which is, curiously enough, not treated elsewhere in the *Patria*. The end of the book is formed by an appendix of some supplementary entries unrelated to Hagia Sophia and the church of the Apostles.

An obvious problem of the *Patria* as compiled in 989/90 was that most entries in Books 2 and 3, which contain the bulk of the information about the monuments and buildings, are not listed in a topographical order. About ninety years later, therefore, an anonymous redactor produced another version of the text, in which Books 2 and 3 were rearranged topographically into three sightseeing tours: the first of them goes along the main street, the Mese, from the August(a)ion (2.15) to the Golden Gate (2.58); the second tour is divided into two sections, one around the Akropolis, and one leading from the Anemodoulion (2.46) to the Blachernai (3.75), with an inserted complementary route from the Forum Tauri (2.38) to the monasteries in the northwest (3.107, 108);

and the third tour leads from the Hippodrome (2.73–79) to the Church of Aimilianos in the southwest (3.88). But still an unordered appendix follows with monasteries within the city and buildings outside the walls. Although this topographical version is much more strictly ordered than the one of 989/90,[29] it is transmitted in relatively few manuscripts.

The *Patria* as a Historical Source

The first topographical description of Constantinople is the so-called *Notitia urbis Constantinopolitanae,* a short text in Latin from the years around 425, in which the fourteen regions of the city are described and the buildings in them listed.[30] After it, no dedicated source about the urban topography of Constantinople is known before the *Patria* was composed in the late tenth century. In the centuries between, building activities of emperors are occasionally described in chronicles and works of historians, and the tenth-century *Synaxarion,* the liturgical calendar of the Constantinopolitan church, mentions the churches at which the commemorations of the saints honored on each day were celebrated.

Only the *Patria,* however, presents a more or less complete and coherent picture of the city as it was in the middle Byzantine period. Despite its notorious historical inexactness and occasionally silly anecdotes, and the fact that it was composed as a piece of light popular fiction rather than as a handbook about the city as it was in the late tenth century, the *Patria* is still the most complete source about the monuments of the city that has come down to us. Later reports of foreign pilgrims, such as the anonymous Englishman in

the late 1070s[31] or the Russians, beginning with Anthony of Novgorod in 1200,[32] are shorter and very much concentrated on churches, monasteries, and the cult of relics, the latter a phenomenon that plays almost no role in the *Patria*.[33]

The *Patria* of Constantinople is a fascinating and almost unique source for the "popular" reception of Constantinople by its inhabitants, with historical notes, anecdotes, and legends attached to the single buildings and objects. The text was widespread in Byzantium and is transmitted by more than sixty manuscripts, either complete or in excerpts.[34] All in all, we may state that the *Patria*, despite its massive problems of historical reliability, is still one of our main sources for the urban history of medieval Constantinople.

Note on the Translation

Of the whole corpus of the *Patria*, only Hesychios's text quoted in Book 1 (chaps. 1–36) and parts of the *Diegesis* (Book 4) have previously been translated into English, by Anthony Kaldellis and Cyril Mango, respectively.[35] For Book 2 I have also consulted the translation of the *Parastaseis* by Averil Cameron and Judith Herrin.[36]

Other translations into other modern languages are my own, of Books 1 (chaps. 51–73), 2, and 3 into German,[37] and that of Gilbert Dagron, of the *Diegesis* (= Book 4) into French.[38]

I am most grateful to Benjamin Anderson, who revised my draft translation, and I give special thanks to Alice-Mary Talbot and Charles Barber, members of the DOML edito-

rial board, who thoroughly reviewed the translation and brought it into its present shape.

1 Following the conventions of Byzantine scholarship, in this volume "Byzantion" refers to the city that is also called Constantinople, while "Byzantium" refers to the Byzantine Empire as a whole and to Byzantine civilization.

2 For the titles of the four books, see p. xii–xvi below.

3 On this phenomenon, see Scheer, *Mythische Vorväter.* An example quoted by the *Patria* is 2.85.

4 Kaldellis, "The Works and Days."

5 Hesychios's *Patria* can be dated by a quotation taken from it (chap. 36 = Book 1, chap. 34 of the *Patria* of Constantinople) in the work *About the Months* of John Lydos (1.12), which was probably written after 540; see Maas, *John Lydus,* 10. For a translation with a more detailed commentary on his text, see Kaldellis, "Hesychios of Miletos," in *Brill's New Jacoby.*

6 Modern edition, with text and translation: Cameron and Herrin, *Constantinople in the Early Eighth Century.* For the interpretation of the text, see now Anderson, "Classified Knowledge."

7 The date is still a matter of discussion: Averil Cameron and Judith Herrin argued for an early eighth-century date; Alexander Kazhdan, reviewing their edition in *Byzantinische Zeitschrift* 80 (1987): 400–403, argued for a late eighth- or early ninth-century date.

8 The only surviving manuscript, Paris. gr. 1336, dates to the eleventh century.

9 James, "Pray Not to Fall."

10 Anderson, "Classified Knowledge." A good example of this attitude is chap. 64, which has passed into the *Patria* as 2.82.

11 Modern editions: Preger, in *Scriptores,* vol. 1; Vitti, *Die Erzählung.* For translations into modern languages, see below.

12 Although no figural mosaics are mentioned in the building, which would suggest a date before the final establishment of the cult of images in 843, the existence of the saints' figures in the tympana, which can safely be dated after the year 886, is apparently presupposed by the text; see the notes to 4.5.

13 Modern edition: Preger, *Scriptores,* vol. 2.

14 1.37, 41, 42, 53, 54–56; 2.54, 55, 59; 3.2, 9, 13, 17, 20, 22–24, 30–32, 37, 40, 41, 59, 62, 63, 81, 125, 142, 152, 155, 172, 182; 4.1, 30.

15 3.152, and 4.30.

16 This is chaps. 1–42 of the Preger edition, on pp. 1–18.

17 Severus, who actually destroyed the city in 196 CE and did not, contrary to the legend, restore it thereafter, is portrayed here as a second founder after Byzas; on which see Dagron, *Constantinople imaginaire,* 62–74.

18 Hesychios's *Patria* has also been incorporated completely into a hagiographical *Life of Constantine,* which was written at roughly the same time as our text; see Opitz, "Die Vita Constantini," 568–76. There too, the text has been "Christianized" at the end by mentioning the Forum and its relics (as here in 2.20), and a number of churches, but this is done, it seems, independently from the *Patria* of Constantinople.

19 This is chaps. 37–73 of the Preger edition, on pp. 135–50.

20 See Halkin, "Une nouvelle vie de Constantin."

21 On which see below, 3.105.

22 See the notes to chaps. 70 and 71 below.

23 The title given in Preger's edition, "The *Patria* of Constantinople: On Statues, together with a Chapter on Adiabene," is contained only in one manuscript family and is probably secondary.

24 Called "x" by Preger, "Beiträge."

25 These sources also include Book 3; 2.62 and 63 are doublets to 3.37 and 91, while 2.72 is a doublet to 3.83.

26 In chaps. 101, 64 and 65, and 71.

27 This book is found on pp. 214–83 of the Preger edition.

28 For the sake of completeness, the Greek text presented and translated here is that of the independently transmitted complete version of the *Diegesis,* found on pp. 74–108 of the Preger edition (chaps. 1–29) and pp. 284–89 (chaps. 30–35).

29 For an analysis, see Berger, *Untersuchungen,* 87–147. The text of the topographical versions is almost identical to the version of 989/90 and differs only in the arrangement of entries. Preger therefore only added a table in an appendix that contains the numbers and titles of the entries.

30 Edited in Seeck, *Notitia dignitatum,* 227–43; analyzed by Berger, "Regionen und Straßen," 350–87.

31 Ciggaar, "Une description de Constantinople."

32 Still unavailable in a reliable modern edition, it has been translated into French by Ehrhard, "Le livre du pèlerin"; for the pilgrims of the late Byzantine period, see Majeska, *Russian Travelers.*

33 One of the exceptions, 3.148, is remarkably similar to the corresponding chapter in the English pilgrim's report.

34 See below in the Note on the Text, p. 281.

35 Kaldellis, "Hesychios of Miletos," in *Brill's New Jacoby;* Mango, *The Art,* 96–102; see also Mango, "Byzantine Writers," 45–50.

36 Cameron and Herrin, *Constantinople in the Early Eighth Century.*

37 Berger, *Studien.*

38 Dagron, *Constantinople imaginaire,* 191–314.

BOOK ONE

Πάτρια Κωνσταντινουπόλεως κατὰ Ἡσύχιον Ἰλλούστριον

[1] Δύο καὶ ἑξήκοντα καὶ τριακοσίων ἀπὸ τῆς Αὐγούστου Καίσαρος μοναρχίας διεληλυθότων ἐνιαυτῶν τῇ πρεσβυτέρᾳ Ῥώμῃ καὶ τῶν πραγμάτων αὐτῆς ἤδη πρὸς πέρας ἀφιγμένων Κωνσταντῖνος ὁ Κωνσταντίου παῖς ἐπιλαβόμενος τῶν σκήπτρων τὴν νέαν ἀνίστησι Ῥώμην ἴσην αὐτὴν τῇ πρώτῃ χρηματίζειν προστάξας. Ἤδη μὲν γὰρ καὶ τυράννοις καὶ βασιλεῦσι χρησαμένην πολλάκις ἀριστοκρατίας τε καὶ δημοκρατίας πολιτευσαμένην τρόπῳ τέλος ἐπὶ τὸ προκείμενον <συνέβη> ἐξενηνοχέναι μέγεθος.

[2] Λεκτέον δὲ ἡμῖν, ὅπως τε ἐξ ἀρχῆς γέγονε καὶ ὑπὸ τίνων ἀπῳκίσθη, ἐκ τῶν ἀρχαίων ποιητῶν καὶ συγγραφέων τὴν ὑπόθεσιν ποιουμένοις.]

1 Φασὶ μὲν Ἀργείους πρώτους χρησάσης αὐτοῖς τῆς Πυθίας οὕτως,

Ὄλβιοι, οἳ κείνην ἱερὴν πόλιν οἰκήσουσιν
ἀκτὴν Θρηικίην στενυγρὸν παρά τε στόμα Πόντου,
ἔνθα δύο σκύλακες διερὴν μάρπτουσι θάλασσαν,
ἔνθ' ἰχθὺς ἔλαφός τε νομὸν βόσκονται ἐς αὐτόν,

πήξασθαι τὰς οἰκήσεις ἐν ἐκείνῳ τῷ χωρίῳ, ἐν ᾧ Κύδαρός τε καὶ Βαρβύσης ποταμοὶ τὰς διεξόδους ποιοῦνται, ὁ μὲν

The *Patria* of Constantinople
According to Hesychios Illoustrios[1]

[W]hen 362 years had passed since the sole reign of the [1]
Caesar Augustus in the elder Rome, and her fortunes were
already coming to an end, Constantine the son of Constantius (306–337) took over the scepters and established the
new Rome, ordering that it should be equal in rank to the
first. For after having been ruled by tyrants and kings, and
often having been governed by the ways of aristocracy and
democracy, it finally achieved its present greatness.

So we should tell how it originated in the beginning and [2]
by whom it was settled, using the old poets and writers as
our basis.][2]

It is said[3] that first the Argives, after having received this 1
prophecy from the Pythia,

> Blessed are those who will inhabit that holy city,
> a narrow strip of the Thracian shore at the mouth of the
>   Pontos,
> where two pups drink of the gray sea,
> where fish and stag graze on the same pasture,[4]

set up their dwellings at the place where the rivers Kydaros
and Barbyses have their estuaries, one flowing from the

τῶν ἀρκτῴων, ὁ δὲ τῶν ἑσπερίων προρρέοντες καὶ κατὰ τὸν τῆς λεγομένης Σεμέστρης νύμφης βωμὸν τῇ θαλάσσῃ μιγνύμενοι.

2 Ἐπεὶ οὖν εἰς τὴν εἱμαρμένην ἀφίκοντο <χώραν> καὶ θυσίαις τοὺς ἐγχωρίους ἐξιλάσκοντο δαίμονας, κόραξ τῆς ἱερουργίας ὑφαρπάσας βραχύ τι μέρος εἰς ἕτερον μετέθηκε τόπον, ὃς ἔχει τὴν τοῦ Βοσπόρου προσηγορίαν βουκόλου τὴν τοῦ ὄρνιθος ὑποδείξαντος πτῆσιν, ἀφ' οὗπερ καὶ Βουκόλια ἐκεῖνο τὸ χωρίον ἐκλήθη.

3 Ἕτεροι δὲ Μεγαρεῖς ἱστόρησαν ἀπὸ Νίσου τὸ γένος κατάγοντας εἴσπλουν ἐν αὐτῷ ποιησαμένους τῷ τόπῳ ὑφ' ἡγεμόνι Βύζαντι, οὗπερ τὴν προσηγορίαν μυθεύουσι τῇ πόλει προστεθῆναι. Ἄλλοι δὲ Σεμέστρης τῆς ἐπιχωρίου νύμφης παῖδά τινα γεγονότα τὸν Βύζαντα ἀναπλάττουσιν.

4 Οἱ μὲν οὖν διαφόροις ἐχρήσαντο λόγοις, ἡμεῖς δὲ πιθανὴν τὴν ἱστορίαν τοῖς ἐντυγχάνειν ἐθέλουσιν παραστῆσαι βουλόμενοι ἐκ τῆς Ἰνάχου θυγατρὸς Ἰοῦς τὴν ἀρχὴν προσφόρως ποιούμεθα. Ἰνάχου γὰρ τοῦ Ἀργείων βασιλέως γέγονε θυγάτηρ Ἰώ. Ταύτης τὴν παρθενίαν ἐφύλαττεν Ἄργος, ὃν πολυόμματον λέγουσιν. Ἐπεὶ δὲ Ζεὺς ἐρασθεὶς τῆς κόρης πείθει τὸν Ἑρμῆν δολοφονῆσαι τὸν Ἄργον, λυθείσης δ' αὐτῇ τῆς παρθενίας ὑπὸ Διὸς εἰς βοῦν μεταβάλλεται.

5 Ἥρα δὲ χολωθεῖσα ἐπὶ τῷ γενομένῳ οἶστρον ἐπιπέμπει τῇ δαμάλει καὶ διὰ πάσης αὐτὴν ἐλαύνει ξηρᾶς τε καὶ ὑγρᾶς.

6 Ἐπειδὴ δὲ πρὸς τὴν Θρακῶν ἀφίκετο χώραν, ὄνομα μὲν τῷ τόπῳ καταλέλοιπε Βόσπορον, αὐτὴ δὲ πρὸς τὸ

north, the other from the west, and merging with the sea at the altar of the nymph called Semestre.

When they had arrived in the destined land and propiti- 2 ated the local demons with sacrifices, a raven snatched away a small piece of the sacrifice and carried it to another place which has the name Bosporos, because a cowherd *(bouko-los)* pointed out the flight of the bird, for which reason this place was also called Boukolia.[5]

Others claim that people from Megara, who derived their 3 descent from Nisos, sailed to this place under their leader Byzas, and invent the fable that his name was attached to the city. Others imagine that Byzas was a child of the local nymph Semestre.[6]

While some have given these different explanations, we 4 intend to present a plausible story to those who may wish to read this, and as such it is appropriate to begin with Io, the daughter of Inachos.[7] For Io was the daughter of Inachos, the king of the Argives. Argos, whom they call the many-eyed, watched over her virginity. But when Zeus, having fallen in love with the girl, persuaded Hermes to kill Argos, and she had lost her virginity to Zeus, she was transformed into a cow.

Hera became angry about what had happened and sent 5 out a gadfly against the heifer, and drove her through every land and sea.

When she arrived in the land of Thrace, she left behind 6 the name Bosporos for the place[8] and then returned to the

καλούμενον Κέρας ἐπανελθοῦσα, καθ' ὃ Κύδαρός τε καὶ Βαρβύσης συμμίσγονται τοῖς ἐνοικοῦσι προθεσπίζοντες τὰ ἐσόμενα, παρὰ τὸν Σεμέστρης βωμὸν τὴν λεγομένην Κερόεσσαν ἀπεκύησε κόρην, ἐξ ἧς καὶ Κέρας ὁ τόπος ὠνόμασται. Ἄλλοι δὲ μᾶλλον τῇ θέσει τοῦ χωρίου τοὔνομα προστιθέασιν, οἱ δὲ τῇ τῶν καρπῶν εὐφορίᾳ τὸ τῆς Ἀμαλθείας αἰγὸς κέρας προσαγορεύουσιν.

7   Ἡ τοίνυν Κερόεσσα παρὰ τῇ Σεμέστρῃ νύμφῃ τραφεῖσα καὶ παραδόξῳ μορφῇ λαμπρυνθεῖσα πολὺ τὰς Θρᾳκικὰς ὑπερέβαλε παρθένους, τῷ τε θαλαττίῳ μιγεῖσα Ποσειδῶνι τίκτει τὸν καλούμενον Βύζαντα, τοὔνομα τοῦτο λαβόντα ἐκ τῆς θρεψάσης αὐτὸν κατὰ τὴν Θρᾴκην νύμφης Βιζύης, ἧς μέχρι καὶ νῦν οἱ πολῖται τῶν ὑδάτων ἀρύονται.

8   Ὡς οὖν ἐπὶ τὴν ἀκμὴν τῆς ἡλικίας ὁ νέος προέβαινεν καὶ τοῖς Θρᾳκίοις ἐνδιέτριβεν ὄρεσι φοβερῶς πρὸς τοὺς θῆρας καὶ τοὺς βαρβάρους φερόμενος, πρεσβείας ὑπὸ τῶν τοπαρχούντων ἐδέχετο σύμμαχος αὐτοῖς εἶναι καὶ φίλος προτρεπόμενος.

9   Ὡς οὖν καὶ Μελίας αὐτὸν ὁ τῶν Θρᾳκῶν βασιλεὺς ἐπὶ τὸν τοῦ θηρὸς ἆθλον μετεπέμψατο καὶ τὰς ἐξ αὐτοῦ δόξας ὁ Βύζας ἀπηνέγκατο τὸν ὑποταγέντα ταῦρον τῇ ἱερουργίᾳ προσφέρων καὶ τοὺς πατρῴους ἐξιλασκόμενος δαίμονας κατὰ τὴν τῶν εἰρημένων ποταμῶν σύμμιξιν, ἀετὸς ἀθρόως φανεὶς τὴν καρδίαν ὑφαρπάζει τοῦ θύματος καὶ κατὰ τὴν ἄκραν τῆς Βοσπορίας ἀκτῆς <ἀποπτὰς ἔστη> ἀντικρὺ τῆς καλουμένης Χρυσοπόλεως, ἣν Χρύσης ὁ παῖς ἐκ Χρυσηΐδος γεγονὼς καὶ Ἀγαμέμνονος φεύγων τὴν

so-called Horn *(keras)*, where the rivers Kydaros and Barbyses mingle with each other and so foretell the future to the
local inhabitants, and, at the altar of Semestre,[9] she gave
birth to a daughter named Keroessa,[10] after whom the place
is also called the Horn. Others rather ascribe the name to
the shape of the place, while still others call it the horn of
the goat Amaltheia[11] because of its abundant harvests.

Keroessa was brought up by the nymph Semestre, and   7
being adorned with amazing beauty, she surpassed the Thracian maidens by far. After uniting with the sea god, Poseidon, she gave birth to the one called Byzas, who received his
name from and was raised in Thrace by the nymph Bizye,
from whom the citizens <of Constantinople> still draw
their water up to this day.[12]

Now when the young man, advancing to the prime of   8
youth, dwelled in the Thracian mountains, he instilled fear
in both beasts and barbarians, and received embassies from
local rulers urging him to be their ally and friend.

Now when Melias, the king of the Thracians,[13] sent him   9
out to do battle against a wild animal, Byzas emerged with
glory from the combat, and offered the vanquished bull as a
sacrifice, thus appeasing the tutelary demons at the confluence of the aforementioned rivers. Suddenly an eagle appeared and snatched the heart of the sacrificial animal, and,
flying to the promontory of the shore of the Bosporos,
landed opposite the place called Chrysopolis.[14] Chryses, the
child born to Chryseis and Agamemnon, left this name

Κλυταιμνήστρης ἐπιβουλὴν μετὰ τὴν τοῦ πατρὸς ἀναίρεσιν καὶ πρὸς τὴν τῆς Ἰφιγενείας ζήτησιν ἐπειγόμενος
μνῆμα τῆς ἑαυτοῦ ταφῆς τοῖς ἐγχωρίοις τοὔνομα τοῦτο
κατέλιπε φθασάσης αὐτὸν ἐκεῖ τῆς τοῦ βίου καταστροφῆς.

10 Ὁ μὲν οὖν Βύζας κατὰ τὴν ἄκραν τῆς Βοσπορίας ἁλὸς
διέγραψεν πόλιν. Ποσειδῶνος δὲ καὶ Ἀπόλλωνος ὥς φασι
συνεργούντων ἀνοικοδομεῖ τὰ τείχη λόγου τε παντὸς
κρείττονα μηχανώμενος.

11 Τοὺς γὰρ ἐν αὐτοῖς πύργους ἑπτὰ ὄντας ἀντιφθέγ-
γεσθαί τε καὶ διηχεῖν ἀλλήλοις συνήρμοζεν. Εἴποτε γὰρ
σάλπιγξ ἢ φωνή τις ἑτέρα τοῖς πύργοις ἐπεφοίτα, ἕτερος
ἐξ ἑτέρου τὴν ἠχὼ μετελάμβανεν, καὶ τῷ πρὸς τὸ πέρας
κειμένῳ παρέπεμπον.

12 Ἀλλὰ μὴν καὶ ἄλλο τι τοῖς ταῦτα συγγράψασιν εἰρημένον οὐ παραλείψομεν· τὸν γὰρ Ἡρακλέους καλούμενον
πύργον τὰ τῶν πολεμίων τοῖς ἐντὸς οὖσι τοῦ τείχους μετα-
διδόναι μυστήρια λέγουσιν.

13 Μετὰ δὲ τὴν τοῦ τείχους στεφάνην καὶ τὰ τεμένη τῶν
θεῶν ἀπειργάζετο· Ῥέας μὲν κατὰ τὸν τῆς Βασιλικῆς
λεγόμενον τόπον νεών τε καὶ ἄγαλμα καθιδρύσατο, ὅπερ
καὶ Τυχαῖον τοῖς πολίταις τετίμηται. Ποσειδῶνος δὲ τέμενος πρὸς τῇ θαλάττῃ ἀνήγειρεν, ἔνθα νῦν ὁ τοῦ μάρτυρος
Μηνᾶ οἶκος διακεκόσμηται, Ἑκάτης δὲ κατὰ τὸν νῦν τοῦ
Ἱπποδρομίου τόπον, τῶν δὲ Διοσκούρων, Κάστορός τέ
φημι καὶ τοῦ Πολυδεύκους, ἐν τῷ τῆς Σεμέστρης βωμῷ
καὶ τῇ τῶν ποταμῶν μίξει, ἐν ᾧ καὶ λύσις τῶν παθῶν τοῖς
ἀνθρώποις ἐγίνετο.

14 Ἐγγὺς δὲ τοῦ καλουμένου Στρατηγίου Αἴαντός τε καὶ

behind to the local people as a memorial of his burial, <for> when he fled the conspiracy of Klytaimnestra, hastening to find Iphigeneia after the slaying of his father, the end of his life suddenly befell him there.

So Byzas laid out a city at the promontory of the Bospo- 10 rian sea. With the help of Poseidon and Apollo, as they say, he built the walls, contriving to make them stronger than words can tell.

For he linked their towers, seven in number, in such a way 11 that they resounded and transmitted sound to one another. Whenever the sound of a trumpet or some other sound reached the towers, one received the echo from the other and transmitted it to the last one.[15]

But we will not omit something else mentioned by those 12 who have written about this: for they say that the so-called tower of Herakles transmitted the secrets of the enemy to those inside the walls.

After completing the circuit of the wall he also built the 13 sanctuaries of the gods. At the place called the Basilike,[16] he consecrated a temple and a statue of Rhea, which is also honored by the citizens as a temple of Tyche.[17] He also erected near the sea a sanctuary of Poseidon, where the splendid house of the martyr Menas has now been built;[18] of Hekate at the present site of the Hippodrome;[19] and of the Dioskouroi, that is Kastor and Polydeukes, at the altar of Semestre and the confluence of the rivers, where people were delivered from their ailments.[20]

Near the so-called Strategion he set up altars of Ajax 14

Ἀχιλλέως βωμοὺς ἀνεθήκατο· ἔνθα καὶ τὸ Ἀχιλλέως χρηματίζει λουτρόν. Ἀμφιάρεω δὲ τοῦ ἥρωος ἐν ταῖς λεγομέναις Συκαῖς ᾠκοδόμησεν, αἳ τὴν ἐπωνυμίαν ἐκ τῶν συκοφόρων δένδρων ἐδέξαντο. Ἀνωτέρω δὲ μικρὸν τοῦ Ποσειδῶνος ναοῦ καὶ τὸ τῆς Ἀφροδίτης προσαγορεύεται τέμενος Ἀρτέμιδός τε πρὸς τὸ τῆς Θρᾴκης ὄρος.

15   Ἐπεὶ δὲ ταῦτα εἰς τὴν αὐτοῦ διῳκήσατο πόλιν, ἐχρῆν δὲ λοιπὸν τοὺς ἐπιόντας ἀπωθεῖσθαι βαρβάρους, μάλιστα τὸν Αἷμον, ὃς τῆς Θρᾴκης τύραννος ἦν καὶ πρὸς αὐτὴν ἧκεν τὴν τοῦ Βύζαντος πόλιν αὐτόν τε τὸν ἥρωα προκαλούμενος εἰς μάχην καὶ διαπορθεῖν ἅπαντα προθυμούμενος. <Ὁ δὲ> οὐχ ὑπομείνας τὴν ἔφοδον τοῦ βαρβάρου μόνος πρὸς μόνον διαγωνίζεται καὶ καταβάλλει τὸν Αἷμον ἐπὶ τὸν ἐπώνυμον αὐτοῦ λόφον.

16   Ὁ μὲν οὖν Βύζας μετὰ τὴν εἰρημένην νίκην ὡς ἐπὶ τὴν Θρᾴκην ἤλαυνε τοὺς πολεμίους, Ὀδρύσης ὁ τῶν Σκυθῶν βασιλεὺς περαιωθεὶς τὸν Ἴστρον καὶ πρὸς αὐτὰ διελθὼν τὰ τῆς πόλεως τείχη ἐπολιόρκει τοὺς ἔνδον. Πρὸς ὃν ἡ τοῦ Βύζαντος γυνή, ἡ θαυμαστὴ Φιδάλεια, μηδέν τι καταπλαγεῖσα τὸ πλῆθος τῶν πολεμίων, ἀλλὰ τῇ γυναικείᾳ χρησαμένη χειρὶ διηγωνίσατο σοφισαμένη τὸν βάρβαρον τῇ τῶν δρακόντων συμμαχίᾳ.

17   Ὡς γὰρ τοὺς κατὰ τὴν πόλιν ὄφεις εἰς ἕν τι χωρίον συλλαβοῦσα ἐφρούρει, ἀθρόως τοῖς ἐναντίοις ἐπιφανεῖσα δίκην βελῶν ἢ ἀκοντίων ἔπεμπε τὰ θηρία καὶ πλείστους λυμηναμένη τούτῳ τῷ τρόπῳ διέσωσε τὴν πόλιν. Ἐντεῦθεν τοίνυν ἀρχαῖος μῦθος φέρεται μὴ δεῖν τοὺς κατὰ τὴν πόλιν

and Achilles, where now the bath of Achilles is.[21] He built
<an altar> of the hero Amphiaraos at the place called Sykai
which has received its name from the fig-bearing trees.[22]
Also, a bit further up from the temple of Poseidon in the di-
rection of the Thracian mountain is the sanctuary named
after both Aphrodite and Artemis.[23]

Having equipped his city with these structures, it was 15
also necessary for him to drive off the invading barbarians,
above all Haimos, the ruler of Thrace who had come to the
city of Byzas, challenging the hero himself to battle with the
intention of destroying the city. Instead of waiting for the
barbarian's onslaught, he engaged him in single combat and
threw Haimos down on the hill which bears his name.[24]

After the aforesaid victory, when Byzas drove his enemies 16
as far as Thrace, Odryses, the king of the Skythians, having
crossed the Istros River, arrived at the very walls of the city
and laid siege to the inhabitants.[25] The wife of Byzas, the
amazing Phidaleia,[26] was not at all terrified by the multitude of enemies, but using her feminine hand devised a way
to overcome the barbarian by making an alliance with serpents.

For after collecting the snakes of the city in one spot and 17
guarding them there, she appeared suddenly before the enemy, hurled the beasts at them like arrows or spears, and by
harming a large number of them in this way saved the city.
Therefore an ancient saying has been handed down to us

ἁλισκομένους ἀπολλύειν ὄφεις, οἷα εὐεργέτας αὐτοὺς γενομένους.

18 Οὐ μετὰ πολὺν δὲ χρόνον Στρόμβος ἀνὴρ τοὔνομα καὶ αὐτὸς ἐκ Κεροέσσης τεχθεὶς πόλεμον ἐπιφέρει τῷ Βύζαντι πολλὴν ἐπαγόμενος δύναμιν. Ἀνεκινεῖτο τοίνυν ἅπαντα τὰ Σκυθικὰ γένη, συνέτρεχον δὲ καὶ οἱ τῆς Ἑλλάδος κρατοῦντες καὶ Ῥοδίων οὐκ εὐκαταφρόνητος δύναμις ὅ τε τῆς γείτονος Χαλκηδόνος τοπάρχης Δίνεως, ἐκ Μεγαρέων ἄποικος ἐκεῖσε γενόμενος δέκα καὶ ἐννέα ἔμπροσθεν ἔτεσιν τῆς Βύζαντος αὐταρχίας.

19 Χαλκηδὼν δὲ ὠνόμασται τὸ χωρίον, ὡς μέν τινές φασιν, ἀπὸ τοῦ Χαλκηδόνος ποταμοῦ, ὡς δὲ ἕτεροι, ἀπὸ τοῦ παιδὸς Κάλχαντος τοῦ μάντεως ὕστερον τοῦ Τρωικοῦ πολέμου γενομένου, ὡς δὲ ἄλλοι, ἀπὸ Χαλκίδος πόλεως τῆς Εὐβοίας ἀποίκων ἐκεῖ πεμφθέντων· οὓς δὴ καὶ τυφλοὺς ἀπεκάλεσαν παρεωρακότας τὸ Βυζάντιον.

20 Ὡς οὖν σὺν πλείοσι ναυσὶν ὁ Δίνεως εἰς συμμαχίαν ἧκεν τοῦ Βύζαντος, μὴ δυνηθεὶς προσορμῆσαι τῇ πόλει ἄρτι τοῦ βασιλέως αὐτῶν Βύζαντος μεταλλάξαντος καὶ τοῦ δήμου παντὸς ἐν ἀγωνίᾳ τυγχάνοντος πρὸς τὸν καλούμενον Ἀνάπλουν ἀφίκετο, ἔνθα καὶ διατρίψας Ἑστίας τὸν τόπον ὠνόμασεν.

21 Μικρῷ γε μὴν ὕστερον διαβὰς ἐν τῇ πόλει καὶ τοὺς βαρβάρους ἀπωσάμενος δεύτερος αὐτὸς ἐστρατήγησε τοῦ δήμου τῶν Βυζαντίων. Καθ᾽ οὓς δὴ χρόνους καὶ δρακόντων πλεῖστα γένη ἐπεφοίτησεν τῇ πόλει, ὡς τοὺς οἰκοῦντας αὐτὴν διαφθείρεσθαι· οὓς δὴ τῇ τῶν καλουμένων

that snakes captured in the city should not be killed, as they are its benefactors.

Shortly afterward a man called Strombos, who was also 18 born to Keroessa,[27] attacked Byzas, leading a great army. Then all the Skythian tribes were incited to war, but also the rulers of Greece came to help him and a not insignificant force of Rhodians, as well as the local lord of neighboring Chalkedon, Dineos,[28] a Megarian colonist who had come there nineteen years before Byzas had established his rule.

The place was called Chalkedon, some say because of the 19 Chalkedon River, while others say <it is> because of the son of Kalchas the seer, who was born after the Trojan war, and yet others say, <it is> after Chalkis, a city of Euboia,[29] for colonists had been sent to that spot, whom they also called "blind" for disregarding the site of Byzantion.[30]

So when Dineos came with many ships to help Byzas, he 20 was unable to come to anchor at the city, for their king Byzas had just passed away and the people were in great anguish, and he went on to the place called Anaplous,[31] where he stayed and called the place Hestia.

Shortly thereafter, he crossed over to the city and re- 21 pelled the barbarians, becoming the second *strategos* of the Byzantine people. In those days so many kinds of serpents came to dwell in the city that its inhabitants perished. But the inhabitants killed them, with the assistance, so they say,

πελαργῶν ὀρνίθων ἐπιφορᾷ διεχρήσαντο Ποσειδῶνος
αὐτοῖς ὥς φασι συνεργήσαντος.

22 Οὐ μετὰ πολὺ δὲ καὶ τῶν ὀρνίθων αὐτοῖς ἐναντία φρο-
νούντων καὶ θανάτων αἰτίαν ἐπαγόντων τούς τε ἁλισκομένους αὐτοῖς ὄφεις πρὸς τὰς τῶν ὑδάτων δεξαμενὰς
ἀκοντιζόντων καὶ τοῖς γε πολίταις ἐν ταῖς λεωφόροις ἀφα-
νῶς ἐπιβαλλόντων ἐν ἀφασίᾳ διετέλουν.

23 Ἀνὴρ δέ τις τῶν ἐκ Τυάνων, τοὔνομα Ἀπολλώνιος, ἐκ
λίθου ξεστοῦ τρεῖς ἀνεστήσατο πελαργοὺς ἀντιπροσώπως
ἀλλήλοις ὁρῶντας, οἳ καὶ μέχρι τῶνδε διαμένουσι τῶν
χρόνων οὐ συγχωροῦντες ἐπιφοιτῆσαι τῇ πόλει τὸ τῶν
πελαργῶν γένος.

24 Ἐπὶ δὲ τοῖς εἰρημένοις Δίνεω τοῦ στρατηγοῦ μεταλλάξαντος Λέων τὴν τῶν Βυζαντίων ἀριστοκρατίαν ἐδέ-
ξατο· ἐφ' οὗπερ Φίλιππος ὁ τῶν Μακεδόνων βασιλεύς, ὁ
Ἀμύντου παῖς γεγονώς, πολλὴν ἐπαγόμενος δύναμιν ἐπολιόρκει τὴν πόλιν διώρυξί τε καὶ παντοίοις πολεμικοῖς μη-
χανήμασι τοῖς τείχεσι προσπελάζων.

25 Καὶ δὴ ἂν ταύτην ἐξεῖλε ῥᾳδίως νυκτὸς ἐπιλαβόμενος
ἀσελήνου καὶ ὄμβρου καταρραγέντος ἐξαισίου, εἰ μή τις
αὐτοῖς τοῦ θείου γέγονε συμμαχία τοὺς κατὰ τὴν πόλιν
κύνας πρὸς ὑλακὴν ἀναστήσαντος καὶ νεφέλας πυρὸς τοῖς
ἀρκτῴοις ἐπαγαγόντος μέρεσιν. Ἐξ οὗπερ οἱ δῆμοι διε-
γερθέντες καὶ θερμῶς τοῖς πολεμίοις συνενεχθέντες ἤδη
τὴν πόλιν ὑπὸ τῷ Φιλίππῳ γενομένην ἐρρύσαντο ἀνα-
λαβόντες τοὺς διαφθαρέντας πύργους τοῖς ἐκ τῶν τάφων
παρακειμένοις λίθοις καὶ ἀνυφάναντες τὰς ἐπάλξεις τοῦ
τείχους· οὗ δὴ χάριν Τυμβοσύνην τὸ τεῖχος ἐκάλεσαν

of Poseidon and by taking advantage of the birds called storks.

But not long afterward the birds too became hostile to- 22
ward them and brought death to them by slinging the captured snakes into the cisterns and by dropping them invisibly onto citizens in the streets, so that they were at their wit's end.

A man from Tyana, however, called Apollonios, set up 23
three storks of hewn stone facing each other, which have remained to our time and do not allow the species of storks to come to the city.[32]

After the said events, when the *strategos* Dineos had 24
passed away, Leo accepted the aristocratic rule over the Byzantines;[33] whereupon Philip, the king of the Macedonians (II, 359–336 BCE), son of Amyntas, led a large force against him and besieged the city, attacking the walls with trenches and all manner of military devices.[34]

And, in fact, he would have easily taken it by an attack on 25
a moonless night with heavy pouring rain, if they had not received some divine assistance which roused the dogs in the city to bark and brought clouds of fire into the northern regions. As a result, the people were awakened and fought fiercely against the enemies, freeing their city which had already fallen into Philip's hands, repairing the ruined towers with the stones from graves that lay about, and rebuilding the battlements of the walls; for this reason, they called

λαμπαδηφόρον Ἑκάτης ἀναστήσαντες ἄγαλμα. Αὖθίς τε πρὸς ναυμαχίας τραπέντες περιφανῶς τοὺς Μακεδόνας ἐνίκησαν. Καὶ τούτῳ τῷ τρόπῳ διαλυθέντος τοῦ πολέμου Φίλιππος παραχωρεῖ Βυζαντίοις.

26   Ἐπειδὴ δὲ καὶ Λέων τὸν βίον μετήλλαξεν, Χάρης ὁ τῶν Ἀθηναίων στρατηγὸς σὺν ναυσὶ τεσσαράκοντα εἰς συμμαχίαν τῶν Βυζαντίων ἐλθὼν πρὸς τὸν κατὰ Φιλίππου πόλεμον κατέλαβε τὴν ἄκραν τῆς Προποντίδος, ἥτις μεταξὺ κεῖται Χρυσοπόλεως καὶ Χαλκηδόνος, καὶ ἐν ἐκείνῳ προσορμήσας τῷ τόπῳ ἀπόπειραν ἐλάμβανε τοῦ πολέμου.

27   Ἔνθα δὴ τὴν ἐπομένην αὐτῷ γυναῖκα νόσῳ βληθεῖσαν ἀποβαλὼν κατέθηκεν ἐν τάφῳ ἀναστήσας αὐτῇ βωμὸν καὶ κίονα σύνθετον, ἐν ᾧ δάμαλις δείκνυται ἐκ ξεστοῦ συγκειμένη λίθου. Οὕτω γὰρ μᾶλλον ἐκείνη τὴν ἐπωνυμίαν ἐκέκλητο, ἥτις διὰ τῶν ἐγγεγραμμένων στίχων μέχρι τῶν καθ' ἡμᾶς διασώζεται χρόνων.

28   Εἰσὶ δὲ οἱ στίχοι οὗτοι·

Ἰναχίης οὐκ εἰμὶ βοὸς τύπος οὐδ' ἀπ' ἐμεῖο
κλήζεται ἀντωπὸν Βοσπόριον πέλαγος.
Κείνην γὰρ τὸ πάροιθε βαρὺς χόλος ἤλασεν Ἥρης
ἐς Φάρον· ἥδε δ' ἐγὼ Κεκροπίς εἰμι νέκυς.
Εὐνέτις ἥν δὲ Χάρητος· ἔπλων δ' ὅτε πλῶεν ἐκεῖνος
τῇδε Φιλιππείων ἀντίπαλος σκαφέων·
Βοίδιον οὔνομα δ' ἥεν ἐμοὶ τότε· νῦν δὲ Χάρητος
εὐνέτις ἠπείροις τέρπομαι ἀμφοτέραις.

the wall Tymbosyne, setting up a torchbearing statue of Hekate.[35] Then again turning to naval war they gloriously defeated the Macedonians. And when the war had ended in this way, Philip surrendered to the Byzantines.

And when Leo too had quitted his life, Chares, the Athe- 26
nian *strategos,* came to support the Byzantines with forty ships in the war with Philip and reached the promontory of the Propontis which lies between Chrysopolis and Chalkedon; and anchoring there he tried his hand at war.[36]

Here he lost the woman who accompanied him, when 27
she was struck down by an illness, and he buried her in a grave and set up an altar for her and a composite column, which shows a heifer of hewn stone.[37] So perhaps she bore the name which has been preserved down to our day in the inscribed verses.

These are the verses: 28

I am not the image of the cow, the daughter of Inachos,[38]
nor is the facing Bosporian sea named after me.
In olden times the severe wrath of Hera drove her
to Pharos, but here I am, a dead descendant of
    Kekrops.[39]
I was the wife of Chares and sailed when he sailed
here, against Philip's ships.
Then my name was "little cow," now Chares's
wife, I am gladdened by both continents.

29 Τοῦ δὲ Χάρητος εἰς Ἀθήνας ἐκπλεύσαντος Πρωτόμα-
χος τὴν στρατηγικὴν ἀρχὴν διαδέχεται, ὃς τοὺς ἐπανα-
στάντας Θρᾷκας καταδουλώσας τοῖς ὅπλοις ἐν τῷ καλουμένῳ τῆς πόλεως Μιλίῳ χάλκεα ἀνέθηκε τρόπαια.

30 Κατοιχομένου δὲ καὶ τούτου Τιμήσιος ἀνὴρ τῶν ἐν
Ἀργείοις τραφέντων πρῶτον μὲν κατὰ τὸν Εὔξεινον
προσαγορευόμενον Πόντον πρὸς τῷ λεγομένῳ Ἐφεσιάτῃ
(ἔνθα ποτὲ Ἐφέσιοι ἀποικίας πέμψαντες καὶ πόλιν οἰκοδο-
μεῖν πειραθέντες αὖθις τοῦ Βυζαντίου ὑπήκουσαν λογίου,

ἔνθα δύο σκύλακες διερὴν μάρπτουσι θάλασσαν,
ἔνθ᾽ ἰχθὺς ἔλαφός τε νομὸν βόσκονται ἐς αὐτόν),

ἀντικαταστῆσαι πόλιν ἐπιχειρήσας καὶ διαμαρτὼν τῆς ἐλ-
πίδος συνοικίζεται Βυζαντίοις· καὶ στρατηγὸς τοῦ παντὸς
ἀναδειχθεὶς δήμου πᾶσαν ὁμοῦ τὴν πόλιν εἰς τὸ μεῖζον καὶ
ὠφέλιμον μετερρύθμισεν, νόμους τε περὶ τῶν καθ᾽ ἡμέραν
συμβόλαιά τε τιθέμενος καὶ ἔθη καθιστὰς πολιτικά τε καὶ
ἥμερα, δι᾽ ὧν ἀστείους τε καὶ φιλανθρώπους τοὺς πολίτας
ἀπέδειξεν.

31 Ἱερά τε θεῶν πλεῖστα τὰ μὲν αὐτὸς ἀνεστήσατο, τὰ δὲ
καὶ πρὶν ὄντα ἐπεκόσμησεν· τὸν γὰρ πρὸς τῇ ἄκρᾳ τῆς
Ποντικῆς θαλάσσης κείμενον ναόν, ὃν Ἰάσων ποτὲ τοῖς
δώδεκα θεοῖς καθιέρωσε, κατηρειπωμένον ἀνήγειρε καὶ
τὸν ἐπὶ τῷ Φρίξου λεγομένῳ λιμένι τῆς Ἀρτέμιδος οἶκον
ἀνεκαίνισεν.

32 Ἐπὶ δὲ τούτῳ Καλλιάδης στρατηγῶν τοῦ Βυζαντίου
ἄριστά τε πρὸς τοὺς ὀθνείους τε καὶ ἐμφυλίους πολεμίους

When Chares had left for Athens by ship, Protomachos 29 succeeded to the office of *strategos*. After subduing the rebellious Thracians by military force, he dedicated bronze trophies at the so-called Milion of the city.[40]

When he too had passed away, a man called Timesios,[41] 30 one of those who had been brought up among the Argives, first made an attempt to found another city instead on the so-called Hospitable Sea, at the place called Ephesiates (where the Ephesians had once sent a colony,[42] and had attempted to build a city, but had then again heard the Byzantine saying,

where two pups drink of the gray sea,
where fish and stag graze on the same pasture),[43]

but when his hopes failed, he joined the Byzantines. And having been appointed *strategos* over the entire people, he reorganized the whole city, making it greater and more prosperous. By establishing laws and regulations concerning daily affairs, and by implementing customs both civil and civilized, he made the citizens urbane and humane.

He himself founded a great number of temples of the 31 gods, and embellished those already existing. He restored the ruined temple which lies on the cape of the Pontic Sea and which Jason had once dedicated to the twelve gods,[44] and renovated the temple of Artemis near the so-called harbor of Phrixos.[45]

After him, Kalliades became *strategos* of Byzantion,[46] and 32 after fighting with distinction against foreign and internal

ἀγωνισάμενος τὸ περιβόητον τοῦ Βύζαντος ἄγαλμα κατὰ
τὴν καλουμένην Βασιλικὴν ἀνέθηκε καὶ ἐπέγραψεν οὕτως·

Τὸν κρατερὸν Βύζαντα καὶ ἱμερτὴν Φιδάλειαν
εἰν ἑνὶ κοσμήσας ἄνθετο Καλλιάδης.

33 Ἀλλὰ ταῦτα μὲν καὶ ἀριστοκρατουμένων καὶ δημοκρα-
τουμένων τῶν Βυζαντίων, ἔτι δὲ καὶ τυραννουμένων κατὰ
διαφόρους συμβέβηκε χρόνους. Ὡς δὲ τῇ τῶν ὑπάτων
ἐπικρατείᾳ ἡ Ῥωμαίων ἀρχὴ πάσας ὑπερεβάλετο τὰς δυναστείας, κατεδούλωσε δὲ καὶ τὰ τῶν Ἑλλήνων ἔθνη,
εἰκότως αὐτῇ καὶ Βυζάντιοι πειθόμενοι διετέλουν.

34 Ἐπειδὴ δὲ μετά τινας χρόνους Σευήρου[1] βασιλεύσαν-
τος τῆς Ῥώμης αὐτοὶ τὴν τοῦ τυραννήσαντος τῶν ἑῴων
Νίγρου προτιμήσαντες ἐλπίδα εἰς χεῖρας ἐλθεῖν ἐτόλμη-
σαν πρὸς τὸν αὐτοκράτορα, ἀφαιρεθέντες παρ᾽ αὐτοῦ τῶν
πολιτικῶν δικαίων καὶ τῆς στεφάνης αὐτοῖς καταλυθείσης
τοῦ τείχους Περινθίοις προσετάχθησαν δουλεύειν τοῖς καλουμένοις Ἡρακλεώταις.

35 Παυσαμένου δὲ τῆς ὀργῆς τοῦ Σευήρου αὖθις εἰς μείζονα κόσμον ἐπανῆλθον λουτρὸν μὲν αὐτοῖς μέγιστον
κατὰ τὸν τοῦ Διὸς Ἱππίου βωμόν, ἤτοι τὸ Ἡρακλέους ἄλ-
σος καλούμενον (ἔνθα τὰς Διομήδους αὐτόν φασι δαμά-
σαντα ἵππους Ζεύξιππον τὸν τόπον ὀνομάσαι), πολυτελῶς
ἐγείραντος καὶ τὸν τούτῳ πλησιάζοντα χῶρον τῆς ἱππο-
δρομίας τοῖς τοῦ Διὸς ἀνακείμενον κούροις ἰκρίοις τε καὶ
στοαῖς διακοσμήσαντος (ἔνθα καὶ νῦν οἱ καμπτῆρες δη-
λοῦσι τὰ τῶν ἐφόρων γνωρίσματα διὰ τῶν ἐπικειμένων

enemies, he set up the famous statue of Byzas at the so-called Basilike,[47] placing this inscription on it:

Strong Byzas and lovely Phidaleia
Kalliades dedicated here, fashioning them in a single
   group.

So that happened at different times when the Byzantines   33
were ruled by aristocracies, democracies and even tyrannies.
When Roman rule superseded all local powers by consular
authority, it also subdued the Greek tribes, and the Byzantines also fittingly submitted to it.

When, after some years, Severus (192–211) became em-   34
peror of Rome, they preferred to put their hope in Niger,
who had seized power in the east, and they dared to rise
against the emperor.[48] They were deprived by him <Seve-
rus> of their civil rights, the crest of their wall was destroyed, and they were ordered to serve the people of Per-
inthos who are called those of Herakleia.[49]

But when Severus's anger had ended, they attained an   35
even greater glory,[50] for he built a huge and luxurious bath
for them at the altar of Zeus Hippios, that is, the so-called
grove of Herakles (where they say that he tamed the horses
of Diomedes and called the place Zeuxippos);[51] also, he
adorned the nearby racecourse, which was dedicated to the
Dioskouroi,[52] with stands and porticoes (where still today
the turning points show the tokens of the games' overseers

ᾠῶν τοῖς χαλκοῖς ὀβελίσκοις), ἐπὶ δὲ τούτοις καὶ στρατιωτικὰ τέλη προσνείμαντος.

36 Μέχρι μὲν οὖν περιῆν Σευῆρος καὶ ὁ τούτου παῖς Ἀντωνῖνος, ἡ πόλις Ἀντωνίνα προσηγορεύετο· ἐπειδὴ δὲ τοῖς θείοις τῶν βασιλέων ἀπεδόθη,[2] αὖθις τὸ Βυζάντιον ὠνομάζετο.

37 Ἀπὸ δὲ τοῦ Βύζαντος μέχρι τοῦ Σευήρου ἔτη χνε'. Ὁ δὲ Σευῆρος εἰρηνικὰς σπονδὰς ποιήσας μετὰ Νιγέρου τοῦ Βυζαντίου βασιλέως, τοῦ υἱοῦ Τιμησίου, εἰσῆλθον[3] οἱ μεγιστᾶνες αὐτοῦ εἰς τὸ Βυζάντιον ἀπὸ Ῥώμης· ἐπεὶ οὖν οἱ Βυζάντιοι ἀπὸ τῶν Μακεδόνων[4] διείποντο, ὁ δὲ Σευῆρος ἀνῆλθε πρὸς τὸ <συμ>πολεμῆσαι τοῖς Βυζαντίοις· ἠγάγετο δὲ γυναῖκα ὁ τοῦ Νιγέρου υἱὸς τὴν θυγατέρα Σευήρου. Τὸν μέντοι στρατὸν αὐτοῦ ὁ Σευῆρος κατέλιπεν ἐν Χρυσοπόλει. Καὶ ποιήσαντες σύλλογον πρὸς ἀλλήλους ὅ τε Νίγερος καὶ ὁ Σευῆρος εἰσῆλθον μετὰ τριακοσίων μόνων.

38 Καὶ εὐωχηθέντες μεγάλως, ἐπὶ τὴν κάτω μοῖραν τῆς τραπέζης ἤγουν τοῦ διαζυγίου ἔστησάν τινες φιλόσοφοι δύο, ὅ τε Φόρτων καὶ Μαρκίων Ῥωμαῖοι καὶ ἠρώτων πρὸς τοὺς Βυζαντίους τοὺς ἐσθίοντας· "ἠγάγομεν χαρὰν ἀκερδῆ καὶ λύπην ἀζήμιον." Προσκαλεσάμενος δὲ ὁ Νίγερος τοὺς φιλοσόφους αὐτοῦ, οὐκ ἠδυνήθησαν τοῦτο φράσαι· εἷς δὲ τῶν ἀνακειμένων ἐν τῷ συμποσίῳ γηραλέος ὢν γνοὺς τὸ ἀπόφθεγμα εἶπεν· "τοῦτό ἐστιν ἱππικὸς καὶ ἀγωνιστικὸς ἀγών."

39 Τότε ὁ Σευῆρος πρὸς θεραπείαν τοῦ συμπενθεροῦ αὐτοῦ Νιγέρου ἔκτισε δύο βαλανεῖα, ἔσωθεν μὲν τῆς πόλεως καὶ πλησίον τοῦ παλατίου τὸ καλούμενον Ζεύξιππον,

by eggs placed on bronze spears);[53] and in addition to these things he granted military tolls.

For as long as Severus and his son Antoninus lived, the 36 city was called Antonina. But when he was enrolled among the divine emperors, it was again called Byzantion.[54]

From Byzas to Severus, 655 years.[55] After Severus had 37 concluded a peace treaty with Niger, the king of Byzantion and son of Timasios,[56] his great men entered Byzantion, <coming> from Rome. For the Byzantines descended from the Macedonians, so Severus went out to fight as an ally of the Byzantines. The son of Niger married the daughter of Severus. Severus left his army behind in Chrysopolis, and having joined forces with each other, Niger and Severus went in with only three hundred men.

And when they had a great banquet, two philosophers 38 stood at the lower part of the table, that is the separate part, Phorton and Markion the Romans, and said to the Byzantines who were dining: "We have brought pleasure without gain and sorrow without loss." When Niger summoned his philosophers, they could not explain this statement, but an old man among the banqueters knew the saying and said: "This means a contest of horse racers and of fighters."[57]

Then Severus built two baths for the treatment of his 39 son-in-law's father, Niger, one inside the city and close to the palace, the so-called Zeuxippos,[58] the other outside the

ἔξωθεν δὲ τῆς πόλεως τὰ νῦν καλούμενα Καμίνια, λουτρὸν εὐμέγεθες καὶ ἀξιοθαύμαστον. Ἐκ δὲ τῆς ὑπερβολῆς τοῦ μεγέθους αὐτοῦ ἑκάστῃ ἡμέρᾳ δύο χιλιάδες ἐλούοντο· ἦπτε δὲ μετὰ τοῦ Μηδικοῦ πυρός.

40 Τὸ δὲ νῦν σωζόμενον Ἱπποδρόμιον ἐκτίσθη παρὰ Σευήρου κήπων ὄντων ἐκεῖσε ἀδελφῶν δύο καὶ χήρας γυναικός. Μέχρι δὲ τοῦ Χαλκοῦ πεδίον ἦν· ἀπὸ δὲ τοῦ Χαλκοῦ μέχρι τοῦ Σφενδόνος κίονες εὐμεγέθεις ἀνηγέρθησαν (ἐξ οὗ καὶ ἡ ψυχρὰ κινστέρνα ἐστί), διότι κρημνώδης ἦν ὁ τόπος.

41 Τὸ δὲ ἓν μέρος τῶν βαθμίδων ἀνεπληρώθη παρὰ Σευήρου, τὸ ἕτερον καταλιπὼν ἀτελὲς διὰ τὸ ἐλθεῖν αὐτῷ ἀγγελίαν ὅτι οἱ Γάλλοι πορθοῦσι τὴν Ῥώμην· <ὃ> ἀκούσας ὁ Σευῆρος παρεγένετο ἐν τῇ Ῥώμῃ· νόσῳ δὲ ἐπιληψίας τελευτᾷ κρατήσας χρόνους ιζ'. Ἀπὸ δὲ τὸν θάνατον αὐτοῦ παρῆλθον χρόνοι ξ' καὶ ἐπέκεινα μέχρι τῆς βασιλείας τοῦ μεγάλου Κωνσταντίνου.

42 Δύο δὲ καὶ ἑξήκοντα καὶ τριακοσίων ἐτῶν ἀπὸ τῆς Αὐγούστου Καίσαρος μοναρχίας διεληλυθότων τῇ πρεσβυτέρᾳ Ῥώμῃ καὶ τῶν πραγμάτων αὐτῆς ἤδη πρὸς πέρας ἀφιγμένων Κωνσταντῖνος ὁ Κωνσταντίου παῖς ἐπιλαβόμενος τῶν σκήπτρων τὴν νέαν ἀνίστησι Ῥώμην Κωνσταντινούπολιν λεγομένην προθύμως ἀνασχομένην τὴν προσηγορίαν.

43 Θαυμαστὴν γὰρ αὐτὴν ἀπεργασάμενος τῷ κάλλει πόρρωθέν τε μεταγαγὼν τὰ τείχη κατὰ τοὺς λεγομένους Τρωαδησίους ἐμβόλους λουτρά τε καὶ ἱεροὺς οἴκους ἀπέδειξεν, καθὰ καὶ ἐν τῷ Στρατηγίῳ λεγομένῳ φόρῳ,

city <and> which is now called The Furnaces, a huge and wonderful bath. Because of its great size, two thousand people bathed there every day, and its ovens were kindled with Median fire.[59]

The Hippodrome, as preserved today, was built by Seve- 40 rus on the site of the gardens belonging to two brothers[60] and a widow. Up to the Brazen <Obelisk>, the ground was flat. From the Brazen <Obelisk> columns of good size were set up as far as the Sphendone,[61] where also the cold cistern is, for the terrain was sloping.

One side of the stands was completed by Severus, who 41 left the other side unfinished, because he had received a message that the Gauls were besieging Rome. When Severus heard this, he went to Rome, but he died of epilepsy, after a reign of seventeen years. After his death, sixty and more years passed until the reign of Constantine the Great.

When 362 years had passed[62] since the sole reign of the 42 Caesar Augustus in elder Rome, and her fortunes were already coming to an end, Constantine, the son of Constantius, took over the scepters and established the new Rome, which was called Constantinople,[63] and gladly accepted this appellation.

For[64] he made its beauty wondrous, moving the walls far 43 away to the so-called Troadesian porticoes[65] and endowing it with baths and holy houses,[66] as he also inscribed on a

ἔνθα ποτὲ οἱ στρατηγοῦντες ἄνδρες τὰς τιμὰς ὑπεδέχοντο, ἐπὶ λιθίνης ἀνέγραψε στήλης.

44 Καὶ τῆς μητρὸς αὐτοῦ Ἑλένης ἐπὶ κίονος ἀνέστησεν ἄγαλμα καὶ τὸν τόπον ὠνόμασεν Αὐγουστίωνα· καὶ τοῖς ἀκολουθήσασιν αὐτῷ ἄρχουσιν ἀπὸ Ῥώμης συγκλητικοῖς ἐφιλοτιμήσατο οἴκους, οὓς αὐτὸς ἔκτισεν ἐξ ἰδίων χρημάτων, οὕσπερ μετ᾽ ὀλίγον ἐροῦμεν.

45 Ἐπὶ δὲ τούτῳ καὶ ὁ τῶν ὑδάτων ὁλκὸς προσετέθη τῇ πόλει, ἀνέστησαν δὲ καὶ αἱ δύο ἁψίδες πρὸς τῷ καλουμένῳ Φόρῳ καὶ ὁ πορφυροῦς καὶ περίβλεπτος κίων, ἐφ᾽ οὗπερ ἵδρυται Κωνσταντῖνος· ὃν ὁρῶμεν δίκην Ἡλίου τοῖς πολίταις ἐκλάμποντα.

45a [Τοῦτο γοῦν τὸ ἄγαλμα κατέπεσεν ἀπὸ τοῦ κίονος καὶ φόνον τῶν ἐκεῖσε παρευρεθέντων ἀνδρῶν τε καὶ γυναικῶν ὡσεὶ δέκα εἰργάσατο κατὰ τὴν πέμπτην δηλαδὴ τοῦ Ἀπριλλίου μηνός, τῆς τεσσαρεσκαιδεκάτης ἰνδικτιῶνος τοῦ ἑξακισχιλιοστοῦ ἑξακοσιοστοῦ τεσσαρεσκαιδεκάτου ἔτους, εἰκοστὸν ἔτος ἀγούσης τῆς βασιλείας τοῦ κυρίου Ἀλεξίου τοῦ Κομνηνοῦ. Ὥρα ἦν ὡσεὶ τρίτη, ὅτε καὶ γνόφος γέγονεν καὶ βίαιος νότος ἔπνευσε σφοδρόν, τοῦ κομήτου ἀστέρος τοῦ Ἀκοντίου κληθέντος καὶ τὸν τοιοῦτον τοῦ ἀέρος τάραχον ἐξεργασαμένου, τοῦ φανέντος κατὰ τὴν ἑσπέραν τῆς Παρασκευῆς τῆς πρώτης ἑβδομάδος· καθ᾽ ἣν ἐνάτην εἶχεν ὁ Φεβρουάριος μὴν τῆς τεσσαρεσκαιδεκάτης ἰνδικτιῶνος τοῦ ἑξακισχιλιοστοῦ ἑξακοσιοστοῦ τεσσαρεσκαιδεκάτου ἔτους· καὶ οὕτω διηρκέσατο.]

46 Ἐπὶ τούτοις καὶ τοὺς τῆς συγκλήτου βουλῆς ἀνῳκοδόμησεν οἴκους Σενάτον τούτους ὀνομάσας, ἐν οἷς καὶ τὸ

stele of stone in the so-called Forum of the Strategion, where once the generals had received their honors.[67]

And[68] he set up a statue of his mother Helena on a col- 44
umn and called the place Augustion,[69] and donated to the officials and senators who had followed him from Rome houses,[70] which he built himself at his own expense, and about which we shall presently speak.

In[71] his time, the water supply channel was also added to 45
the city. In addition they built the two arches at the so-called Forum and the conspicuous porphyry column, on which is set <the statue of> Constantine, whom we see shining like the sun upon the citizens.[72]

[This statue fell from the column and caused the death of 45a
the men and women who happened to be there, about ten in number, on the fifth of April of the fourteenth indiction, in the year 6614 (1106), the twentieth year of the reign of the lord Alexios Komnenos (1081–1118). About the third hour, it became dark and a violent southern wind blew fiercely, for a comet, which is called the Spear, had caused this turbulence of the air. It appeared in the evening of the Friday of the first week, on the ninth of February of the fourteenth indiction, in the year 6614, and then stayed.][73]

In addition to this, he also built the houses of the senate 46
council, calling them the Senate.[74] There he set up the statue

THE PATRIA

Δωδωναίου Διὸς ἀνέστησεν ἄγαλμα καὶ δύο τῆς Παλλάδος ἱδρύματα, καὶ τὴν τῶν βασιλείων αὐλήν.

47   Ἐφιλοτιμήσατο δὲ τῷ δήμῳ καθ' ὃν ὑπάτευσε χρόνον ἄρτους ἡμερησίους, ὀνομάσας αὐτοὺς παλατίνους ὡς ἐκ τοῦ παλατίου χορηγουμένους, καὶ οἶνον καὶ κρέας καὶ ἔλαιον καὶ σιτηρέσια τάξας, ὧν καὶ μέχρι τοῦ νῦν ἡ πόλις ἀπολαύει τῶν ὑπ' αὐτοῦ ῥιφέντων καλάμων φέρουσα τὰ γνωρίσματα, νόμους τε πολλοὺς καὶ συμβόλαια <περὶ τῶν> καθ' ἑκάστην τιθεὶς ἀπὸ τοῦ βελτίστου καὶ δικαίου, τείχεσίν τε μεγίστοις περιβαλὼν τὴν πόλιν καὶ διαφόροις κοσμήσας τρόποις ὡς πρὸς ζῆλον ἀπεργάσασθαι τῆς πρεσβυτέρας Ῥώμης.

48   Ὠικοδόμησεν δὲ παραχρῆμα καὶ ἱεροὺς οἴκους ἕνα μὲν ἐπώνυμον τῆς ἁγίας Εἰρήνης, ἕτερον δὲ τῶν Ἀποστόλων· καὶ τὰ τῶν Ἑλλήνων πάντα καθεῖλε θρησκεύματα, πολλοὺς δὲ ναοὺς ἀνήγειρεν, οὕστινας εἴπωμεν μετ' ὀλίγον.

49   Ἔκτισε δὲ δρομικὴν τὴν ἁγίαν Σοφίαν καὶ ξυλόστεγον. Ἀπὸ δὲ τῆς ἁγίας Σοφίας στῆλαι ἀφηρέθησαν ἐξ αὐτῆς υκζ', πλεῖαι μὲν Ἑλλήνων ὑπάρχουσαι, αἵτινες ἐκ τῶν πολλῶν ὑπάρχουσιν τοῦ τε Διὸς καὶ Κάρου τοῦ πατροιοῦ Διοκλητιανοῦ καὶ τὸ δωδεκάζῳδον καὶ ἡ Σελήνη καὶ ἡ Ἀφροδίτη καὶ ὁ Ἀρκτοῦρος ἀστὴρ παρὰ δύο Περσικῶν στηλῶν βασταζόμενος καὶ ὁ νότιος πόλος καὶ ἱέρεια τῆς Ἀθηνᾶς ἀπὸ τοῦ πλευροῦ τὸν Ἥρωνα φιλόσοφον μαντεύουσα· ἐκ δὲ τῶν Χριστιανῶν ὀλίγαι μὲν ὡσεὶ π'.

50   Ἔκτισεν δὲ καὶ τὸν ἅγιον Ἀγαθόνικον καὶ τὸν ἅγιον Ἀκάκιον καὶ τοὺς ἁγίους Ἀποστόλους σὺν τῇ μητρὶ αὐτοῦ,

of the Zeus of Dodone and two of Pallas, and built the emperor's palace.

In the year of his consulate he donated loaves of bread 47 daily to the people, calling the loaves "palatine," as they were distributed from the palace, and he assigned wine and meat and oil and grain allowances to them, which the city enjoys to this day, bearing the marks of the reeds thrown by him.[75] He issued many laws and decrees about daily life, from the best and most lawful, and surrounded the city with very big walls and adorned it in different ways, fashioning it so that the older Rome should envy it.

He also immediately built holy houses, one in the name 48 of Saint Eirene, and another of the Apostles.[76] And he destroyed the whole religion of the pagans, and built many churches on which we shall report presently.

He[77] built Hagia Sophia as a basilica with a wooden roof. 49 From Hagia Sophia 427 statues were removed, most of them pagan ones. Among the multitude of them, there are those of Zeus and Carus, the stepfather of Diocletian, and the zodiac, Selene, Aphrodite, the star Arktouros, held by two Persian statues, the South Pole and a priestess of Athene, soothsaying the philosopher Heron from the side. Of the Christian statues there were few, about eighty.

He[78] also built <the churches of> Saint Agathonikos and 50 Saint Akakios and, together with his mother, the <church of

δρομικὴν ξυλόστεγον ποιήσας, καὶ μνημοθέσιον τῶν βασιλέων, ἐν ᾧ κεῖται αὐτός.

51   Χρὴ δὲ γινώσκειν ὅτι τοῦ Βύζαντος τὰ παλάτια ἐν τῇ ἀκροπόλει ἦσαν. Ὁ δὲ ναὸς τοῦ ἁγίου Μηνᾶ ὑπῆρχε πρότερον τοῦ Διός· ἐξ οὗ καὶ εἰς τὰς μαρμαρίνους ἀψίδας τὰς ὕπερθεν τῶν μεγάλων δύο κιόνων ὑπάρχουσι τοῦ μεγάλου Διὸς καὶ τοῦ Κρόνου αἱ στῆλαι. Ἔθος γὰρ ἦν τοῖς παλαιοῖς εἰς τὰς ἀκροπόλεις κτίζειν τὰς ἑαυτῶν κατοικίας ἤγουν παλάτια.

52   Ἤρχετο δὲ τὸ τεῖχος ἀπὸ τοῦ τείχους τῆς ἀκροπόλεως καὶ διήρχετο εἰς τὸν Εὐγενίου πύργον καὶ ἀνέβαινεν μέχρι τοῦ Στρατηγίου καὶ ἤρχετο εἰς τὸ Ἀχιλλέως λοετρόν· ἡ δὲ ἐκεῖσε ἀψὶς ἡ λεγομένη νῦν Οὐρβίκιος πόρτα ἦν χερσαία τῶν Βυζαντίων. Καὶ ἀνέβαινεν εἰς τὰ Χαλκοπρατεῖα τὸ τεῖχος ἕως τοῦ Μιλίου· ἦν δὲ κἀκεῖσε πόρτα τῶν Βυζαντίων χερσαία· καὶ διήρχετο εἰς τοὺς πλεκτοὺς κίονας τῶν Τζυκαλαρείων καὶ κατέβαινε τὸ τεῖχος εἰς τοὺς Τόπους καὶ ὑπέκαμπτεν εἰς ἀκρόπολιν διά τε τῶν Μαγγάνων καὶ Ἀρκαδιανῶν. Εἶχεν δὲ πύργους τὸ ὅλον τεῖχος κζ΄. Αὕτη δέ ἐστιν ἡ σχηματογραφία τοῦ Βύζαντος.

53   Ἡ δευτέρα σχηματογραφία, ἣν μετέθηκεν ὁ μέγας Κωνσταντῖνος, ἐστὶν αὕτη· προσέθηκεν τὸ τεῖχος ἀπὸ μὲν τοῦ Εὐγενίου μέχρι τοῦ ἁγίου Ἀντωνίου, ἀπὸ δὲ τοὺς Τόπους μέχρι τῆς παναγίας Θεοτόκου τῆς Ῥάβδου. Καὶ ἀνέβαινεν ἕως τοῦ Ἐξακιονίου τὸ χερσαῖον τεῖχος ἀπὸ τῆς Ῥάβδου καὶ κατέβαινεν μέχρι τῆς παλαιᾶς πόρτας τοῦ Προδρόμου καὶ τῆς μονῆς τοῦ Δίου καὶ τὰ Ἰκασίας καὶ διήρχετο μέχρι τῆς Βώνου καὶ εἰς τὸν ἅγιον Μανουήλ,

the> Apostles, making it a basilica with a wooden roof, and the mausoleum of the emperors where he is laid to rest.

One[79] should know that the palaces of Byzas were on the Akropolis. The church of Saint Menas was previously a temple of Zeus, and from it are also the statues of the great Zeus and Kronos on the marble arches which are above the two great columns.[80] For it was a custom of the ancients to build their houses, that is palaces, on their Akropolises. 51

The wall started from the Akropolis wall and extended to the tower of Eugenios, then went up to the Strategion, and went on to the Bath of Achilles;[81] the arch there, which is now called the gate of Ourbikios, was a land gate of the Byzantines. And the wall went up to the Chalkoprateia and the Milion; also there was a land gate of the Byzantines. And the wall went on to the Plaited Columns of the Tzykalareia, and descended to the Topoi, and returned to the Akropolis by way of the Mangana and the Arkadianai. It had altogether twenty-seven towers. This is the town plan of Byzas. 52

The second town plan, which Constantine the Great laid out, is this one:[82] He added a wall from <the tower of> Eugenios to Saint Antonios, and from the Topoi to the most holy <church of the> Mother of God of the Rod.[83] And the land wall went up to the Exakionion from the Rod, went down to the old gate of <Saint John> the Precursor, to the monasteries of Dios and Ikasia, passed on to <the cistern of> Bonos and to <the church of> Saints Manuel, Sabel, and Ismael (at 53

Σαβὲλ καὶ Ἰσμαὴλ (ἐν ᾧ τόπῳ ἀνηρέθησαν οἱ ἅγιοι) καὶ διήρχετο εἰς τὰ Ἀρματίου καὶ μέχρι τοῦ ἁγίου Ἀντωνίου καὶ ἔκαμπτεν ἕως τοῦ Εὐγενίου. Διήρκεσε δὲ οὕτως τὸ τεῖχος ἔτη ρλβ΄, δέκα βασιλέων αὐτοκρατορησάντων. Αὕτη τοῦ μεγάλου Κωνσταντίνου ἡ σχηματογραφία.

54 [Δεῖ εἰδέναι ὅτι ὁ μέγας Κωνσταντῖνος ἤρξατο κτίζειν τὴν Κωνσταντινούπολιν ἐν ἔτει ἀπὸ κτίσεως κόσμου ͵εωκη΄, κρατήσας ἐν αὐτῇ χρόνους ιθ΄. Περαιωθέντος οὖν τοῦ ἑνδεκάτου ἐνιαυτοῦ τοῦ αὐτοῦ βασιλέως καὶ ἀρχὴν λαβόντος τοῦ δωδεκάτου ἔτους ἐπεχείρησεν ἡ Βύζαντος πόλις κτίζεσθαι.]

55 Χρὴ δὲ γινώσκειν ὅτι τῷ ͵εωλζ΄ ἔτει τοῦ κόσμου, τῷ τρίτῳ μηνὶ τῆς δευτέρας ἐπινεμήσεως, τῇ εἰκοστῇ ἕκτῃ τοῦ Νοεμβρίου μηνός, ἡμέρᾳ Τετάρτῃ, ὄντος τοῦ ἡλίου εἰς τοῦ τοξότου τὸ ζῷδον (ὡροσκόπει δὲ Καρκῖνος), τὸ πρῶτον ἔτος τῆς σξε΄ ὀλυμπιάδος, ἐπήξαντο τοὺς θεμελίους τῶν δυσικῶν τειχῶν τῆς Κωνσταντινουπόλεως. Καὶ ιθ΄ μησὶ τό τε χερσαῖον καὶ παράλιον τεῖχος μετὰ καὶ πλείστων οἰκοδομημάτων τῶν ἐν τῇ πόλει δομηθέντων ἀπαρτίσαντες, τῇ ἑνδεκάτῃ τοῦ Μαΐου μηνὸς τὰ ἐγκαίνια τῆς πόλεως γεγόνασι καὶ προσηγορεύθη ἡ πόλις Κωνσταντινούπολις.

56 [Ὁ αὐτὸς ⟦ἡμέρας Δευτέρας ἰνδικτιῶνος τρίτης ἔτους ͵εωλη΄⟧ ἦρξεν ἐν Ῥώμῃ μετὰ Μαξιμιανοῦ καὶ Μαξεντίου ἔτη ἑπτά, μόνος δὲ ἔτη ἕτερα ἕξ, ὡς εἶναι ὁμοῦ τὰ ὅλα ἔτη τῆς αὐτοῦ βασιλείας τριάκοντα δύο, ἐν Ῥώμῃ δὲ δεκατρία, καὶ ἐν Κωνσταντινουπόλει δεκαεννέα.]

57 Ἐπὶ δὲ τῇ τῶν ἐγκαινίων ἡμέρᾳ διέταξεν ἐπὶ τοὺς ἐφεξῆς χρόνους τὴν αὐτοῦ στήλην ὁρᾶσθαι μετὰ τῆς

the place where the saints were executed). And it passed on to Ta Armatiou as far as Saint Antonios, and then turned to <the tower of> Eugenios.[84] This wall lasted for 132 years during the reigns of ten emperors.[85] This is the town plan of Constantine the Great.

[One should know that Constantine the Great began to build Constantinople in the year 5828 from the beginning of the world, reigning there nineteen years.[86] When the eleventh year of his reign had been completed and the twelfth began, he undertook to rebuild the city of Byzas.] 54

One should know that the foundations of the western walls of Constantinople were laid in the year of <the creation of> the world 5837, in the third month of the second indiction, on the 26th of the month of November, a Wednesday, when the sun stood in the sign of Sagittarius (in the horoscope of Cancer), the first year of the 265th Olympiad. And completing within nineteen months the land and sea wall with most of the edifices which had to be built in the city, the inauguration of the city was celebrated on the eleventh of May and the city received the name Constantinople, [a Monday of the third indiction, the year 5838.[87] 55

He reigned in Rome with Maximian and Maxentius seven years, alone another six, so that all the years of his reign are thirty-two, thirteen in Rome, and in Constantinople nineteen.][88] 56

On the day of the inauguration, he decreed that in future years his statue should be shown with the usual honor at a 57

εἰθισμένης τιμῆς ἱππικοῦ ἀγομένου τῷ κατὰ καιρὸν βασι-
λεύοντι καὶ τῷ δήμῳ καὶ ἀνέρχεσθαι μέχρι τοῦ Στάματος.

58   Ταῦτα ἐπράχθη τῷ δωδεκάτῳ ἔτει τῆς βασιλείας τοῦ
μεγάλου καὶ ἐν ἁγίοις Κωνσταντίνου, συμπραττόντων καὶ
συνευδοκούντων εἰς τὴν οἰκοδομὴν τῆς θεοφρουρήτου
Κωνσταντινουπόλεως Εὐφρατᾶ τε φημὶ τοῦ παρακοιμωμένου καὶ Οὐρβικίου καὶ Ὀλυβρίου πραιποσίτου καὶ
Ἰσιδώρου καὶ Εὐστοργίου καὶ Μιχαὴλ πρωτοβεστιαρίου
ἀμφοτέρων πατρικίων, καὶ Ὀνωρησίου ἐπάρχου, καθὼς
ἱστοροῦσιν Εὐτυχιανὸς πρωτοασηκρήτης ὁ γραμματικός,
ὁ συμπαρὼν τῷ παραβάτῃ Ἰουλιανῷ ἐν Περσίδι, Εὐτρό-
πιός τε ὁ σοφιστὴς καὶ ἐπιστολογράφος Κωνσταντίνου,
Ἐλεύσιός τε διάκονος ὁ φιλόσοφος καὶ Τρωΐλος ὁ ῥήτωρ
ὁ πολλὰς ἀρχὰς διανύσας μετὰ δόξης καὶ Ἡσύχιος ὁ ταχυ-
γράφος—οὗτοι πάντες αὐτόπται καὶ θεαταὶ γενόμενοι
τῶν τηνικαῦτα πραχθέντων ἀκριβῶς.

59   Ἐν δὲ τῷ αὐτῷ δωδεκάτῳ ἔτει τῆς βασιλείας αὐτοῦ
ἐποίησεν ὡς εἴρηται μείζονα τὴν Βυζαντίων πόλιν, ἐκάλε-
σέν τε αὐτὴν Κωνσταντινούπολιν· ἔκτισέ τε τὰ παλάτια
ἀπό τε τῆς Χαλκῆς καὶ τῶν Ἐξκουβίτων καὶ τῶν Σχολῶν·
καὶ τοῖς ἁγίοις Ἀποστόλοις ναὸν ἀνήγειρεν ἐκεῖσε καὶ τὴν
θόλον τῆς Ἑπταλύχνου, ἣ καὶ μέχρι τοῦ νῦν σώζεται
ἔσωθεν τῶν Σχολῶν, καὶ τὸ Τριβουνάλιον καὶ τὰ νῦν ὀνο-
μαζόμενα Νούμερα, καὶ αὐτὰ εἰς παλάτιον, καὶ τὰ ιθʹ
Ἀκούβιτα καὶ τὸ Στέψιμον καὶ τὸν ναὸν τοῦ ἁγίου Στεφάνου, ὅνπερ εἶχεν χειμέριον κοιτῶνα.

60   Ἀνήγειρεν δὲ καὶ τὴν Μαγναῦραν καὶ τοῦ Κυρίου τὴν
ἐκκλησίαν καὶ τὸ Γενικὸν καὶ τὸ Ἰδικὸν καὶ τὸ Βεστιάριον

chariot race, to the then reigning emperor and the people, and should be brought up to the Stama.[89]

This was done in the twelfth year of the reign of Constan- 58 tine the Great who is reckoned among the saints. To the building of the God-protected city of Constantinople, Euphratas the *parakoimomenos* contributed and collaborated, I say, and Ourbikios, the prefect Olybrios, Isidoros, Eustorgios, and the *protobestiarios* Michael, all of them patricians, and Honoresios the prefect, as reported by Eutychianos the chief of the chancellery and man of letters who was also in Persia with the apostate Julian, Eutropios the sophist and letter writer of Constantine, Eleusios the deacon and philosopher, Troilos the rhetor who held many positions with great honor, and Hesychios the stenographer—they all were eyewitnesses and precise observers of the events which happened at that time.[90]

In the same twelfth year of his reign he expanded, as has 59 been said, the city of the Byzantines, called it Constantinople and built the palaces[91] from the Chalke <Gate>, the Exkoubita and the Scholai. And he built a church of the Apostles there and the Dome of the Seven Candelabra which is preserved to this day within the Scholai, as well as the Tribunal and what is now called the Noumera, which are also in the palace, and the Nineteen Couches, the Stepsimon, and the church of Saint Stephen which he had as a winter apartment.

He also built the Magnaura and the church of the 60 Lord, the Genikon and the Idikon, the Bestiarion, the

καὶ τὸν Καβαλλάριν καὶ τὸ Σῖγμα καὶ τὸ Ὠάτον τὸ πρὸς τὴν Νέαν κείμενον καὶ μέχρι τῆς Σιδηρᾶς ὀνομαζομένης καὶ τὸ Κάτοπτρον τὸ λοετρὸν καὶ τὰ παλάτια τὰ ἐπάνω μέχρι τοῦ Γερανίου καὶ τὸ Χρυσόκλαβον καὶ τὸ μέγα λοετρὸν τοῦ Οἰκονομίου τὸ πλησιάζον εἰς τὸ Τζυκανιστήριον, ἔχον ἑπτὰ ἐνθήκας καὶ δώδεκα στοὰς καὶ κολυμβήθραν εὐμεγέθη· ἔνζωδον δὲ ὑπῆρχεν· καὶ αἱ μὲν ἑπτὰ ἐνθῆκαι εἰς μίμησιν τῶν ἑπτὰ πλανήτων, αἱ δὲ δώδεκα στοαὶ κατὰ τῶν ιβ' μηνῶν τὰς κράσεις. Ἐσώζετο δὲ καὶ ἧπτε μέχρι τοῦ Νικηφόρου τοῦ Φωκᾶ. Ὁ δὲ Ἰωάννης ὁ Τζιμισκῆς κατέλυσεν αὐτὸ καὶ ἐκ τῆς ὕλης ἔκτισεν τὴν Χαλκῆν, ἐν ᾗ καὶ ἐτάφη.

61   Βουλόμενος δὲ κτίσαι ἱππικὸν κατὰ μίμησιν τῆς Ῥώμης εὗρεν τὸ τοῦ Σευήρου καὶ ἀνεπλήρωσεν αὐτὸ ἤγουν τὸ ἓν μέρος τῶν βαθμίδων καὶ τῶν δύο περιπάτων καὶ τὸ ἄνω τῶν καγκέλλων καὶ τὸν Σφενδόνα καὶ τοὺς καμπτῆρας καὶ τοὺς δήμους.

62   Πάντα δὲ τὰ χαλκουργεύματα καὶ τὰ ξόανα ἐκ διαφόρων ναῶν καὶ πόλεων ἀθροίσας ἔστησεν αὐτὰ εἰς διακόσμησιν τῆς πόλεως, ὁμοίως δὲ καὶ τοὺς κίονας τῶν περιπάτων· ἐπάτωσε δὲ τοὺς αὐτοὺς περιπάτους μετὰ συγκοπῆς. Καὶ ἐπετέλεσεν αὐτὸς πρῶτος γυμνικὸν καὶ ἱππικὸν ἀγῶνα. Ὁ δὲ ἔχων τοὺς ὀνικοὺς πόδας ἧκεν ἀπὸ τῆς μεγάλης Ἀντιοχείας· ἔστιν δὲ ὁ Βελλεροφόντης καὶ ἐσέβοντο αὐτὸν ἐκεῖσε. Ὅσα δὲ ἀγάλματα καὶ τίνες εἰσὶ καὶ πόθεν ἥκασιν ἕκαστον καὶ διὰ τί ἐστηλώθησαν, ἔσχατον λεπτομερῶς ἐροῦμεν εἰς τὰ περὶ κτισμάτων.

Kaballarios, the Sigma, and the Oaton which lies toward the New Church, and <the buildings> up to the so-called Iron Gate, and the bath of the Mirror and the upper palaces, up to the Geranion and the Chrysoklabon, and the great bath of the Oikonomion which is close to the Tzykanisterion,[92] which had seven halls and twelve porticoes and a great pool. It was decorated with statues, and the seven halls imitated the seven planets, while the twelve porticoes were built according to the climate of the twelve months. It was intact and in operation until Nikephoros Phokas (963–969). John Tzimiskes (969–976) dismantled it and built from its materials the <chapel of the> Chalke, where he was also buried.

When he wanted to build the Hippodrome, imitating 61 that of Rome, he found the Hippodrome of Severus and completed it, that is, the one side of the tribunes and the two galleries, the upper part of the starting gate, the Sphendone, the turning points and the <seats assigned to the> circus factions.[93]

All the bronze statues and images he collected from dif- 62 ferent temples and cities for the embellishment of the city, and also the columns of the galleries; he also paved the galleries with cut stone.[94] And he first sponsored a sporting and chariot contest. The <statue> that has the donkey's feet came from Antioch the Great; it is Bellerophon, whom they worshipped there.[95] How many statues there are, their identification, the origin of each, and why they were set up, we will later tell in detail in the book about the buildings.

63 Θέλων δὲ οἰκίσαι ὁ μέγας Κωνσταντῖνος τὴν πόλιν αὐτοῦ, μάλιστα δὲ τοὺς Ῥωμαίους εἰς τὸ Βυζάντιον ἀγαγεῖν, ἔλαβεν ἐξ αὐτῶν λαθραίως τὰ δακτυλίδια αὐτῶν, ἑνὸς ἑκάστου ἰδίως, καὶ ἀπέστειλεν αὐτοὺς ἐπὶ τὸν βασιλέα τῶν Περσῶν, ὅστις ἐκαλεῖτο Σάρβαρος, τέσσαρας μὲν μαγίστρους, τὸν Ἄδδαν, τὸν Πρωτάσιον, τὸν Σκόμβρον, τὸν Φιλόξενον, ὀκτὼ δὲ πατρικίους, τὸν Δομνῖνον, τὸν Πρόβον, τὸν Δαρεῖον, τὸν Μαῦρον, τὸν Ῥοδανόν, τὸν Σαλλούστιον τὸν ἔπαρχον, τὸν Μόδεστον, τὸν Εὔβουλον.

64 Μετὰ πλείστου στρατοῦ, ὡς εἴρηται, ἐξαπέστειλεν αὐτοὺς ποιήσαντας ις΄ μῆνας ἐν τῇ Περσίδι. Ὁ δὲ μέγας Κωνσταντῖνος ἀποστείλας εἰς Ῥώμην ἀνελάβετο τὰς γυναῖκας καὶ τὰ τέκνα καὶ τὰς φαμιλίας αὐτῶν· ὥρισε δὲ καὶ κτίστας μηχανικούς, ἵνα θεάσωνται τοὺς οἴκους αὐτῶν καὶ τοὺς τόπους ἑνὸς ἑκάστου πῶς κεῖνται. Καὶ ὡς εἶδον τὰς οἰκίας αὐτῶν, ἑτέρας ἐπὶ τὸν αἰγιαλὸν τῆς θαλάσσης, ἄλλας ἐπὶ τὰς ἠπείρους, καὶ τὰ σχήματα τῶν κτισμάτων καὶ τὰς ἀνόδους οἷαι ἦσαν κοχλιοειδεῖς, καὶ λαβόντες τὰς φαμιλίας αὐτῶν τῶν συγκλητικῶν ἀνῆλθον ἐπὶ τὸ Βυζάντιον καὶ ἀνθομοίους ἔκτισαν τοὺς οἴκους αὐτῶν· καὶ ἐκάθισεν ἐκεῖσε τὰς φαμιλίας αὐτῶν.

65 Ἐλθόντες οὖν ἀπὸ τῆς Περσίδος μετὰ νίκης ἀναλαβόμενοι καὶ πάκτα κεντηνάρια τξε΄, δεξάμενος δὲ αὐτοὺς ὁ βασιλεὺς καὶ ποιήσας εὐωχίας εἶπεν αὐτοῖς· "θέλετε ἀπελθεῖν εἰς Ῥώμην;" δοκιμάζων αὐτούς· οἵτινες ἔφησαν μὴ κατελθεῖν μέχρι δύο μηνῶν. Ὁ δὲ βασιλεὺς ἔφη· "ἀπόψε ἔχω δοῦναι ὑμῖν τὰς οἰκίας ὑμῶν." Προστάξας δὲ Εὐφρατᾶν τὸν παρακοιμώμενον αὐτοῦ, ὅστις ἐποίησεν τὸν

Constantine the Great wanted to colonize his city, and 63
especially to bring the Romans to Byzantion.[96] So he secretly took away their rings, from each one separately,
and sent them to the king of the Persians who was called
Sarbaros, namely four *magistroi,* Addas, Protasios, Skombros, and Philoxenos, and eight patricians, Domninos, Probos, Dareios, Mauros, Rhodanos, Salloustios the prefect,
Modestos, and Euboulos.[97]

He sent them out, as it is said, with a very great army, 64
and they stayed sixteen months in Persia.[98] Constantine the
Great sent to Rome and took their wives and children and
families. He also ordered master builders to survey their
houses and the site of each house to see how they were situated. And when they observed their houses, some on the
seashore, others on the mainland, and the shapes of the
buildings and their staircases, <to see> which of them were
spiral, they took the families of these senators with them,
went to Byzantion and built similar houses for them. And he
settled their families there.

When they returned victoriously from Persia, having re- 65
ceived also a tribute of 365 hundredweights *(kentenaria)* of
gold,[99] the emperor received them, gave a banquet for them,
and said to them: "Do you want to go to Rome?" In this
way he tested them, and they said they would not go there
for another two months. The emperor said: "This evening
I will give you your houses." He gave an order to his

Κωνσταντῖνον Χριστιανόν, ἕνα ἕκαστον ἀπέδωκεν τοὺς αὐτῶν οἴκους.

66 Ἰδόντες δὲ τοὺς πυλῶνας αὐτῶν καὶ τὰς αὐλὰς καὶ τὰς ἀνόδους ὅτι ὅμοια Ῥώμης εἰσὶ καὶ τὰ μέτρα καὶ τὰ σχήματα καὶ τὰ ὕψη, καὶ τὴν ἀπόβλεψιν τῶν θυρίδων, ἔδοξαν εἶναι ἐν φαντασίᾳ ἐν Ῥώμῃ. Εὑρόντες δὲ καὶ τὰς φαμιλίας αὐτῶν ἐξεπλάγησαν· ὁμιλησάντων δὲ ἑκάστου αὐτῶν τὰς φαμιλίας αὐτῶν, τότε ἐπίστευσαν, ὅτι οὐκ ἔστιν φάντα-σμα, ἀλλὰ φρόνησις τοῦ βασιλέως, "ὅτι ἄκοντας καὶ μὴ βουλομένους ἡμᾶς ἐνῴκισεν ἐνθάδε."

67 Ἐκ δὲ τῶν ὀνομάτων αὐτῶν εἴληφαν οἱ τόποι τὰς προσ-ηγορίας. Ὁ δὲ Φιλόξενος ἔκτισεν κινστέρναν τὴν ἐπονο-μαζομένην Φιλόξενον. Ὁ Πρόβος ἀνήγειρεν ναὸν τοῦ Προδρόμου, ὅνπερ ὁ Καβαλλῖνος ἐποίησεν ἐργοστάσιον, τὰ λεγόμενα Πρόβου. Ὁ Δομνῖνος ἔκτισεν οἶκον εἰς τὰ Μαυριανοῦ, ὃν εἶχεν ὁ Ἀγρικόλαος. Ὁ Δαρεῖος ἔκτισεν οἶκον τῆς Ἰκανατίσσης τοῦ Σκληροῦ. Ὁ Μαῦρος ἔκτισεν οἶκον, ὅπερ εἶχεν ὁ Βελονᾶς. Ὁ Ῥοδανὸς ἔκτισεν οἶκον, ὅσπερ καλεῖται τὰ Εὐουράνης· ἔστι δὲ τῆς Μαμαίνης. Ὁ Σαλλούστιος ἔκτισεν οἶκον, ὅστις καλεῖται τοῦ Κοντο-μύτου. Ὁ Μόδεστος ἔκτισεν οἶκον εἰς τοὺς ἁγίους Ἀπο-στόλους τοῦ Λαμπροῦ. Οἱ δὲ τρεῖς πυλῶνες ἐκτίσθησαν παρὰ τοῦ Εὐβούλου.

68 Ἔκτισε δὲ καὶ τέσσαρας ἐμβόλους ἀπὸ τοῦ παλατίου μέχρι τῶν χερσαίων τειχῶν, ἐγχορήγους θόλους· ὁ εἷς ἤρχετο ἀπὸ τοῦ Τζυκανιστηρίου καὶ τῶν Μαγγάνων καὶ τῆς ἀκροπόλεως καὶ τῶν Εὐγενίου καὶ διήρχετο μέχρι τοῦ ἁγίου Ἀντωνίου· ὁ δὲ ἕτερος ἀπὸ τῆς Δάφνης καὶ τῶν

parakoimomenos Euphratas, who had made Constantine a Christian, and he gave everyone his house.[100]

When they saw their gates, their courtyards and their 66 staircases, <realizing> that their size, shapes and height were the same as in Rome, and also the view from the windows, they imagined that they were in Rome. When they also found their families there, they were amazed, and as they talked to their families, they understood that this was no phantasm, but a plan of the emperor "who has settled us here against our will and without our consent."

The sites received their names from the names <of the 67 Romans>. Philoxenos built a cistern, the so-called Philoxenos. Probos built a church of the Precursor, which <Constantine V> Kaballinos (741–775) turned into a workshop, called Ta Probou. Domninos built at Ta Maurianou a house which was owned by Agrikolaos. Dareios built the house of the *hikanatissa* of Skleros. Mauros built a house which was owned by Belonas. Rhodanos built a house which is called Ta Euouranes; it is owned by Mamaina. Salloustios built a house which is called that of Kontomytes. Modestos built at <the church of> the Holy Apostles a house <which is owned by> Lampros.[101] The three gates were built by Euboulos.

He also built four porticoes from the palace to the land 68 walls, with spacious vaults.[102] One began from the Tzykanisterion, the Mangana, the Akropolis and Ta Eugeniou, and went to Saint Antonios.[103] The second went from <the

41

Σοφιῶν μέχρι τῆς Ῥάβδου· οἱ δὲ ἕτεροι δύο ἔμβολοι ἀπὸ τῆς Χαλκῆς καὶ τοῦ Μιλίου καὶ τοῦ Φόρου μέχρι τοῦ Ταύρου καὶ τοῦ Βοὸς καὶ τοῦ Ἐξακιονίου. Ἐπάνω δὲ τῶν ἐμβόλων περίπατοι πλακωτοὶ λίθινοι καὶ στῆλαι χαλκαῖ ἄπειροι εἰς διακόσμησιν τῆς πόλεως ἵσταντο.

69 Ἔκτισε δὲ καὶ τοὺς μ' ὑδρῶνας[5] καὶ τοὺς ἀγωγοὺς ἔφερεν ἀπὸ Βουλγαρίας· ἐποίησεν δὲ καὶ καράβους ἐγχορήγους ἐπὶ πᾶσαν τὴν πόλιν βαθεῖς, τῷ ὕψει ὅσον τῶν ἐμβόλων, διὰ τὸ μὴ εἶναι δυσωδία τις καὶ ἐνσκήπτουσιν νόσοι πολλαί, ἀλλ' εἰς τὸ βάθος διέρχεσθαι τὰς δυσώδεις ὕλας καὶ κατέρχεσθαι εἰς τὴν θάλασσαν.

70 Ταῦτα δὲ ἐκτίσθησαν ὡς εἴρηται παρὰ Οὐρβικίου πραιποσίτου καὶ Σαλλουστίου ἐπάρχου καὶ τῶν λοιπῶν, καταλιπὼν αὐτοῖς κεντηνάρια χρυσίου ἑξακόσια εἴς τε τοὺς ἐμβόλους καὶ τοὺς ἀγωγοὺς καὶ εἰς τὰ τείχη. Ἐκεῖνος δὲ ἦν κατὰ τῶν Σκυθῶν καὶ ὑποτάξας αὐτοὺς ἔκτισεν πόλιν τὴν Περσθλάβαν καὶ τὴν Δίστραν καὶ τὴν Πλίσκουβαν καὶ τὴν Κωνσταντίαν. Ταῦτα δὲ ἐκτίσθησαν παρισταμένου τοῦ Οὐρβικίου εἰς χρόνους δύο ἥμισυ ἀπὸ φωνῆς Ἑρμείου.

71 Ἔκτισε δὲ καὶ τὰ Ἁρματίου δι' ὧν ἔπηξεν τὴν κόρτην αὐτοῦ καὶ τὰ ἅρματα αὐτοῦ ἐκεῖσε ἀπέθετο, ὅτε ὑπέταξεν τοὺς Βυζαντίους. Εἰς δὲ τὰ ὀνόματα τῶν τριῶν αὐτοῦ υἱῶν ἔκτισεν παλάτια τὰ καλούμενα Κωνσταντιανὰς καὶ τὰ καλούμενα Κώνσταντος· ἔστιν δὲ ὁ οἶκος τοῦ Τουβάκη καὶ τοῦ Ἰβερίτζη, ὅνπερ ἔχει ὁ Ἀκροπολίτης. Τοὺς δὲ ναοὺς καὶ τὰ λοιπά, ὅσα ἀνήγειρεν ὁ μέγας Κωνσταντῖνος, ὕστερον εἰς τὰ περὶ κτισμάτων ἐροῦμεν.

72 Ὁ δὲ μικρὸς Θεοδόσιος εἰς τὸν πέμπτον χρόνον τῆς

palaces of> Daphne and Sophia to the <church of the> Rod.[104] The other two porticoes went from the Chalke, the Milion and the Forum to the <fora of> Tauros, Bous and the Exakionion.[105] On top of the porticoes were paved walkways of stone, and innumerable bronze statues stood there for the embellishment of the city.

He also built the forty water distributors and brought the water supply line in from Bulgaria. He also made spacious and deep wastewater channels in the whole city, of the same height as the porticoes, so as to prevent a stench and many harmful diseases, but the noxious substances passed deep underground and went down to the sea. 69

All this was built, as has been said, by the *praipositos* Ourbikios, the prefect Salloustios and the others, <as Constantine> had left them six hundred hundredweights of gold for the porticoes, the water supply lines and the walls. He himself went against the Scythians, subdued them and built the cities of Persthlaba, Distra, Pliskouba, and Konstantia.[106] These were built, as Hermeias says, with the help of Ourbikios within two and a half years. 70

He also built Ta Armatiou where he had set up his camp and stored his weapons when he subdued the Byzantines. In the names of his three sons he built palaces, called Konstantianai and Ta Konstantos. This is the house of Toubakes and Iberitzes,[107] which is now owned by Akropolites. About the churches and the other structures, which Constantine the Great built, we will later tell in <the book> about the buildings. 71

An earthquake happened in the fifth year of Theodosios 72

βασιλείας αὐτοῦ σεισμοῦ γεγονότος καὶ τῶν τειχῶν εἰς γῆν καταπιπτόντων διὰ τὸ τοὺς Ἀμαληκίτας τοὺς Χατζιτζαρίους οἰκῆσαι ἐν τῇ πόλει καὶ βλασφημεῖν σφοδρῶς εἰς τὸ Τρισάγιον—ποιήσας ὁ αὐτὸς βασιλεὺς ἱκεσίαν καὶ λιτὴν εἰς τὸν Κάμπον τοῦ Τριβουναλίου μετὰ τοῦ πατριάρχου Πρόκλου κραζόντων τὸ "Κύριε ἐλέησον" ἐπὶ πολλὰς ὥρας, πάντων ὁρώντων ἐπήρθη παιδίον εἰς τὸν ἀέρα καὶ ἤκουσεν ἀγγέλων μελῳδούντων καὶ ὑμνούντων· "ἅγιος ὁ Θεός, ἅγιος ἰσχυρός, ἅγιος ἀθάνατος, ἐλέησον ἡμᾶς." Κατελθόντος δὲ τοῦ παιδίου ὁ λαὸς ἐμελῴδει οὕτως καὶ ἔστη ὁ σεισμὸς ἔκτοτε.

73   Καὶ ἐξέωσεν ὁ βασιλεὺς πάντας τοὺς αἱρετικοὺς ἐκ τῆς πόλεως καὶ παρεξέβαλεν τὰ τείχη ἀπὸ τοῦ Ἐξακιονίου μέχρι Χρυσείας· ἐξ οὗ καὶ στήλην ἔστησεν αὐτοῦ ὄπισθεν τῶν ἐλεφάντων. Καὶ ἀνεβίβασεν τὸ παράλιον τεῖχος ἀπὸ τῆς Ῥάβδου μέχρι Χρυσείας καὶ ἀπὸ τὸν ἅγιον Ἀντώνιον τὰ Ἀρματίου μέχρι τῶν Βλαχερνῶν καὶ τῆς Χρυσείας. Οἱ δὲ δύο δῆμοι ἔκτισαν τὰ τείχη παρ' αὐτοῦ ὁρισθέντες, καθὼς εἰς τὰ περὶ κτισμάτων ἐροῦμεν.

the Younger's reign,[108] and the walls collapsed to the ground, because the Amalekites, the Chatzitzarians,[109] lived inside the city and slandered the Trisagion vehemently. When the emperor made a litany and a procession to the Camp of the Tribunal[110] together with the patriarch Proklos, shouting "Lord, have mercy" for many hours, a child was lifted up into the air in the sight of all, and he heard the angels singing and chanting: "Holy is God, holy and strong, holy and immortal, have mercy upon us." When the child came back down, the people sang this, and henceforth the earthquake stopped.

And the emperor expelled all the heretics from the city and extended the walls from the Exakionion to the Golden Gate, where he also set up his statue behind the elephants.[111] And he extended the sea wall from the <church of the> Rod to the Golden Gate and from Saint Antonios of Ta Armatiou to the Blachernai and the Golden Gate. The two circus factions built the walls at his command, as we shall describe in the book about the buildings.

BOOK TWO

Πάτρια τῆς Κωνσταντινουπόλεως· περὶ στηλῶν, ἐν ᾧ καὶ περὶ Ἀδιαβηνῆς

Περὶ Ἀδιαβηνῆς.—Αὕτη ἡ χώρα κεῖται πρὸ τῆς Μεσοποταμίας ὡς ἐπὶ ἀνατολὴν πέραν τοῦ Τίγριδος. Ἀντικρὺς δέ ἐστιν ἡ ἄσφαλτος ἡ λεγομένη <ν>άφθα· λέγεται δὲ Ἀδιαβηνὴ διὰ τὸ εἶναι πλείονας ποταμοὺς ἐν αὐτῇ καὶ δυσχερεστέραν ποιεῖν τὴν διάβασιν. Ἐκεῖ ἐστιν ἡ Νινευή· τοσαύτην δὲ ἀσφάλειαν ποιεῖ τοῖς κτίσμασιν ἡ ἄσφαλτος, ὥστε ταῖς ὀπταῖς πλίνθοις καὶ τοῖς λεπτοῖς λίθοις συμμιγεῖσα ἰσχυροτέρα γίνεται παντὸς σιδήρου. Ἐκεῖσε δέ ἐστιν <τὸ> Ἄορνον στόμιον, ἐξ οὗ δεινὸν πνεῦμα ἀναδίδοται, ὥστε ἐπίγειόν ζῷον ἅπαν καὶ πᾶν πτηνὸν ἀποφθείρειν, εἰ προστύχοι ὀσφρανθῆναι. Καὶ σκεδάννυται[1] καὶ οὐ κατ' εὐθεῖαν ἐξέρχεται καὶ ὀλίγον ἀνερχόμενον ἄνεισιν καὶ πάλιν ἀντανακλᾶται· καὶ ἐκ τούτου τὰ ἐν ὑψηλοῖς πετόμενα σῴζεται καὶ τὰ πέριξ <νεμόμενα. Λέγει δὲ ὁ Δίων τοιοῦτόν τι ἑωρακέναι ἐν Ἱεραπόλει τῆς> Ἀσίας, ὥστε πάντα τὰ ὀσφραινόμενα φθείρει πλὴν τῶν εὐνούχων. Ἔστιν δὲ ἐν τῇ Ἀδιαβηνῇ ἡ Κτησιφῶν.

2   Περὶ ἀγάλματος Ἰανουαρίου.—Τὸ ἄγαλμα τοῦ Ἰανουαρίου ἱστοροῦσι τετράμορφον διὰ τὰς τέσσαρας τροπάς· ἄλλοι δὲ πλάττουσιν αὐτὸν ἐν τῇ δεξιᾷ χειρὶ κλεῖδα

The *Patria* of Constantinople:
On Statues, Together with a
Chapter on Adiabene

On Adiabene.[1]—This country lies before Mesopotamia, to the east beyond the Tigris. On the opposite side, there is the asphalt which is called *naphtha*. It is called Adiabene, because there are many rivers which make its passage difficult. Nineveh is there. The asphalt makes the buildings very secure so that, when mixed with baked brick and small stones, it becomes harder than any iron. The Aornon estuary is there, whence a terrible wind emerges, killing every land animal and every bird which happens to smell it. And it is dispersed, and does not gush out directly, but rises a bit when coming out and falls back down again. For this reason creatures that fly high and <those that graze> in the vicinity are saved. <Dion says that he also saw such a wind in Hierapolis in>[2] Asia, that it kills all who smell it except eunuchs. Ktesiphon is also in Adiabene.

On the statue of January.—The statue of January is represented as a tetramorph because of the four seasons. Others fashion him holding a key in his right hand, as the beginning

2

κατέχον<τα> ὡς ἀρχὴν τοῦ χρόνου καὶ ἄνοιξιν τοῦ ἐνιαυτοῦ καὶ θυρεόν, ἕτεροι δὲ τῇ δεξιᾷ χειρὶ ψήφων κρατοῦντα τ', τῇ δὲ εὐωνύμῳ ξε' ὥσ<περ τὸν ἐνιαυτόν· ὅθεν
καὶ ὁ Λογγῖνος Αἰωνάριον αὐτὸν ἑρμηνεῦσαι βιάζεται
ὡσ>ανεὶ αἰῶνος πατέρα.

3 Περὶ ἀγάλματος κρατοῦντος δόρυ.—Τῆς Ἀθηνᾶς τὸ
ἄγαλμα δόρυ κρατεῖ καὶ ἀσπίδα παρὰ τὸ σταθερὸν καὶ ἀν-
δρεῖον καὶ διὰ τὸ πᾶσαν ἐπιβουλὴν διὰ τῆς σοφίας ἀπω-
θεῖσθαι· ἡ αὐτὴ γάρ ἐστι τῷ νῷ. Καὶ περικεφαλαίαν διδόασιν αὐτῇ διὰ τὸ εἶναι τῆς σοφίας τὸ ἀκρότατον ἀθέατον·
καὶ ἐλαίαν ὡς καθαρωτάτης αὐτῆς οὐσίας οὔσης· φωτὸς
γὰρ ὕλη ἡ ἐλαία· καὶ Γοργόνα διδόασιν ἐπὶ τὸ στῆθος
αὐτῆς διὰ τὸ ταχὺ τοῦ νοός.

4 Περὶ ἀγάλματος κρατοῦντος κιθάραν.—Κιθάραν ἐπὶ
χειρῶν πλάττουσι τοῦ Ἀπόλλωνος, οἱονεὶ τὸν ἥλιον τὴν
τοῦ παντὸς ἁρμονίαν· κιρνώμενος γὰρ τοῖς λοιποῖς
ἀστράσι καὶ τίκτει καὶ ζῳογονεῖ.

5 Περὶ ἀγάλματος κρατοῦντος ψαλίδα χαλκῆν.—Τὴν
Ἥραν λέγουσιν εἶναι τὸν ἀέρα· καὶ ἐπεὶ ὁ ἀὴρ καθαίρει,
ποιοῦσι τῆς Ἥρας τὸ ἄγαλμα βαστάζειν ψαλίδα ἀπὸ
μεταφορᾶς ψαλίδος τῆς ἀποκειρούσης τὰς τρίχας καὶ
καθαρὸν ἀποδεικνυούσης τὸ σῶμα.

6 Περὶ ἀγάλματος βαστάζοντος πύργον.—Τὴν Δήμητραν
οἱ παλαιοὶ τὴν γῆν καλοῦσιν· καὶ ἐπειδὴ ἕδρα πάσης
πόλεως ἡ γῆ ἐστιν, ὡς βαστάζουσα τὰς πόλεις πλάττεται
πυργοφόρος.

7 Περὶ ἀγάλματος κτένα φέροντος.—Τῆς Ἀφροδίτης τὸ
ἄγαλμα κτένα φέρει. Ἐπειδὴ συνέβη ποτὲ ταῖς τῶν

of the year, as both the opening of the year and its door-keeper, while others show him holding three hundred pebbles in his right hand, and sixty-five in his left, <like the year. Hence Longinos attempts to interpret him as being Aionarios>, the father of time.

On a statue holding a spear.—The statue of Athene holds 3
a spear and a shield because of her steadfastness and courage, and because she wards off every scheme by her wisdom, for she herself is prudent. And they give her a helmet, for the peak of wisdom is invisible, and an olive branch, as this is the most pure substance, for olive branch wood is the material of light. And they place a Gorgon's head on her breast because of the quickness of her mind.

On a statue holding a lyre.—They put a lyre into the 4
hands of Apollo, as he is the sun, the harmony of the universe. For when united with the other stars he both gives birth and creates life.

On a statue holding bronze scissors.—They say that Hera 5
is the air, and since the air cleanses, they make the statue of Hera holding scissors, using the metaphor that the scissors cut the hair and render the body clean.

On a statue holding a tower.—The ancients call Demeter 6
the earth, and as the earth is the abode of every town, she is depicted bearing a tower, as if she were holding the towns.

On a statue holding a comb.—The statue of Aphrodite 7
holds a comb, for it once happened that the women of the

Ῥωμαίων γυναιξὶ κνήφην λοιμώδη γενέσθαι, καὶ ξυρου-
μένων αὐτῶν πασῶν γεγόνασιν <αὐταῖς οἱ κτένες> ἀχρεῖοι·
εὐξαμένας δὲ τῇ Ἀφροδίτῃ ἀνατριχωθῆναι, τιμῆσαί τε αὐτὴν ἀγάλματι κτένα φέρουσαν. Πλάττουσιν δὲ αὐτὴν καὶ
γένειον ἔχειν, ὅτι τε καὶ ἄρρενος καὶ θηλείας ὄργανα ἔχει·
αὐτὴν γὰρ λέγουσιν τὴν ἔφορον γενέσεως τοῦ παντός, καὶ
ἀπὸ τῆς ὀσφύος καὶ ἄνωθεν λέγουσιν αὐτὴν ἄρρενα, τὰ δὲ
κάτω θήλειαν. Πλάττουσι δὲ αὐτὴν καὶ ἔφιππον, ἐπειδὴ
καὶ ὁ Αἰνείας ὁ υἱὸς αὐτῆς πλεύσας μέχρι τῆς δύσεως
μετὰ τοῦτο ἵππῳ ἐπέβη καὶ τὴν μητέρα ἐτίμησε τοιούτῳ
ἀγάλματι.

8   Περὶ ἀγάλματος τοῦ Διός.—Ἄγαλμα πλάττουσι τοῦ
Διὸς καθήμενον, ἔχον τὰ ἄνω γυμνά, τὰ δὲ κάτω ἐσκεπα-
σμένα· κρατεῖ δὲ τῇ μὲν εὐωνύμῳ σκῆπτρον, τῇ δὲ δεξιᾷ
ἀετὸν προτείνει· καὶ τὸ μὲν καθέζεσθαι τὸ ἑδραῖον τῆς
δυνάμεως αἰνίττεται, τὸ δὲ τὰ ἄνω γυμνὰ ἔχειν, ὅτι φανερὸς
τοῖς νοεροῖς καὶ τοῖς οὐρανίοις τοῦ κόσμου μέρεσι· τὰ δὲ
λοιπὰ σκέπεται, ὅτι τοῖς χαμαιζήλοις ὁ θεὸς ἄγνωστος· τὸ
δὲ τῇ λαιᾷ σκῆπτρον κατέχειν τὸ ἐξουσιαστικὸν σημαίνει,
τὸ δὲ τῇ ἑτέρᾳ προτείνειν ἀετόν, ὡς τῶν ἀεροφόρων
πνευμάτων κρατεῖ, ὡς ἀετὸς τῶν μεταρσίων ὀρνέων.

8a   <Περὶ ἀγάλματος Ἡρακλέους βαστάζοντος τρία
μῆλα.>— . . . διὰ δὲ τῶν τριῶν μήλων δηλοῖ, ὡς σφαίρας
εἰς τρία κλίματα κατέχειν τὴν πᾶσαν διακόσμησιν.

9   Περὶ ἀγάλματος πτερωτοῦ τοῦ Ἑρμοῦ.—Τὸν Ἑρμῆν οἱ
Ἕλληνες καὶ οἱ λοιποὶ τῶν ἀρχαίων [Ῥωμαίων] κατὰ τὴν
αὐτῶν πεπλανημένην μυθολογίαν υἱὸν Διὸς λέγουσι καὶ
Μαίας· Διὸς μὲν οἷον τοῦ νοῦ, Μαίας <δὲ τῆς φρονήσεως·

Romans got a pestilential itch, and when they all shaved themselves, <their combs> became useless. When they prayed to Aphrodite to get their hair back, they also honored her with a statue holding a comb. They also depict her with a beard, for she has the body parts of both a man and a woman. They call her the guardian of the creation of the universe, and they say she is a male from the loins and above, and below a female. They also depict her on horseback, for her son Aineias, after he had sailed to the west, got on a horse and honored his mother with such a statue.

On the statue of Zeus.—They make a seated statue of Zeus, having the upper part naked, and the lower covered. He holds a scepter in his left hand, and holds out an eagle with his right. His seated posture signifies his steadfastness, and the nakedness of his upper part means that he is visible to the spiritual and the heavenly parts of the world. He has the rest of his body covered, for the god is unknown to the lowly. His holding a scepter in his left hand means that he is powerful, and his holding forth an eagle with the other, that he controls the air-bearing winds, as the eagle controls the birds in the air.

<On the statue of Herakles holding three apples.>— ... showing by the three apples that spheres hold the whole order in three regions of the world.

On the winged statue of Hermes.—The Greeks and the other ancients [the Romans] say that Hermes, according to their erroneous mythology, is the son of Zeus and Maia, from the intellect of Zeus, and the <prudence of Maia; for

ἐκ νοῦ γὰρ καὶ> φρονήσεως ὁ λόγος γεννᾶται. Διὰ τοῦτο καὶ πτερωτὸν αὐτὸν <ποιοῦσιν ὡς ταχύν· οὐδὲν γὰρ λόγου ταχύτερον· ὅθεν καὶ Ὅμηρος ἔφη "ἔπεα πτερόεντα" καὶ "ὡσεὶ πτερὸν ἠὲ νόημα." Πάντων δὲ νεώτατον αὐτὸν> ἐργάζονται διὰ τὸ μὴ γηράσκειν τὸν λόγον· ἀλλὰ καὶ τετράγωνον αὐτὸν ποιοῦσι διὰ τὴν στερρότητα τοῦ ἀληθοῦς λόγου.

10   Περὶ ἀγάλματος Ἑρμοῦ βαστάζοντος μάρσιππον.—Τοῦ κέρδους αἴτιον λέγουσι καὶ τῶν ἐμποριῶν τὸν Ἑρμῆν· ὅθεν καὶ τὸ ἄγαλμα αὐτοῦ ἱστῶσι βαστάζοντα μάρσιππον· ἀλλὰ καὶ οἱ Φοίνικες τοὺς θεοὺς αὐτῶν πλάττουσιν ἐπιφέροντας βαλάντιον χρυσοῦ συμβόλου ὄντος δυναστείας· οἱ δὲ Ἕλληνες σιδηροφοροῦντας αὐτοὺς πλάττουσιν ὡς τοῖς ὅπλοις ὑποταττομένων τῶν ἀνθρώπων.

11   Περὶ ἀγάλματος Εὐγνωμοσύνης.—Ἄγαλμα τῆς Εὐγνωμοσύνης τῇ δεξιᾷ χειρὶ σκῆπτρον κατέχει ὡς ἀγχίνου οὔσης τῆς εὐγνωμοσύνης, τῇ δὲ ἀριστερᾷ βιβλίον διὰ τὸ τὸν εὐγνώμονα δέεσθαι ἀναμνήσεως, ἥτις διὰ βιβλίων γίνεται.

12   Περὶ ἀγάλματος τοῦ Πριάπου.—Τὸ ἄγαλμα τοῦ Πριάπου τοῦ Ὥρου παρ' Αἰγυπτίοις κεκλημένου ἀνθρωποειδὲς ποιοῦσι, τῇ δεξιᾷ σκῆπτρον κατέχον, ὡσανεὶ παρ' αὐτοῦ φανῆναι τὴν ξηρὰν καὶ τὴν θάλασσαν· ἐν δὲ τῇ εὐωνύμῳ κρατῶν τὸ αἰδοῖον αὐτοῦ ἐντεταμένον, ὅτι τὰ κρυπτὰ ἐν τῇ γῇ σπέρματα φανερὰ καθίστησιν. ἔχει δὲ καὶ πτερὰ διὰ τὴν ταχυτῆτα τῆς κινήσεως· τὸν δὲ κύκλον τοῦ δίσκου <διὰ> τὴν περιφέρειαν· ταὐτὸν γὰρ εἶναι τῷ ἡλίῳ αὐτὸν δοξάζουσιν· ὡς εἴρηται γάρ, ἀνθρωπόμορφον ἔχει ἄγαλμα

the word is born from intellect> and from prudence. Therefore they also <make him winged as he is quick, for nothing is quicker than the word, wherefore Homer also spoke
of "winged words" and "winged like a thought." They make
him youngest of all>, for the word never ages. But they also
make him square because of the strength of the true word.

On the statue of Hermes holding a pouch.—They say ₁₀
that Hermes is the cause of profit and commerce. Therefore
they set up his statue holding a pouch. But the Phoenicians
also make their gods holding a pouch of gold as a symbol of
power, while the Greeks make them holding iron objects,
for men are subdued by weapons.

About the statue of Honesty.—The statue of Honesty ₁₁
holds a scepter in her right hand, for Honesty is shrewd, and
in her left hand a book, for an honest man needs a reminder
which is provided by books.

On the statue of Priapos.—The statue of Priapos, who is ₁₂
called Horos by the Egyptians, is made in the form of a man;
he holds a scepter in his right hand, as land and sea were
shown by this; and he holds in his left hand his erect private
parts, for he clearly reveals the seed hidden in the earth. He
also has wings because of his quick movements, and the circle of a disk because of its roundness, as they believe that he
is identical to the Sun. For it is said that he has a human-

τῇ δεξιᾷ χειρὶ σκῆπτρον κατέχον, τῇ δὲ εὐωνύμῳ τὸ
αἰδοῖον αὐτοῦ ἐντεταμένον· ἐπὶ δὲ τούτῳ πτερά· κατὰ
μέσον δὲ τῶν πτερῶν δισκοειδὴς κύκλος.

13 Περὶ ἀγάλματος τῆς Γῆς.—Ὅτι γυναῖκα λέγουσι τὴν
Ἑστίαν καὶ πλάττουσιν οἱονεὶ τὴν Γῆν τύμπανον βαστά-
ζουσαν, ἐπειδὴ τοὺς ἀνέμους ἡ γῆ ὑφ' ἑαυτὴν συγκλείει.

14 Περὶ ἀγάλματος ἔχοντος ἐν τῇ κεφαλῇ κέρατα.—Τὸ δὲ
ἄγαλμα τοῦ Σελεύκου τοῦ δι' ἀνδρείαν ὀνομασθέντος
Νικάνορος τοῦ δόντος τῷ υἱῷ αὐτοῦ Ἀντιόχῳ Στρατονίκην
τὴν ἑαυτοῦ γυναῖκα ἐρασθέντι αὐτῆς καὶ διὰ τὸν πρὸς
αὐτὴν ἔρωτα ἀσθενήσαντι καὶ ἐπικρυπτομένῳ, γνωσθέντι
δὲ ὑπὸ Ἐρασιστράτου τοῦ ἰατροῦ. Φασὶ συνόντα Σέλευκον
Ἀλεξάνδρῳ τῷ Μακεδονικῷ ταῦρον θυομένῳ ἀποδράντα
μόνον Σέλευκον περιγενέσθαι αὐτοῦ τῶν κεράτων κρα-
τήσαντα· καὶ διὰ τοῦτο τῷ ἀγάλματι αὐτοῦ περιτιθέασι
κέρατα ἐν τῇ κεφαλῇ.

14a Περὶ ἀτραβατικῶν.—Ἐν ταῖς ἑορταῖς καὶ ἐπινικίοις καὶ
παρόντων πρέσβεων ἐνεδύοντο χλαμύδας ποικίλας ἀπὸ
χρυσοῦ καὶ πορφύρας ἢ ἄλλως πως πολυτελεῖς· ἐν δὲ ταῖς
κοιναῖς συνόδοις ξηραμπελίνας τῷ χρώματι, ἃς ἐκάλουν
ἀτραβατικὰς ἢ ἀπὸ τοῦ χρώματος—τὸ γὰρ μέλαν ἄτρον
ἐκάλουν—ἢ ὅτι μετὰ τὰς τραβέας ταύταις εἰώθασι χρῆσθαι·
τραβέαι δὲ λέγονται αἱ πολυτελεῖς χλαμύδες.

15 Περὶ Αὐγουστίωνος.—Τῇ πέμπτῃ τοῦ Ὀκτωβρίου μηνὸς ἐχόρευον οἱ ῥηγεωνάρχαι ἐν τῷ {αὐ}γουστίωνι ἤγουν
τῷ ὀψοπωλείῳ εἰς τιμὴν τοῦ βασιλεύοντος κατὰ τὸν
καιρόν. Τὸν αὐτὸν οὖν τόπον νῦν οἱ ἰδιῶται Αὐγουστίωνα
καλοῦσιν· ἐν ᾧ καὶ στήλην ὁ μέγας Κωνσταντῖνος ἔστησεν

shaped statue holding a scepter in his right hand and his erect private parts in his left hand, as well as wings and a disk-shaped sphere between the wings.

On the statue of the Earth.—They say that Hestia is a 13 woman, and make her statue like the Earth holding a drum, for the Earth encloses the winds within herself.

On a statue having horns on its head.—This is the statue 14 of Seleukos (305–281 BCE) who was called Nikanor because of his bravery,[3] and who gave his own wife Stratonike to his son Antiochos, when he fell in love with her, and became ill because of his love for her and dissembled this, but was found out by the physician Erasistratos. They say that Seleukos was together with Alexander the Macedonian when he sacrificed a bull, and when the bull ran away only Seleukos could subdue it by grabbing its horns, and therefore they put horns on the head of his statue.

On *atrabatika.*—At feasts and victory celebrations, and 14a whenever ambassadors were present, they wore multicolored mantles of gold and purple, or with costly ornament of some other kind. At ordinary meetings <they wore> mantles in the color of withered vine leaves which they called *atrabatika,* either from the color—for they called the black *atron*—, or because they used to wear them after the *trabeai;* the costly mantles are called *trabeai.*

On the Augoustion.—On the fifth of October, the re- 15 gionarchs used to dance in the {Au}goustion, that is, in the food market, in honor of the emperor of that time. Now the uneducated people call this same place the Augoustion. Constantine the Great set up a statue there of his mother,

τῆς ἑαυτοῦ μητρός· διὸ καὶ ἐπωνόμασε τὸν τόπον Αὐγουστίωνα, πρότερον Γουστίωνα λεγόμενον ἤγουν ὀψο-
πωλεῖον.

16   Περὶ τῶν στηλῶν τῶν ἐν τῇ ἀψίδι τῆς καμάρας τοῦ Φόρου.—Ὅτι ἐν τῇ ἀψίδι τῆς καμάρας τοῦ Φόρου ἵστανται
δύο στῆλαι Ἑλένης καὶ Κωνσταντίνου καὶ σταυρὸς μέσον
αὐτῶν γράφων· "εἷς ἅγιος, εἷς κύριος Ἰησοῦς Χριστὸς εἰς
δόξαν Θεοῦ Πατρός· ἀμήν." Καὶ δύο ταχυδρόμων ὁμοίως
στῆλαι πτερωτῶν· ἀνετέθησαν δὲ παρὰ τοῦ τὸν Φόρον
ἐπαρχοῦντος.

17   Περὶ τοῦ ἀγάλματος τοῦ ἐν τῷ Αὐγουστίωνι ἐφίππου
κρατοῦντος σταυρὸν καὶ σφαῖραν.—Κτίσας ὁ Ἰουστινιανὸς
τὴν ἁγίαν Σοφίαν ἐκάθηρεν τὴν αὐλὴν καὶ ἐμαρμάρωσεν
αὐτὴν τὸ πρώην οὖσαν γουστεῖον ἤγουν ὀψοπωλεῖον· διὸ
καὶ ἔστησεν τὴν ἑαυτοῦ εἰκόνα ἔφιππον ἐπὶ κίονος· καὶ τῇ
μὲν ἀριστερᾷ χειρὶ φέρει σφαῖραν ἐμπεπηγότος σταυροῦ
ἐν αὐτῇ καὶ ὑποσημαίνοντος, ὡς διὰ τῆς εἰς τὸν σταυρὸν
πίστεως τῆς γῆς πάσης ἐγκρατὴς γέγονε· σφαῖρα μὲν γὰρ
ἡ γῆ διὰ τὸ σφαιροειδὲς τοῦ αὐτῆς σχήματος, πίστις δὲ ὁ
σταυρὸς διὰ τὸν ἐν αὐτῷ προσηλωθέντα σαρκὶ Θεόν. Τὴν
δὲ δεξιὰν χεῖρα ἀνατεταμένην ἔχει κατὰ ἀνατολὰς στάσιν
τῶν Περσῶν σημαίνων καὶ μὴ μεταβαίνειν ἐπὶ τῆς Ῥω-
μαϊκῆς γῆς, διὰ τῆς ἀνατάσεως καὶ ἀπώσεως τῆς χειρὸς
βοῶν· "στῆτε, Πέρσαι, καὶ μὴ πρόσω χωρεῖτε· οὐ γὰρ
συνοίσει ὑμῖν."

[Τὸν οὖν αὐτὸν Ἰουστινιανὸν λέγεται ἐπαρθῆναι τοῖς
τοῦ Βελισαρίου εὐτυχήμασιν. Οὗτος οὖν σταλεὶς κατὰ
τῶν Περσῶν καὶ τῶν λοιπῶν τῶν τῆς ἀνατολῆς παρὰ τοῦ

and therefore he also called Augoustion the place which had
previously been called *goustion,* that is, food market.[4]

On the statues on the arch of the vault of the Forum.— 16
On the arch of the vault of the Forum there stand two statues of Constantine and Helena, and a cross between them
on which is written: "One holy, one lord Jesus Christ to the
glory of God the Father, Amen." And also the statues of two
winged messengers. They were set up by the supervisor of
the Forum.[5]

On the statue of the rider in the Augustion who holds a 17
cross and a globe.[6]—When Justinian (I, 527–565) built Hagia
Sophia, he cleared the courtyard and paved with marble
what had previously been a *gousteion,* that is a food market.[7]
He therefore also set up his own image on horseback on a
column. And he holds in his left hand a globe which has a
cross fixed on it and means that he had become lord of all
the earth because of his faith in the cross—for the earth is
a globe because of its spherical shape, and the cross is faith
because God was nailed to it in the flesh. He has his right
hand extended to the east, giving the Persians a sign that
they should stop and not advance into Roman territory, saying, by raising and warding off with his hand: "Stop, Persians, and do not go further, for this will be of no benefit
for you."

[They say also that the same Justinian became arrogant
because of Belisarios's successes. So he was sent by the emperor against the Persians and the other people of the east,

βασιλέως καὶ πάντας κατατροπωσάμενος καὶ Γελίμερα κρατήσας ἀπέστειλεν αὐτὸν εἰς Μαυρουσίαν ἐκεῖσε τηρεῖσθαι ὑπὸ τοῦ Φαρές, ὃς εἰς μεγάλην ἔνδειαν ἄρτου γεγονὼς διὰ τὸ μὴ ἐν τῷ τόπῳ τῆς Μαυρουσίας σῖτον γεωργεῖσθαι, ἀλλ᾽ ἑφθὰς τὰς ὀλύρας σιτεῖσθαι, ἔγραψε τῷ βασιλεῖ στεῖλαι αὐτῷ ἄρτον καὶ σπόγγον καὶ κιθάραν. Ὁ δὲ ἐκπλαγεὶς ἐπὶ τούτοις ἤρετο τὸν ἐπιστολέα, τίνος χάριν ταῦτά γε ἐπιζητεῖ. Καὶ ἐξεῖπεν, ὅτι ἄρτον μὲν διὰ τὸ αὐτὸν ἐπιθυμεῖν τοῦ ἰδεῖν τε καὶ φαγεῖν, σπόγγον διὰ τὸ λούειν τὸ ἅπαν αὐτοῦ σῶμα ὑπὸ τῶν δακρύων, τὴν δὲ κιθάραν διὰ τὸ παραμυθεῖσθαι ἑαυτοῦ ταῖς συμφοραῖς. Ὁ δὲ βασιλεὺς ἐκπλαγεὶς καὶ θαυμάσας ἔστειλε τοῦτον τὰ αἰτηθέντα. Διὰ ταῦτα οὖν Ἰουστινιανὸς ἐπαρθεὶς ἔφιππον ἑαυτὸν ἔστησεν ἐπὶ κίονος. Ὃς ὕστερον φθονήσας τῷ ῥηθέντι στρατηγικωτάτῳ Βελισαρίῳ ἐξώρυξε τοῦτον τοὺς ὀφθαλμοὺς καὶ προσέταξε τοῦτον καθεσθῆναι εἰς τὰ Λαύσου καὶ ἐπιδοῦναι αὐτῷ σκεῦος ὀστράκινον καὶ ἐπιρρίπτειν αὐτῷ τοὺς διερχομένους ὀβολόν.]

18   Περὶ τοῦ ἐν τῷ βορείῳ μέρει τοῦ Φόρου σταυροῦ.— Ὅτι ἐπὶ τὸ βόρειον μέρος τοῦ Φόρου ἵσταται σταυρός, ὡς εἶδεν αὐτὸν Κωνσταντῖνος ἐν τῷ οὐρανῷ, χρυσέμπλαστος ἐν τοῖς ἀκρωτηριακοῖς στρογγύλοις μήλοις· ἔνθεν καὶ αὐτὸς καὶ οἱ υἱοὶ αὐτοῦ καθορῶνται χρυσέμβαφοι μέχρι τοῦ νῦν.

19   Περὶ τοῦ Ξηρολόφου.—Ὅτι τὸν Ξηρόλοφον πρώην τινὲς θέαμα ἐκάλουν· ἐν αὐτῷ γὰρ ἔστησαν κοχλίαι ις´ καὶ Ἀρτέμιδος συνθετὴ στήλη καὶ Σευήρου τοῦ κτίσαντος καὶ θεμάτιον τρίπουν. Ἔνθα ἐθυσίαζεν πολλὰς θυσίας

defeated them all, took Gelimer prisoner and sent him to Maurousia, to be guarded by Phares. When he was in great need of bread, as there was no grain grown in Maurousia, such that they had to eat cooked spelt, he wrote to the emperor that he should send him a loaf of bread, a sponge and a lyre. The emperor was amazed and asked his correspondent why he had asked for this. And he said that he longed for bread to see and eat it, for the sponge to wash his whole body with tears, and for the lyre to comfort himself in his misfortune. The emperor was amazed and impressed, and sent him what he wished. Therefore Justinian became arrogant and had himself set up on horseback on the column. Later he developed a grudge against the aforementioned most successful general Belisarios, had his eyes torn out and ordered him to be seated at Ta Lausou, to be given a clay bowl, and to let the passersby throw in an obol.][8]

On the cross at the northern side of the Forum. — On the 18 northern side of the Forum stands a cross, as Constantine saw it in the sky, with gilded spherical apples at the ends. Also he and his sons can be seen there, gold plated, [9] up to this day.

On the Xerolophos. — The Xerolophos was formerly 19 called a spectacle. For sixteen spiral columns stood there,[10] a composite statue of Artemis, one of the founder Severus (195–211), and a horoscope on three feet. Severus often

Σευῆρος· ἔνθα καὶ χρησμοὶ πολλοὶ τῷ τόπῳ γεγόνασιν·
καθ᾽ ὃν καὶ κόρη παρθένος ἐτύθη. Καὶ θέσις ἦν ἀστρονομικὴ
λς᾽ χρόνους διαρκέσασα. Ὁ αὐτὸς δὲ Ξηρόλοφος, καθὼς
ὁ Διακρινόμενος λέγει, στήλην εἶχεν τοῦ μικροῦ Θεοδοσίου
καὶ Οὐαλεντινιανοῦ καὶ Μαρκιανοῦ κάτωθεν τοῦ κίονος·
σεισμοῦ δὲ γενομένου πεπτωκέναι τὰς στήλας.

20   Περὶ τῶν δύο σταυρῶν τῶν λῃστῶν.—Ὅτι κάτωθεν τοῦ
Φόρου κεχωσμένοι ὑπάρχουσιν οὗτοι οἱ δύο σταυροὶ καὶ
βικίον μύρου, ᾧ ἠλείψατο ὁ Χριστός· καὶ πολλὰ ἕτερα
σημειοφορικά, τεθέντα μὲν παρὰ Κωνσταντίνου τοῦ μεγάλου, ἀσφαλισθέντα δὲ ὑπὸ Θεοδοσίου τοῦ μεγάλου.

21   Περὶ τῆς γεφύρας τῆς πέραν τῆς πόλεως τοῦ ἁγίου
Μάμαντος.—Ὅτι εἰς τὸν ἅγιον Μάμαντα τὸν πέραν
ἵστατο γέφυρα μεγάλη οἵα τῆς Χαλκηδόνος, δώδεκα
καμάρας ἔχουσα. Ποταμὸς γὰρ κατήρχετο παμμεγέθης
καὶ μάλιστα τῷ Φεβρουαρίῳ μηνί. Ἔνθα καὶ δράκων
ἵστατο χαλκοῦς· διὰ δὲ τὸ λέγειν τινὰς δράκοντα οἰκεῖν ἐν
τῇ γεφύρᾳ, πολλαὶ παρθένοι ἐτύθησαν καὶ πλῆθος προ-
βάτων καὶ βοῶν καὶ ὀρνέων. Βασιλίσκος γάρ τις ἐρασθεὶς
τοῦ τόπου, ὃς ἦν εἷς τῶν ἀπὸ Νουμεριανοῦ Καίσαρος,
κτίσας κατῴκησεν ἐν αὐτῷ· ἔνθα καὶ ναὸν τοῦ Διὸς ἤγειρεν
παμμεγέθη. Ταῦτα δὲ πάντα Ζήνων τῷ δευτέρῳ ἔτει τῆς
βασιλείας αὐτοῦ κατέστρεψεν.

22   Περὶ τῶν ὀστῶν τῶν γιγάντων.—Ὅτι ἐν τῷ ναῷ τοῦ
ἁγίου Μηνᾶ ἐν τῇ ἀκροπόλει ὄρυγμα εὑρέθη, ὅτε ἐκαθαί-
ρετο, καὶ ὀστᾶ ἀνθρώπων γιγάντων εἰς πλῆθος· ἅτινα
θεασάμενος Ἀναστάσιος ὁ βασιλεὺς καὶ ἐκπλαγεὶς εἰς τὸ
παλάτιον κατέθετο εἰς θαῦμα ἐξαίσιον.

sacrificed there, and many oracles happened at this place, where also a maiden was sacrificed. And there was an astronomical installation which encompasses thirty-six years.[11] This same Xerolophos had, according to Diakrinomenos, a statue of Theodosios the Younger (II, 408–450), and of Valentinian (I, 364–375) and Markianos (450–457) below the column, but they fell down during an earthquake.[12]

On the two crosses of the thieves.—These two crosses 20 and a glass vessel of the perfumed oil with which Christ was anointed, are buried underneath the Forum, and many other miraculous things, placed there by Constantine the Great and secured by Theodosios the Great (I, 379–395).[13]

On the bridge of Saint Mamas on the other side of the 21 city.—At Saint Mamas on the other side there stood a large bridge similar to the one at Chalkedon, with twelve arches. For a very big river used to flow there, especially in the month of February. A bronze dragon also stood there, and since some said that a dragon lived in that bridge, many virgins were sacrificed as well as a great number of sheep and oxen and birds. For a certain Basiliskos, who was one of the descendants of the Caesar Numerianus (283–284), fell in love with the place, built it up and lived there; he also erected a very large temple to Zeus there. But Zeno (474–491) destroyed all this in the second year of his reign.[14]

On the giants' bones.—A great trench was found in the 22 church of Saint Menas when it was being cleansed, and many bones of giant men. The emperor Anastasios (491–518) saw them and marveled at them, and deposited them in the palace as an extraordinary wonder.[15]

23   Περὶ στήλης εὐνούχου ἐν τῇ Χελώνῃ.—Ἐν τῷ ναῷ τοῦ
ἁγίου Προκοπίου ἐν τῇ Χελώνῃ στήλη ἵστατο εὐνούχου
τινός, ἣ ἐν τῷ στήθει ἔγραφεν· "ὁ μετατιθεὶς θεμάτια τῷ
βρόχῳ παραδοθήτω." Ἦν δὲ ἡ στήλη Πλάτωνος κουβικουλαρίου, ὃς ἐν ταῖς ἡμέραις τοῦ βασιλέως Βασιλίσκου πυρίκαυστος γέγονε· τῶν δὲ γονέων αὐτοῦ αἰτησάντων τῷ
βασιλεῖ εἰς μνημόσυνον τοῖς ἀνταίρουσιν βασιλεῖ στηλω-
θῆναι τὸν εὐνοῦχον Πλάτωνα, οὐκ ἐκώλυσεν. Ἐν δὲ τῷ
ἀνακαινίζεσθαι τὸν τοῦ ἁγίου μάρτυρος ναὸν μετετέθη εἰς
τὸ Ἱπποδρόμιον. Οἱ δὲ οἶκοι τοῦ αὐτοῦ εὐνούχου σώζονται
ἐν τῇ Χελώνῃ ἕως τῆς σήμερον.

24   Περὶ τοῦ τόπου τοῦ Κυνηγίου.—Ἐν τῷ Κυνηγίῳ τὸ
πρότερον ἐρρίπτοντο οἱ βιοθάνατοι· ἦσαν δέ τινες ἐκεῖσε
στῆλαι. Ἀπελθὼν δὲ Θεόδωρος ὁ ἀναγνώστης μετὰ Ἱμε-
ρίου χαρτουλαρίου εἶδεν ἐκεῖσε στήλην μικρὰν τῷ μήκει
καὶ πλατεῖαν πάνυ. "Ἐμοῦ δὲ θαυμάζοντός φησιν ὁ Ἱμέριος·
'θαύμαζε, ὅτι ὁ κτίσας τὸ Κυνήγιόν ἐστιν.' Ἐμοῦ δὲ εἰπόντος, 'Μαξιμῖνος ὁ κτίσας καὶ Ἀριστείδης ὁ καταμετρήσας,'
παρευθὺ πεσεῖν τὴν στήλην ἐκ τοῦ ἐκεῖσε ὕψους καὶ δοῦναι
τῷ Ἱμερίῳ καὶ παραυτὰ θανατῶσαι. Ἐμοῦ δὲ φοβηθέντος
καὶ πρὸς τὴν ἐκκλησίαν φυγόντος καὶ καταγγέλλοντος τὰ
πραχθέντα, οὐδείς μοι ἐπίστευσεν, ἕως ὅρκοις αὐτοὺς
ἐβεβαίωσα τὸ γεγονός. Οἱ οὖν οἰκεῖοι τοῦ τελευτήσαντος
καὶ οἱ φίλοι τοῦ βασιλέως σὺν ἐμοὶ ἐπορεύθησαν ἐν τῷ
Κυνηγίῳ καὶ πρὸ τοῦ τὸ πτῶμα τοῦ ἀνδρὸς ἐγγίσαι <τὸ
πτῶμα> τῆς στήλης ἐθαύμαζον." Ἰωάννης δέ τις φιλόσοφός
φησιν, ὅτι "εὗρον ὑπὸ τούτου τοῦ ζώδου ἔνζωδον καὶ
ἐνίστορον ἐγγεγλυμμένον ἄνδρα τεθνηξόμενον." Ἐξ οὗ

On the statue of the eunuch at the Chelone.—At the   23
church of Saint Prokopios at the Chelone[16] stood a statue of
a eunuch which had written on his chest: "Let him who dis-
turbs monuments be hanged." The statue was of the chamberlain Platon, who was burned alive in the days of the emperor Basiliskos (474–475). When his parents requested of
the emperor that the eunuch Platon be commemorated in a
statue as a reminder to those who opposed the emperor, he
did not forbid it. When the church of the holy martyr was
renovated, it was removed to the Hippodrome. The houses
of the same eunuch survive to this day at the Chelone.[17]

On the Kynegion.—Formerly, the condemned were   24
thrown into the Kynegion; there were also some statues
there. When the lector Theodore went there with Himerios
the *chartoularios,* he saw a statue that was small in stature
and very squat. "While I was marveling, Himerios said: 'You
are right to marvel, for he is the builder of the Kynegion.'
When I said: 'Maximinos was the builder and Aristides the
architect,' the statue immediately fell from the height there
and dealt Himerios a great blow and killed him on the spot.
In my terror I sought asylum in the <Great> Church, and
when I recounted what had happened, I was not believed
until I resorted to confirmation by oath. So the dead man's
relatives and the friends of the emperor went with me to the
Kynegion and, before approaching the man's body, marveled
at the fallen statue." A certain John, a philosopher, said that
"I found beneath this statue the depicted relief image of
a man who will be killed." When the emperor Philippikos

Φιλιππικὸς ὁ βασιλεὺς πληροφορηθεὶς ἐκέλευσεν τὸ αὐτὸ ζῷδον ἐν τῷ αὐτῷ τόπῳ καταχωσθῆναι.

25 Περὶ τῶν δύο στηλῶν Βηρίνης τῆς γυναικὸς τοῦ μεγά-λου Λέοντος.—Δύο στῆλαί εἰσιν τῆς Βηρίνης, μία μὲν νοτιωτέρα τοῦ ἁγίου μάρτυρος Ἀγαθονίκου μετὰ τὴν ἄνο-δον τῶν ἐκεῖσε βαθμίδων, ἑτέρα δὲ βορειοτέρα ἄντικρυς αὐτῆς πλησίον τοῦ ναοῦ τῆς ἁγίας Βαρβάρας τοῦ Ἀρτοτυ-ριανοῦ τόπου. Καὶ ἡ μὲν τοῦ ἁγίου Ἀγαθονίκου γέγονεν ζῶντος Λέοντος τοῦ Μακέλλη τοῦ ἀνδρὸς αὐτῆς, ἡ δὲ τῆς ἁγίας Βαρβάρας μετὰ τὴν τελευτὴν αὐτοῦ, ἡνίκα Βασι-λίσκον τὸν ἀδελφὸν αὐτῆς ἔστεψεν φυγόντος Ζήνωνος τοῦ γαμβροῦ αὐτῆς.

26 <Περὶ Εὐφημίας τῆς γυναικὸς Ἰουστίνου.>—Εὐφημίας τῆς γυναικὸς Ἰουστίνου τοῦ Θρᾳκὸς στήλη ἵσταται ἐν τῇ ἁγίᾳ Εὐφημίᾳ τῇ ὑπ' αὐτῆς κτισθείσῃ.

27 Περὶ τῶν Ἀρκαδιανῶν.—Ἀρκαδίας τῆς γυναικὸς Ζή-νωνος τῆς ἐν τῷ δευτέρῳ συνοικεσίῳ ἐν τοῖς πλησίον μέρεσι τῶν βάθρων τῶν λεγομένων <Τόπων> ἐν τοῖς τοῦ Ἀρχιστρατήγου μέρεσιν εἰς Ἀρκαδιανὰς ἐστηλώθη· ἔνθα Ζήνων ἔκρινε τοὺς μετὰ Βασιλίσκου καὶ σέκρητον τὸν τόπον ἐποίησε. Τῆς δὲ πρώτης αὐτοῦ γυναικὸς Ἀριάδνης καὶ τοῦ Ζήνωνος ἐν τῇ βασιλικῇ πύλῃ τῆς Χαλκῆς ἔστη-σαν.

28 Περὶ τῆς Χαλκῆς.—Ὅτι ἐν τῇ Χαλκῇ πλησίον Πουλ-χερίας τῆς ἀοιδίμου ὡς πρὸς τὸν περίπατον τοῦ παλατίου ἀνηγέρθη στήλη αὐτῆς. Ἐν αὐτῷ δὲ τῷ τόπῳ καὶ ὁ Ζήνων καὶ ἡ Ἀριάδνη ἵστανται καὶ ἕτεραι δύο στῆλαι πεζαὶ ἐπὶ κιόνων βραχέων, ἐλεγεῖα ἔχουσαι Σεκούνδου φιλοσόφου.

(711–713) was informed about this, he ordered that the same statue be buried in the same place.[18]

On the two statues of Verina, the wife of Leo the Great 25 (I, 457–474).—There are two statues of Verina, one to the south of <the church of> the holy martyr Agathonikos above the steps, and the other more to the north opposite her, near the church of Saint Barbara of the Artotyrianos Topos.[19] The statue at Saint Agathonikos was erected during the lifetime of Leo Makelles, her husband; the one at Saint Barbara after his death, when she crowned her brother Basiliskos (474–475) after the flight of her son-in-law Zeno.[20]

On Euphemia, the wife of Justin.—A statue of Euphemia, 26 the wife of Justin the Thracian (I, 518–527), stands near Saint Euphemia, which she herself founded.[21]

On the Arkadianai.—<A statue> of Arkadia, the second 27 wife of Zeno (474–491), was erected near the steps known as <Topoi>, in the neighborhood of the holy Archangel at the Arkadianai. Here Zeno gave judgment against the supporters of Basiliskos (474–475) and turned the place into a court. They also erected <a statue> of his first wife Ariadne with Zeno himself on the imperial gate of the Chalke.[22]

On the Chalke.[23]—A statue of the famous Pulcheria (d. 28 453) was erected near the Chalke gate, at the gallery in front of the palace.[24] At the same place, there are also statues of Zeno (474–491) and Ariadne, and two statues on foot on short pillars, bearing elegiac verses by Sekoundos the phi-

Ἀντικρὺ δὲ τῆς Χαλκῆς ἐπὶ ἀψίδος γοργονοειδεῖς κεφαλαὶ
ἡμίσειαί εἰσιν δύο χρυσέμβαφοι γυναικοειδεῖς· ἥκασι δὲ
ἀπὸ Ἐφέσου ἐκ τοῦ ναοῦ τῆς Ἀρτέμιδος στῆλαι ὀκτώ· καὶ
αἱ μὲν τέσσαρες ἐν τοῖς τοῦ Ταύρου μέρεσιν ἐν τοῖς
παλατίοις προσεπάγησαν Κωνσταντίνου καὶ Ἰουλιανοῦ
καὶ τῆς γυναικὸς αὐτοῦ καὶ τῶν υἱῶν αὐτοῦ καὶ Γάλλου·
τὰ δὲ τέσσαρα ἐν τῇ Χαλκῇ ἐν τῷ εὐωνύμῳ μέρει. Ἔνθα
καὶ σταυρὸς ὑπὸ Ἰουστινιανοῦ πέπηγε καὶ στήλη
χρυσέμβαφος Βελισαρίου καὶ Τιβερίου [καὶ] τοῦ κυρ-
τοειδοῦς Θρᾳκός, καὶ Ἰουστῖνος ὁ πρῶτος λεπτοειδὴς καὶ
τῶν συγγενῶν αὐτοῦ στῆλαι ἑπτά, αἱ μὲν ἀπὸ μαρμάρων,
αἱ δὲ χαλκαῖ. Οἱ δὲ δύο ἵπποι οἱ ἐπάνω τῶν γοργονοειδῶν
ἱστάμενοι ἐν τῇ ἀψίδι καὶ οὗτοι ἐκ τοῦ τῆς Ἀρτέμιδος ναοῦ
ἀπὸ Ἐφέσου ἥκασι παρὰ Ἰουστινιανοῦ τοῦ κτίσαντος τὴν
ἁγίαν Σοφίαν καὶ ἐστήλωσεν αὐτὰ διὰ τὸ μὴ ἀντιζηλοῦν
ἀλλήλοις τοὺς ἵππους· ὁμοίως καὶ τὸν σταυρὸν διὰ τὸ
ἑδραῖον· καὶ Μαξιμιανοῦ στήλη ἐν αὐτῇ τῇ Χαλκῇ ἵσταται
βαρυτάτη· ἔνθα νῦν καὶ τὸ γένος ἅπαν τοῦ μεγάλου
Θεοδοσίου ὑπάρχει καὶ τοῦ Μαυρικίου καὶ τῆς γυναικὸς
αὐτοῦ καὶ τῶν τέκνων.

29   Περὶ τοῦ Μιλίου.—Ἐν τῇ καμάρᾳ τοῦ Μιλίου στῆλαι
Κωνσταντίνου καὶ Ἑλένης εἰσίν· ἔνθα καὶ σταυρὸς ὁρᾶται
πρὸς ἀνατολὰς βασταζόμενος ὑπ' αὐτῶν· μέσον δὲ τοῦ
σταυροῦ ἡ Τύχη τῆς πόλεως, κατήνιον κλειδωμένον καὶ
ἐστοιχειωμένον, τοῦ ἅπαντος εἴδους ἀνελλιπῆ εἶναι καὶ
νίκην πᾶσαν τῶν ἐθνῶν ἐπιφέρειν, τοῦ μηκέτι ἰσχύειν
προσεγγίσαι ἢ προσψαῦσαι ἐντὸς ἢ ἐπιφοιτῆσαι, ἀλλὰ

losopher.[25] On an arch opposite the Chalke are two gorgon-like gilded female relief heads. Eight statues came from Ephesos, from the temple of Artemis,[26] and four of these were set up in the palace in the area of the Tauros <Forum>, <namely> Constantine, Julian (361–363) and his wife, his sons and Gallos. The other four are on the left of the Chalke. There is also a cross set up under Justinian (I, 527–565), a gilded statue of Belisarios, Tiberios the Thracian (II, 578–582) with a hunched back, and the first Justin (518–527), slender in appearance, and seven statues of relatives, some in marble and some in bronze.[27] The two horses which stand above the gorgon-like <heads> on the arch were also brought from the temple of Artemis in Ephesos by Justinian (I, 527–565) who built Hagia Sophia. And he set them up so that the horses would not become jealous of each other, and also the cross on account of its steadfastness. A very heavy statue of Maximian stands at the same Chalke. The whole family of Theodosios the Great (I, 379–395) is still here,[28] also Maurikios (582–602), his wife and his children.

On the Milion. — Statues of Constantine and Helena are ₂₉ on the arch of the Milion. They hold a cross that can also be seen there to the east, and the Tyche of the city is in the middle of the cross,[29] a small chain which is locked and enchanted. It ensures that no commodity of any kind is lacking, and brings all victory over the pagans, so that they are unable to approach, to get inside or to come again and again,

πόρρω ἀπέχειν καὶ ὑπονοστεῖν ὡς ἡττωμένους. Ἡ δὲ κλεὶς
τοῦ κατηνίου κατεχώσθη εἰς τὰς βάσεις τῶν κιόνων.

30 Ἐν αὐτῷ δὲ τῷ Μιλίῳ στῆλαι ἵστανται Σοφίας τῆς γυναικὸς Ἰουστίνου τοῦ Θρᾳκὸς καὶ Ἀραβίας τῆς θυγατρὸς
αὐτῆς καὶ Ἑλένης ἀνεψιᾶς αὐτῆς.

31 Περὶ τοῦ Πιττάκη.—Ὁ δὲ λεγόμενος Πιττάκης στήλη
ἐστὶν τοῦ μεγάλου Λέοντος τοῦ Μακέλλη, ἣν ἀνήγειρεν
Εὐφημία ἡ τούτου ἀδελφή, διότι οἶκος ἦν αὐτῆς ἐκεῖσε·
καὶ ἑκάστη ἑβδομάδι εἰς αὐτὴν ἀπήρχετο ὁ βασιλεὺς Λέων
διὰ τὸ εἶναι σώφρονα καὶ παρθένον· καὶ πάντες οἱ ἀδικού-
μενοι εἴτε πολῖται εἴτε θεματικοὶ ἀπὸ πάσης οἰκουμένης
ἐκεῖσε εἰς τὰς βαθμίδας τοῦ κίονος ἐτίθουν τὰ πιττάκια
αὐτῶν, φυλαττόντων αὐτὰ ἐκεῖσε τῶν ταξεωτῶν. καὶ ὅταν
ἤρχετο ὁ βασιλεύς, ἐδίδουν ἅπαντα ταῦτα οἱ ταξεῶται τῷ
βασιλεῖ, καὶ παρευθὺ ἐλάμβανον τὰς λύσεις αὐτῶν ἕκαστος
ἐκεῖσε. Ὅταν δὲ ἦν ὁ βασιλεὺς ἐν παλατίῳ, καθ᾽ ἑκάστην
πρωῖαν ἔπεμπεν ἑβδομάριόν τινα· καὶ ἀνελαμβάνετο ἐκ
τῶν ταξεωτῶν καὶ ἐκόμιζεν τὰ ῥιπτόμενα δεητικὰ πιττάκια.
Καὶ ἐδίδου καθ᾽ ἑκάστην ὁ βασιλεὺς τὰς λύσεις καὶ τὰς
ἀποφάσεις τῶν πιττακίων τοῖς ἑβδομαρίοις ἢ κοιτωνίταις
καὶ ἀπήγοντο πρὸς τὴν αὐλὴν τοῦ Πιττακίου καὶ ἐδίδουν
τοῖς φυλάττουσιν στρατιώταις κἀκεῖνοι τοῖς δεομένοις.
Διὸ καὶ οἱ μέλλοντες διοικεῖσθαι ταχέως ἑσπέρας ἐτίθουν
τὰς δεήσεις καὶ τῇ ἐπαύριον ἐλάμβανον τὸ πέρας· ὅθεν
ἐκλήθη ὁ τόπος Πιττάκια.

32 Ἐν τῷ τριβουναλίῳ τοῦ παλατίου Εὐδοκίας τῆς γυναικὸς Θεοδοσίου καὶ αὐτοῦ Θεοδοσίου Μαρκιανοῦ τε καὶ

but stay far away and return home in defeat. The chain's key was buried at the bases of the columns.

At the same Milion stand statues of Sophia, the wife of 30 Justin the Thracian (565–578), and Arabia her daughter and Helena her niece.[30]

On the Pittakes.—The so-called Pittakes is the statue of 31 the great Leo Makelles (I, 457–474)[31] which his sister Euphemia erected, because her house was there. And the emperor used to visit her every week, for she was wise and a virgin. And all those who had suffered injustice, be they citizens or provincials from anywhere in the world, placed their petitions (*pittakia*) there on the steps at the foot of the column, and the constables guarded them there. And when the emperor came, the constables gave them all to the emperor, and everybody received his decision there immediately. When the emperor was in the palace, he sent every morning a *hebdomarios* who collected the supplicatory petitions, which had been thrown there, from the constables and carried them off. And every day the emperor gave rulings and decisions on the petitions to the *hebdomarioi* or chamberlains, and they went to the court of Pittakios, and gave them to the soldiers who were on guard, who gave them in turn to the supplicants. Therefore, those who wanted a prompt decision placed the petitions there in the evening and received the result the next day, and for this reason the place was called Pittakia.

In the Tribunal of the palace stood statues of Eudokia, 32 the wife of Theodosios (II, 408–450), of Theodosios

Κωνσταντίνου στῆλαι ἔστησαν· ἔνθα καὶ ὀρχήσεις τῶν δύο δημοτικῶν μερῶν ἐγένοντο ἕως Ἡρακλείου.

33   Περὶ τοῦ Ζευξίππου.—Ὁ δὲ Ζεύξιππος τὸ λοετρὸν ὑπὸ Σευήρου κατεσκευάσθη καὶ ἐστοιχειώθη μετὰ κανδήλας ὑελίνης ἅπτεσθαι, τὸ δὲ ὕδωρ ζέειν σφοδρῶς καὶ τὸν ἀέρα τοῦ λοετροῦ. Ἀλόγιστοι δέ τινες ἐλθόντες τοῦτο κατέστρεψαν.

34   Ἡ στήλη ἡ ἱσταμένη εἰς τὰ Ἀρμαμέντου Φωκᾶ τοῦ στρατιώτου ἐστίν· καὶ ἐν τῷ ἑβδόμῳ ἔτει τῆς βασιλείας αὐτοῦ περὶ τὸ τέλος σπουδάζων ἀναγαγεῖν αὐτὴν ἐν τῷ κτιστῷ κίονι μετὰ τὸ ἀναγαγεῖν αὐτὴν δεκαοκτὼ παρελθουσῶν ἡμερῶν κατηνέχθη τῆς βασιλείας. Τότε δὲ ἦν καὶ ὁ Σικεὼν ὁ ὅσιος.

35   Περὶ τοῦ Διιππίου, τοῦ ἁγίου Ἰωάννου τοῦ θεολόγου.—Ὁ αὐτὸς δὲ Φωκᾶς ἔκτισεν τὸν ναὸν τοῦ ἁγίου Φωκᾶ ἐν τῷ Μιλίῳ μήπω ὀροφώσας αὐτόν. <...>² Ἐκεῖσε δὲ ἦν ἕως τότε ἡ ἀλλαγὴ τῶν κουντούρων· καὶ καθ' ὃν τόπον ἠντζοκόπησεν τὰ κούντουρα ἐκ τῶν ἐκεῖσε ἄρας· καὶ γὰρ ἀλλαγὴ χερσαία ἦν· καὶ ἐκ τῶν ἐκεῖσε ἤλλαξεν μέχρι τῆς Χρυσείας πύλης. Μετὰ δὲ τὸ ἀνελθεῖν καὶ βασιλεῦσαι ἔστησεν ἐκεῖσε δύο ἵππους κουντούρους ἀντζοκοπημένους ἐπὶ βωμοὺς λιθίνους τετραδικοὺς σύνεγγυς τοῦ ναοῦ τοῦ ἁγίου Φωκᾶ· ὃν αὐτὸς ἀνήγειρεν Δίιππιον αὐτὸν ὀνομάσας τὸν τόπον. Ἐκεῖσε γὰρ καὶ δύο κίονας διὰ ψηφίδων χρυσῶν Κωνσταντίνου καὶ Ἑλένης ἱστόρησεν. Ὁ δὲ Ἡράκλειος ἐλθὼν καὶ κρατήσας ἐτίμησεν τὸν ναόν, σκεπάσας αὐτὸν καὶ μετονομάσας εἰς τὸ ὄνομα τοῦ ἁγίου Ἰωάννου τοῦ θεολόγου.

himself, of Markianos (450–457) and Constantine; here the dances of the two factions took place until Herakleios (610–641).[32]

On the Zeuxippos.—The Zeuxippos was built as a bath 33 by Severus (195–211)[33] and was enchanted, so that it was heated by a glass lamp, and the water and air of the bath were very hot. Some irrational people came and destroyed this.

The statue which stands at Ta Armamentou is of Phokas 34 the soldier (602–610). And in the seventh year of his reign, toward its end, he strove to set it up on the column that had been built, and eighteen days after it had been set up he was deposed from imperial power. The blessed <Theodore of> Sykeon also lived at that time.[34]

On the Diippion, Saint John the Theologian.[35]—The 35 same Phokas built the church of Saint Phokas at the Milion, but had not yet roofed it, <. . .>[36] Up to that time, a station for changing post-horses had been there, and at this place he took short-tailed horses and cut the tendons <of the remaining ones>, for it was a changing station on the solid land. And from there he rode as far as the Golden Gate. When he returned and became emperor, he set up two short-tailed lame post-horses on square stone plinths near the church of Saint Phokas, which he had built himself, calling the place Diippion. He also decorated the two columns of Constantine and Helena there with golden mosaic. When Herakleios (610–641) arrived and came to power, he honored the church, roofing it and renaming it in the name of Saint John the Theologian.

36 Τὰ δὲ Λαύσου οἶκος ἦν Λαύσου πατρικίου καὶ πραιποσίτου, ὅστις ἀρχὰς πολλὰς καὶ δόξας διήνυσεν ἐν τοῖς χρόνοις Ἀρκαδίου υἱοῦ τοῦ μεγάλου Θεοδοσίου. Ἐκόσμησεν δὲ αὐτὸν διὰ ποικίλων καὶ πολυτελῶν μικρῶν κιόνων καὶ μαρμάρων. Οὗτος δὲ ὁ οἶκος ἐκ τῶν δώδεκα τοῦ μεγάλου Κωνσταντίνου ὑπῆρχεν· ἐν ᾧ καὶ ἀετοὶ λίθινοι καὶ φιάλαι καὶ βαθμοὶ καὶ βωμοὶ τετράγωνοι ἐκχέοντες ὕδωρ εἰς διακόσμησιν τῆς πόλεως· ἵστανται δὲ μέχρι τῆς σήμερον.

37 Πλησίον δὲ τοῦ Μιλίου τῆς ἁψίδος στήλη ἔφιππος Τραιανοῦ ἐστιν καὶ πλησίον αὐτοῦ στήλη ἔφιππος Θεοδοσίου τοῦ μικροῦ.

38 Ἀρκαδίου δὲ καὶ Θεοδοσίου τοῦ υἱοῦ αὐτοῦ καὶ Ἀδριανοῦ πλησίον τῆς στήλης Θεοδοσίου τοῦ μεγάλου ἀμφότεροι ἔφιπποι ἵστανται ἐν τοῖς Ταύρου μέρεσιν πλησίον τοῦ κίονος κάτωθεν.

39 Ἡ δὲ ἐν τῷ Ζευξίππῳ λουτρῷ ἱσταμένη στήλη ἐκ χρωμάτων τοῦ Φιλιππικοῦ ἐστιν τοῦ πραοτάτου.

40 Περὶ τῆς βασιλικῆς κινστέρνης.—Ἡ δὲ λεγομένη βασιλικὴ κινστέρνα ἐκτίσθη ὑπὸ τοῦ μεγάλου Κωνσταντίνου. Ἡ δὲ καθεζομένη ἐπὶ δίφρου ἐκεῖσε μεγάλη στήλη ἐστὶν τοῦ Σολομῶντος, ἣν ἀνέστησεν ὁ μέγας Ἰουστινιανὸς κρατοῦντα τὴν σιαγόνα αὐτοῦ καὶ ὁρῶντα τὴν ἁγίαν Σοφίαν, ὅτι ἐνικήθη εἰς μῆκος καὶ κάλλος ὑπὲρ τὸν παρ' αὐτοῦ κτισθέντα ναὸν ἐν Ἱερουσαλήμ. Ἐκεῖσε δὲ ἵσταται στήλη τοῦ μεγάλου Θεοδοσίου ἐπὶ δύο κιόνων τετραδικῶν χρυσεμβάφων ὄπισθεν τῆς Βασιλικῆς πλησίον τοῦ Μιλίου.

41 Θέαμα α'.—Τὸ δὲ ἐν αὐτῇ τῇ Βασιλικῇ χρυσορόφῳ

74

Ta Lausou was the house of Lausos the patrician and *prai-* 36
positos, who received many offices and honors in the time of
Arkadios (395–408), the son of Theodosios the Great (I,
379–395). He decorated it with multicolored and costly
small columns and marbles. This house was one of the
twelve of Constantine the Great.[37] <In it were> also stone
eagles, fountains, steps and square plinths which gushed
forth water for the adornment of the city, and they stand to
this day.

A statue of Trajan (96–117) on horseback is near the Mi- 37
lion arch, and close by is a statue of Theodosios the Younger
(II, 408–450) on horseback.

<Statues> of Arkadios (395–408), Theodosios his son (II, 38
408–450) and Hadrian (117–138) stand near the statue of
Theodosios the Great (I, 379–395), all equestrian, in the region of the Tauros, on the ground near the column.[38]

The colored image[39] in the Zeuxippos bath is Philippikos 39
(711–713) the most gentle.

On the Basilike cistern.—The so-called Basilike cistern 40
was built by Constantine the Great. The great statue which
sits on a chariot there is Solomon, which Justinian the Great
(I, 527–565) erected; Solomon is holding his cheek and looking at Hagia Sophia, as he was outdone by its size and beauty,
which is greater than that of the temple he built in Jerusalem. A statue of Theodosios the Great (I, 379–395) stands
there on two square gilded pillars, behind the Basilike near
the Milion.

Spectacle number one.[40]—In the golden-roofed Basilike 41

ὀπίσω τοῦ Μιλίου ἦν ἀνδροείκελον ἄγαλμα χρυσέμβαφον· ἔνθα ἦν τὸ ἔξαμον Ἡρακλείου τοῦ βασιλέως· καὶ γονυ-κλινὲς Ἰουστινιανοῦ τοῦ τυράννου. Ἐν ᾗ ὁ Τερβέλις ἐδη-μηγόρησεν· ἐν οἷς ἐλέφας ἵστατο παμμεγέθης ὑπὸ Σευήρου κατεσκευασμένος· ὄρος δὲ ἦν πρὸ τοῦ μέρους τῶν ἀνα-βαθμῶν· ἔνθα καὶ σχολὴ φυλαττόντων πολλή· ἔμενε δὲ ἐκεῖσε ἀργυροκόπος ἐν πλαστοῖς ζυγοῖς τὴν πρᾶσιν ποι-ούμενος· καὶ τοῦ οἰκήματος αὐτοῦ πορθουμένου, ἠπείλει τῷ τὸν ἐλέφαντα φυλάττοντι θάνατον, εἰ μὴ τοῦτον κρα-τήσει. Ὁ δὲ θηροκόμος οὐκ ἐνεδίδου· ὃν φονεύσας ὁ ζυγοπλάστης δέδωκε βορὰν τῷ ἐλέφαντι· τὸ δὲ θηρίον ἀτίθασον ὂν καὶ αὐτὸν ἀνεῖλεν. Καὶ ὁ Σευῆρος ἀκούσας τῷ θηρίῳ θυσίας ἤνεγκεν. Ἐν αὐτῷ δὲ τῷ τόπῳ παρευθὺ καὶ ἀνετυπώθησαν τό τε θηρίον καὶ ὁ θηροκόμος. Ἔνθα καὶ Ἡρακλῆς ἐλατρεύθη πολλὰς θυσίας δεξάμενος· ὃς ἐν τῷ Ἱπποδρομίῳ μετετέθη. Ἐπὶ δὲ Ἰουλιανοῦ ὑπατικοῦ ἀπὸ Ῥώμης ἦλθεν ἐπὶ τὸ Βυζάντιον καὶ εἰσήχθη ἐν ἀπήνῃ καὶ νηΐ μετὰ στηλῶν ι'.

42   Θέαμα β'. — Ὅτι ἅρμα Ἡλίου ἐν τέτρασιν ἵπποις πυρί-νοις ἱστάμενον[3] παρὰ δύο στηλῶν ἐκ παλαιῶν τῶν χρόνων ὑπῆρχεν ἐν τῷ ὡρέῳ Μιλίῳ. Ἔνθα εὐφημίσθη ὁ μέγας Κωνσταντῖνος μετὰ τὸ νικῆσαι Ἀζώτιον· ἐπειδὴ καὶ Βύζας ἐκεῖσε εὐφημίσθη. Κατενεχθὲν δὲ τὸ ἅρμα ἐν τῷ Ἱππο-δρομίῳ δορυφορούμενον στηλίδιον καινὸν παρὰ Κωνσταν-τίνου κατασκευασθὲν ὑπὸ Ἡλίου φερόμενον, Τύχη πό-λεως, εἰς τὸ Στάμα εἰσῄει καὶ στεφανωθὲν ἔξῄει. Ἐτίθετο δὲ ἐν τῷ Σενάτῳ ἕως τῶν ἐπιόντων γενεθλίων τῆς πόλεως.

behind the Milion, where the measure of the emperor Herakleios (610–641) was set up, was the gilded statue of a man
and a kneeling one of Justinian the Tyrant (II, 685–695 and
705–711). Tervelis <of Bulgaria> spoke publicly there. A huge
elephant, which was made by Severus (195–211), also stood
there. There was an enclosure in front of the steps, and
there was also a large company of guards. A silversmith who
used rigged scales in his business lived there, and when his
house was damaged, he threatened to kill the elephant's
keeper if he did not keep the animal under control. But the
keeper would not give way, so the user of rigged scales killed
him and offered him to the elephant as fodder, but the animal, being wild, killed the silversmith too. And when Severus heard this, he offered sacrifices to the animal, and both
of them, the animal and its keeper, were immediately commemorated in statues in that place. Herakles was also worshipped there and received many sacrifices. His statue was
transferred to the Hippodrome. It came from Rome to Byzantion in the time of the *consularis* Julian (322), and was
brought on a chariot and a boat with ten statues.[41]

Spectacle number two.—A chariot of Helios with four fi-
ery horses, borne on two columns, has stood at the golden
Milion since ancient times. Constantine the Great was acclaimed there after defeating Azotios, for Byzas was also acclaimed there. When the chariot was brought down into the
Hippodrome with an escort, a new little statue that Constantine had made and Helios carried, the Tyche of the city,
came to the Stama, and after being crowned, it went out. It
was then placed in the Senate until the next birthday of the

42

Διότι δὲ ἐπὶ κεφαλῆς σταυρὸν εἶχεν, ὃν ἐχάραξε Κωνσταντῖνος, Ἰουλιανὸς αὐτὸ βοθύνῳ κατέχωσεν.

43   Περὶ Ἀρείου.—Ἔνθα Ἄρειος τὸν ἔχθιστον ὑπέστη
θάνατον, ἀπὸ τῆς καμάρας τοῦ Φόρου τοῦ Σενάτου ὡσεὶ
κθʹ παλαιστάς, ἐτυπώθη ὑπὸ τοῦ θεοφιλοῦς Θεοδοσίου
Ἄρειος ἐν μαρμάρῳ ἀναγλύφῳ γειτνιῶντι τῇ γῇ καὶ σὺν
τῇ τοῦ Ἀρείου Μακεδονίου, Σαβελλίου καὶ Εὐνομίου
πρὸς αἰσχύνην αὐτῶν, ὡς ἂν οἱ παρερχόμενοι κόπρον καὶ
οὖρα καὶ ἐμπτύσματα ἐπιρρίπτωσιν αὐτοῖς.

44   Περὶ τοῦ Σενάτου.—Ὅτι τὸ Σενάτον ὡς οἶμαι λέγει,
ὅτι ἐξ ἀρχῆς τοὺς κωδικέλλους οἱ πατρίκιοι ἐκεῖσε
ἐλάμβανον ἕως Κωνσταντίνου· πρῶτος δὲ Καλλίστρατος
τὴν ἀξίαν τοῦ ὑπάτου ἐκεῖσε ἐδέξατο τοῦ δήμου κράξαντος·
"Καλλίστρατος εὐτυχὴς καὶ εἰς ἄλλο προκόψει." Ὁ δὲ
φοβηθεὶς προσέφυγε τῇ ἐκκλησίᾳ. Κωνσταντῖνος δὲ
ἐξωμόσατο μὴ ἀδικῆσαι αὐτόν. Ὁ δὲ μὴ ἀνασχόμενος
ἐχειροτονήθη πρεσβύτερος, εἶτα ἐπίσκοπος· ὅθεν τὰ
πολλά μοι ἐκφέρεται διηγήματα.

45   Περὶ τοῦ πορφυροῦ κίονος.—Ὑποκάτω δὲ τοῦ κίονος
τοῦ Φόρου ἐτέθη καὶ τὸ Παλλάδιον στοιχεῖον καὶ ἕτερα
πολλὰ σημειοφορικά. Ὁ δὲ κύκλος τοῦ Φόρου ἐστὶν τὸ
ἴσον τῆς ποδέας τῆς κόρτης τοῦ μεγάλου Κωνσταντίνου,
ἐν ᾧ αὐτὴν ἐκεῖσε ἔπηξεν, ὅτε ἀνῆλθεν ἀπὸ Ῥώμης. Οἱ δὲ
σιγματοειδεῖς δύο ἔμβολοι ἐτύγχανον τότε σταῦλοι γύροθεν τῆς κόρτης. Καὶ ὁ περίβλεπτος οὗτος κίων καὶ ἡ
στήλη τοῦ Ἀπόλλωνος, δίκην Ἡλίου ἔστησεν αὐτὴν ὁ
μέγας Κωνσταντῖνος εἰς τὸ ὄνομα αὐτοῦ, θήσας ἐν τῇ

city. But because of the cross, which Constantine had engraved on its head, Julian buried it in a pit.[42]

On Areios.—Where Areios met his disgusting death, a distance of about twenty-nine palm widths from the arch of the Senate at the Forum, Areios was represented by the God-loving Theodosios (I, 379–395) on a marble relief close to the ground, and with Areios also Makedonios, Sabellios and Eunomios for their shame, so that passersby may hurl dung and urine and spittle at them.[43]

On the Senate.—The Senate has this name, I think, because from the beginning until the reign of Constantine the patricians received their codicils there. Kallistratos was the first to receive the office of consul there, while the faction shouted, "Kallistratos is fortunate and will advance to another <office>." But he was afraid, and fled into a church. Constantine swore that he would not harm him, but he was not satisfied and was ordained a presbyter, later also a bishop. Many accounts of this have reached me.[44]

On the porphyry column.—Both the talismanic Palladion and many other miraculous objects were placed beneath the column of the Forum.[45] The circle of the Forum corresponds to the surface area of Constantine the Great's camp which he established there when he came from Rome. The two sigma-shaped porticoes were at that time stables around the camp. And Constantine the Great set up this lofty column and the statue of Apollo as Helios in his name,

43

44

45

κεφαλῇ ἥλους ἐκ τῶν τοῦ Χριστοῦ δίκην ἀκτίνων, ὡς Ἥλιος τοῖς πολίταις ἐκλάμπων.

46 Περὶ τῶν Ἀρτοπωλείων.—Ἐν δὲ τοῖς Ἀρτοπωλείοις κυνάριόν ἐστιν οὔθατα μέχρι τῶν εἴκοσι περιφέρον· καὶ ταῶνες καὶ ἀετοὶ καὶ λέαιναι, λαγωοί τε καὶ κριῶν κάραι καὶ στρουθῶν καὶ κορωνῶν καὶ τρυγόνος μιᾶς καὶ γαλῆς καὶ δαμάλεως καὶ Γοργόναι δύο, μία μὲν ἐκ δεξιῶν καὶ ἑτέρα ἐξ εὐωνύμων, ἡ μία τῇ ἑτέρᾳ κατ' ὄψιν βλεπόμεναι, ἀπὸ μαρμάρων ἐγγεγλυμμέναι [καὶ χοίρων πλῆθος ἀγέλαι]· ἵσταντο δὲ μέχρι Ζήνωνος. Γαληνὸς δέ τις, ἰατρὸς καὶ φιλόσοφος ὑπάρχων, ἐκεῖσε περαιωθεὶς τὰς Γοργόνας ἔλεγεν ἱερογλυφικὰ καὶ ἀστρονομικὰ ὄντα τῶν μελλόντων δηλούσας τὰς ἱστορίας πάσας σὺν τῶν ὀνομάτων, Κωνσταντίνου τοῦ μεγάλου τυπώσαντος ταῦτα. Τοῦ δὲ αὐτοῦ Γαληνοῦ ἐπὶ πλεῖστον συχνάσαντος καὶ τοῖς ἀναγνώσμασιν προσέχοντος τὰ μέλλοντα συμβαίνειν Ζήνωνι παρὰ Βηρίνης καὶ γελάσαντος, Καλλίστρατός τις συρφετὸς τῷ γένει, κάπηλος τῇ τέχνῃ, μετὰ τὴν ἐπάνοδον Ζήνωνος διαβάλλει τὸν Γαληνόν· ὁ δὲ Ζήνων τοῦτον ἀνῃρήκει.

46a Λέγουσιν δὲ καὶ τοῦτο καί ἐστιν ἀληθές, ὅτι αἱ ἀγέλαι τῶν χοίρων ἐκεῖσε διερχόμεναι εἰς τὸν Ἀρτοτυριανὸν τόπον μέσον τῆς καμάρας, ὅθεν ἀνέρχονται, ἵστανται ἐνεοὶ καὶ οὐ δύνανται διέρχεσθαι, ἕως ὅτου οἱ χοιροδέται οἱ τούτους ἐλαύνοντες τύψωσιν τὴν ἀγέλην σφοδρῶς· μέχρι ὅτου αἷμα ἐκχυθῇ ἀπὸ τῶν ῥινῶν αὐτῶν εἰς θυσίαν τοῦ τόπου ἐκείνου, οὐ μεθίστανται ἐκ τῶν ἐκεῖσε· ἡνίκα δὲ χυθῇ αἷμα ὀλίγον, ἀθρόως ὁρμᾷ καὶ κινεῖ ἡ ἀγέλη τῶν χοίρων. Καὶ οὕτως ἐστὶν ἀληθές.

affixing nails from those of Christ<'s crucifixion> as rays on its head, shining like Helios on the citizens.[46]

On the Artopoleia.[47]— In the Artopoleia, there is a small 46 dog, bearing as many as twenty teats, and peacocks and eagles and lionesses and hares and ram's heads, and sparrows and crows and one turtle dove and a weasel and a heifer, as well as two Gorgons, one on the right and one on the left, one looking into the face of the other, carved from marble in relief [, and a large herd of pigs].[48] They were there until the time of Zeno (474–491). But a certain Galenos, a doctor and philosopher, proceeded thither and ascertained that the <writings on the> Gorgons were hieroglyphic and astronomical, recording all the future fates <of the emperors> with their names, this having been done by Constantine the Great. When this Galenos passed by there often and observed in the inscriptions what was destined to happen to Zeno at the hands of Verina, and laughed, a certain Kallistratos, of lowly birth and a peddler by trade, denounced Galenos after the return of Zeno. And Zeno had him executed.[49]

And this is also told, and it is true: When the herds of 46a pigs cross into the Artotyrianos place through the arch,[50] as they come up, they come to a standstill and cannot go through, until the swineherds, who are driving them, beat the herd severely. Until some blood is shed from their noses as a sacrifice for that place, they will not move from there, but as soon as a little bit of blood is shed, the herd of pigs suddenly moves forward in a rush. And this is true in this way.

THE PATRIA

47 Περὶ τοῦ Ταύρου.—Ὅτι ἐν τῷ Ταύρῳ στήλη τοῦ μεγάλου Θεοδοσίου ἵσταται· ἥν δὲ πρώην ἀργυρᾶ· ἔνθα τοὺς
ἀπὸ τῶν ἐθνῶν ἥκοντας ἐδέχετο· ἐκεῖσε δὲ πρώην παλάτια
ὑπῆρχον καὶ ξενοδοχεῖον τῶν Ῥωμαίων, δηλονότι εἰς τὸ
καλούμενον Ἀλωνίτζιν. Ἐπάνω δὲ τοῦ μεγάλου κίονος
ἐστήλωται Θεοδόσιος· οἱ δὲ υἱοὶ αὐτοῦ, ὁ μὲν Ὀνώριος
ἐπάνω τῆς λιθίνης ἀψίδος τῆς πρὸς δυσμάς, ὁ δὲ Ἀρκάδιος
ἐν τῇ πρὸς ἀνατολὰς λιθίνῃ ἀψίδι ὕπερθεν τῶν περιβλέπτων
μεγάλων κιόνων τῶν τετραδησίων. Μέσον δὲ τῆς αὐλῆς
ἐστιν ἔφιππος μεγαλαῖος, ὃν οἱ μὲν λέγουσιν Ἰησοῦν τὸν
υἱὸν τοῦ Ναυῆ, ἕτεροι δὲ τὸν Βελλεροφόντην· ἤχθη δὲ
ἀπὸ τῆς μεγάλης Ἀντιοχείας. Τὸ δὲ τετράπλευρον τοῦ
ἐφίππου τὸ λιθόξεστον ἔχει ἐγγεγλυμμένας ἱστορίας τῶν
ἐσχάτων τῆς πόλεως, τῶν Ῥῶς τῶν μελλόντων πορθεῖν
αὐτὴν τὴν πόλιν. Καὶ τὸ ἐμπόδιον,[4] ὅπερ ἀνθρωποειδὲς
χαλκούργημα βραχὺ παντελῶς καὶ δεδεμένον γονυκλινὲς
ἔχει ὁ ποὺς ὁ εὐώνυμος τοῦ ἵππου τοῦ μεγαλιαίου, καὶ
αὐτὸ σημαίνει, τί ἐστιν ἐκεῖσε γεγραμμένον. Ὁμοίως καὶ ὁ
κοῦφος κίων ὁ μεγαλαῖος ὁ ἐκεῖσε καὶ ὁ Ξηρόλοφος τὰς
ἐσχάτας ἱστορίας τῆς πόλεως καὶ τὰς ἁλώσεις ἔχουσιν ἐν-
ίστορας ἐγγεγλυμμένας.

48 Περὶ τοῦ Φιλαδελφίου.—Ὅτι τὸ καλούμενον Φιλαδέλφιον υἱοί εἰσιν τοῦ μεγάλου Κωνσταντίνου. Ὁπόταν δὲ
ὁ μέγας Κωνσταντῖνος ἐτελεύτησεν, τοῦ Κωνσταντίου
ὄντος ἐν τοῖς ἀνατολικοῖς μέρεσιν, Κώνσταντος δὲ ἀπὸ
δύσεως καὶ τῶν Γαλλιῶν ἐρχομένου, συνήφθησαν ἐκεῖσε
καὶ ἀσπάζονται ἀλλήλους· οὐχ ὅτι ἐκεῖ συνήφθησαν, ἀλλὰ
τῆς ὑπαντῆς αὐτῶν ἐκεῖσε ἀναστηλωθείσης. Ὡς δὲ ἕτεροί

82

On the Tauros.[51]—A statue of Theodosios the Great (I, 47
379–395), which was formerly silver, stands in the Tauros
where he used to receive those who came from the foreigners.[52] Formerly, palaces and a hostel of the Romans were
there, that is, at the place called the threshing floor (Halonitzin). Theodosios is installed on top of the big column.
His sons are above the lofty great quadruple columns: Hon-
orios (395–423) stands on the stone arch to the west, Arkadios (395–408) on the stone arch to the east.[53] In the middle
of the courtyard is a huge equestrian statue, which some
people call Joshua son of Nun, others Bellerophon. It was
brought from Antioch the Great.[54] The four-sided stonecut
plinth of the rider has relief narratives of the final days of
the city, of the Rhos (Russians) who will conquer this city.
And that impediment, which is the very short man-shaped
bronze object tied in a kneeling position under the left foot
of the huge horse, signifies the same as that which is depicted there.[55] Similarly, both the huge, hollow column there
and the Xerolophos have the story of the final days of the
city and its conquests depicted as reliefs.

On the Philadelphion.—The so-called Philadelphion is 48
the sons of Constantine the Great. When Constantine the
Great died, Constantius (337–361) was in the eastern parts,
and Constans came from the West and Gaul, and they
met there and embraced each other.[56] Not that they would
have met there, but that their meeting was commemorated

φασιν, ὅτι νῦν τὸ καλούμενον Φιλαδέλφιον, ἐν ᾧ ἐστὶ βόρροθεν ἀψίς, προτείχισμα ἦν καὶ χερσαία πόρτα τὸ παλαιόν, ὑπὸ Κάρου κατασκευασθεῖσα.

49 Περὶ τοῦ Ἀνηλίου τοῦ ἐν τῷ Φόρῳ.—Ἐκεῖ οὖν ἵστατο πρῶτον ἡ στήλη τοῦ Φόρου, ἣν εἰς καροῦχαν ἤνεγκαν ἀπὸ τοῦ Φιλαδελφίου, ὡς δὲ ὁ Διακρινόμενος λέγει, ἀπὸ τῆς Μαγναύρας. Ἡ ἐν τῷ Φόρῳ τεθεῖσα στήλη πολλὰς ὑμνῳ-δίας δεξαμένη εἰς Τύχην τῆς πόλεως προσεκυνήθη παρὰ πάντων, ὑψωθεῖσα ἐν τῷ κίονι, τοῦ ἱερέως μετὰ τῆς λιτῆς παρεστηκότος καὶ μετὰ κραυγῆς τὸ "Κύριε ἐλέησον" βο-ώντων ἑκατοντάκις. Καὶ ἄνωθεν ἐκεῖσε ἐπὶ τὴν κεφαλὴν τοῦ κίονος πολλὰ ἐτέθησαν θαυμαστὰ καὶ παράδοξα. Πα-νήγυρις δὲ περὶ τούτου γέγονεν τεσσαρακονθήμερος καὶ σιτηρέσια πολλὰ τότε ὁ βασιλεὺς δέδωκεν. Τῇ δὲ ἐπαύριον τὸ γενέθλιον τῆς πόλεως γέγονεν καὶ μέγα ἱπποδρόμιον· ὅτε καὶ ἡ πόλις ὠνομάσθη Κωνσταντινούπολις.

50 Περὶ τοῦ σταυροῦ τοῦ Φιλαδελφίου.—Τὸν δὲ εἰς τὸ Φιλαδέλφιον ὄντα σταυρὸν ἀνέστησεν ὁ ἅγιος Κωνσταν-τῖνος ἐπὶ κίονος κεχρυσωμένον διὰ λίθων καὶ ὑέλων κατὰ τὸν σταυροειδῆ τύπον, ὃν εἶδεν ἐν τῷ οὐρανῷ. Καὶ ἐκ τοῦ κίονος ἐκείνου τοῦ πορφυροῦ ἐποίησεν στήλας τῶν υἱῶν αὐτοῦ καὶ ἀνετύπωσεν ἐπὶ θρόνου καθέζεσθαι. Ἐποίησεν δὲ εἰς τὸν κίονα ἐκεῖνον ἱστορίας τὰς ἑαυτοῦ ἐνζώδους καὶ γράμματα Ῥωμαῖα τὰ ἔσχατα σημαίνοντα. Ἵσταται δὲ ἀντικρὺ τῶν δύο υἱῶν αὐτοῦ τῶν ἐπὶ θρόνου καθεζομένων καὶ τῶν ἄλλων τῶν ἀσπαζομένων.

51 Περὶ τοῦ Μοδίου καὶ τῶν χειρῶν.—Ὅτι τὸ λεγόμενον Μόδιον ὡρολογεῖον ἦν, ἤγουν τὸ ἔξαμον τοῦ Μοδίου·

there. Others say that what is now called the Philadelphion, in which there is an arch to the north, was formerly an out-work and a land gate built by Carus (282–283).[57]

On the Sunless (Anelios)[58] in the Forum.—Formerly, the 49 statue of the Forum stood there, which they brought on a carriage from the Philadelphion, or as Diakrinomenos says,[59] from the Magnaura. When the statue was set up in the Forum, it received many hymns and was revered as the Tyche of the city by all, and finally it was raised on the column in the presence of the priest and the procession, with everyone crying out the "Lord, have mercy" a hundred times. And above, on top of the column, many miraculous and remarkable objects were placed. A celebration of forty days took place on this occasion, and the emperor bestowed many gifts of grain on the people. On the next day the birthday of the city took place and a great race in the Hippodrome, and the city was given the name of Constantinople.[60]

On the cross of the Philadelphion.—Saint Constantine 50 set up the cross, gilded with precious stones and glass, and in accordance with the cruciform figure he had seen in the sky, on a column in the Philadelphion. And he made statues of his sons next to that porphyry column, showing them seated on a throne.[61] He made relief pictures of his deeds on that column, and Latin inscriptions which indicate the final days. It stands opposite his two sons who are seated on a throne, and the others who embrace each other.

On the Bushel and the hands.—The so-called Bushel was 51 a clock,[62] that is, an official measure. It stood on the arch

ἵστατο δὲ ἐπάνω τῆς ἁψίδος τοῦ Ἀμαστριανοῦ μέσον τῶν δύο χειρῶν κατασκευασθὲν ὑπὸ Οὐαλεντινιανοῦ διὰ τὸ καὶ τὴν Λαμίαν εἶναι ἐγγὺς αὐτῶν. Ὑποκάτω δὲ ἐν τῷ εἰλήματι τῶν χειρῶν ἱστορίαι εἰσίν· οἱ δὲ πεπειραμένοι εὑρήσουσιν αὐτάς. Ὡρίσθη δὲ τὸ μόδιον κούμουλον πιπράσκεσθαι· εἷς δὲ τῶν ἐμπόρων πέπρακέ τινι τὸ μόδιον ῥῆγλον· γνοὺς δὲ τοῦτο ὁ βασιλεὺς ἐχειροκόπησεν αὐτοῦ τὰς δύο χεῖρας καὶ ἔστησεν ὁρᾶσθαι, ὁμοίως καὶ τὸ μόδιον· ἐχρημάτισεν δὲ ὡρολογεῖον.

52 Περὶ τοῦ Ἀμαστριανοῦ.—Ἐν τῷ τόπῳ τοῦ Ἀμαστριανοῦ Ζεὺς Ἥλιος ἵστατο ἐν αὐτῷ ἐν ἅρματι μαρμαρίνῳ στηλωθεὶς καὶ Ἡρακλῆς ὁ ἀνακείμενος· ἔνθα καὶ ποταμὸς ὁ ἀπὸ Λύκου λατρευόμενος καὶ χελῶναι ἐκεῖσε μεσταὶ ὀρνίθων καὶ δράκαιναι ιη' καὶ μαρμάρινος στήλη ἱσταμένη ἐκ χώρας Παφλαγονίας δεσπότου, καὶ ἑτέρα, κεχωσμένη τῇ κόπρῳ καὶ τοῖς οὔροις καὶ τῷ χοΐ, δούλου τοῦ ἐκ χώρας Ἀμάστριδος Παφλαγόνος. Ἐν αὐτῷ δὲ τῷ τόπῳ ἐτύθησαν τοῖς δαίμοσιν ἀμφότεροι καὶ ἀνεστηλώθησαν εἰς θάμβος. Ἐκεῖσε δὲ καὶ καλλωπισμὸς κιόνων λεπτῶν σιγματοειδῶς ἀνεγερθέντων. Ἐγένοντο δὲ ἐκεῖσε δαιμόνων ἐπιστασίαι πολλαί.

53 Περὶ τοῦ Βοός.—Εἰς δὲ τὸν καλούμενον Βοῦν κάμινος ἦν ἐκεῖσε παμμεγέθης ἐκτισμένη βοὸς ἔχουσα κεφαλήν· ἔνθα καὶ οἱ κακοῦργοι ἐτιμωροῦντο· ὅθεν καὶ ὁ Ἰουλιανὸς προφάσει τῶν καταδίκων πολλοὺς ἐν αὐτῷ κατέκαυσεν Χριστιανούς. Ἦν δὲ ἡ κάμινος βοὸς τύπος παμμεγεθεστάτου θεάματος· οὗ κατὰ μίμησιν καὶ ἐν τῷ Νεωρίῳ βοῦς ἀπετυπώθη. Ἦν δὲ ἡ κάμινος ἕως Φωκᾶ, ἀλλ' ὑπὸ

of the Amastrianon between the two hands, and had been made by Valentinian (I, 364–375) because the Lamia was also nearby. Under them, in the arch of the hands, there are representations, and experienced ones will find them. It was decreed that the bushel should be sold as a heaped measure, but one of the merchants sold the bushel as a level measure. When the emperor learned this, he cut off both <the merchant's> hands and displayed them to be seen, and likewise the bushel as well.[63] But it was a clock.

On the Amastrianon. — In the place of the Amastrianon 52 Zeus Helios stood on a chariot of marble, and a reclining Herakles. There was also a river worshipped by a wolf,[64] and tortoises full of birds and eighteen she-serpents,[65] and the standing marble statue of a lord who came from the land of Paphlagonia, and another one, buried in dung and urine and dust, the slave of the Paphlagonian from Amastris. Both were sacrificed to the demons at this place and set up as a source of wonder.[66] There is also an adornment of slender columns, erected in a hemicycle. Many apparitions of demons occurred there.

About the Ox. — A huge furnace, which had the head of 53 an ox, was built at the so-called Ox. Criminals were punished there, and Julian (361–363) burned many Christians in it on the pretext of their being convicted criminals. The furnace bore as a spectacle the figure of a huge ox, in imitation of which the ox at the Neorion harbor was made. The ox existed up to the time of Phokas (602–610), but was

Ἡρακλείου ἐχωνεύθη λόγῳ φόλλεων. Ἐν αὐτῷ δὲ τῷ τόπῳ καὶ ἁψίδες ὅμοιαι τῷ Ξηρολόφῳ, ἔχουσαι ἀγάλματα πολλὰ καὶ ἱστορίας λιθίνας· ἃς οἱ διερχόμενοι εὑρήσουσιν οὐκ ὀλίγας.

54   Περὶ τοῦ Ἐξακιονίου.—Τὸ δὲ Ἐξακιόνιον χερσαῖον ἦν τεῖχος παρὰ τοῦ μεγάλου Κωνσταντίνου κτισθέν· διήρκεσε δὲ χρόνους ρλβ΄ μέχρι τῆς βασιλείας Θεοδοσίου τοῦ μικροῦ. Ἔξωθεν δὲ ἵστατο κίων ἔχων στήλην τοῦ μεγάλου Κωνσταντίνου καὶ τούτου χάριν λέγεται Ἐξακιόνιον. Ἵσταντο δὲ ἐκεῖσε στῆλαι πολλαί· συνέτριψε δὲ ταύτας ὁ βασιλεὺς Μαυρίκιος. Εἰς δὲ τοὺς νῦν σωζομένους κίονας ἵσταντο αἱ ἀπὸ Κυζίκου ἐλθοῦσαι στῆλαι.

55   Περὶ τοῦ Τετραπύλου.—Τὸ δὲ νῦν λεγόμενον Τετρά-πυλον πρῴην ὠνομάζετο Τετράβηλον καὶ διήρκεσεν ἔτη ρξ΄ μέχρι Ζήνωνος· ἦν δὲ ἐκεῖσε κουβούκλιον ἐπάνω τῶν κιόνων ὑπὸ τοῦ μεγάλου Κωνσταντίνου κτισθὲν καθ᾽ ὁμοίωσιν τῆς Ῥώμης. Οἱ δὲ συγγενεῖς τοῦ τελευτήσαντος βασιλέως καὶ ἡ Αὐγούστα προελάμβανον τὸ ἐξόδιον καὶ ἐθρήνουν ἐκεῖσε τὸν τελευτήσαντα ἔσωθεν· ἐρχομένη δὲ ἡ κλίνη ἔσωθεν τοῦ κουβουκλίου, ἀπελύοντο τὰ βῆλα εἰς τὸ μὴ εἰσέρχεσθαι ἢ κατοπτεύειν τοῦ λαοῦ τινα καὶ κατ᾽ ἰδίαν ἐκόπτοντο οἰμωγὰς καὶ θρήνους ἕως ὡρῶν ἕξ· καὶ ἔκτοτε ἀνελάμβανον αὐτὸν τὸν ἀποιχόμενον μέχρι τῶν ἁγίων Ἀποστόλων καὶ ἐκήδευον αὐτόν· καὶ εἶθ᾽ οὕτως ὑπέστρεφον αἱ γυναῖκες.

56   Περὶ τοῦ Ἐξακιονίου.—Ἡ δὲ ἱσταμένη εἰς τὸ Ἐξακιό-νιον στήλη ἐπὶ βραχέος κίονος κατὰ τὸ βόρειον μέρος

melted down by Herakleios (610–641) for bronze coins.[67] At this place are also arches similar to those of the Xerolophos, which have many statues and stone reliefs, of which passersby will find a good number.

On the Exakionion.—The Exakionion was a land wall 54 built by Constantine the Great. It lasted for 132 years up to the reign of Theodosios the Younger (II, 408–450).[68] Outside it stood a column which had a statue of Constantine the Great, and therefore it is called Exakionion.[69] Many statues stood there, but Emperor Maurikios (582–602) destroyed them. On the columns preserved today stand the statues which came from Kyzikos.

On the Tetrapylon.[70]—What is called today Tetrapylon 55 [with four arches] was formerly called Tetrabelon [with four curtains] and lasted for 160 years until the reign of Zeno (474–491).[71] There was a chamber on top of the columns, built by Constantine the Great in imitation of Rome. When an emperor died, his relatives and the Augusta went ahead of the funeral procession and lamented the deceased inside there. When the bier was brought into the chamber, the curtains were closed so that none of the people could come or look in, and they wailed and lamented privately for up to six hours, then they brought the deceased to the Holy Apostles and buried him, and then the women returned.

On the Exakionion.—The statue which stands on a short 56 column at the Exakionion on the northern side is Constan-

ὑπάρχει Κωνσταντίνου τοῦ τυφλοῦ τοῦ νεωτερίζοντος, τοῦ υἱοῦ Εἰρήνης.

57 Ἡ δὲ ἱσταμένη εἰς τὸ Σίγμα στήλη ἐπὶ κίονος ὑπάρχει Θεοδοσίου τοῦ μικροῦ τοῦ υἱοῦ Ἀρκαδίου· ἣν ἀνήγειρεν Χρυσάφιος ὁ εὐνοῦχος ὁ Τζουμᾶς καὶ παρακοιμώμενος.

58 Περὶ τῶν Ἐλεφάντων.—Αἱ δὲ στῆλαι τῶν ἐλεφάντων τῆς Χρυσείας πόρτας ἥκασιν ἐκ τοῦ ναοῦ τοῦ Ἄρεως ἀπὸ Ἀθήνας παρὰ Θεοδοσίου τοῦ μικροῦ τοῦ κτίτορος τοῦ χερσαίου τείχους μέχρι τῶν Βλαχερνῶν· ὅπερ ἔκτισεν εἰς ἑξήκοντα ἡμέρας· ἐχόντων τῶν δύο μερῶν τῶν δήμων ἀπὸ χιλιάδων ὀκτώ, ὄντων δημάρχων Μαγδαλᾶ μέρους τῶν Βενέτων καὶ Χαρισίου ἀδελφοῦ αὐτοῦ μέρους τῶν Πρασίνων μετὰ καὶ Εὐλαμπίου συγγενοῦς αὐτῶν. Καὶ ἤρξαντο κτίζειν οἱ μὲν Βένετοι ἀπὸ Βλαχέρνας, οἱ δὲ Πράσινοι ἐκ τῆς Χρυσείας πόρτης· καὶ ἡνώθησαν ἀμφότεροι εἰς τὴν Μυρίανδρον πόρταν τὴν καλουμένην Πολύανδρον, τῶν ἰδιωτῶν δὲ καλούντων αὐτὴν Κολίανδρον· οὕτως δὲ ἐκλήθη Πολύανδρος διὰ τὸ ἀμφότερα τὰ μέρη ἐκεῖσε ἑνωθῆναι.

58a Περὶ τῶν λοιπῶν στηλῶν τῆς Χρυσείας.—Αἱ λοιπαὶ στῆλαι αἱ ἱστάμεναι εἰς τὴν Χρυσείαν ἥκασιν παρὰ Βιγιλίου ἀσηκρήτου καὶ ἀστρονόμου, μετὰ καὶ τῆς γυναικείας τῆς κατεχούσης τὸν στέφανον εἰς τύπον τῆς πόλεως. Ἄνωθεν δὲ καὶ κάτωθέν εἰσι καὶ λοιπὰ μικρὰ ξόανα, ἅτινα σημαίνουσιν τοῖς πεπειραμένοις ἀκριβῶς πολλὴν γνῶσιν.

59 Περὶ τοῦ Στρατηγίου.—Τὸ καλούμενον Στρατήγιον ἡ στήλη ὑπάρχει Ἀλεξάνδρου τοῦ Μακεδόνος, ἡ ἐν τῷ μεγάλῳ ἱσταμένη· ἥτις ἵστατο πρώην εἰς Χρυσόπολιν, ὅτι

tine the Blind, the Rebellious (VI, 780–797), the son of Eirene (797–802).

The statue which stands on a column at the Sigma[72] is   57
Theodosios the Younger (II, 408–450), the son of Arkadios
(395–408), erected by the eunuch Chrysaphios the Tzoumas[73] and chamberlain.

On the Elephants.—The statues of the elephants of the   58
Golden Gate were brought from the temple of Ares in Athens by Theodosios the Younger (II, 408–450) who built the
land wall up to the Blachernai. He built it in sixty days: both
factions had eight thousand men each, with Magdalas being the leader of the Blues and his brother Charisios of the
Greens, together with their relative Eulampios.[74] The Blues
started to build from the Blachernai, the Greens from the
Golden Gate, and they met at the Myriandros Gate which is
called Polyandros, even though uneducated people call it
Koliandron. It was called Polyandros because both factions
were united there.[75]

On the remaining statues of the Golden Gate.—The re-   58a
maining statues which stand at the Golden Gate were
brought by Vigilios the *asekretis* and astronomer,[76] including
the female one which holds the wreath as a representation
of the city. Above and below are also other small sculptures
which disclose much knowledge very exactly to the experienced.

On the Strategion.—The statue called Strategion, which   59
stands on the great <square>, is Alexander of Macedonia
(339–323 BCE).[77] It stood previously in Chrysopolis, as he

τὸν στρατὸν αὐτοῦ ἐκεῖσε ἐρρόγευσε διπλῆν ῥόγαν τὸν
ἕνα χρόνον· καὶ διὰ τοῦτο ὠνομάσθη Χρυσόπολις παρὰ
τῶν Μακεδόνων· ἐκ δὲ τοῦ στρατοῦ ὠνομάσθη Στρατήγιον.
Ἵστατο δὲ ἡ στήλη εἰς Χρυσόπολιν, ὡς ἀνήγειραν αὐτὴν
οἱ λαοί, χρόνους χμη'· ὁ δὲ μέγας Κωνσταντῖνος ἔφερεν
αὐτὴν ἐν τῇ πόλει. Ἐκεῖσε δὲ ἀπεδοκιμάζοντο οἱ στρα-
τιῶται, ὅτι πεδίον ἦν ὁ τόπος.

60   Τὸ δὲ Μονόλιθον τὸ ἱστάμενον ἐκεῖσε ἀπόκλασμα ἦν
τοῦ ἱσταμένου εἰς τὸ Ἱππικόν· ἧκε δὲ ἀπὸ Ἀθήνας παρὰ
Πρόκλου πατρικίου ἐν τοῖς χρόνοις τοῦ μικροῦ Θεοδοσίου.

61   Ἵστατο δὲ εἰς τὸ αὐτὸ Στρατήγιον καὶ ὁ τρίπους <ὁ>
ἔχων τὰ παρῳχηκότα καὶ τὰ ἐνεστῶτα καὶ τὰ μέλλοντα
ἔσεσθαι· καὶ ὁ νότιος πόλος καὶ ἡ λεκάνη τοῦ τρικακκάβου
ἡ τεθεῖσα εἰς τὰ Στείρου· εἰς μαντεῖον γὰρ ἦν ὁ τόπος·
πλησίον δὲ ἐκεῖσε καὶ ἡ Τύχη τῆς πόλεως. Ὁ δὲ Βάρδας ὁ
Καῖσαρ ὁ θεῖος Μιχαὴλ τοῦ βασιλέως μετατέθηκεν καὶ
παρέλυσεν αὐτὰ καὶ συνέτριψεν.—Περὶ δὲ τοῦ Μονολίθου
ὁ χρονικὸς δηλοῖ τὴν αὐτοῦ ἱστορίαν. Ὁ δὲ μικρὸς Στρατήγιος ὑπάρχει ἡ στήλη τοῦ Λεωμακέλλη.

62   Περὶ τῶν Σοφιῶν.—Ὁ λιμὴν τῶν Σοφιῶν ἐκτίσθη παρὰ
Ἰουστίνου τοῦ ἀποκουροπαλάτου, τοῦ ἀνδρὸς Σοφίας τῆς
Λωβῆς. Μέσον δὲ τοῦ λιμένος ἵστανται στῆλαι τέσσαρες,
Σοφίας καὶ Ἰουστίνου καὶ Ἀραβίας καὶ Βιγλεντίας τῆς μη-
τρὸς αὐτοῦ· καὶ αἱ μὲν δύο ἀφηρέθησαν παρὰ Φιλιππικοῦ·
εἶχον δὲ γράμματα τῶν μελλόντων.

63   Περὶ τοῦ Ἐλευθερίου.—Ὁ δὲ λιμὴν τοῦ Ἐλευθερίου
ἐκτίσθη παρὰ τοῦ μεγάλου Κωνσταντίνου· ἵστατο δὲ
στήλη λιθίνη Ἐλευθερίου ἀσηκρήτου, φέρουσα ἐπὶ ὤμων

had offered his army double pay for one year there. And because of this it was called Chrysopolis by the Macedonians, and was called Strategion on account of the army. The statue stood in Chrysopolis, as the people had set it up, for 648 years,[78] but Constantine the Great brought it into the city. Soldiers were dismissed there, for the place was flat.

The obelisk which stands there was a broken piece of the one which stands in the Hippodrome; it was brought from Athens by the patrician Proklos in the time of Theodosios the Younger (II, 408–450).[79] 60

On the same Strategion also stood: the tripod which has the past, the present and the future on it; the South Pole[80] and the basin of the tripod which was set up at Ta Steirou,[81] for the place was an oracle; and nearby the Tyche of the city. The Caesar Bardas, the uncle of Emperor Michael (III, 842–867), removed, disassembled, and destroyed them.— The chronographer tells the history of the obelisk. The small Strategios is the statue of Leomakelles (Leo I, 457–474).[82] 61

On the Sophiai.—The harbor of the Sophiai was built by Justin (II, 565–578), the former *kouropalates,* the husband of Sophia the Maimed. Four statues stand in the middle of the harbor, of Sophia, Justin, Arabia and Biglentia his mother. And these two were removed by Philippikos (711–713), for they had inscriptions about the future[83]. 62

On Eleutherios.—The harbor of Eleutherios was built by Constantine the Great. A stone statue of the *asekretis* Eleutherios stood there, bearing a basket on his shoulders and a 63

καπούλιον καὶ πτύον ἐν τῇ χειρί, ἀμφότερα λίθινα. Κτισθείσης δὲ τῆς στήλης τοῦ Θεοδοσίου ἐπὶ τοῦ κίονος τοῦ Ταύρου ὁ χοῦς ἐχύνετο εἰς τὸν λιμένα καὶ ἐγεμίσθη.

64   Περὶ τοῦ σταυρίου.—Τὸ δὲ σταυρίον τὸ ἰδρυμένον ἐπὶ τοῦ κίονος πλησίον τῶν Ἀρτοπωλείων ἐν τῇ αὐλῇ τῇ λιθο-στρώτῳ ἀνηγέρθη παρὰ τοῦ μεγάλου Κωνσταντίνου, ὅταν ἐκτίσθη ἡ πόλις. Τὸ δὲ παλαιὸν ἔφερον ἐκεῖσε τοὺς ἵππους ἑκατέρων τῶν μερῶν οἱ ἡνίοχοι καὶ εὐφημίζοντες ἔλεγον· "τοῦ σταυροῦ ἡ δύναμις, βοήθει αὐτοῖς." Ἐκεῖσε δὲ ἵσταντο καὶ πύλαι χαλκαῖ τέσσαρες ἐκ τῶν τεσσάρων μερῶν καὶ περίπατοι γύροθεν τέσσαρες καὶ σημειοφορικὰ πολλά· καὶ διήρκεσαν μέχρι Θεοφίλου. Ἔκτοτε δὲ ἐκλήθη "κοιλὰς κλαυθμῶνος" παρ' αὐτοῦ καὶ προσετάγησαν οἱ σωματοπρᾶται ἐκεῖσε πιπράσκειν τὰ οἰκετικὰ πρόσωπα.

65   Περὶ τοῦ ξενῶνος τῶν Θεοφίλου.—Ἐν τῷ καλουμένῳ Ζεύγματι ἐπάνω τοῦ λόφου, ὅπερ ὁρᾶται εὔμηκες κτίσμα νοσοκομείου, ὁ μέγας Κωνσταντῖνος ἀνήγειρεν αὐτὸ εἰς πορνεῖον. [Γέγονε δὲ καὶ οἶκος Ἰσιδώρου πατρικίου, εἶτα μοναστήριον γυναικεῖον· καὶ ὁ Θεόφιλος ἐποίησεν αὐτὸ ξενῶνα.] Ἵστατο δὲ στήλη ἐπὶ κλωστοῦ λιθίνου κίονος, ἡ Ἀφροδίτη· τῶν δὲ ἐρώντων ἀπερχομένων καὶ συνουσιαζόν-των τὰς ἐκεῖσε οἰκούσας μοιχαλίδας, ἔξω δὲ τοῦ οἴκου μὴ εὑρίσκεσθαι ἕτερον πορνεῖον ἢ τοιαύτην μοιχαλίδα γυ-ναῖκα· ἔσωθεν δὲ τοῦ αὐτοῦ οἴκου ἦσαν διάχωρα ἐπὶ τοὺς κίονας μετὰ κρικίων καὶ κορτίνων· καὶ οὕτως οἱ ἐν ἀσωτίᾳ ἐκεῖσε ἐρώμενοι ἐτέρποντο. Ἦν δὲ σημεῖον ἡ στήλη τῶν ἐν ὑπολήψει ὄντων καθαρῶν γυναικῶν καὶ παρθένων, πλουσίων τε καὶ πενήτων· ἐάν τις ἔλυσεν τὴν παρθενίαν

shovel in his hand, all of stone. When the statue of Theodosios (I, 379–395) was set up on the column of Tauros, the earth was dumped into the harbor, and it was filled up.[84]

On the cross.—The cross which stands on the column 64 near the Artopoleia in the paved courtyard was erected by Constantine the Great, when the city was built. Formerly, charioteers brought the horses of both factions there, acclaimed <the cross> and said: "Power of the cross, help them." There were bronze gates on all four sides and four porticoes all around and many miracle-working objects, and they survived until the reign of Theophilos (829–842). From then on, the place was called "a vale of tears" by him, and the slave dealers were ordered to sell household slaves there.[85]

On the hospital of Theophilos.—Constantine the Great 65 built the big hospital building that can be seen on top of the hill, near the so-called Zeugma, as a brothel. [It then became the house of the patrician Isidoros, and later a nunnery, and Theophilos (829–842) turned it into a hospital.][86] A statue of Aphrodite stood there on a braided stone column.[87] Lovers went there and consorted with the adulterous women living there, for there was no other brothel than this house nor such adulterous women elsewhere. Inside the house were compartments separated at the columns with rings and curtains, and in this way the profligate lovers enjoyed themselves. The statue was a touchstone for chaste women and virgins, both rich and poor, who were held in suspicion. If someone defiled a girl's virginity, and many or

τινός, ἐκείνων πολλῶν τε καὶ ὀλίγων μὴ ὁμολογούντων
ἔλεγον αὐταῖς οἱ γονεῖς καὶ φίλοι· "ἀπέλθωμεν εἰς τὸ
τῆς Ἀφροδίτης ἄγαλμα καὶ, εἰ καθαρὰ εἴης, ἐλεγχθήσει."
Ἐκεῖσε δὲ ὑπὸ τῆς στήλης πλησιαζουσῶν, εἰ μὲν ἄμεμπτος
ὑπῆρχεν, διήρχετο ἀβλαβής, εἰ δὲ ἐμιάνθη ἢ ἐλύθη αὐτῆς
ἡ παρθενία, ἡνίκα ἐπὶ τὸν κίονα τοῦ ἀγάλματος ἐπλησίασαν,
ἄκουσαν καὶ μὴ βουλομένην ἐπιστασία ἀθρόα ἐσκότιζεν
αὐτὴν καὶ σηκώνουσα ἐν πᾶσιν τὰ ἱμάτια αὐτῆς, ἐδείκνυεν
πᾶσιν τὸ ἑαυτῆς αἰδοῖον· ὁμοίως δὲ καὶ αἱ ὕπανδροι, ἐὰν
λαθραίως ἐμοιχεύοντο, τοῦτο καὶ ἐν αὐταῖς ἐγένετο. Καὶ
ἐθαύμαζον πάντες καὶ ἐπίστευον πάντες τῇ γενομένῃ πορ-
νείᾳ ἐκείνων ὁμολογουσῶν. Ἡ δὲ γυναικαδέλφη Ἰουστίνου
τοῦ ἀποκουροπαλάτου συνέτριψε τὴν στήλην διὰ τὸ καὶ
αὐτῆς τὸ αἰδοῖον φανῆναι μοιχευσάσης καὶ διερχομένης
ἐφίππου ἐκεῖσε ἐν τῷ λούματι τῶν Βλαχερνῶν διὰ τὸ ἐξαίσιον ὄμβρον γενέσθαι καὶ μηκέτι δύνασθαί τινα πλεῖν ἐν
τοῖς βασιλικοῖς δρομωνίοις.

66 Τὰ δὲ λεγόμενα Κοντάρια, βίγλα ἦν ἐκεῖ μεγάλη τὸ
πρότερον καὶ ἕως ἑπτὰ χρόνων ἐφυλάττετο ἐκεῖσε· καὶ
πολέμου γενομένου δύο ἔτη, ναὸς ᾠκοδομήθη εἰδώλων
μικρὸς ὑπὸ Γαλλίνου· ὃν καθελὼν ὁ μέγας Κωνσταντῖνος
τῆς Θεοτόκου ναὸν ἤγειρεν καὶ ἐχάραξε τὸν Χριστὸν καὶ
τὴν Θεοτόκον καὶ τὴν αὐτοῦ μητέρα καὶ ἑαυτὸν καὶ ἐπετέλεσεν πανήγυριν ἡμέρας δώδεκα. Ὅστις ναὸς μετωνο-
μάσθη ἡ ἁγία Θέκλα. Τότε δὲ καὶ τοῦ Μιλίου ἡ καμάρα
χερσαία ἦν πόρτα· καὶ εἰς τὸ Διίππιν ἦν ἡ ἀλλαγή. Αὐτὰ
δὲ τὰ λεγόμενα Κοντάρια μέγα ὄρος ἦν, ἐξ οὗ καὶ

few of them did not admit this, their parents and friends would say to them: "Let's go to the statue of Aphrodite, and you will be tested as to whether you are chaste." When they approached <the place> below the column, if she was without blame, she passed by unharmed, but if she was defiled or her virginity destroyed, a sudden apparition would confuse her, reluctantly and against her will, as soon as they approached the column with the statue, and lifting her dress in front of all, she would show her genitals to all. A similar phenomenon befell married women, if they had secretly committed adultery. And all were amazed, and all believed when the women confessed the adultery they had committed. The sister-in-law of the former *kouropalates* Justin (II, 565–578) smashed this statue, for her genitals too had been revealed when she had committed adultery and had passed by on horseback en route to the bath of the Blachernai, because an extraordinary rain had fallen, and it was impossible to go in the imperial galleys.

At the so-called Kontaria, there was formerly a great watchtower which was guarded for seven years. And when a war broke out for two years, a small temple of idols was built there by Gallienus (260–268). Constantine the Great pulled it down and built a church of the Mother of God, and he made pictures of Christ, of the Mother of God, of his mother [Helena] and himself, and celebrated a festival for twelve days.[88] This church was renamed Saint Thekla. At that time as well, the vaulted chamber of the Milion was a land gate, and there was a place for changing horses at the Diippion.[89] The so-called Kontaria was a big hill, whose

66

ἐφυλάττετο ἡ βίγλα τῶν Βυζαντίων πτοουμένων τοὺς δυσικούς.

67 Ὅτι τὰ λεγόμενα Βιγλεντίου ἰσχυροτάτη βίγλα ἦν τοῦ ἁγίου Κωνσταντίνου, ὅτε τὸ Βυζάντιον ἐπόρθει.

68 Περὶ τοῦ Νεωρίου.—Ὅτι τὸ Νεώριον ὁ Κόνων ἐστοι-χειώσατο· ἐν ᾧ καὶ ἀγορὰ τῶν θαλασσίων ἐμπόρων πρῶτον ἦν· ἐπὶ δὲ Ἰουστινιανοῦ μετεποιήθη εἰς τὸν Ἰουλιανοῦ λιμένα.

69 Ὁ δὲ ἀγωγὸς τῶν μεγάλων ἁψίδων ὑπὸ Οὐάλεντος ἐκτίσθη ὡς ὁρᾶται.

70 Ἐν τῇ καλουμένῃ Ἀετίου κινστέρνῃ, ἥτις ὑπὸ Ἀετίου πατρικίου ἐκτίσθη ἐπὶ Οὐάλεντος, στήλη ἵστατο τοῦ αὐτοῦ Ἀετίου.

71 Ἡ δὲ λεγομένη Ἄσπαρος κινστέρνα ὑπὸ Ἄσπαρος καὶ Ἀρδαβουρίου ἐκτίσθη ἐπὶ τοῦ μεγάλου Λέοντος· καθ᾽ ἣν ἀμφότεροι πληρωθείσης αὐτῆς ἀνηρέθησαν [παρὰ τοῦ αὐτοῦ βασιλέως· οἵτινες ἐβούλοντο μετὰ τοῦ δήμου κατα-βιβάσαι Λέοντα τῆς βασιλείας, εἰ μὴ ἐξ ἀγχινοίας οὗτος τούτους ἀνεῖλε δόλῳ.] Ὁ δὲ οἶκος τοῦ Ἄσπαρος ἦν, ὅνπερ εἶχεν Βασίλειος ὁ παρακοιμώμενος.

72 Τὴν δὲ Βώνου κινστέρναν ἔκτισε Βῶνος πατρίκιος ἀνελθὼν ἀπὸ Ῥώμης καὶ ἐσκέπασεν αὐτὴν διὰ κυλινδρικῶν θόλων. Ὁ δὲ οἶκος αὐτοῦ ἐκεῖσε ἦν· ὁ αὐτὸς δὲ ἦν ἐπὶ Ἡρακλείου βασιλέως.

73 Περὶ τοῦ Ἱπποδρομίου.—Ὅτι ἀπὸ Ῥώμης πολλὰ ἐνε-χθέντα εἴδωλα ἔστησαν ἐν τῷ Ἱπποδρομίῳ, ἐξαίρετα δὲ ἑξήκοντα, ἐν οἷς καὶ τὸ τοῦ Αὐγούστου. Ἀπὸ δὲ Νικομηδείας στῆλαι πολλαὶ ἥκασιν, ὅθεν καὶ Διοκλητιανοῦ ἐν τῷ

watchtower provided protection for the Byzantines who feared the people from the west.

The place called Ta Biglentiou was a very strong watch- 67 tower of Saint Constantine when he besieged Byzantion.[90]

On the Neorion.—The Neorion was enchanted by Ko- 68 non (Leo III, 717–741). A market for mercantile traders was also there, but under Justinian (I, 527–565) it was moved to the harbor of Julian.[91]

The aqueduct with the great arches was built by Valens 69 (364–378), as can be seen.[92]

At the so-called Cistern of Aetios, which was built by the 70 patrician Aetios under Valens, a statue stood of this Aetios.[93]

The so-called cistern of Aspar was built by Aspar and Ar- 71 dabourios under Leo the Great (I, 457–474). When it was finished they were both executed there[94] [by the same emperor, for they had planned together with the people to depose Leo from his imperial rule, except that he had shrewdly killed them through treachery.][95] Aspar's house was there, which was owned by the *parakoimomenos* Basil.[96]

The patrician Bonos built the cistern of Bonos when he 72 came from Rome, and covered it with barrel vaults. His house was there, and he lived under the emperor Herakleios (610–641).[97]

On the Hippodrome.—Many idols which had been 73 brought from Rome stood in the Hippodrome, sixty of them extraordinary pieces, among them even that of Augustus (31 BCE–14 CE). Many statues came from Nikomedeia, including that of Diocletian (284–305) which is preserved to

Ἱπποδρομίῳ σῴζεται ἕως νῦν, ἐπίκυφος οὖσα ἀναμέσον
τοῦ καθίσματος ἱσταμένη τοῦ βασιλικοῦ. Ὁμοίως καὶ ἀπὸ
Ἀθήνας καὶ Κυζίκου καὶ Καισαρείας καὶ Τράλλης καὶ Σάρ-
δης καὶ Μωκησοῦ καὶ ἀπὸ Σεβαστείας καὶ Σατάλων καὶ
Χαλδείας καὶ Ἀντιοχείας τῆς μεγάλης καὶ Κύπρου καὶ ἀπὸ
Κρήτης καὶ Ῥόδου καὶ Χίου καὶ Ἀτταλείας καὶ Σμύρνης
καὶ Σελευκείας καὶ ἀπὸ Τυάνων καὶ Ἰκονίου καὶ ἀπὸ Βιθυ-
νῶν Νικαίας καὶ ἀπὸ Σικελίας καὶ ἀπὸ πασῶν τῶν πόλεων
ἀνατολῆς καὶ δύσεως ἥκασι διάφοραι στῆλαι παρὰ τοῦ
μεγάλου Κωνσταντίνου, αἳ καὶ ἐτέθησαν καὶ ἐστηλώθησαν, ἐν ᾧ οἱ διερχόμενοι ταῦτα καὶ πεπειραμένοι ἔχωσιν τὸ
ἀλάθητον τῶν ἐσχάτων.

74 Ἀρτέμιδος δὲ ἡ στήλη ἐν τῷ Ἱππικῷ ἐστιν· ἔνθα οἱ πα-
λαίοντες δοκιμάζονται.

75 Οἱ δὲ τέσσαρες κεχρυσωμένοι ἵπποι οἱ ὕπερθεν τῶν
καγκέλλων ὁρώμενοι ἐκ τῆς Χίου ἥκασιν ἐπὶ Θεοδοσίου
τοῦ μικροῦ.

76 Αἱ δὲ ἐν τῷ Περιπάτῳ τῶν δύο μερῶν ἔφιπποι στῆλαι
καὶ πεζαὶ Γρατιανοῦ καὶ Οὐαλεντινιανοῦ καὶ Θεοδοσίου
καὶ τοῦ κυρτοῦ Φιρμιλλιανοῦ πρὸς γέλωτα ἔστησαν.

77 Αἱ δὲ γεννῶσαι θῆρας καὶ ἀνθρώπους ἐσθίουσαι ἡ μὲν
μία ἐστὶν Ἰουστινιανοῦ τοῦ τυράννου, δηλοῦσα τὴν ἱστορίαν τῶν δευτέρων αὐτοῦ πράξεων· ἡ δὲ ἑτέρα, ἐν οἷς καὶ
πλοῖον ὑπάρχει, οἱ μὲν λέγουσιν ὅτι ἡ Σκύλλα ἐστὶν ἡ ἐκ
τῆς Χαρύβδεως, ἐσθίουσα τοὺς ἀνθρώπους· καί ἐστιν ὁ
Ὀδυσσεύς, ὃν κατέχει τῇ χειρὶ ἐκ τῆς κορυφῆς· ἕτεροι δὲ
λέγουσιν, ὅτι ἡ γῆ καὶ ἡ θάλασσα καὶ οἱ ἑπτὰ αἰῶνές εἰσιν

this day in the Hippodrome; stooping, it stands in the middle of the imperial box.⁹⁸ Various statues were also brought by Constantine the Great from Athens, Kyzikos, Kaisareia, Tralles, Sardis, Mokesos, Sebasteia, Satala, Chaldeia, Antioch the Great, Cyprus, Crete, Rhodes, Chios, Attaleia, Smyrna and Seleukeia, and from Tyana, Ikonion, Nicaea in Bithynia, Sicily and all the towns of the east and west,⁹⁹ which were set up and enchanted, and those that pass by and are experienced find there infallible <knowledge> of the last days.

The statue of Artemis is in the Hippodrome where the wrestlers are tested.¹⁰⁰   74

The four gilded horses which can be seen above the starting gates came from Chios under Theodosios the Younger (II, 408–450).¹⁰¹   75

The statues of people on horseback and on foot in the Gallery on both sides are those of Gratian (375–383), Valentinian (I, 364–375), Theodosios (I, 379–395), and of the crooked Firmilianus for his derision.¹⁰²   76

Of those that give birth to wild beasts and devour men is one of the tyrant Justinian (II, 685–695 and 705–711), showing the story of his deeds in his second reign. The other, where there is also a boat,¹⁰³ is, according to some, Scylla who devours the men thrown out by Charybdis, and it is Odysseus whose head she holds in her hand.¹⁰⁴ Others say that this is the earth, the sea and the seven ages of the world   77

οἱ ἐσθιόμενοι διὰ κατακλυσμόν· ὁ περιὼν δὲ ὁ ἕβδομος οὗτος αἰών.

78 Ἡ δὲ καθεζομένη εἰς τὸ σελλίον τὸ χαλκοῦν, ὁ μὲν Ἡρωδίων τὴν Βηρίναν λέγει τὴν γυναῖκα τοῦ μεγάλου Λέοντος· ἄλλοι δέ φασιν Ἀθηνᾶν ἐξ Ἑλλάδος ἐλθοῦσαν.

79 Ἡ δὲ ὕαινα ἀπὸ τῆς μεγάλης Ἀντιοχείας ἤχθη ὑπὸ τοῦ μεγάλου Κωνσταντίνου. Τὰ δὲ λοιπὰ ἀγάλματα τοῦ Ἱππικοῦ τά τε ἄρρενα καὶ θήλεα, καὶ οἱ διάφοροι ἵπποι καὶ τῶν καμπτήρων οἱ κίονες οἱ λίθινοι καὶ οἱ χαλκοῖ, καὶ οἱ ὀβελίσκοι τῶν καμπτήρων οἱ χαλκοῖ, καὶ αἱ ἱστορίαι τοῦ μονολίθου καὶ αἱ ἡνιοχευτικαὶ στῆλαι σὺν ταῖς βάσεσιν αὐτῶν ταῖς ἐνιστόροις, καὶ τῶν περιπάτων οἱ κίονες σὺν τῶν κεφαλαίων καὶ ποδίσκων αὐτῶν καὶ τῶν ἐν Σφενδόνι καὶ τῶν στηθαίων⁵ καὶ συστεμάτων αὐτῶν καὶ σκαλίων καὶ σωλέων, καὶ ἁπλῶς ὁπόθεν ἐκεῖσε εὑρίσκεται γραφή, κατ' ἐξαίρετον εἰς τὰς χαλκᾶς στήλας—τῶν ἐσχάτων ἡμερῶν καὶ τῶν μελλόντων εἰσὶν πᾶσαι αἱ ἱστορίαι· ἃς ἐστηλώσατο Ἀπολλώνιος ὁ Τυανεὺς εἰς μνήμην τῶν ἐντυγχανόντων διὰ τὸ ἀνεξάλειπτα εἶναι· ὁμοίως καὶ ἐπὶ πάσης τῆς πόλεως τὰ ἀγάλματα ἐστοιχειώσατο. Οἱ δὲ ἔχοντες δοκιμὴν τῶν στηλωτικῶν τῶν ἀποτελεσμάτων εὑρήσουσιν πάντα ἀλαθήτως. Ὁμοίως καὶ οἱ τρίποδες τῶν Δελφικῶν κακκάβων καὶ αἱ ἔφιπποι στῆλαι γράφουσιν, δι' ἣν αἰτίαν ἔστησαν καὶ τί σημαίνουσιν.

80 Ὁ Αὔγουστος ὁ Ὀκταούιος Αὐγούστῳ μηνὶ ὑπάτευσε καὶ ἐτίμησεν αὐτόν, Σεξτίλιον πρώην λεγόμενον, ὀνομάσας Αὔγουστον· ἐν αὐτῷ δὲ καὶ ἐτελεύτησε τῇ ιθ' τοῦ μηνός. Τῷ δὲ Σεπτεμβρίῳ ἐγεννήθη τῇ κγ', καὶ τῇ β' τοῦ

which are devoured by the floods, and the present age is the seventh one.

While Herodion[105] says that the <woman> seated on a   78
bronze throne is Verina, the wife of Leo the Great (I, 457–474), others say she is an Athene which came from Greece.[106]

The hyena was brought from Antioch the Great by Con-   79
stantine the Great.[107] The other statues of the Hippodrome, both male and female, the various horses, the stone and bronze columns of the turning points, the bronze obelisks of the turning points, the reliefs on the obelisk, the charioteer's statues with their relief bases, the columns of the galleries with their capitals and bases, those in the Sphendone, their balustrades and wall revetments, their steps and podia, and simply every place where an inscription can be found, especially on the bronze statues—all these are depictions of the last days and of the future. Apollonios of Tyana[108] set them up to commemorate these events as they are imperishable. In a similar way, he also enchanted the statues throughout the city. Those who are experienced with the workings of statues will find everything without missing anything. The tripods of the Delphic pots and the equestrian statues also bear inscriptions, explaining why they have been set up and what they mean.

Augustus Octavius (31 BCE–14 CE) became consul in the   80
month of August and so he honored it; it had previously been called Sextilios, but he gave it the name August, in which he also died, on the 19th of the month. He was born

Σεπτεμβρίου Ἀντώνιον ἐνίκησε καὶ ἤρξατο τῆς μοναρχίας· καὶ ἐτίμησεν αὐτόν, ἀρχὴν ἰνδικτιῶνος ποιησάμενος αὐτὸν ἤτοι ἀρχὴν χρόνου, ὅθεν ὁ Σεπτέμβριος τετίμηται.

81   Φησὶν Ἀππιανός, Δίων τε καὶ ἄλλοι οἱ τὰ Ῥωμαϊκὰ ἱστορήσαντες, ὡς ὁ Καῖσαρ ἀπὸ Νικοπόλεως πρὸς τὸ Δυρράχιον περῶν μεγάλου κλύδωνος γενομένου καὶ τοῦ κυβερνήτου ἐξαπορήσαντος, ἀγνοοῦντος ὡς τὸν Καίσαρα φέρει—ἦν γὰρ κεκαλυμμένος τοῦ μὴ γνωρίζεσθαι—ἀνα-καλυψάμενος εἶπεν πρὸς τὸν κυβερνήτην· "ἴθι πρὸς τὸν κλύδωνα· Καίσαρα φέρεις καὶ τὴν Καίσαρος τύχην."

82   Κράνος ὁ φιλόσοφος, εἷς ὢν τῶν ζ΄ φιλοσόφων τῶν σὺν τῇ Εὐδοκίᾳ ἀνελθόντων ἐξ Ἀθηνῶν, ᾔτησε τὸν Θεοδόσιον ἰδεῖν τὰ ἐν τῷ Ἱπποδρομίῳ στοιχεῖα· καὶ ἰδὼν τὸν Περι-χύτην λεγόμενον καὶ τὸν ἔμπροσθεν αὐτοῦ ἱστάμενον Ὄνον εἶπεν, "τίς ὁ στήσας;" Τοῦ δὲ ἀναγνώστου εἰπόντος, "Οὐαλεντινιανός," "ὢ συμφορά," φησίν, "ὅτι ἄνθρωπος ὄνῳ ἀκολουθεῖ."—Ἦσαν δὲ οἱ φιλόσοφοι οὗτοι· Κράνος, Κάρος, Πέλοψ, Ἀπελλῆς, Νερούας, Σιλβανὸς καὶ Κύρβος. Θεωρούντων δὲ ἱππεύοντα τὸν βασιλέα καὶ θαυμαζόντων, ἔφη ὁ βασιλεύς· "τί θαυμάζετε;" Ἀπεκρίθη δὲ Ἀπελλῆς· "θαυμάζω εἰδώς, ὅτι τῶν Ὀλυμπίων ἀλλασσομένων ἵπποι γενήσονται ἀνθρώπων ἐπιβάται." Νερούας ἔφη· "κακὸν τῇ βασιλίδι, ὅτι τὸ στοιχεῖον τοῖς στοιχείοις συντρέχει." Καὶ ὁ Σιλβανὸς τὸ ὀκλάζον ζώδιον ἰδών, "καιροὶ ἐπὶ τού-του," ἔφη, "ἀγόνατοι ἔσονται." Ὁ δὲ Κύρβος τὸν Δῆμον ἰδὼν εἶπεν· "ὢ Δῆμος, δι' ὃν δήμιοι περισσεύουσι." Ὁ δὲ Κράνος ἰδὼν τὸ γυμνὸν ἀνδρείκελον, περικεφαλαίαν τῇ

on the 23rd of September, and on the second day of September he defeated Antonius and became sole ruler, and he honored this month by making it the beginning of the indiction, that is, the beginning of the year, wherefore September is honored.[109]

Appianos, Dion, and others who wrote Roman histories, 81 say that when Caesar went from Nikopolis to Dyrrhachion, a great storm arose and the helmsman was at a loss, not being aware that he had Caesar on board—for the latter had covered his head in order not to be recognized; so he uncovered himself and said to the helmsman: "Go into the storm; you are carrying Caesar and Caesar's good fortune."[110]

Kranos the philosopher, one of the seven philosophers 82 who came with <the empress> Eudokia from Athens, asked Theodosios (II, 408–450) if he could inspect the statues in the Hippodrome. When he saw the so-called Bath Attendant and the Donkey standing in front of him, he said, "Who set it up?," and when a lector replied, "Valentinian (I, 364–375)," he said, "What a disaster for a man to follow a donkey!"[111] These were the philosophers: Kranos, Karos, Pelops, Apelles, Nerva, Silvanos, and Kyrbos. When they saw the emperor riding on horseback and were amazed, the emperor said, "Why are you amazed?" Apelles replied, "I am surprised, for I see that horses will be the riders of men when the Olympians change." Nerva said, "<This is> a bad sign for the queen <of cities>, if the statue is like its meaning." And Silvanos said, looking at the kneeling statue, "Times will be barren under his rule." When Kyrbos looked at <the statue> of the People, he said, "O People, on account of whom public executioners are unnecessary." When Kranos saw the naked male statue with a helmet on its head and

κεφαλῇ περιφέρον, καὶ τὸν ὄνον ἔμπροσθεν εἶπεν, "ὥς
ποτε ὄνος ἄνθρωπος ἔσται," καὶ "ὦ τῆς συμφορᾶς ὅτι
ἄνθρωπος ὄνῳ ἀκολουθεῖν οὐκ αἰσχύνεται." Πέλοψ δὲ
τοὺς ὅρους τῶν ἵππων ἰδὼν ἠρώτησε· "τίνος τὸ πρόβλημα;"
Τοῦ δὲ Θεοδοσίου εἰπόντος, "Κωνσταντίνου," ἐκεῖνον
φάναι, "ἢ φιλόσοφος ἄκυρος ἢ βασιλεὺς οὐκ ἀληθής."
Ἑώρα γάρ τι ὁ φιλόσοφος θηλύμορφον ζῴδιον τετραμερέσι
ζῳδιακοῖς γράμμασι γεγραμμένον καὶ εἶπεν· "ὦ
τετραπέρατε, ἐξ οὗ Κωνσταντῖνος καὶ <. . .> ἀπέρατοι
ἔσονται." Κάρος δὲ προτραπεὶς εἶπε· "δυστυχῆ μοι τὰ
πάντα φαίνεται· εἰ γὰρ ταῦτα τὰ στοιχεῖα, ὡς πειρῶνται,
ἀληθεύουσιν, ἵνα τί ἡ πόλις συνέστηκεν;"

83   Ἀσκληπιόδωρος δὲ ὁ φιλόσοφος ἐπὶ Ἀναστασίου, ἰδὼν
τὸ μέγα ζῴδιον τὸ ἐν τῷ Ἱππικῷ τὴν χεῖρα κατέχον ἐπὶ τοῦ
προσώπου, ἔφη· "ὦ βία, ὅτι πᾶσα ἀνθρωπίνη ἔνδεια εἰς
μίαν ἀνθρώπου φρόνησιν ἐζυμώθη." Καί τις αὐτῷ ὑπέδειξε
γράμματα ἐν τῷ μαρμάρῳ· ὁ δὲ ὑπαναγνοὺς φησιν· "ἀγα-
θὸν μὴ φθάσαι τὰ τότε μέλλοντα γενέσθαι, ὡς καὶ ἐμοὶ
κέρδος ἦν τοῦ μὴ ἀναγνῶναι."

84   Θεοσάρης θεὸς σέβεται· Ἄραβες δὲ μάλιστα τιμῶσι· τὸ
δὲ ἄγαλμα αὐτοῦ λίθος ἐστὶ μέγας τετράγωνος ἀτύπωτος
ὕψος ποδῶν τεσσάρων, εὖρος δύο, βάθος ἑνός· ἀνάκειται
δὲ ἐπὶ βάσεως χρυσηλάτου. Τούτῳ θύουσι καὶ τὸ αἷμα τῶν
ἱερείων προχέουσι· τοῦτο αὐτοῖς ἐστιν ἡ σπονδή· ὁ δὲ
οἶκος ἅπας ἐστὶν ὁλόχρυσος· οἵ τε γὰρ τοῖχοι χρύσεοι καὶ
τὰ ἀναθήματα πολλά εἰσιν. Ἔστι δὲ τὸ ἄγαλμα ἐν Πέτρᾳ
τῆς Ἀραβίας· καὶ αὐτοὶ σέβονται αὐτόν.

85   Στῆλαι Περσέως καὶ Ἀνδρομέδας.—Ἐκ τοῦ Ἰκονίου

the donkey standing in front of him, he said, "One day a donkey will be like a man," and "What a disaster if a man is not ashamed to follow a donkey!" Pelops, looking at the starting gates of the horses, said, "Who posed the riddle?" And when Theodosios replied, "Constantine," he said, "Either the philosopher has erred or the emperor did not tell the truth." For the philosopher saw a female statue inscribed with zodiacal inscriptions on all four sides, and he said, "O four-sides, through whom Constantine and <. . .> will come to naught." Karos, urged to speak, said, "All this appears to be bad in my opinion, for if these statues tell the truth when they are put to the test, why does Constantinople still stand?"[112]

In the time of Anastasios (491–518), the philosopher 83 Asklepiodoros looked at the large statue in the Hippodrome which holds its hand up to its face, and said, "O might! To think that all human need should have arisen in the singular mind of a man." And someone showed him the writing on the marble; when he had read it, he said, "It would be good not to know in advance what is going to happen; so too I would have been better off if I had not read the inscription."[113]

Theosares is venerated as a god, and the Arabs honor him 84 especially. His statue is a large unworked four-sided stone, four feet high, two wide and one deep, and rests on a plinth of beaten gold. They offer him sacrifices and pour forth the blood of sacrificial animals, and this is their libation. And the whole house is of pure gold; for the walls are golden and there are many votive offerings. The statue stands in Petra in Arabia, and they worship it.[114]

Statues of Perseus and Andromeda.—The statues of 85

Περσέως στῆλαι καὶ Ἀνδρομέδας θυγατρὸς Βασιλίσκου, ὑπαρχούσης ὡς οἱ μῦθοί φασιν δίδοσθαι θυσίαν τῷ ἐκεῖσε ἐμφωλεύοντι δράκοντι. Οὕτως γὰρ ἦν ἐκ παλαιᾶς συνηθείας δίδοσθαι παρθένον κόρην τῷ θηρίῳ· καθ' ἣν Ἀνδρομέδα δεθεῖσα ἔμελλε τῷ θηρίῳ βορὰ δίδοσθαι. Ὁ γοῦν προειρημένος Περσεὺς ἐκεῖσε ἥκων πύθεται κλαιούσης τῆς Ἀνδρομέδας, τί ἂν ὠδύρετο· ἡ δὲ τὸ συμβὰν ἐξηγήσατο. Τοῦ δὲ καθίσαντος <ἧκε τὸ θηρίον>· αὐτὸς δὲ Γοργόνης κεφαλὴν ἐν πήρᾳ κατέχων ὀπισθοφανῶς στραφεὶς δείκνυσιν τὸ θηρίον τὸ δηλητήριον· ὅθεν ἰδὸν ἐκεῖνο ἀπέψυξεν. Ὅθεν καὶ ἐκλήθη Ἰκόνιον ἡ πόλις παρὰ Φιλοδώρου λογιστοῦ διὰ τὸ τὸν Περσέα δεῖξαι τὴν εἰκόνα ἐκεῖσε. Ἦν δὲ τῇ πόλει ὄνομα ἀπὸ γενέσεως Δάνεια· ἔπειτα ἐκλήθη Θρηνῳδία, παρὰ δὲ Φιλοδώρου Ἰκόνιον. Ἔνθα καὶ ἐτελειώθη ὁ αὐτὸς Περσεὺς σὺν τῇ Ἀνδρομέδᾳ· ἐπάνω οὖν τῆς πύλης τῆς πόλεως ἐστηλώθησαν ἀμφότεροι. Ἥκασιν οὖν αἱ στῆλαι ἐπὶ Κωνσταντίου μετὰ τὸ πληρωθῆναι τὴν Ἀντιοχέων ἐκκλησίαν, ἐν τῷ μεγάλῳ τοῦ Κωνσταντίνου λοετρῷ καὶ ἔστησαν πλησίον τοῦ Τζυκανιστηρίου.

86 Ἐν τῇ κατωγαίᾳ πόρτῃ τῇ πληρεστάτῃ στοιχεῖον ἵστατό τινος Φιδαλίας Ἑλληνίδος. Ἀρθείσης δὲ τῆς στήλης θαῦμα ἦν ἰδεῖν μέγα, σείεσθαι τὸν τόπον ἐκεῖνον ἐπὶ πολύ, ὥστε καὶ τὸν βασιλέα θαυμάσαι καὶ λιτὴν ἀπελθεῖν ἐν τῷ τόπῳ καὶ οὕτως παῦσαι τὸν σεισμὸν Σάβα τοῦ ὁσίου δι' εὐχῶν.

87 Ἐπὶ ἅρματος ἵστατο εἰς τοὺς πλεκτοὺς κίονας ἐν τῇ λεγομένῃ Νεολαίᾳ στήλη γυναικεία καὶ βωμὸς μετὰ μοσχαρίου· ἐν οἷς καὶ ἵπποι χρυσολαμπεῖς τέσσαρες· ἐπὶ δίφρου καὶ διφρελάτου γυναικὸς <στήλη> ἐν τῇ δεξιᾷ χειρὶ

Perseus and Andromeda, the daughter of Basiliskos, came from Ikonion; as the myths say, she was given as a sacrifice to the dragon that lived there. For this was an ancient custom, for a young maiden to be offered to the beast. Accordingly, Andromeda was bound and about to be given to the beast. The aforementioned Perseus, passing that way, asked the weeping Andromeda why she was lamenting, and she told him what had happened. But as he sat down, <the beast came>. Turning away and facing backward, he showed the Gorgon's head he was carrying in his satchel to the poisonous beast, which expired on seeing it. So the city was called Ikonion by Philodoros the *logistes* because Perseus had shown the image (*eikon*) there. The name of the city from its foundation was Daneia; then it was called Threnodia, but by Philodoros it was called Ikonion. The same Perseus died there together with Andromeda, and both were depicted over the city gate. The statues came during the reign of Constantius (II, 337–361) after the completion of the church of Antioch, to the great bath of Constantine[115] and stood near the Tzykanisterion.[116]

At the ground-level gate, which has been filled up, stood 86 the enchanted statue of a certain pagan woman, Phidalia. When the statue was removed, a great wonder was to be seen, namely that the place shook for a long time, so that even the emperor marveled and a procession went to the place, and only by the prayers of Saint Sabas was the earthquake stopped.[117]

A female statue stood on a chariot at the place called 87 Neolaia on the braided columns, and an altar with a calf. Four horses, shining with gold, were also with these; and on a chariot with a charioteer was a <statue> of a woman hold-

κατέχουσα στηλίδιόν τι, ἄγαλμα διατρέχον. Τοῦτο οἱ μὲν λέγουσι Κωνσταντίνου κατασκευήν, <οἱ δὲ> τὴν ζεῦξιν μόνην, τὴν δὲ λοιπὴν ἀρχαίαν εἶναι καὶ μηδὲν παρὰ Κωνσταντίνου κατασκευασθῆναι. Ἕως γὰρ Θεοδοσίου τοῦ μεγάλου θέαμα παρὰ τῶν πολιτῶν γέγονεν ἐν τῷ Ἱπποδρομίῳ ἀνὰ κηρῶν καὶ λευκῶν χλαμύδων φοροῦντας πάντας εἰσέρχεσθαι τὴν αὐτὴν στήλην μόνην ἐπάνω ἅρματος ἕως τοῦ Στάματος ἀπὸ τῶν καγκέλλων. Τοῦτο δὲ ἐξετέλουν, ὅτε τὸ γενέθλιον τῆς πόλεως ἑορτάζετο. Ἐκεῖ δὲ ἐν ζῴδοις ἐστηλώθησαν εἰς τοὺς κίονας ὁ Ἀδὰμ καὶ ἡ Εὔα καὶ ἡ Εὐθηνία καὶ ὁ Λιμός.

88   Περὶ λίμνης τοῦ Νεωρίου.—Ἐν τῇ λεγομένῃ λίμνῃ τοῦ Νεωρίου βοῦς ἵστατο χαλκοῦς παμμεγεθέστατος πάνυ· κράζειν δὲ ἔλεγον αὐτὸν ὡς βοῦν μίαν τοῦ ἐνιαυτοῦ, καὶ γίνεσθαι παραπτώματα ἐν τῇ ἡμέρᾳ ἐκείνῃ, ἐν ᾗ ἔκραξεν· ἐπὶ δὲ Μαυρικίου τοῦ βασιλέως ἐν αὐτῇ τῇ λίμνῃ κατεχώσθη.

89   Περὶ τῶν στηλῶν τῶν ἐν τῇ Χαλκῇ.—Τοῦ Μαυρικίου στήλη καὶ τῆς γυναικὸς καὶ τῶν τέκνων αὐτοῦ ἐν τῇ Χαλκῇ ἵσταται ἄνωθεν τῆς θεανδρικῆς εἰκόνος τοῦ Ἰησοῦ Χριστοῦ· ὑπ' αὐτοῦ γὰρ κατεσκευάσθησαν. Αἱ δὲ δύο στήλαι αἱ ἐκτεταμέναι τὰς χεῖρας ὁ εἷς τῷ ἑτέρῳ ἐκ τῆς Ἀθηναίων γῆς ἥκασιν· φιλοσόφων δέ φασιν εἶναι, ὥς φησιν Λιγύριος ὁ Ἑλληνικός.

89a   Μετὰ τὸ ἀποθανεῖν Μαρκιανὸν τὸν βασιλέα ἐγένετο Εὐτύχους τινὸς μαθητὴς ὀνόματι Ἄκατος, διάκονος ὑπάρχων τοῦ ναοῦ τῆς ἁγίας Εὐφημίας· ὃς ἰδὼν ἡττηθέντας τοὺς κατὰ Εὐτύχην κατέλαβε Σεραπίωνα τὸ κάστρον·

ing in her right hand a small statue, a running figure. While some say that it was set up by Constantine, <others say> only the group of horses, while the rest is antique and not made by Constantine. For up to the time of Theodosios the Great (I, 379–395) there was a spectacle enacted by the citizens in the Hippodrome, when everyone entered with candles and white cloaks, conveying this same statue alone on a chariot from the starting gates as far as the Stama. They used to perform this each time that the birthday of the city was celebrated. And Adam and Eve and Plenty and Famine were represented there by statues on columns.[118]

About the harbor of Neorion. — A bronze ox of enormous 88 size stood at the harbor called Neorion. They said that it bellowed like an ox once a year and that on the day on which it bellowed, disasters happened. In the reign of the emperor Maurikios (582–602) it was sunk in this harbor.[119]

About the statues on the Chalke. — The statues of Mau- 89 rikios (582–602) and his wife and children at the Chalke stand above the theandric icon of Jesus Christ; for they were made by him. The two statues whose hands are outstretched toward each other came from the land of the Athenians; they say they are of philosophers, as Ligyrios the pagan says.[120]

After the death of the emperor Markianos (450–457) a 89a man named Akatos, a deacon of the church of Saint Euphemia, became a disciple of a certain Eutyches. When he saw that the followers of Eutyches were defeated, he went to the

τοῦτο δὲ ἦν ἓν τῶν Περσῶν, Ῥήγιον τοὔνομα. Ἐμήνυσε δὲ Περιττίῳ τῷ καστροφύλακι τὰ τῆς ἀσθενείας τῶν ἐν Καλχηδόνι οἰκούντων· ὃς παρευθὺ τοῦ ἅρματος ἐπιβὰς— οὕτως γὰρ τοῖς ἐν Ῥηγίῳ καστροφύλαξι πέφυκε—μετὰ ἑβδομήκοντα χιλιάδων ἔρχεται ἐπὶ τὴν Καλχηδονίων μητρόπολιν· οἱ δὲ ἐκεῖσε προγνόντες ἔφυγον ἐν τῷ Βυζαντίῳ, ἄραντες μεθ᾽ ἑαυτῶν καὶ τὰ τίμια λείψανα τῆς ἁγίας Εὐφημίας· ὅπερ αὐτὸς Ἄκατος ἀμυνόμενος διὰ τὸ μὴ συγχωρηθῆναι Εὐτύχει τὴν ἐκκλησίαν κατὰ ταύτης τὸν Πέρσην Περιττίωνα ἤγαγε. Τότε ἡρπάγη παρὰ τῶν Περσῶν ὁ Ἥλιος θεὸς ὁ λεγόμενος Κρόνος, χρυσέγκαυστος, ὃς ἵστατο ἐν Καλχηδόνι· ὃν καὶ ἀπήγαγον εἰς Περσίαν.

90 Περὶ στηλῶν τῶν ἐν τῷ ἁγίῳ Μωκίῳ.—Ἐπὶ Λέοντος τοῦ Ἰσαύρου πολλὰ θεμάτια παρελύθησαν ἀρχαῖα διὰ τὸ τὸν ἄνδρα ἀλόγιστον εἶναι.

91 Τότε τὸ λεγόμενον Τρίζωδον τὸ εἰς τὰ κοῦφα τοῦ ἁγίου Μωκίου κάτωθεν ὑπάρχον ἐπήρθη· ἐν αὐτῷ ἠστρονόμουν ἕως τότε πολλοί· καὶ τύμβοι Ἑλλήνων καὶ Ἀρειανῶν ὑπάρχουσι κεχωσμένοι καὶ ἄλλα εἰς πλῆθος σκηνώματα.

92 Τὸ δὲ Πάνορμον διπλότειχον κάστρον ὑπάρχει ὑπὸ τοῦ Πανόρμου Ἕλληνος κτισθὲν δίκην σιδήρου καὶ χαλκοῦ ἀναμεμιγμένου. Ἐν δὲ τῇ πρὸς βορρᾶν πόρτῃ τοῦ αὐτοῦ κάστρου ἵστατο στυράκιον ἰκμοειδὲς καὶ στήλη γυναικεία δικέφαλος. Ἔνθα καὶ θέαμα γέγονεν· ἐμπρησμοῦ γάρ ποτε τὸ κάστρον κατειληφότος καὶ πάσης τῆς πόλεως ἐδαφισθείσης μετὰ καὶ τῶν τειχῶν ἵστασθαι τὸ πυργίον ἐκεῖνο τῆς πόρτης, ἔνθα καὶ ἡ στήλη συνίστατο. Ἀλλὰ μὴν πολλάκις καὶ τοῦ πυρὸς προσεγγίζοντος τῷ προσώπῳ, ὥς

fort of Serapion. This was one of those held by the Persians, called Rhegion. He told Perittios, the commander of the fort, about the vulnerability of the inhabitants of Chalkedon. Perittios immediately mounted his chariot—for this was the equipment of the commanders of Rhegion—and with seventy thousand men he made for the metropolis of Chalkedon. The people learned in advance and fled to Byzantion, taking with them the precious relics of Saint Euphemia. It was in revenge that Akatos, because the church had not been given over to Eutyches, led the Persian Perittios against it. It was then that the Sun god, the so-called Kronos, in gold-niello, which stood in Chalkedon, was seized by the Persians, who took it away to Persia.[121]

About the statues at Saint Mokios.—Under Leo the Isaurian (III, 717–741) many ancient horoscopes were destroyed, because the man was irrational. 90

At that time the quadrant of the zodiac, as it is called, was removed; this had been in the hollow place below Saint Mokios. Up to that time many people used to perform astronomical calculations by it. And the tombs of pagans and Arians are there underground, and many other corpses.[122] 91

Panormon is a fort with a double wall, built by Panormos the pagan, as if from iron and bronze welded together. At the north gate of the same fort stood a small moist spike and a statue of a woman with two heads. Here a spectacle took place: when a fire engulfed the fort and the whole city burned down together with the walls, that tower of the gate where the statue stood remained standing. And many times the fire indeed came very near the face <of the statue>, but 92

ὑπό τινος διώκοντος αὐτὸ ὄπισθεν, ὡς ὀργυιὰς ε΄ ὑπεχώρει τῆς στήλης. Αὕτη δὲ παρελήφθη ὑπὸ Χοσρόου τοῦ Περσῶν τυράννου καί ἐστιν ἐν Περσίδι λατρευομένη μέχρι τοῦ νῦν. Τῷ αὐτῷ δὲ χρόνῳ ἠχμαλώτευσεν ὁ Χοσρόης καὶ τὰ Ἱεροσόλυμα λαβὼν μεθ᾿ αὐτοῦ καὶ τὸν τίμιον καὶ ζωοποιὸν σταυρὸν σὺν τῷ πατριάρχῃ Ζαχαρίᾳ. Ὁ δὲ Ἡράκλειος τῷ εἰκοστῷ ἔτει τῆς βασιλείας αὐτοῦ τὸν Χοσρόην ἀνελὼν καὶ τὴν αἰχμαλωσίαν ἣν ἠχμαλώτευσεν ὁ Χοσρόης, καὶ τὸν τίμιον σταυρὸν εἰς τοὺς ἰδίους ἀπεκατέστησεν τόπους καὶ σπουδῇ καὶ χάριτι Θεοῦ, Μοδέστου τοῦ ἐν ἁγίοις πατριάρχου Κωνσταντινουπόλεως τοῦτο δι᾿ εὐχῆς αὐτοῦ σπεύσαντος γενέσθαι.

93   Περὶ τοῦ Ὀκταγώνου.—Τὸ δὲ καλούμενον Σμύρνιον πλησίον τοῦ Τετραδησίου ἐμβόλου ἔχει ὑποκάτω τῆς γῆς τὸ πρὸς βορρᾶν μέρος ὀργυιὰς ι΄, στήλας θ΄· ἔστι δὲ πλησίον τοῦ ναοῦ τοῦ ἁγίου Θεοδώρου τῶν Σφωρακίου. Εἰσὶ δὲ αἱ στῆλαι αἱ μὲν τρεῖς Κωνσταντίνου τοῦ μεγάλου καὶ τῆς γυναικὸς αὐτοῦ Φαύστας καὶ Ἱλαρίωνος πραιποσίτου καὶ τοῦ παιδὸς αὐτοῦ τοῦ τρίτου, ὁμωνύμου Κωνσταντίνου, Κρίσκεντος ὀνομαζομένου, ὃν Ἡρόδοτος καὶ Ἱππόλυτος χρονογράφοι λέγουσιν ἀποκεφαλισθῆναι ὑπὸ τοῦ πατρὸς διὰ τὸ εἰς ὑποψίαν ἐλθεῖν ἐπὶ Φαύστῃ τῇ μητρὶ αὐτοῦ. Ἐκείνην μὲν βαλανεῖον ἐκπυρώσας ἐκέλευσεν ἔσωθεν κατακαῆναι, τὸν δὲ υἱὸν αὐτοῦ ἀποτμηθῆναι ἄκριτον διὰ ὑποψίαν τινά. Διὸ καὶ τῆς μητρὸς Ἑλένης μὴ φερούσης τὴν ἀναίρεσιν τοῦ νέου, ἤδη τῆς τοῦ καίσαρος ἀξιωθέντος τιμῆς, ἠδολέσχει ἐπὶ τῇ ἀκρίτῳ ἀποφάσει· καὶ ἐστήλωσεν τὸν υἱὸν αὐτοῦ ὁ Κωνσταντῖνος καὶ λυπηθεὶς μετενόησεν

retreated five fathoms from the statue as if forced back by something pursuing it. The statue was taken by Chosroes (II, 591–628), tyrant of the Persians, and is worshipped in Persia to this day.[123] At the same time, Chosroes also conquered Jerusalem and took away the venerable and life-giving cross, together with the patriarch Zacharias. In the twentieth year of his reign, Herakleios (610–641) killed Chosroes and returned to their proper places the captives whom Chosroes had taken and the venerable cross, with zeal and the grace of God, because Modestos, the saintly patriarch of Constantinople, urged him to do so by his prayer.

On the Octagon.—The so-called Smyrnion near the Tet- 93
radesion portico has nine statues below ground in the part ten fathoms to the north. It is near the church of Saint Theodore of Sphorakios. Of these statues three are of Constantine the Great and his wife Fausta, and Hilarion the *praipositos* and his third son, also named Constantine, called Kriskes, whom Herodotus and Hippolytus the chronographers say was beheaded by his father, because he came under suspicion with respect to his mother Fausta. He [Constantine the Great] let a bath be heated and ordered that she should be burned inside, and that his son be beheaded without a formal judgment, because of a suspicion. His mother Helena was unable to bear the execution of the young man, who had already been honored by the dignity of *caesar,* and criticized the decision made without a trial. And Constantine set up a statue for his son, and in his grief

καὶ ἔκλαυσεν ἐπ᾽ αὐτῷ μ᾽ ἡμέρας καὶ μ᾽ νύκτας μὴ λουσάμενος τὸ σῶμα καὶ μὴ ἀναψύξας ἐν κοίτῃ. Ἐποίησεν δὲ τὴν στήλην αὐτοῦ ἐξ ἀργύρου καθαροῦ βάψας αὐτὴν ἐκ χρυσίου πλείστου, τὴν δὲ κεφαλὴν αὐτοῦ μόνην ἐκ χρυσίου τελείου, γράφουσαν ἐν τῷ μετώπῳ, "ἠδικημένος υἱός μου." Ταύτην στήσας μετάνοιαν βάλλων ἐλιπάρει τὸν Θεὸν ὑπὲρ ὧν ἐπλημμέλησεν.—Αἱ δὲ λοιπαὶ στῆλαι ὑπάρχουσιν Σευήρου, Ἁρματίου, Ζευξίππου, Βιγλεντίου τοῦ καὶ τὰ Βιγλεντίου κτίσαντος καὶ Ἐλευθερίου τοῦ εἰς τὸ Σινάτον παλάτια κτίσαντος. Οὗτοι δὲ πάντες παρ᾽ αὐτοῦ ἐστηλώθησαν ὡς ἀποτμηθέντες· οἱ δὲ Ἀρειανοὶ εὑρόντες αὐτὰς ἐπὶ Οὐάλῃ κατέχωσαν ἐκεῖ τὰς αὐτὰς στήλας.

94 Περὶ τοῦ Σινάτου.—Ἐν δὲ τῷ Σινάτῳ ἀπετέθησαν ἡνίοχοι ἐν ζευξίπποις καὶ ἐτέθησαν ἐν τῷ ἀστρονομικῷ ὀργάνῳ, ἔνθα τῆς Ἀρτέμιδος καὶ τῆς Ἀφροδίτης ἵστανται στῆλαι· ἐν αἷς σκυτάλαις ἀπεκεφαλίσθησαν ὑπὸ τῶν Ἀρειανῶν. Αἱ δὲ καροῦχαι ἐν τῷ εἰλήματι κατεχώσθησαν ὑπὸ Θεοδοσίου τοῦ βασιλέως.

95 Οἱ δὲ δώδεκα κόφινοι τῶν περισσευμάτων δέκα ἔτη ἐν τῷ παλατίῳ τοῦ Σινάτου κατέκειντο· μετὰ δὲ ταῦτα ἐν τῷ εἰλήματι κατεχώσθησαν.

96 Στῆλαι τῆς ἁγίας Σοφίας.—Ἐν τῇ Μεγάλῃ Ἐκκλησίᾳ τῇ νῦν ὀνομαζομένῃ ἁγίᾳ Σοφίᾳ στῆλαι ἵσταντο υκζ᾽, αἱ πλεῖαι μὲν Ἑλλήνων ὑπάρχουσαι· αἵτινες ἐκ τῶν πολλῶν ὑπῆρχον τοῦ τε Διὸς καὶ Κάρου τοῦ πατροιοῦ Διοκλητιανοῦ καὶ τὸ δωδεκάζωδον καὶ ἡ Σελήνη καὶ ἡ Ἀφροδίτη καὶ ὁ Ἀρκτοῦρος ἀστὴρ παρὰ δύο Περσικῶν στηλῶν βασταζόμενος καὶ ὁ νότιος πόλος καὶ ἡ ἱέρεια τῆς Ἀθηνᾶς ἀπὸ

he had a change of heart and wept for forty days and forty nights, neither washing his body nor resting on his bed. He made the statue of pure silver and coated it with much gold, and the head itself was made of pure gold, having inscribed on the forehead, "My son who was wronged." When he had erected this, he prostrated himself in penance and prayed to God for his sins. The remaining statues are of Severus, Armatios, Zeuxippos, Biglentios the builder of Ta Biglentiou, and Eleutherios who built a palace near the Senate. All these people were commemorated in statues after having been beheaded. When the Arians found them under Valens (364–378), they buried the same statues there.[124]

On the Senate.—In the Senate, charioteers were put in 94 their chariots and set on the astronomical instrument, where the statues of Artemis and Aphrodite stand. There they were beheaded with clubs by the Arians. The chariots were buried under the arch under the emperor Theodosios (I, 379–395).[125]

The twelve baskets of surplus <bread> lay ten years in the 95 palace of the Senate. After this they were buried under the arch.[126]

Statues of Hagia Sophia.—At the Great Church which is 96 now called Hagia Sophia stood 427 statues, most of them of pagans. Among this great number were those of Zeus, and of Carus (282–283), the stepfather of Diocletian, and the Zodiac, and Selene and Aphrodite and the star Arktouros, supported by two Persian statues, and the South Pole, and a

τοῦ πλευροῦ τὸν Ἥρωνα φιλόσοφον μαντεύουσα. Ἐκ δὲ
τῶν Χριστιανῶν ὀλίγαι μὲν ὡσεὶ π'· καὶ δέον ἐκ τῶν πολλῶν ὀλίγας μνημονεῦσαι· Κωνσταντίνου τοῦ μεγάλου καὶ
Κωνσταντίου καὶ Κώνσταντος καὶ Γαληνοῦ κυαίστορος
καὶ Ἰουλιανοῦ Καίσαρος καὶ ἑτέρου Ἰουλιανοῦ ἐπάρχου
καὶ Λικινίου Αὐγούστου καὶ Οὐαλεντινιανοῦ καὶ Θεοδοσίου καὶ Ἀρκαδίου τοῦ υἱοῦ αὐτοῦ καὶ Σεραπίωνος
ὑπατικοῦ καὶ Ἑλένης μητρὸς Κωνσταντίνου τρεῖς· ἡ μὲν
μία πορφυρᾶ διὰ μαρμάρων, ἡ δὲ ἑτέρα διὰ ψηφίδων
ἀργυρῶν ἐν χαλκῷ κίονι καὶ ἡ ἄλλη ἐλεφαντώδης Κύπρου
ῥήτορος προσενέγκαντος· ἅστινας Ἰουστινιανὸς μερίσας
τῇ πόλει τὸν ναὸν μέγιστον ἀνήγειρεν μετὰ πίστεως καὶ
πόνου. Οἱ δὲ πεπειραμένοι τῶν προειρημένων περιερ-
χόμενοι τὴν πόλιν καὶ ζητοῦντες εὑρήσουσιν οὐκ ὀλίγας.

97   Μαναναῆ στρατηγοῦ μετὰ τὸ νικῆσαι Σκύθας κατὰ
κράτος στήλη ἠξιώθη τιμηθῆναι ἐν τῷ καλουμένῳ Ὠρείῳ,
ὅ τινες καλοῦσι Μόδιον· ἦν δὲ καλούμενον ὡρολόγιον·
ἔνθα νῦν ἵστανται κίονες καὶ ἀψὶς πρὸς τὸν οἶκον τὸν νῦν
λεγόμενον Κρατεροῦ· ἔνθα ἵσταται καὶ μόδιος χαλκοῦς
καὶ ὡρεῖον καὶ δύο χεῖραι χαλκαῖ ἐπὶ ἀκοντίων. Τὸν δὲ
μόδιον δέον ἐστὶ μὴ παραδραμεῖν ἡμᾶς ὅτι ἐπὶ Οὐαλεντινιανοῦ ἐτυπώθη· τότε γὰρ καὶ ἀρχιμόδιον ἐπὶ τῶν ἐν τῇ
Κωνσταντινουπόλει οἰκούντων ἀνηρευνήθη † τοῦτο τοῦ
ἀργύρου τυπώσαντος· ἄργυρος δὲ ἀπ' ἀρχῆς ἐτυπώθη τὸ
νόμισμα. Τοῦτο δὲ καὶ Θεοδώρητος διασαφεῖ τρανότατα.
Αἱ δὲ χαλκαῖ χεῖραι ἔκτοτε ἄνωθεν προετυπώθησαν. Τοῦ
δὲ βασιλέως τὸ κουμούλιον μόδιον νομοθετήσαντος, μὴ
ἀνταίρειν δὲ τοῖς ναυτιῶσι προστάξαντος καὶ σιτηρέσια

priestess of Athene prophesying to Hero the philosopher, standing beside him. There were only a few Christians, about eighty. It is worth mentioning a few among them: Constantine the Great, Constantius, Constans, Galen the *quaestor* and Julian Caesar (361–363) and another Julian, the eparch, Licinius Augustus (308–324), Valentinian (I, 364–375) and Theodosios (I, 379–395) and his son Arkadios (395–408), Serapion the *consularis,* and three of Helena, the mother of Constantine: a porphyry one of marble, another with silver inlay on a bronze column and the other of ivory, given by Kypros the rhetor. Justinian (I, 527–565) distributed these statues about the city when he built the Great Church with faith and effort. Those who are experienced with the foregoing will find a good number of them if they go around the city and look for them.[127]

When Mananaes the general had mightily defeated the 97
Scythians,[128] he was considered worthy of being honored with a statue in the so-called Horeion, which some call the Bushel; it was also called a clock. Here now stand columns and an arch, near the house now called the house of Krateros.[129] A bronze bushel also stands there, and a granary, and two bronze hands on spears. As for the bushel, we must not omit the fact that it was created in the time of Valentinian (I, 364–375). For at that time an official measure was established for the people of Constantinople, and he linked it to the silver coin, for the *nomisma* was originally struck of silver. Theodoretos describes this most clearly. The bronze hands were then set up above it, for when the emperor had issued a decree <to use> the heaped measure, and had in-

εἷς ἐξ ἀμφοτέρων τῶν ναυτῶν τῷ βασιλεῖ τὸν σῖτον ἀπεμπωλῶν ἐν τοῖς ἐκεῖσε δίκην ἄδικον καταγγείλαντος ἐν τῷ κατωγαίῳ Μοδίῳ τὴν δεξιὰν χεῖρα ἀπώλεσεν· ὅθεν καὶ ἐτυπώθησαν αἱ χεῖραι τοῖς λαμβάνουσιν καὶ τοῖς διδοῦσιν ἀμφοτέρους ἐκ τῶν προστεταγμένων μὴ ἀγανακτεῖν.

97a Ἔνθεν τοῦ αὐτοῦ Οὐαλεντινιανοῦ στήλη ἵστατο εἰς τὴν ἀψίδα, ἔξαμον ἐν τῇ δεξιᾷ χειρὶ κατέχουσα· ἡρπάγη δὲ εἰς πάκτον διὰ τὸ καὶ αὐτὴν ἀργυρᾶν εἶναι ὑπὸ Κουρίου προτίκτορος ἐπὶ Ἰουστινιανοῦ τῷ δευτέρῳ ἔτει.

98 Περὶ στήλης τῶν Ἀρτοπωλείων.—Μενάνδρου μάντεως στήλη ἧκεν ἐν Κωνσταντινουπόλει, ἣν ἔστησαν ἐπὶ τὸν Ἀρτοτυριανὸν οἶκον εἰς θέαν διὰ τὸ εἶναι τὴν στήλην εἰς μῆκος πηχῶν ιε', πλάτος δὲ πηχῶν η'· ἥντινα χυμευτὴν ὑπάρχουσαν καὶ ἀργυροελάτην καθαρὰν Μαρκιανὸς ὁ εὐσεβὴς εἰς ἀργύρια ἐχάραξεν καὶ τοῖς πένησιν διένειμεν.

99 Ἀρδαβούριος στρατηγὸς ἐπὶ Λέοντος τοῦ εὐσεβοῦς ἐν τοῖς Θρακῴοις μέρεσιν Ἡρωδιανοῦ στήλην εὑρὼν ἐπίκυρτον πάνυ καὶ παχεῖαν θυμωθεὶς ὤλεσεν· ἥντινα ὀλέσας εὗρεν χρυσίου τάλαντα, λίτρας ρλγ'· ἃ μετὰ προθυμίας τῷ βασιλεῖ κατεμήνυσεν. Ὁ δὲ ὑπ' αὐτοῦ ἐσφάττετο καὶ ὀδυνώμενος ἔλεγεν· "οὐδεὶς μολίβδῳ χρυσὸν καταμίξας ἐπὶ ζημίας † ἠνδρίζετο, οἷα παρὰ τῷ κυρτῷ τούτῳ βασιλεῖ εἰς ἐμὲ συμβέβηκεν." Ἔνθεν καὶ οἱ διερχόμενοι τὸν τόπον <καὶ> μάλιστα φιλόσοφοι οὐ τοῖς προτέροις κακοῖς <τῷ θανάτῳ> Ἀρδαβούριον ἔβαλον, ἀλλ' ἕνεκεν τῆς στήλης

structed the shippers not to resist, one of the shippers who was selling his grain to the emperor for the grain dole lost his right hand at the foot of the Bushel when <someone> unjustly accused him of cheating. Therefore the hands were set up for buyers and sellers, warning both not to protest against the decree.[130]

A statue of the same emperor Valentinian (I, 364–375) also   97a
stood on the arch, holding a measure in his right hand. Because it was silver, it was removed by Kourios the Protector in order to pay tribute in the second year of Justinian (I, 527–565).[131]

On the statue of the Artopoleia.—The statue of Menan-   98
der the seer came to Constantinople, and they placed it on the Artotyrianos house so that it could be seen, because the statue was fifteen cubits high and eight cubits broad. As it was <both> cast and of pure beaten silver, Markianos the Pious (450–457) struck it into silver coins and gave them to the poor.[132]

Ardabourios, a general under Leo the Pious (I, 457–474),   99
found in the region of Thrace a statue of Herodian which was very hunchbacked and heavy. In a fit of anger he broke it, and on breaking it he found gold talents of 133 pounds, which he enthusiastically reported to the emperor. But <Ardabourios> was killed by him, and in his agony he said, "Not even one debasing gold with lead has received such a punishment as I have suffered at the hands of this hunchbacked emperor!" And so those who pass by the place, especially philosophers, did not attribute the death of Ardabourios to his previous misdeeds, but thought it was because <of his

THE PATRIA

Ἡρωδιανοῦ· ὅτε καὶ Ἄσπαρ σὺν αὐτῷ τὸ πέρας ἐδέξατο.
Ἄσπαρος δὲ στήλη ἐν τοῖς τοῦ Ταύρου μέρεσιν σώζεται
ἕως τῆς δεῦρο ἐν ἵππῳ ἐρρωμένῳ δεξιολαβεῖ καθεζόμενος
<ὡς> ὁρᾶται.

100 Ἐν δὲ τῷ Φόρῳ τῷ δεξιῷ μέρει τῆς ἀνατολῆς ἐδέξατο
στήλας πορφυρᾶς διὰ μαρμάρων ιβ' καὶ σειρῆνας ιβ'· ἄστι-
νας σειρῆνας οἱ πολλοὶ ἵππους θαλασσίους καλοῦσι· χρυσέμβαφοι δὲ ἦσαν. Ἐπὶ δὲ ἡμῶν ἑπτὰ μόναι καθορῶνται·
τὰς δὲ τρεῖς ἐξ αὐτῶν ἐν τοῖς τοῦ ἁγίου Μάμαντος μέρεσιν
τέθεικαν καὶ αἱ λοιπαὶ σώζονται.

101 Ἡ δὲ Τύχη τῆς πόλεως χαλκῆ μετὰ μοδίου ἵσταται ἐν
τῇ ἀνατολικῇ ἀψίδι· ἣν ἔφησαν <ὑπὸ> Μιχαὴλ τοῦ Ῥαγγαβὲ χειροκοπηθῆναι αὐτὴν τὴν στήλην διὰ τὸ μὴ ἰσχύειν
τὰ δημοτικὰ μέρη κατὰ τῶν ἀνακτόρων.

102 Περὶ τοῦ Φόρου.—Ἰστέον ὅτι ὁ σταυρὸς ὁ μεσοσυλ-
λαβῶν ἀναγινωσκόμενος, "ἅγιος, ἅγιος, ἅγιος," παρὰ τοῦ
προστατοῦντος τῷ Φόρῳ ἀνηγέρθη· ἔνθεν καὶ δύο ταχυδρόμων καὶ [τῶν υἱῶν] Κωνσταντίνου καὶ Ἑλένης ἐκ
δεξιῶν καὶ ἐξ εὐωνύμων σώζονται στῆλαι. Εἰς δὲ τὴν ἀνα-
τολικὴν ἀψίδα τοῦ Κωνσταντινιακοῦ Φόρου σταυρὸς ἀρ-
γυρέμπλαστος ἐν τοῖς ἀκρωτηριακοῖς στρογγύλοις μήλοις
ἐν αὐτῷ τῷ τόπῳ <ὑπὸ Κωνσταντίνου> ἀνηγέρθη, ὡς
ἐθεάσατο αὐτὸν ἐν τῷ οὐρανῷ. Οἱ δὲ χρυσέμβαφοι υἱοί
εἰσιν αὐτοῦ.

102a Καὶ ἐλέφαντος στήλη ἵστατο φοβερὰ ἐν τοῖς εὐωνύμοις
μέρεσιν πλησίον τῆς μεγάλης στήλης· ἔνθα καὶ παράδοξον
ἐδείκνυτο θέαμα. Σεισμοῦ γὰρ γενομένου καὶ αὐτὸς πέ-
πτωκεν καὶ ἀπώλεσεν τὸν ἕνα πόδα τὸν ὄπισθεν. Οἱ δὲ τοῦ

destruction> of Herodian's statue. This was when Aspar also met his death with him. A statue of Aspar is preserved up to the present day in the region of the Tauros, mounted on a strong powerful war horse, as can be seen.[133]

In the Forum on the right part of the eastern side, <Constantine the Great> received twelve statues of porphyry and marble and twelve sirens, which most people call sea horses; and they were gilded. In our time only seven are to be seen; three of them were moved into the region of Saint Mamas, but the others are preserved in place.[134]

The bronze Tyche of the city with a bushel stands on the eastern arch. They say that Michael Rhangabe (I, 811–813) cut off her hands, so that the popular factions would not rise up against the palace.

On the Forum.—One should know that the cross which is held in the middle, and on which can be read "Holy, Holy, Holy," was set up by the patron of the Forum. The statues of two angels and of Constantine on the right and of Helena on the left are preserved there. A silver-inlaid cross on whose extremities are circular orbs was erected in this very spot on the eastern arch of the Forum of Constantine <by Constantine the Great>, just as he saw it in the sky. The gilded <statues> are his sons.[135]

And an awe-inspiring statue of an elephant stood on the left near the great statue. This manifested a strange spectacle. For once there was an earthquake and the elephant fell over and lost one hind foot. The soldiers of the prefect—for

100

101

102

102a

ἐπάρχου ταξεῶται—ἔθος γὰρ τὸν Φόρον παρ' αὐτῶν
φυλάττεσθαι—συνδραμόντες ἐγεῖραι τὸν ἐλέφαντα εὖρον
ἐν αὐτῷ ἀνθρώπου ὀστᾶ ἀμφότερα ὅλου τοῦ σώματος καὶ
πυξίον μικρόν, οὗ ἐν τῇ κεφαλῇ ἔγραφεν· "Ἀφροδίτης
παρθένου ἱέραος οὐδὲ θανοῦσα χωρίζομαι." Ὅπερ ὁ ἔπαρχος τῷ δημοσίῳ προσέθηκεν εἰς νουμία τοῖς προαναδεδηλο-
κόσιν.

103 Ἀλλὰ καὶ χοῖρος ἵστατο σημαίνων τὴν κραυγὴν τῆς
πανηγύρεως, καὶ γυμνὴ στήλη σημαίνουσα τὸ ἀναίσχυντον
τῶν ἀγοραζόντων καὶ τῶν πωλούντων· συστεμάτια δὲ μέσον τοῦ Φόρου ἔνζωδα ἐπὶ κιόνων ἱστάμενα καὶ ἐν αὐτοῖς
δηλοῦντα τὰς ἱστορίας τῶν μελλόντων ἐσχάτως γενέσθαι
ἐπὶ τὴν πόλιν. Οἱ δὲ στηλωτικοὶ τῶν ἀποτελεσμάτων
ταῦτα πάντα συνιᾶσιν. Ἐστήλωσε δὲ ἅπαντα ταῦτα Ἀπολλώνιος ὁ Τυανεὺς παρακληθεὶς παρὰ Κωνσταντίνου τοῦ
μεγάλου· καὶ εἰσελθὼν ἐστοιχειώσατο ὀνόματα ἐπικρατείας
ἕως τέλους αἰῶνος.

104 Περὶ τοῦ Μιλίου.—Ἐν τῷ λεγομένῳ Μιλίῳ Θεοδοσίου
στήλη ἵσταται ἐφ' ἵππου χαλκοῦ· καὶ ἐν τῇ χειρὶ κατέχει
μῆλον καὶ στήλην ἑτέραν, ἀνδροείκελον ἄγαλμα ἔχον καὶ
στέφανον· ἣν ἀνεγείρας πολλὰ σιτηρέσια τῇ πόλει δέδωκεν. Οἱ δὲ κίονες ὀκτὼ καὶ οἱ ποδίσκοι, ὁμοίως καὶ τῶν
Ἀρτοπωλείων οἱ ὀκτὼ κίονες καὶ τῶν Τζυκαλαρείων <καὶ>
τῆς Χαλκῆς ἔχουσιν ἱστορίας πολλὰς ἃς καλλύνας ἐχρύσωσε.

104a Περὶ τοῦ Περιπάτου.—Ἐν τῷ Περιπάτῳ ἔφιπποι στῆλαι
γένος Γρατιανοῦ ἅπαν καὶ Θεοδοσίου καὶ Οὐαλεντινια-
νοῦ· ἐξ αὐτῶν καὶ τοῦ κυρτοῦ Φιρμιλλιανοῦ πρὸς γέλωτα
γέγονεν· καὶ σώζεται ἕως τῆς σήμερον.

they used to guard the Forum—came running to reerect the elephant, and found inside it all the bones of a human body, and a small box, which had written at the top: "Not even in death am I separated from the holy maiden Aphrodite." The prefect added this to the public treasury for coins, in addition to the above cases.[136]

A pig stood there as well signifying the shouts of the market; and a naked statue signifying the shamelessness of the buyers and sellers. And there are relief slabs on columns in the middle of the Forum and on them are shown stories of what will finally happen to the city. The prophetic records confirm all this. Apollonios of Tyana recorded these things at the request of Constantine the Great, and when he came in he enchanted them with the power of words <that will last> until the end of time.   103

On the Milion.—A bronze equestrian statue of Theodosios (I, 379–395) stands at the so-called Milion. He has an apple in his hand and another man-shaped statue and a wreath. When he erected it, he donated much grain to the city.[137] The eight columns and the bases, as well as the eight columns of the Artopoleia and the Tzykalareia[138] and the Chalke, have many reliefs on them which he embellished by gilding them.   104

On the Gallery (Peripatos).—The equestrian statues in the Gallery are of the whole family of Gratian (375–383), Theodosios (I, 379–395) and Valentinian (I, 364–375). Among them, one of the crooked Firmillianus was made for his derision; and it is preserved to the present day.[139]   104a

105 Περὶ τοῦ Ξηρολόφου.—Τὸν δὲ Ξηρόλοφον πρώην θέαμά τινες ἐκάλουν· ἐν αὐτῷ γὰρ κοχλίαι ις' καὶ συνθετὴ Ἄρτεμις καὶ ἔτεραι πολλαὶ εἰς τὰς ἀψίδας· ἔσχατον δὲ ἐκλήθη Θεοδοσιακὸς Φόρος καὶ ἦν μέχρι Κωνσταντίνου τοῦ Κοπρωνύμου.

106 Ὅτι Μητροφάνους καὶ Ἀλεξάνδρου καὶ Παύλου αἱ εἰκόνες ἐν σανίσι γεγόνασιν ὑπὸ τοῦ μεγάλου Κωνσταντίνου· καὶ ἵστανται ἐν τῷ μεγάλῳ κίονι τῷ πορφυρῷ πλησίον κατὰ ἀνατολάς· ἅστινας οἱ Ἀρειανοὶ μετὰ τὸ κρατῆσαι πυρὶ παραδεδώκασιν ἐν τῷ κορωνίῳ Μιλίῳ μετὰ καὶ τοῦ τῆς Θεοτόκου ἀπεικονίσματος καὶ αὐτοῦ τοῦ νηπιάσαντος σαρκὶ Ἰησοῦ Χριστοῦ, καθὼς Ἀγκυριανὸς χρονογράφος ἐν τῷ Δεκαλόγῳ αὐτοῦ καὶ Ἀναστάσιος ἡμῖν παραδέδωκαν.

107 Ὁ δὲ ἅγιος Ἀγαθόνικος ὑπὸ Ἀναστασίου τὸ πρότερον καὶ Ἰουστινιανοῦ τοῦ μεγάλου τὸ δεύτερον ἀνεκαινίσθη· ἐν αὐτῷ δὲ τῷ ναῷ καὶ πατριάρχαι ἐπισκόπησαν ἑπτὰ ἐπὶ χρόνους πεντήκοντα· καὶ βασιλεῖς στεφηφοροῦσιν ἐκεῖσε. Δι' ἣν δὲ αἰτίαν μετεποιήθη † ὑπὸ θυμοῦ,[6] οὐ γινώσκεται. Καὶ παλάτιον δὲ ἦν πλησίον τοῦ ναοῦ μέγιστον· ὑπὸ δὲ Τιβερίου τοῦ πρώτου μετεποιήθη διολεσθὲν εἰς τὰ βασίλεια.

108 Τὰ δὲ τείχη τῆς δύσεως τῶν μεγάλων πορτῶν ἐπὶ Λέοντος τοῦ μεγάλου καὶ εὐσεβοῦς ἀνεκαινίσθησαν· καθ' ἣν καὶ ἐλιτάνευσαν καὶ τὸ "Κύριε ἐλέησον" τεσσαρακοντάκις ἐξεβόησαν καὶ ὁ δῆμος τῶν Πρασίνων ἔκραξαν· "Λέων Κωνσταντῖνον καὶ Θεοδόσιον εἰς κράτος ἐνίκησεν." Οὗτος γὰρ ἐνομοθέτησεν· ἡ ἁγία κυριακὴ τῇ ἀπραξίᾳ τιμᾶσθαι· πρὸ γὰρ αὐτοῦ πάντες ἔκαμνον.

On the Xerolophos.—Formerly, some people called the   105
Xerolophos a spectacle. For in it were sixteen spiral columns, and a composite statue of Artemis,[140] and many others on the arches. Finally, it was called the Forum of Theodosios (I, 379–395), and lasted until Constantine Kopronymos (V, 741–775).

Icons of Metrophanes (306–314) and Alexander (314–337)   106
and Paul (337–339, 341–342, 346–351) were depicted on wooden panels under Constantine the Great. They stand near the great porphyry column on the eastern side. The Arians, after they had prevailed, delivered them up to the fire in the vaulted Milion, together with the likeness of the Mother of God with Jesus Christ himself who had become an infant in the flesh, as Ankyrianos the historian in his Decalogue and Anastasios have handed down to us.[141]

Saint Agathonikos was repaired first by Anastasios (491–   107
518) and a second time by Justinian the Great (I, 527–565). For fifty years seven patriarchs held office in this same church, and emperors wear crowns there.[142] The reason for which it was altered by wrath[143] is not known. There was also a large palace near this church, and being in a ruined state it was converted by the first Tiberios (578–582) into the present palace.

The western walls, those of the great gates, were restored   108
under Leo the Great and Pious (I, 457–474); on that occasion they also held a religious procession and chanted the "Lord, have mercy" forty times, and the faction of the Greens shouted, "Leo has surpassed Constantine[144] and Theodosios." For he made a law that the holy Sunday should be honored by a day of rest; before that, everyone worked.

109 Τὰ δὲ τείχη τὰ πρὸς τὴν θάλασσαν ἀνακαινίζονται ἐπὶ
Τιβερίου Ἀψιμάρου· ἕως γὰρ αὐτοῦ ἠμελημένα ἦσαν πάνυ·
καὶ ἐκ δευτέρου ἀνεκαινίσθησαν ἐπὶ Θεοφίλου.

110 Περὶ τοῦ ἁγίου Μωκίου.—Δέον γινώσκειν ὅτι ὁ ἅγιος
Μώκιος πρῶτον μὲν ὑπὸ τοῦ μεγάλου Κωνσταντίνου
ἀνῳκοδομήθη Ἑλλήνων πλήθη ἐκεῖσε κατοικούντων
πολλά· καὶ ναὸς ἦν τοῦ Διός, καθὼς καὶ ἐκ τῶν αὐτῶν λίθων ἐκτίσθη ὁ ναός. Ἐν δὲ ταῖς ἡμέραις Θεοδοσίου τοῦ
μεγάλου ἐξορίζονται οἱ Ἀρειανοὶ ἀπὸ τῆς ἁγίας ἐκκλησίας
καὶ ἐλθόντες ἐν τῷ ναῷ τοῦ ἁγίου Μωκίου ἠράσθησαν καὶ
παρακαλοῦσι τῷ βασιλεῖ κατοικεῖν αὐτοὺς ἐκεῖ, ὃ καὶ γέγονεν. Παρευθὺ οὖν ἀνεγείρουσι τὸν ναὸν οἱ Ἀρειανοὶ καὶ
δοξάζεται παρ' αὐτῶν ἔτη ζ'· καὶ πίπτει λειτουργούντων
αὐτῶν ἐν τῷ ζ' ἔτει, καθ' ὃν πολλοὶ Ἀρειανοὶ ἀπεκτάνθησαν.
Ἐν δὲ ταῖς ἡμέραις Ἰουστινιανοῦ τοῦ μεγάλου ἀνεγείρεται
ὁ αὐτὸς ναὸς καὶ ἵσταται ἕως ἡμῶν.

The sea walls were repaired under Tiberios Apsimar 109
(698–705), as they had been completely neglected before
him.[145] And they were repaired a second time under
Theophilos (829–842).

On Saint Mokios.—Note that Saint Mokios was origi- 110
nally built by Constantine the Great, when a large number
of pagans lived there. And there was a temple of Zeus there,
so the church was built with its stones. In the days of Theodosios the Great (I, 379–395) the Arians were expelled from
the holy church, and coming to the church of Saint Mokios
they desired it and asked the emperor for permission to
dwell there, which indeed happened. So the Arians immediately rebuilt the church, and it was used by them for seven
years. It collapsed in the seventh year as they were celebrat-
ing the liturgy; and many Arians were killed. But in the days
of Justinian the Great (I, 527–565) the same church was rebuilt and stands to our own day.[146]

APPENDIX TO
BOOK TWO

Περὶ συνόδων

Σύνοδος ἐν Νικαίᾳ τοῦ ἁγίου Κωνσταντίνου.—Ἡ πρώτη σύνοδος γέγονεν ἐν τῇ Νικαίᾳ τῆς Βιθυνίας ὑπὸ τοῦ μεγάλου Κωνσταντίνου, συνελθόντων τῶν τρια-κοσίων δέκα καὶ ὀκτὼ ἁγίων πατέρων καὶ Σιλβέστρου πάπα Ῥώμης· οἳ καὶ καθεῖλαν Ἄρειον, ὅστις ἦν πρῶτος πρεσβύτερος Ἀλεξανδρείας· τὸν γὰρ Κύριον ἡμῶν Ἰησοῦν Χριστὸν ψιλὸν ἄνθρωπον ἔλεγεν εἶναι· Ἴβηρες δὲ καὶ Ἰνδοὶ τότε ἐχριστιάνισαν. Ἐπὶ δὲ τούτου εἰσῆλθον καὶ τὰ λείψανα τῶν ἁγίων ἀποστόλων· ἐβούλετο δὲ καὶ τὴν τοῦ καλουμένου χρυσαργύρου συντέλειαν ἐκκόψαι, ἣν ἀπὸ τῆς πρεσβυτέρας Ῥώμης ἡ πόλις κατέλαβεν.

2   Σύνοδος δευτέρα.—Σύνοδος δευτέρα Θεοδοσίου τοῦ μεγάλου ἐν Κωνσταντινουπόλει τῶν ρν' ἁγίων πατέρων καὶ Δαμάσου πάπα Ῥώμης καὶ Νεκταρίου Κωνσταντινου-πόλεως καὶ Γρηγορίου τοῦ θεολόγου κατὰ Μακεδονίου τοῦ πνευματομάχου· τὸ γὰρ ἅγιον Πνεῦμα οὐκ ἔλεγεν Θέον, ἀλλὰ ἀλλότριον τῆς θεότητος· ἥτις καὶ προέθηκεν τὸ σύμβολον τῆς πίστεως οὕτως· "καὶ εἰς τὸ Πνεῦμα τὸ ἅγιον τὸ κύριον καὶ ζωοποιόν." Ἐπὶ τοῦ αὐτοῦ τοῦ μεγάλου Θεοδοσίου ἀπετέθησαν λείψανα εἰς τὸν ναὸν τῆς ἁγίας Εὐφημίας Τερεντίου καὶ Ἀφρικανοῦ· καὶ τοῦ προφήτου Σαμουὴλ τὸ ἅγιον λείψανον εἰσῆλθεν ἐν τῇ πόλει ἐπὶ

On Councils[1]

Council in Nicaea, of Saint Constantine (325).—The First
Council was held at Nicaea in Bithynia by Constantine the
Great, with 318 holy fathers and Silvester, the pope of Rome,
in attendance.[2] They deposed Areios, who was the first
priest of Alexandria, for he said that our Lord Jesus Christ
was a simple man. Then, the Iberians and Indians became
Christians.[3] In <Constantine's> time the relics of the apostles were also brought in <to the city>. He also decided to
abolish the so-called tax of the *chrysargyron*, which the city
had taken over from the older Rome.[4]

Second Council (381).—The Second Council of Theodo- 2
sios the Great <was held> at Constantinople, with 150 holy
fathers, Damasus pope of Rome, Nektarios of Constantinople, and Gregory the Theologian against Makedonios the
Pneumatomach, for he said that the Holy Spirit was not
God, but different from divinity. <The Council> also added
this to the creed: "And in the Holy Spirit, the Lord, the giver
of life." Under the same Theodosios the Great, relics of
Terentius and Africanus were placed in the church of Saint
Euphemia.[5] And the holy relic of the prophet Samuel was

Ἀρκαδίου τοῦ υἱοῦ αὐτοῦ καὶ ἐτέθη εἰς τὸν ναὸν τοῦ
Ἑβδόμου· ὁ δὲ Ἀττικὸς ἦν πατριάρχης τῷ τότε καιρῷ καὶ
κατέθετο ταῦτα ὡς εἴρηται εἰς τὸ Ἕβδομον.

3 Σύνοδος τρίτη.—Ἐπὶ Θεοδοσίου τοῦ μικροῦ γέγονεν ἡ
τρίτη σύνοδος ἡ ἐν Ἐφέσῳ τῶν διακοσίων ἁγίων πατέρων,
ἐπὶ καθαιρέσει Νεστορίου· τὸν γὰρ Χριστὸν καὶ αὐτὸς
ψιλὸν ἄνθρωπον ἔλεγεν εἶναι· οἳ καὶ συνελθόντες ἀνε-
θεμάτισαν αὐτόν· καὶ τελείως ἐκήρυξαν καὶ ἐδίδαξαν τὴν
ἀθόλωτον πίστιν τὴν ἐν Τριάδι θεότητα ἀνυμνουμένην ἀεί.

4 Σύνοδος τετάρτη.—Ἐπὶ Μαρκιανοῦ καὶ Οὐαλεντινιανοῦ γέγονεν ἡ τετάρτη σύνοδος ἐν Καλχηδόνι τῶν ἑξα-
κοσίων τριάκοντα ἁγίων πατέρων, Λέοντος πάπα Ῥώμης
καὶ Ἀνατολίου Κωνσταντινουπόλεως κατὰ Διοσκόρου
Ἀλεξανδρέων πατριάρχου καὶ Εὐτυχοῦς ἀρχιμανδρίτου·
οὗτοι γὰρ τὴν ἐνανθρώπησιν τοῦ Κυρίου ἡμῶν Ἰησοῦ
Χριστοῦ παρῃτοῦντο καὶ ἐν φαντασίᾳ αὐτοῦ τὴν σάρκα
ἐμυθολόγουν.

5 Σύνοδος πέμπτη.—Ἐπὶ δὲ Ἰουστινιανοῦ τοῦ μεγάλου
γέγονεν ἡ πέμπτη σύνοδος ἐν Κωνσταντινουπόλει τῶν
ἑκατὸν ἑξήκοντα ἁγίων πατέρων καὶ Εὐτυχίου ἀρχιε-
πισκόπου Κωνσταντινουπόλεως· οἳ καὶ καθεῖλον Ὠριγέ-
νην, Εὐάγριον καὶ Δίδυμον τοὺς παράφρονας· τὰ γὰρ σώματα ἡμῶν μὴ ἀνίστασθαι ἐδυσφήμουν καὶ παράδεισον
αἰσθητὸν μὴ γενέσθαι ὑπὸ τοῦ Θεοῦ μήτε εἶναι· καὶ ἐν
σαρκὶ μὴ πλασθῆναι τὸν Ἀδάμ, καὶ τέλος εἶναι τῆς κολά-
σεως καὶ δαίμονας ἐλθεῖν εἰς τὴν ἀρχαίαν ἀποκατάστασιν.

6 Σύνοδος ἕκτη.—Ἐπὶ δὲ Κωνσταντίνου καὶ Ἡρακλείου
καὶ Τιβερίου [υἱοῦ αὐτοῦ] γέγονεν ἡ ἕκτη σύνοδος τῶν

brought into the city under his son Arkadios (395–408), and was placed in the church of the Hebdomon.[6] At that time, Attikos was patriarch (406–426), and he placed them, as it is said, at the Hebdomon.

Third Council (431).—The Third Council of the two hundred holy fathers was held at Ephesos under Theodosios the Younger (II, 408–450), in order to depose Nestorios. For he too said that Christ was a simple man.[7] They assembled and anathematized him, and perfectly proclaimed and taught the unsullied belief in the Deity in the Trinity, which is praised forever. 3

Fourth Council (451).—Under Markianos (450–457) and Valentinian (III, western emperor 425–455) the Fourth Council of 630 holy fathers was held at Chalkedon with Leo, pope of Rome (I, 440–61), and Anatolios of Constantinople (449–458), against Dioskoros, patriarch of Alexandria (444–451), and the archimandrite Eutyches. For these denied the incarnation of our Lord Jesus Christ and invented the story that his flesh existed only in imagination.[8] 4

Fifth Council (553).—Under Justinian the Great (I, 527–565) the Fifth Council was held at Constantinople with 160 holy fathers and Eutychios (552–565, 577–582), patriarch of Constantinople. They condemned the insane Origenes, Euagrios and Didymos, for they blasphemed that our bodies would not rise <from the dead>, and that a perceptible paradise was neither created by God, nor existed, and that Adam was not created in the flesh, that there would be a finite end to punishment <in Hell>, and that the demons would be restored to their former state.[9] 5

Sixth Council (680–681).—Under Constantine (IV, 668–685) and Herakleios and Tiberios [his son][10] was held the 6

ἑκατὸν πεντήκοντα ἁγίων πατέρων, ἐπὶ Ἀγάθωνος πάπα Ῥώμης, κατὰ Κύρου Ἀλεξανδρείας, Σεργίου καὶ Πύρου, Πέτρου καὶ Παύλου Κωνσταντινουπόλεως γενομένων ἐπισκόπων· οὗτοι ἀπετόλμησαν εἰπεῖν ἓν θέλημα καὶ μίαν ἐνέργειαν τὸν Κύριον ἡμῶν Ἰησοῦν Χριστὸν ἔχειν καὶ μετὰ σάρκωσιν, τὸν σύνδεσμον τῆς ὀρθοδοξίας διαλῦσαι βουληθέντες οἱ παράφρονες· συνῆσαν δὲ αὐτοῖς καὶ Μακάριος ὁ νομοθέτης Ἀντιοχείας καὶ Ἰσίδωρος, φησίν, ὁ μαθητὴς αὐτοῦ.

7 Σύνοδος ἑβδόμη Εἰρήνης.—Ἐπὶ Εἰρήνης τῆς μητρὸς Κωνσταντίνου τοῦ τυφλοῦ γέγονεν ἡ ἑβδόμη σύνοδος τῶν ἁγίων τη' πατέρων ἐπὶ Ταρασίου πατριάρχου Κωνσταντινουπόλεως ἐν τῇ Νικαέων πολίχνῃ, ἐπὶ τῇ καθαιρέσει Θεοδοσίου· παρ' ἧς δὲ καὶ ἐξέθεντο ὅρους τῆς ἁγίας πίστεως.

8 Σύνοδος ὀγδόη Θεοδώρας καὶ Μιχαὴλ τοῦ υἱοῦ αὐτῆς.—Ἐπὶ Θεοδώρας Αὐγούστης μετὰ θάνατον Θεοφίλου τοῦ ἀνδρὸς αὐτῆς σὺν Μιχαὴλ τῷ υἱῷ αὐτῆς γέγονεν ἡ ὀγδόη σύνοδος ἐν Κωνσταντινουπόλει τῆς ὀρθοδοξίας· ἥτις ᾄδεται ἕως τῆς σήμερον.

Sixth Council of 150 holy fathers, under Agathon, pope of Rome (677–681), against Kyros of Alexandria, Sergios and Pyrrhos, Peter and Paul, who had been bishops of Constantinople. They dared to say that our Lord Jesus Christ had one volition and one power of action even after incarnation.[11] Thus these insane ones wanted to dissolve the bond of orthodoxy. They were joined also by Makarios, the lawgiver of Antioch, and Isidoros, he says, his pupil.[12]

Seventh Council of Eirene (787).—Under Eirene (780– 7
802), the mother of Constantine the Blind (VI, 780–797), the Seventh Council of the holy 308 fathers was held, under Tarasios, patriarch of Constantinople (784–806), in the small town of Nicaea, for the deposition of Theodosios.[13] Definitions of the holy faith were also proclaimed by this <council>.

Eighth Council, of Theodora and her son Michael (843).[14] 8
—Under the Augusta Theodora, after the death of her husband Theophilos and together with her son Michael, the eighth Council of orthodoxy was held in Constantinople, which is praised to this day.

BOOK THREE

Περὶ κτισμάτων

Κωνσταντῖνος ὁ μέγας ἀνήγειρεν τὴν ἁγίαν Εἰρήνην τὴν παλαιὰν καὶ τὴν ἁγίαν Σοφίαν δρομικὴν καὶ τὸν ἅγιον Ἀγαθόνικον καὶ τὸν ἅγιον Ἀκάκιον. Τοὺς δὲ ἁγίους Ἀποστόλους ἔκτισεν ἡ μήτηρ αὐτοῦ σὺν αὐτῷ δρομικὴν ξυλόστεγον, ποιήσασα καὶ μνημοθέσιον τῶν βασιλέων ἐν ᾧ κεῖνται καὶ αὐτοί.

2　Τὸν δὲ ἅγιον Μηνᾶν καὶ τὸν ἅγιον Μώκιον εὗρεν ὅτι ἦσαν ναοὶ εἰδώλων. Καὶ τὸν μὲν ἅγιον Μηνᾶν καθὼς ἦν εἴασεν, ἐδίωξεν δὲ τὰ ἀγάλματα καὶ ἐπωνόμασεν αὐτὸν οὕτως· τὴν δὲ τελείαν αὐτοῦ ἀνοικοδομὴν ἐποίησεν μετὰ ρξθ΄ χρόνους Πουλχερία καὶ Μαρκιανὸς σὺν τοῖς προαστείοις καὶ ἱεροῖς σκεύεσι.

3　Ὁ δὲ ἅγιος Μώκιος ὑπῆρχεν ἄλλα δύο μήκη εἰς μέγεθος παρ' ὅ ἐστιν, ἀλλ' ἔκοψε τὸ δίμοιρον μέρος τοῦ ναοῦ καὶ ἀνήγειρεν τὸ θυσιαστήριον Κωνσταντῖνος ὁ μέγας καὶ ἡ τούτου μήτηρ Ἑλένη· διότι δὲ ἀνηρέθη ὁ ἅγιος Μώκιος ἐκεῖσε, τούτου χάριν ἀνήγειρεν καὶ τὸν ναὸν ὡς ἴδιον αὐτοῦ καὶ τὸ σῶμα αὐτοῦ ἐκεῖσε ἔφερεν.

4　Ἡ ἁγία Ἑλένη ἔκτισεν τὴν Βηθλεὲμ καὶ τὰ Γαστρία. Καλοῦνται δὲ τὰ Γαστρία οὕτως, ὅτι κομίσασα ἀπὸ Ἰερουσαλὴμ τὸν τίμιον σταυρὸν εἰσήγαγεν αὐτὸν ἀπὸ τῆς πόρτας τοῦ Ψωμαθέου· καὶ τὰ εὑρεθέντα ἐκεῖσε ἐπάνω τοῦ

On Buildings

Constantine the Great built old Saint Eirene and Hagia Sophia as basilicas, and also Saint Agathonikos and Saint Akakios. His mother together with him built the Holy Apostles as a basilica with a wooden roof, constructing also a mausoleum of the emperors in which they are also laid to rest.[1]

He found Saint Menas and Saint Mokios as temples for idols.[2] And he left Saint Menas as it was, but removed the statues and gave it this name. Its final rebuilding was completed 169 years later[3] by Pulcheria and Markianos (450–457), with estates and holy vessels <bestowed upon it>. 2

Saint Mokios was two times longer than it is today, but Constantine the Great with his mother Helena cut away two-thirds of the temple and set up the altar.[4] It was because Saint Mokios was executed there that he both rebuilt the church for him and brought his body there. 3

Saint Helena built Bethlehem and the Gastria.[5] These are called Gastria, because when she secured the venerable Cross from Jerusalem, she brought it in through the gate of Psomatheas.[6] And she planted the lilies and cinnamon 4

σταυροῦ κρίνα τε καὶ φύλλα καὶ κῶνστοι καὶ βασιλικὰ καὶ
τριαντάφυλλα καὶ σάμψυχα καὶ βαλσάματα, ἐφύτευσεν
αὐτὰ εἰς γάστρας διὰ τὸ διασῶσαι αὐτά· καὶ ἐκεῖσε εἰς τὴν
μονὴν ἀπληκεύσασα ὠνόμασε τὸν τόπον Γαστρία καὶ μονὴν ἀνήγειρεν.

5 Τὸν δὲ Ψωμαθέαν τὰ παλάτια καὶ τὸ γηροκομεῖον ἀνήγειρεν ἡ ἁγία Ἑλένη, ὁμοίως καὶ τὸν ἅγιον Θεόδωρον τὰ
Κλαυδίου.

6 Τὸν δὲ ἅγιον Ἰουλιανὸν ἀνήγειρεν Οὐρβίκιος ὁ παριστάμενος εἰς τὰ κτίσματα ἐξ οἰκείων ἐξόδων· ἐν ᾧ καὶ
ἦσαν ἄπληκτα τῶν Ῥωμαίων.

7 Εἰς τὸ καλούμενον Ἀλωνίτζιν παλάτια ἦσαν παρὰ τοῦ
μεγάλου Κωνσταντίνου κτισθέντα οὐδαμινά, εἰς τὸ ἀπλη-
κεύειν τοὺς προκρίτους τῶν Ῥωμαίων· ἐξ οὗ καὶ Θεοδόσιος ὁ μέγας, ὄντος αὐτοῦ πένητος καὶ ἀνελθόντος ἐν
Κωνσταντινουπόλει, ἔξωθεν τοῦ παλατίου ἠπλήκευσεν εἰς
τοῦ Ῥουφίνου τοῦ σκυτοτόμου εἰς τὴν βάσιν τοῦ κίονος
τοῦ Ταύρου. Ὁ δὲ αὐτὸς Ῥουφῖνος ἔσχατον ἐγένετο παρὰ
Θεοδοσίου μάγιστρος· ἐξ οὗ καὶ ἔκτισεν τὰς Ῥουφινιανάς.

8 Ὁ μέγας Κωνσταντῖνος ἔκτισε τὰ Μάγγανα εἰς βασιλι-
κὸν ἐργοδόσιον· ἐκλήθησαν δὲ Μάγγανα, ὅτι τὰ μάγγανα
τῶν πολεμίων πάντων καὶ αἱ μηχανικαὶ βίβλοι ἐκεῖσε ἀπ-
έκειντο καὶ τὰ πρὸς τειχομαχίαν σκεύη.

9 Ὁ μέγας Κωνσταντῖνος ἀνήγειρεν τῆς ἁγίας Εὐφημίας
τῆς πανευφήμου τὸν ναὸν ἐν τῷ Ἱπποδρομίῳ τιμήσας
αὐτὸν διὰ πολυτελοῦς ὕλης· παρελθόντων δὲ υμβ' χρόνων,
ἐλθόντος τοῦ μισοθέου Κοπρωνύμου, ἀρμαμέντον καὶ
κοπροθέσιον τοῦτον ἐποίησεν καὶ τὸ λείψανον τῆς ἁγίας

leaves and crepe ginger and basil and roses and marjoram and balsam, which were found there on the cross, in flower-pots (*gastrai*) in order to preserve them. And when she retired to the monastery, she called the place Gastria and built a monastery.

Saint Helena built the palaces of the Psomatheas and the 5 home for old people, and likewise Saint Theodore of Klaudios.[7]

Ourbikios, who assisted <Constantine when Constanti- 6 nople> was built, erected Saint Julian at his own expense.[8] A Roman military camp was also there.

At the so-called Halonitzin (threshing floor) were worth- 7 less palaces, built by Constantine the Great, in which the leaders of the Romans lodged.[9] Therefore, even Theodosios the Great [I, 379–395], when he was poor and first came to Constantinople, camped outside the palace at the place of Rouphinos the leather cutter, at the foot of the column of Tauros.[10] Rouphinos was eventually promoted to the rank of *magistros* by Theodosios, and built the Rouphinianai.

Constantine the Great built the Mangana as an imperial 8 factory. It was called the Mangana because the equipment for all the soldiers as well as the technical books for warfare, and the siege engines, were stored there.

Constantine the Great built the church of Saint Euphe- 9 mia the wholly blessed at the Hippodrome and honored it with precious materials.[11] When 442 years had passed, the God-hating <Constantine V (741–775)> Kopronymos came and made it an armory and a garbage dump, and threw the

σὺν τῇ λάρνακι εἰς τὸν βυθὸν τῆς θαλάσσης ἀπέρριψεν·
μετὰ δὲ χρόνους λζ' Εἰρήνη ἡ εὐσεβεστάτη ἄνασσα ἡ
Ἀθηναία τοῦτον πάλιν ἀνῳκοδόμησεν καὶ τὸ λείψανον
εὑροῦσα ἔφερεν.

10   Ὅτι μέλλων κτίσαι πόλιν ὁ μέγας Κωνσταντῖνος, ὀφείλων πῆξαι τὸ θεμέλιον καὶ καταμετρῆσαι τὴν πόλιν, πεζὸς
ἐξῆλθεν μετὰ τῶν μεγιστάνων αὐτοῦ· καὶ ἐλθὼν εἰς τὸν
Φόρον λέγουσιν αὐτῷ οἱ ἄρχοντες· "ποίησον τέλος τοῦ
τείχους." Ἐκεῖνος δὲ ἔφη· "ἕως οὗ στῇ ὁ προαγωγός μου,
οὐ μὴ στήσω τὸ θεμέλιον." Μόνος γὰρ ἐκεῖνος ἑώρα τὸν
ἄγγελον. Ἀπελθὼν δὲ μέχρι τοῦ Ἐξακιονίου πεζὸς μετὰ
πάσης τῆς συγκλήτου ἐκεῖσε ἐθεάσατο τὸν ἄγγελον τὴν
ῥομφαίαν αὐτοῦ πήξαντα, μηνύοντα ἕως ἐκεῖ στῆναι
αὐτόν. Καὶ διὰ τοῦτο ἔπηξεν ἐκεῖσε τὸ τεῖχος.

11   Ὁ δὲ Φόρος κατὰ μίμησιν τοῦ Ὠκεανοῦ ἐκτίσθη κυκλο-
ειδῶς.

12   Καὶ ὡρολογεῖον ἐκεῖσε ἦν, ὅπερ ἔφερεν ἀπὸ Κυζίκου
χαλκοῦν.

13   Ὁ ἅγιος Ἀνδρέας εἰς τὸ Στρατήγιον. Ὅτι εὑρὼν τὰς
φυλακὰς ὁ μέγας Κωνσταντῖνος τῶν Βυζαντίων εἰς τὸ
Στρατήγιον ἐκεῖσε ἐφρούρει καὶ αὐτὸς τοὺς τιμωρουμέ-
νους. Διήρκεσε δὲ χρόνους σπγ' μέχρι τῆς βασιλείας
Φωκᾶ τοῦ Καππάδοκος.

14   Τὸ δὲ νῦν πραιτώριον οἶκος ἦν πατρικίας χήρας τοὔνομα
Μαρκίας. Διὰ δὲ τὸ εἶναι πνιγηρὰς τὰς φυλακὰς καὶ ἐκ τοῦ
ζόφου καὶ τῆς δυσωδίας μὴ ὑποφέρειν τοὺς ἐκεῖσε δέδωκεν αὐτὸν εἰς μισθὸν Φωκᾶ τῷ βασιλεῖ· καὶ ἐποίησεν
αὐτὸν πραιτώριον.

relic of the saint with its chest into the depths of the sea. After thirty-seven years, the most pious empress Eirene the Athenian (780–802) restored it, found the relic and brought it there.[12]

When Constantine the Great wanted to build the city 10 and had to lay the foundations and to measure out the city, he went out on foot with his great men. And when he came to the Forum, the officials said to him: "End the wall here." But he said: "As long as the one who goes before me does not stop, I will not set the foundations." For he alone saw the angel. And when he had walked on foot with the whole senate as far as the Exakionion, he saw there how the angel planted his sword, thus indicating that he would stop there. And therefore he set up the wall in that place.[13]

The Forum was built in a circular shape imitating the 11 Ocean.

And there was a bronze clock in that place which he 12 brought from Kyzikos.

Saint Andrew at the Strategion.—When Constantine the 13 Great found the prison of Byzantion at the Strategion, he also kept the convicts imprisoned there. This lasted 283 years until the reign of Phokas the Cappadocian (602–610).[14]

The prison of today was the house of a patrician, a widow 14 called Markia.[15] Because the prisons were stifling and the inmates could not bear it because of the darkness and the stench, she rented it to the emperor Phokas, and he turned it into a jail.

15   Καὶ τὰ μὲν Νούμερα ὁμοίως καὶ τὴν Χαλκῆν ἔκτισεν ὁ
μέγας Κωνσταντῖνος καὶ διὰ τὸ εἶναι αὐτὰ ἀργὰ ἐποίησαν
αὐτὰ φυλακὰς οἱ περὶ τὸν Ἡράκλειον καὶ τοὺς καθεξῆς.

16   Τὸν δὲ ἅγιον Φιλήμονα ἀνήγειρεν Εὐδόξιος πατρίκιος
καὶ ἔπαρχος τοῦ μεγάλου Κωνσταντίνου.

17   Τὸν δὲ ἅγιον Ἀναστάσιον λέγουσιν παρὰ Εἰρήνης καὶ
τοῦ υἱοῦ αὐτῆς κτισθῆναι, ἐπεὶ ὁ ἅγιος Ἀναστάσιος ἐν τοῖς
χρόνοις τοῦ Ἡρακλείου ἐμαρτύρησεν μετὰ σς΄ ἔτη τοῦ
μεγάλου Κωνσταντίνου.

18   Τὴν Χελῶνα τὸν ἅγιον Προκόπιον καὶ τὸν ἅγιον Ἀκάκιον τὸ Ἑπτάσκαλον ὁ ἐν ἁγίοις καὶ μέγας Κωνσταντῖνος
ἀνήγειρεν· ὁ δὲ Ἰουστινιανὸς τῆς μεγάλης ἐκκλησίας ὁ
κτίτωρ κατεκάλλυνεν αὐτὸν τὸν ἅγιον Ἀκάκιον.

19   Τὸ καλούμενον Μεσόλοφον μέσον ἐστὶ τῶν ἑπτὰ λό-
φων· ἤγουν ἡ μία μοῖρα τῆς πόλεως ἔχει τρεῖς λόφους καὶ
ἡ ἑτέρα τρεῖς λόφους, καὶ μέσον ἐστὶ τοῦτο· οἱ δὲ ἰδιῶται
Μεσόμφαλον καλοῦσιν αὐτό.

20   Ἐν τῇ λεγομένῃ Χαλκῇ στήλη χαλκῇ ἦν τοῦ Κυρίου
ἡμῶν Ἰησοῦ Χριστοῦ παρὰ τοῦ μεγάλου Κωνσταντίνου
κτισθεῖσα· ὁ δὲ Λέων ὁ πατὴρ τοῦ Καβαλλίνου ταύτην
κατήγαγεν. Ἡ δὲ νῦν διὰ ψηφίδων ὁρωμένη εἰκὼν τοῦ
Χριστοῦ ἀνιστορήθη παρὰ Εἰρήνης τῆς Ἀθηναίας. Ἡ δὲ
χαλκῆ ἐτύγχανεν χρόνους υιε΄· ἐξ οὗ καὶ γυνὴ αἱμόρρους
ἰάθη καὶ ἕτερα θαύματα ἐπετελοῦντο εἰς ὄνομα τοῦ Χριστοῦ.

21   Ἡ Θεοτόκος τὰ Εὐγενίου οἶκος ἦν Εὐγενίου πατρικίου
ἐν τοῖς χρόνοις τοῦ μεγάλου Θεοδοσίου· καὶ ἀνήγειρεν
αὐτὸν ναὸν τῆς Θεοτόκου.

And Constantine the Great likewise built the Noumera 15
and the Chalke, and since they were not used, those around
Herakleios (610–641) and his successors turned them into
prisons.[16]

The patrician Eudoxios, prefect of Constantine the 16
Great, built Saint Philemon.

It is said that Saint Anastasios was built by Eirene (780– 17
802) and her son, for Saint Anastasios was martyred in the
time of Herakleios (610–641), 206 years after Constantine
the Great.[17]

The saintly Constantine the Great built Saint Prokopios 18
at the Chelone[18] and Saint Akakios at the Heptaskalon. Justinian (I, 527–565), the builder of the Great Church, embellished this same Saint Akakios.[19]

The so-called Mesolophon is between the seven hills, 19
that is to say that one part of the city has three hills and the
other <part has> three hills, and it is between them. Uedu-
cated people call it the Mesomphalon.[20]

At the so-called Brazen Gate was a bronze sculpture of 20
our Lord Jesus Christ, which had been set up by Constantine the Great, but Leo (III, 717–741), the father of Kaballinos, tore it down. The mosaic image of Christ which can be
seen today was made by Eirene the Athenian (780–802).[21]
The bronze <sculpture> existed for 415 years.[22] A woman
with an issue of blood was also healed there, and other miracles were accomplished there in Christ's name.

The Mother of God Ta Eugeniou was the house of the pa- 21
trician Eugenios in the years of Theodosios the Great (I,
379–395), and he converted it into a church of the Mother of
God.[23]

147

22   Τὰ δὲ λεγόμενα Οὐρβικίου ἡ Θεοτόκος παρὰ ἄλλου
Οὐρβικίου πατρικίου ἐκτίσθη καὶ στρατηλάτου τῆς ἀνατολῆς βαρβάτου, τοῦ ἱστορήσαντος στρατηγικὰ ἐν τοῖς
χρόνοις Ἀναστασίου τοῦ Δικόρου μετὰ ρπ' χρόνους τοῦ
κτισθῆναι τὴν Κωνσταντινούπολιν. Ὁ δὲ οἶκος αὐτοῦ ἦν
εἰς τὰ Χαμένου καὶ ὁ ἕτερος οἶκος αὐτοῦ εἰς τὸ Στρατήγιον.

23   Τὰ δὲ λεγόμενα Πρωτασίου ὁ μὲν τόπος ἐκ τοῦ ἀνωτέρω εἰρημένου Πρωτασίου ἐκλήθη· ἡ δὲ νῦν ἐκκλησία
τῆς ἁγίας Θεοτόκου ἐκτίσθη παρὰ Ἰουστίνου τοῦ βασιλέως, τοῦ ἀνδρὸς Σοφίας τῆς Λωβῆς, τοῦ ἀποκουροπαλάτου, τοῦ ἀνεψιοῦ τοῦ μεγάλου Ἰουστινιανοῦ· ἐπεὶ
ἀπὸ τοῦ Πρωτασίου ἕως τοῦ κτίτορος Ἰουστίνου διῆλθον
χρόνοι σνβ'.

24   Ὅτι τὰ νῦν καλούμενα Στείρου, οἱ ναοὶ τῶν Ἀρχαγ-
γέλων, ἀπὸ στείρας γυναικὸς ἔλαβον τὴν προσηγορίαν
πατρικίας οὔσης· καὶ ἐν τοῖς χρόνοις τοῦ Λέοντος Μακέλλη εὐκτήριον μικρὸν ἦν· ἀπὸ δὲ τῆς γυναικὸς ὠνομάσθη
ὁ τόπος οὕτως. Καὶ τελευτησάσης διῆλθον χρόνοι οε' καὶ
ἐκτίσθησαν οἱ ναοὶ παρὰ Ἰουστινιανοῦ τοῦ κτίτορος τῆς
μεγάλης ἐκκλησίας. Συμπτωθέντων δὲ αὐτῶν ὑπὸ σεισμοῦ
μετὰ χρόνους τλη' ἀνεκαίνισεν αὐτοὺς Βασίλειος ὁ βασι-
λεύς· ἐξ οὗπερ ἐκ τοῦ Στρατηγίου ἄρας τὴν φιάλην τὴν
χαλκῆν τέθηκεν αὐτὴν ἐκεῖσε. Παρέλυσε δὲ καὶ τὸν Κωνω-
πίωνα, ὅσπερ ἦν ἐστηλωμένος μετὰ μυιῶν καὶ κωνώπων
καὶ ἐμπίδων καὶ φύλλων καὶ κορίδων.

25   Ὁ δὲ ἅγιος Ἰωάννης αἱ Ἀρκαδιαναὶ παρὰ Ἀρκαδίου
ἐκτίσθη, καὶ ἐπιλεξάμενος ἐκ τῶν πολιτῶν χιλιάδας ἕξ,
ὠψίκευον αὐτὸν εἰς τὰ πρόκενσα ἤγουν μεταστασίματα·

The Mother of God called Ta Ourbikiou was built by an- 22
other patrician Ourbikios, a commander of the east who
was bearded, who wrote on strategy in the time of Anastasios the Dikoros (491–518),[24] 180 years after Constantinople
had been built.[25] His house was at Ta Chamenou and his
other house at the Strategion.

The place called Ta Protasiou was named after the afore- 23
mentioned Protasios.[26] The present church of the Mother
of God was built by Emperor Justin (II, 565–578), the husband of Sophia the Maimed, the former *kouropalates,* the
nephew of Justinian the Great (I, 527–565), when 252 years
had passed from Protasios to the founder Justin.[27]

The place now called Ta Steirou, the churches of the 24
Archangels, received its name from an infertile woman who
was a patrician of rank.[28] It was a small chapel in the time of
Leo Makelles (I, 457–474), and the place received its name
from the woman. And after she had died, seventy-five years
passed, and the churches were built by Justinian (527–565),
the founder of the Great Church <Hagia Sophia>. When
they collapsed in an earthquake after 338 years,[29] Emperor
Basil (I, 867–886) restored them, also removing the bronze
fountain from the Strategion and setting it up there. He also
destroyed the Konopion which was enchanted with flies,
mosquitoes, gnats, fleas and bugs.[30]

Saint John of the Arkadianai was built by Arkadios (395– 25
408).[31] Having selected six thousand of the citizens, they
served him at his progresses, that is the processions; he

ἐκάλει δὲ αὐτοὺς Ἀρκαδιακούς· πάνυ γὰρ ἐφίλει αὐτοὺς καὶ εὐεργέτει.

26   Οἱ δὲ λεγόμενοι Τόποι πλησίον τοῦ ἁγίου Λαζάρου· ὁπόταν ἐπανέστη Βασιλίσκος δρουγγάριος καὶ πατρίκιος Ζήνωνι τῷ βασιλεῖ ἐν τῷ δευτέρῳ ἔτει καὶ δεκάτῳ μηνὶ τῆς βασιλείας αὐτοῦ καὶ ἐδίωξεν αὐτὸν καὶ ἐκράτει ὁ Βασιλίσκος τῆς βασιλείας χρόνους δύο ἥμισυ, ὑποστρέψας ὁ Ζήνων μετὰ δυναστείας στρατοπέδου ἀπὸ τῆς μεγάλης Ἀντιοχείας καὶ ἐλθὼν ἀτάραχος ἐν τῇ πόλει προδόσας Ἁρμάτιος τὸν στρατὸν τοῦ Βασιλίσκου φρονῶν τὰ τοῦ Ζήνωνος, ἔφυγεν ὁ Βασιλίσκος σὺν τῇ γυναικὶ καὶ τοῖς τέκνοις αὐτοῦ εἰς τὴν ἁγίαν Εἰρήνην τὴν παλαιάν. Ὁ δὲ Ζήνων ὥρισεν τοῦ γενέσθαι τόπους κριτηρίων εἰς θρόνους τοῦ ἱερατικοῦ καταλόγου καὶ τῆς συγκλήτου· καὶ καθεσθέντων ἐκεῖ πάντων κατεδίκασαν τὸν Βασιλίσκον καὶ ἐξώρισαν αὐτὸν εἰς Λίμνας, εἰς χωρίον Καππαδοκίας, ἔσωθεν καστελλίου. Τῆς δὲ θύρας ἀναφραγείσης ἀπὸ λιμοῦ καὶ δίψης καὶ ψύχους παρέδωκαν τὰς ἑαυτῶν ψυχάς. Καὶ τούτου χάριν ἐκλήθησαν Τόποι ὁ τόπος διὰ τὸ καθεσθῆναι κριτὰς ἐκεῖσε καὶ ἱερεῖς.—Ἔφθασαν δὲ ἐκεῖ τὰ κτίσματα τῶν Τρικλίνων παρὰ τοῦ μεγάλου Κωνσταντίνου κτισθέντα.

27   Οἱ δὲ Ὁδηγοὶ ἐκτίσθησαν παρὰ Μιχαὴλ τοῦ ἀναιρεθέντος ὑπὸ Βασιλείου· πρότερον εὐκτήριον ὑπῆρχεν καὶ τυφλῶν πολλῶν ἐν τῇ ἐκεῖσε πηγῇ βλεψάντων καὶ θαύματα πολλὰ γεγόνασιν.

28   Τὸ Καραβίτζιν τὴν Θεοτόκον Μιχαὴλ ἔκτισεν· ἐκλήθη δὲ οὕτως, ὅτι χήρα γυνὴ ἦν ἐν τοῖς χρόνοις Θεοφίλου τοῦ

called them Arkadiakoi, for he loved them greatly and did many good things for them.

The so-called Topoi near Saint Lazaros.[32]—The *droungarios* and patrician Basiliskos (474–475) revolted against Emperor Zeno (474–491) in the second year and tenth month of his reign and drove him out, and Basiliskos was in power for two and a half years. Zeno returned with a powerful army from Antioch the Great and reached the city unhindered. Armatios[33] betrayed the army of Basiliskos, for he was on Zeno's side, and Basiliskos fled with his wife and children into Old Saint Eirene. Zeno ordered that a place of judgment should be set up with thrones for the ranks of the clergy and the senate, and after they all were seated there, they condemned Basiliskos and exiled him to a castle at Limnai, a place in Cappadocia. As the doors had been sealed, they delivered up their souls as a result of hunger and thirst and cold. And for this reason the place was named Topoi, because judges and priests had sat there.—The hall of the Triklinoi built by Constantine the Great extended to there.

The Hodegoi were built by Michael (III, 842–867) who was murdered by Basil. A chapel was previously there, and many blind men saw again at the spring there, and many miracles happened.[34]

Michael (III, 842–867) built the Mother of God To Karabitzin (the small ship).[35] It was so named, because there

THE PATRIA

πατρὸς αὐτοῦ· καὶ καθήρπαξεν αὐτῆς κουμπάραν παμμε-
γεθεστάτην Νικηφόρος πραιπόσιτος αὐτοῦ· ἥτις γυνὴ
πολλὰ ἐγκαλέσασα τὸν Θεόφιλον ἔμεινεν ἀδιοίκητος διὰ
τὸ κωλύειν αὐτὴν τὸν Νικηφόρον. Ἡ δὲ ἀποροῦσά τινας
τῶν παιγνιωτῶν τοῦ Ἱπποδρομίου παρεκάλεσεν· ὑπ-
έσχοντο δὲ αὐτῇ διὰ μηχανῆς τινος διοικηθῆναι. Ποιήσαντες δὲ οἱ παιγνιῶται καράβιον μικρὸν μετὰ ἀρμένου καὶ
θέντες αὐτὸ ἐπάνω ἁμάξης μετὰ τροχῶν, γινομένου ἱππικοῦ λαχανικοῦ ἔστησαν ἔμπροσθεν τοῦ βασιλικοῦ στάματος, φωνοῦντες εἰς τῷ ἑτέρῳ· "χάνε κατάπιε αὐτό." Τοῦ δὲ
ἀντιλέγοντος ὅτι "οὐ δύναμαι τοῦτο ποιῆσαι," πάλιν ἔφη
ὁ ἕτερος ὅτι "ὁ Νικηφόρος ὁ πραιπόσιτος τῆς χήρας τὸ
καράβιν γεμάτον κατέπιεν καὶ σὺ οὐκ ἰσχύεις φαγεῖν
τοῦτο;" Ταῦτα ἐποίουν καὶ ἔλεγον πρὸς τὸ φανερῶσαι τῷ
βασιλεῖ περὶ τοῦ καραβίου τῆς χήρας. Ταῦτα γνοὺς ὁ
βασιλεὺς ἠρώτησεν, ὅτι "ἀκμὴν οὐκ ἐδιοικήθη ἡ γυνή;"
Καὶ ἡ γυνὴ προσπεσοῦσα (ἵστατο γὰρ εἰς τὰς βαθμίδας),
πάνυ χολωθεὶς ὁ βασιλεὺς ἐκέλευσεν Θεοδώρῳ πρωτο-
σπαθαρίῳ καὶ ἐπάρχῳ τῷ λεγομένῳ Μυγιάρῃ πληρωθῆναι
ξύλον καὶ φρύγανον ἐν τῷ Σφενδόνι καὶ συλλαβέσθαι τὸν
πραιπόσιτον καὶ καῆναι παρευθὺ μετὰ τῆς στολῆς αὐτοῦ·
ὃ καὶ γέγονεν παραυτά. Καὶ ἡ γυνὴ ἀπέλαβεν τὸ ἴδιον καὶ
ἐκ τῆς ὑποστάσεως αὐτοῦ πολλά. Διὰ δὲ τὸ καταμένειν
ἐκεῖσε εἰς τὸν ἀπὸ μαρμάρου οἶκον τὰ Μαυριανοῦ τὴν
γυναῖκαν, ἐκάλεσαν τὸν τόπον Καραβίτζιν.

29   Τὸ δὲ Τζυκανιστήριον ἔκτισεν ὁ μικρὸς Θεοδόσιος,
μικρὸν δέ· τὸν δὲ σταῦλον τὸν τρουλωτὸν ἔκτισεν Μιχαὴλ
ὁ υἱὸς Θεοφίλου κοσμήσας διὰ μαρμάρων πολυτελῶν. Ὁ

152

was a widow in the time of his father Theophilos (829–842), and his chamberlain Nikephoros seized her very large cargo ship. The woman often wrote petitions to Theophilos, but remained without judicial hearing, for Nikephoros prevented that. As she did not know what to do, she asked some of the jesters from the Hippodrome who promised that she would receive her hearing by a trick. The buffoons made a small ship with a sail and put it on a carriage with wheels. When the Vegetable Race was held, they set it up before the imperial loge, and one cried to the other, "Open your mouth and swallow it." When the other answered, "I cannot do that," the other one said again, "The chamberlain Nikephoros has swallowed the widow's fully loaded ship, and you cannot eat this one?" They did this in order to make the <case of the> widow's ship clear to the emperor. When the emperor realized this, he said: "Did the woman not yet receive her hearing?" And the woman fell at his feet, for she was standing at the steps, and the emperor became very angry and ordered the *protospatharios* and prefect Theodore, surnamed Mygiares, to heap up wood and kindling in the Sphendone, to arrest the chamberlain and to burn him immediately together with his robe, and that happened on the spot. And the woman recovered her property and many of his possessions as well. Because the woman lived there in the marble house of Ta Maurianou,[36] they called the place Karabitzin (little ship).

Theodosios the Younger (II, 408–450) built the Tzykanis-   29
terion,[37] but on a small scale. Michael (III, 842–867), the son of Theophilos, built the domed stable and decorated it with

δὲ Βασίλειος παρεξέβαλεν τὸ Τζυκανιστήριον καὶ ὁ
Μιχαὴλ ἐπλάτυνεν. [Ἐν δὲ τοῖς ἡμετέροις χρόνοις πλεῖον
τούτων ἐπλάτυνε Κωνσταντῖνος ὁ Δούκας κτίσας καὶ τὸν
μέγαν Τρίκλινον, τὸν Ἱππόδρομον καὶ τὸν ἕνα κούβουκλον.]
29a   Τὴν δὲ ἐκκλησίαν τὴν Νέαν καὶ τὸν Φόρον τὴν Θεοτόκον καὶ τὰ Στείρου καὶ τὸν ἅγιον Διομήδην ἔκτισεν
Βασίλειος ὁ βασιλεύς.
30   Τὸν δὲ ἅγιον Θεόδωρον τὰ Σφωρακίου ἔκτισεν Σφωράκιος πατρίκιος ἐν τοῖς χρόνοις Ἀρκαδίου καὶ Θεοδοσίου τοῦ υἱοῦ αὐτοῦ. Εἰς δὲ μέρος τῆς ἐκκλησίας εἰς πινσὸν
τῶν κατηχουμένων ἀπέθηκεν χρυσίου κεντηνάρια τρία·
καὶ παρῆλθον χρόνοι ρλγ'· ἐν δὲ τοῖς χρόνοις τοῦ Μαυρικίου ἐπυρκαήθη μέρος τοῦ ναοῦ, καὶ ἀνῳκοδόμησεν αὐτό,
κτίσας καὶ ναὸν τοῦ ἁγίου Γεωργίου. Ἐπὶ δὲ τῆς αὐτοκρα-
τορίας Λέοντος τοῦ υἱοῦ Βασιλείου ἀνελθὼν Ῥωμαῖός τις
τοῦ εὔξασθαι εἰς τοὺς ναοὺς τῆς πόλεως εἶδεν Ῥωμαϊκὰ
γράμματα λίθινα ἐπὶ τοῦ πινσοῦ, καὶ τὴν δύναμιν αὐτῶν
γνοὺς ἐγνώρισεν τῷ βασιλεῖ· καὶ δέδωκεν αὐτῷ χρῆμα καὶ
ἐποίησεν αὐτὸν ἰλλούστριον δοὺς αὐτῷ χάραγμα λίτρας
λ'.—Ὁ δὲ Πρόδρομος ὁ εἰς τὴν κόγχην αὐτοῦ, ὁ Σφωράκιος
ἀνήγειρεν αὐτόν.
31   Τὸ δὲ τετραδήσιον τὸ Ὀκτάγωνον, εἰς ὃ ἦσαν στοαὶ
ὀκτὼ ἤγουν καμαροειδεῖς τόποι, διδασκαλεῖον ἐκεῖσε
ἐτύγχανεν οἰκουμενικόν· καὶ οἱ βασιλεύοντες αὐτοὺς
ἐβουλεύοντο καὶ οὐδὲν ἔπραττον χωρὶς αὐτῶν· ἐξ οὗ καὶ
ἐξ αὐτῶν ἐγένοντο πατριάρχαι καὶ ἀρχιεπίσκοποι. Πλησίον
δὲ τῆς Βασιλικῆς ἦν καὶ διήρκεσε ἔτη υιδ' μέχρι τοῦ
δεκάτου χρόνου Λέοντος τοῦ Συρογενοῦς τοῦ πατρὸς

precious marbles. Basil relocated the Tzykanisterion and Michael expanded it even more. [In our times Constantine Doukas (X, 1059–1067) expanded it beyond that, also building the great Hall, the Hippodrome and one of the chambers.][38]

Emperor Basil (I, 867–886) built the New Church, the Mother of God on the Forum, Ta Steirou and Saint Diomedes.[39] 29a

The patrician Sphorakios built Saint Theodore Ta Sphorakiou in the time of Arkadios (395–408) and his son Theodosios (II, 408–450). On one side of the church, in a pier of the galleries, he deposited three hundredweight of gold, and 133 years passed.[40] And in the time of Maurikios (582–602) a part of the church burned down, and he rebuilt it, also adding the church of Saint George. In the reign of Leo (VI, 886–912), the son of Basil, a Roman came to pray in the churches of the city, and when he saw Latin letters in stone on the pier, he understood their meaning and revealed it to the emperor, and he gave him properties and made him an *illoustrios,* giving him thirty pounds of gold coins.—Sphorakios also built the <chapel of the> Holy Forerunner at its apse. 30

The four-sided Octagon, in which there were eight halls, that is vaulted places,[41] was once a public school, and the emperors were advised by them and did nothing without them. Therefore patriarchs and archbishops were also chosen from their numbers. It was close to the Basilike and lasted for 414 years, until the tenth year of Leo (III, 717–741),[42] the one of Syrian origin, the father of Kaballinos. 31

Καβαλλίνου. Παρατραπεὶς δὲ τῆς θείας χάριτος καὶ γυμνωθεὶς τοῦ Θεοῦ διὰ τὸ μὴ συγκοινωνεῖν αὐτῷ τοὺς μοναχοὺς τῇ ματαίᾳ αὐτοῦ βουλῇ πλησθεὶς ὀργῆς φρύγανα καὶ ξύλα ἀθροίσας κατέκαυσεν ἐκεῖσε τοὺς διδάσκοντας δεκαὲξ μοναχούς.

32   Ἡ δὲ ἁγία Θεοτόκος τὰ Χαλκοπρατεῖα· πρότερον ἐπὶ τοῦ μεγάλου Κωνσταντίνου κατῴκουν Ἰουδαῖοι· ἦσαν δὲ ἐκεῖσε χρόνους ρλβ' καὶ ἐπίπρασκον τὰ χαλκώματα. Ὁ δὲ Θεοδόσιος ὁ μικρὸς ἐξέωσεν αὐτοὺς ἐκ τοῦ τόπου καὶ ἀνακαθάρας τὸν τόπον ναὸν τῆς Θεομήτορος ἀνήγειρεν. Ὑπὸ σεισμοῦ δὲ συμπτωθεὶς ὁ ναός, Ἰουστῖνος ὁ ἀποκουροπαλάτης ἀνήγειρεν αὐτὸν καὶ ἀκίνητα κτήματα ἐπεκύρωσεν.

33   Ὅτι τὰ καλούμενα Ἴλλου ὁ ἅγιος Ἰωάννης οἶκος ἦν Ἴλλου μαγίστρου πολλὰς ἀρχὰς διανύσαντος μετὰ πολλῆς δόξης ἐν τοῖς χρόνοις τοῦ Λέοντος Μακέλλη καὶ Ζήνωνος. Τυραννήσας δὲ ὁ αὐτὸς Ἴλλος καὶ λαὸν ἀθροίσας ο' χιλιάδας εἰς Ἀντιόχειαν τὴν μεγάλην κατὰ Ζήνωνος ἀντῆρεν. Ὁ δὲ Ζήνων ἀποστείλας Λογγῖνον μάγιστρον τὸν ἀδελφὸν αὐτοῦ μετὰ πλήθους στρατιωτῶν καὶ συμβολῆς πολέμου γενομένης πλησίον Ἀντιοχείας, ἐνίκησεν Ἴλλος καὶ τὸν Λογγίνου λαὸν κατέσφαξε· μόνου δὲ αὐτοῦ περισωθέντος εἰσῆλθεν ἐν Ἀντιοχείᾳ. Καὶ κατεδυνάστευσεν ὁ Ἴλλος σφόδρα. Ὁ δὲ Ζήνων ἀπέστειλεν Ἰωάννην πατρίκιον τὸν ἐπίκλην Κυρτὸν μετὰ Σκυθῶν καὶ Μακεδόνων ἐν Σελευκίᾳ καὶ συμβαλόντες πόλεμον ἡττήθησαν οἱ τοῦ μέρους τοῦ Ἴλλου· καὶ αὐτὸς φυγὼν ἔν τινι φρουρίῳ παρεδόθη ὑπὸ τῶν οἰκείων αὐτοῦ ἀνθρώπων καὶ ἀπετμήθη παρὰ

When he turned away from the divine grace and separated from God, he was filled with wrath because the monks did not share his foolish opinion, and so he gathered kindling and wood, and burned the sixteen monks who taught there.[43]

The holy Mother of God Ta Chalkoprateia (the Bronze 32 Shops).—Previously, under Constantine the Great, Jews lived there. They were there for 132 years and sold bronze wares. Theodosios the Younger (II, 408–450) drove them out of this place, cleared the site and built the church of the Mother of God.[44] When the church collapsed in an earthquake, Justin (II, 565–578), the former *kouropalates,* restored it and bestowed properties upon it.

Saint John called Ta Illou was the house of the *magistros* 33 Illos, who held many offices with great glory in the time of Leo Makelles (I, 457–474) and Zeno (474–491).[45] This Illos revolted, and, having gathered an army of seventy thousand in Antioch the Great, he rebelled against Zeno. Zeno sent out the *magistros* Longinos, his brother, with an army. A military engagement took place near Antioch, Illos won and killed Longinos's men, and Longinos alone survived and went to Antioch. And Illos ruled very despotically. Zeno sent the patrician John called Kyrtos with Scythians and Macedonians to Seleukeia, and when war began, those on Illos's side were defeated. He fled into a castle but was betrayed by his own people, and was beheaded by John. He

Ἰωάννου. Συλλαβόμενος δὲ καὶ τοὺς ἄρχοντας αὐτοῦ μετὰ καὶ τῆς αὐτοῦ κάρας εἰσήγαγεν ἐν Κωνσταντινουπόλει ἐπὶ δοράτων τὰς κεφαλὰς αὐτῶν. Ἐτυράννησε δὲ Ἴλλος μῆνας κη΄.

34   Τὸ καλούμενον Φωκόλισθον οὕτως ἐκλήθη· λέγουσι γάρ τινες, ὅτι Φωκᾶ τοῦ βασιλέως ἐφ᾽ ἵππου βαδίζοντος ὀλισθῆσαι τὸν ἵππον αὐτοῦ ἐκεῖσε καὶ πεσεῖν καὶ διὰ τοῦτο κληθῆναι τὸν τόπον Φωκόλισθον, καθώς φησι Πανόδωρος ὁ Αἰγύπτιος. Θεόδωρος δὲ ὁ Θηβαῖος φιλόσοφός φησιν ὅτι πρὸ τοῦ μεγάλου Κωνσταντίνου ὁ τόπος οὗτος ἔξωθεν τοῦ Βυζαντίου ἦν καὶ λῃσταὶ πολλοὶ ἦσαν ἐκεῖσε καὶ πολλοὺς Βυζαντίους ἀνεῖλον· ὁ δὲ μέγας Κωνσταντῖνος μετὰ τὸ κρατῆσαι καὶ κτίσαι τὴν πόλιν μαθὼν περὶ αὐτῶν καὶ πολλὴν ποιησάμενος ἔρευναν εὗρεν ἐκεῖσε τούτους καὶ συνελάβετο· καὶ οὕτως ἀνεσκολόπισεν ἤγουν ἐφούλκισε καὶ διὰ τοῦτο ἐκλήθη ὁ τόπος Φουλκόληστος.

35   Τὰ δὲ Κοντάρια ἡ ἁγία Θέκλα· ὁπότε ἦλθεν Αἶμος ὁ βασιλεὺς Θρᾴκης πρὸς Βύζαντα, ἔκοψαν οἱ Βυζάντιοι ἐκ τῶν ἐκεῖσε κοντάρια καὶ οὕτως ἐκλήθη. Ὁ δὲ μέγας Κωνσταντῖνος ἀνήγειρεν ναὸν ἐκεῖσε τῆς Θεοτόκου· ὁ δὲ Ἰουστῖνος ὁ ἀποκουροπαλάτης εἰς κάλλος καὶ εἰς μέγεθος ἐπλάτυνεν αὐτὸν καὶ ἐκλήθη ναὸς τῆς ἁγίας Θέκλης.

36   Ὁ δὲ ἀρχιστράτηγος τὰ Ἄδδα ἐκτίσθη ὑπὸ τοῦ αὐτοῦ Ἰουστίνου· τὸ δὲ ὄνομα ἐδέξατο ἐκ τοῦ Ἄδδα τοῦ μαγίστρου τοῦ ἐκεῖσε κτίσαντος οἰκίας [πρότερον ναὸς ὢν οὗτος ὁ ἅγιος Θωμᾶς ὁ τοῦ Ἀμαντίου καλούμενος].

37   Τὸν δὲ λιμένα Σοφίας ὁ αὐτὸς ἔκτισεν Ἰουστῖνος εἰς πρόσωπον τῆς γυναικὸς αὐτοῦ Σοφίας. Πρὸ δὲ τοῦ κτίσαι

also captured his officials and, together with his head, he brought their heads on spears to Constantinople. Illos's insurrection lasted for twenty-eight months.

The so-called Phokolisthon was named for this reason.[46]   34
Some say that when the emperor Phokas (602–610) was riding a horse, his horse slipped there and fell down, and therefore the place was called Phokolisthon (where Phokas slipped), as the Egyptian Panodoros says. The philosopher Theodore from Thebes says that this place was outside of Byzantion before Constantine the Great, and that many robbers were there and killed many Byzantines. Constantine the Great, when he had taken over and built the city, learned about them, and after an intensive search he found them there and captured them. And he affixed them to a stake, that is, hanged them on the *furca*,[47] and therefore the place was called Phoulkolestos (where the robbers are hanged).

Saint Thekla Ta Kontaria (the Spears.)[48]—When Haimos,   35
the king of Thrace, came to Byzas, the Byzantines cut spears there, and so it received its name. Constantine the Great built a church of the Mother of God there. The former *kouropalates* Justin (II, 565–578) enlarged it beautifully and at a larger size, and called it a church of Saint Thekla.

The commander in chief (Michael) at Ta Adda was built   36
by the same Justin. It received its name from the *magistros* Addas who built houses there.[49] [Previously this was the church of Saint Thomas, called that of Amantios.][50]

The same Justin (II, 565–578) built the harbor of Sophia   37
in the name of his wife, Sophia. Before the harbor was built,

THE PATRIA

τὸν λιμένα ὑπῆρχεν στοὰ καμαροειδής, ἣν ἔκτισεν ὁ μέγας
Κωνσταντῖνος, καὶ ἀνήρχοντο οἱ φιλόσοφοι οἱ δυσικοὶ
Θηβαῖοί τε καὶ Ἀθηναῖοι καὶ Ἑλλαδικοὶ καὶ διελέγοντο
ἐκεῖσε μετὰ τῶν Κωνσταντινουπολιτῶν. Καὶ διήρκεσε
τοῦτο μέχρι Ἰουστίνου καὶ πάντοτε ἐνίκων οἱ δυσικοί. Ἐπὶ
δὲ Ἰουστίνου ἡττηθέντες οὐδέποτε ἀνῆλθον μέχρι τῆς σήμερον. Χρόνων δὲ τεσσάρων ἔκτοτε διελθόντων ἐγένετο
Σοφίαν τὴν Αὐγούσταν ἵστασθαι εἰς τὸν ἡλιακὸν τοῦ πα-
λατίου· καὶ ὁρῶσα τὰ πλοῖα κλυδωνιζόμενα ἐν τῇ θαλάσσῃ,
σπλαγχνισθεῖσα ἤρξατο ὀδύρεσθαι· καὶ εἰσελθοῦσα εἰς
τὸν βασιλέα τὸν ἄνδρα αὐτῆς ἱκέτευεν αὐτόν, ὅπως παρά-
σχῃ αὐτῇ χρυσίον ἱκανὸν εἰς τὸ ποιῆσαι λιμένα. Καὶ
καμφθεὶς τῇ αἰτήσει αὐτῆς, προσέταξε Ναρσῆν τὸν πατρίκιον καὶ πραιπόσιτον καὶ Τρώιλον τὸν πρωτοβεστιάριον
αὐτοῦ κτίσαι τὸν λιμένα· οἳ καὶ βόθυνον μέγαν ὀρύξαντες
ἀνῳκοδόμησαν τοῦτον. Διὸ καὶ τὴν προσηγορίαν εἴληφεν
τῆς Σοφίας [ὁ Σοφιανῶν καλούμενος λιμήν· ὃν δὴ καὶ
ἀναχωσθέντα τῷ χρόνῳ ἀνώρυξε καὶ ἀνηνέωσε τοῦτον
νῦν ὁ ἐν τοῖς βασιλεῦσι διαφανέστατος, ὁ τῆς ὀρθοδοξίας
ὄντως λιμήν, ὁ αὐτοκράτωρ ἡμῶν κύριος Ἀνδρόνικος
Κομνηνὸς ὁ Παλαιολόγος· ἀνακαθήρας γὰρ τὸν τοιοῦτον
λιμένα καὶ εὐρύνας καὶ βαθύτατον ποιήσας καὶ θριγγεῖον
τοῦτο ἀξιεπαινετώτατον ἤγειρε καὶ τὸν λιμένα διὰ πυλῶν
σιδηρέων κατησφαλίσατο, τὰς βασιλικὰς τριήρεις ἀνεπι-
βούλους ἐν τούτῳ μεῖναι θεσπίσας <καὶ μὴ> σαλεύεσθαι·
ὅπερ ὁρᾶται τῇ πόλει μέγιστον ἔργον καὶ ἀξιορατώτατον].
Μέσον δὲ τοῦ λιμένος ἀνήγειρεν δ΄ στήλας ἐπάνω τῶν δ΄
κιόνων, Σοφίας καὶ Ἀραβίας ἀνεψιᾶς αὐτοῦ, Ἰουστίνου

a vaulted hall was there which Constantine the Great had built, and the western philosophers, the Thebans and Athenians and those from Greece, came and held debates there with the Constantinopolitans. And this lasted until Justin and the westerners always won. Since their defeat under Justin they have not returned to this day.[51] When four years had passed after that, it happened that the Augusta Sophia was standing on the terrace of the palace. And when she saw how the ships were tossed about on the sea, she took pity on them and started to lament. And she went to the emperor, her husband, and beseeched him to give her enough money to build a harbor. And he acceded to her request, and ordered the patrician and chamberlain Narses and his *protobestiarios* Troilos to build the harbor. They dug a big hole and built it. Therefore it also received the name of Sophia [, the so-called harbor of the Sophianai. Since it had filled up over time, it has now been dredged and restored by the most illustrious among the emperors, the true harbor of Orthodoxy, our emperor Lord Andronikos Komnenos Palaiologos (II, 1282–1328). For after having cleared this harbor, he widened it and made it very deep, and he built a most praiseworthy battlement and secured the harbor with iron gates, and decreed that the imperial galleys should stay there free from harm and not be tossed about. This is a very great work for the city, most worthy to be seen.][52] In the midst of the harbor he set up four statues on four columns, of Sophia and his niece Arabia, the emperor Justin and Narses who had

τοῦ βασιλέως καὶ Νάρση τοῦ ἐκεῖσε παρισταμένου [ἐξ ὧν
αἱ δύο ἐπήρθησαν παρὰ Φιλιππικοῦ· εἶχον δὲ γράμματα
περὶ τῶν μελλόντων]. Μετὰ δὲ τὸ κτισθῆναι τὴν Κωνσταντινούπολιν παρῆλθον σνβ' χρόνοι καὶ οὕτως ἐκτίσθη ὁ
λιμήν.

38   Ὅτι τὸ λεγόμενον Βούκινον τὸ παλαιὸν σάλπιγγες
ἦσαν ἐπάνω τοῦ τείχους· τὸ δὲ τεῖχος ὑποκάτω ἦν κοῦφον
κινστερνοειδές· καὶ ὁπόταν ἦν νότος ἢ βορρᾶς σφοδρός,
ἐκ τῶν κυμάτων τῆς θαλάσσης ἀποκρουομένων τῶν τειχῶν ἀνήρχοντο πνεύματα βίαια καὶ ἤχει μελῳδίαν Σειρή-
νων· καὶ ἀντέλεγεν ὁ ἕτερος πύργος ὁ ἄντικρυς. Ὅταν δὲ
ἤθελεν κινῆσαι ὁ Ῥωμαϊκὸς στόλος, ἐκεῖσε ἠθροίζετο καὶ
κατὰ τὸν ἦχον τῶν πύργων ἐσάλπιζον αἱ νῆες καὶ ἀπεκί-
νουν.

39   Ὁ ἅγιος Σέργιος καὶ Βάκχος· ὅτι τὰ καλούμενα Ὁρ-
μίσδου λιμὴν ἐτύγχανεν μικρός· ἐν ᾧ ὥρμουν αἱ νῆες πρὸ
τοῦ τὰ Σοφίας κτισθῆναι· ἐκ δὲ τῶν πολλῶν χρόνων ἀμε-
ληθεὶς ἐγεμίσθη. Ἐκεῖσε δὲ ὁ μέγας Ἰουστινιανὸς ὁ κτίτωρ
τῆς ἁγίας Σοφίας ἔμενεν· ἐν ᾧ καὶ ἐχρημάτιζεν κοιτὼν
αὐτοῦ, ὠνόμασέ τε Σεργίου καὶ Βάκχου· ὑπῆρχεν δὲ τότε
τῶν ἁγίων Ἀποστόλων, ὁπόταν τὸν χρησμὸν ἔλαβεν ὑποκάτω τῶν βαθμίδων, ὅταν τὴν σφαγὴν ἐποίει εἰς τὸ
Ἱππικόν.

39a   Ἐκλήθη δὲ Ἰουλιανοῦ λιμήν, ὅτι ὁ ὑπατικὸς ὁ κτίσας
αὐτὸν οὕτως ἐκαλεῖτο.

40   Τὸν ἅγιον Πλάτωνα ἀνήγειρεν Ἀναστάσιος ὁ Δίκορος
εἰς τὴν ἀρχὴν τοῦ ἑβδόμου αἰῶνος· τοὺς δὲ κίονας τοὺς
ἐνζώδους τοὺς δέκα ἔφερεν ἀπὸ Θεσσαλονίκης· καὶ οἱ μὲν

helped him[53] [, of which two were removed by Philippikos, for they had letters on them concerning the future.][54] After Constantinople had been built, 252 years passed, and the harbor was built.[55]

The so-called Boukinon (trumpet.)[56] — In olden times, there were trumpets on top of the walls. Underneath, the wall was hollow like a cistern, and when a heavy south or north wind blew, strong currents of air came up as the waves of the sea were repulsed from the walls, and a melody of the sirens was heard, and the tower opposite responded. When the Roman fleet was ready to depart, it assembled there, and the ships sounded together with the sound of the towers, and departed. 38

Saints Sergios and Bacchos. — The place called Ta Hormisdou was a small harbor where the ships anchored before Ta Sophias was built. Neglected for a long time, it was filled up. There lived Justinian the Great (I, 527–565), the founder of Hagia Sophia. There too was his dwelling which he called Sergios and Bacchos. It was <a church> of the Holy Apostles at the time when he received the oracle at the foot of the steps <of the tribune> when he carried out the massacre in the Hippodrome.[57] 39

The harbor of Julian was so called because this was the name of the *consularis* who built it.[58] 39a

Anastasios Dikoros (I, 491–518) built Saint Platon at the beginning of the seventh millennium.[59] He brought ten columns carved with reliefs from Thessalonike. Eight of them 40

ὀκτὼ ἵστανται εἰς τὸν αὐτὸν ναόν, οἱ δὲ δύο εἰς τὴν Χαλκῆν ἐτέθησαν παρὰ Ῥωμανοῦ τοῦ γέροντος.

41 Ὁ δὲ καλούμενος Διηγηστέας· ἀθροίσεις ἐκεῖσε ἐγένοντο τὸ παλαιὸν τῶν δύο δημοτικῶν μερῶν καὶ τρίκλινος ἦν ἐκεῖσε παμμεγεθέστατος καὶ ὁπότε οἱ δήμαρχοι ἤθελον ποιῆσαι ἐκλογήν, ἐκεῖσε ἠθροίζοντο. Διήρκεσε δὲ χρόνους πεντακοσίους. Θεοδώρα δὲ ἡ Αὐγούστη τοῦ Θεοφίλου ἀπερχομένη ἐν Βλαχέρναις, ὠλίσθησεν ὁ ἵππος αὐτῆς ἐν τῷ ἐμβόλῳ τῷ ὄντι πρὸ τοῦ νάρθηκος τοῦ ναοῦ· καὶ πάλιν ὑποστρεφομένη εἰς αὐτὸν τὸν τόπον ὀλισθήσασα ἔγκυος οὖσα καὶ ἀποκαλυφθεῖσα ἀνήγειρεν ναὸν τῆς ἁγίας Ἄννης.

42 Τὰ Μαυριανοῦ ὁ τόπος· Μαυρικίου τοῦ βασιλέως ἔτι ὄντος πατρικίου καὶ ἐξκουβίτορος ἐκεῖσε ἦν ὁ οἶκος αὐτοῦ. Μετὰ δὲ τὸ βασιλεῦσαι αὐτὸν ὠνομάσθη ὁ τόπος τὰ Μαυριανοῦ.

43 Τὸν δὲ ναὸν τῆς ἁγίας Ἀναστασίας τῆς Ῥωμαίας τὸν ὄντα εἰς τὰ Μαυριανοῦ Μαρκιανὸς ὁ ὅσιος ἔκτισεν ἐκ τοῦ πλούτου Ἄσπαρος τοῦ ἀναιρεθέντος παρὰ τοῦ Λέοντος Μακέλλη. Τὸν δὲ ναὸν ὀφείλων κτίσαι ὁ ὅσιος εἰς τὰ Ψηφᾶ, ἐν οἷς καὶ ψηφάδας ἐπώλουν, ὠνήσατο τὸν τόπον εἰς δύο χιλιάδας νομίσματα διὰ τὸ εἶναι τὸν τόπον μυσαρὸν καὶ διὰ τὰ ὑπομνήματα τὰ εὑρεθέντα ἐκεῖσε τοῦ ἁγίου Γρηγορίου τοῦ θεολόγου πρὸ ἐτῶν ρ' γράφοντα οὕτως ὅτι "ἀνακαινισθήσεται ὁ ναὸς οὗτος εἰς κάλλος καὶ εἰς μέγεθος εὖ οἶδα· τάδε μοι λέγει τὸ Πνεῦμα τὸ ἅγιον." Πρώην γὰρ μικρὸν εὐκτήριον ἦν. Ὑπῆρχεν δὲ ἡ ἁγία Ἀναστασία ξυλόστεγος· ὁ δὲ Βασίλειος ἐσκέπασεν αὐτὴν δι' ὀρόφου χρυσοῦ.

stand in this church, while two were set up in the Chalke by
Romanos the Elder (I, 920–944).[60]

The so-called Diegesteas.[61]—Meetings of the two popu-   41
lar factions took place there of old, and there was a very
great hall, and whenever the faction leaders wanted to hold
an election, they assembled there. It lasted for five hundred
years.[62] When Theodora, the Augusta of Theophilos (829–
842), was going to the Blachernai, her horse slipped in the
portico in front of the narthex of the church; and again,
when she returned, she slipped at the same place, being
pregnant, and had a vision and built the church of Saint
Anna.[63]

The place Ta Maurianou.—When the emperor Maurikios   42
(582–602) was still a patrician and *exkoubitor* his house was
there. After he had become emperor, the place was called Ta
Maurianou.[64]

The blessed Markianos built the church of Saint Anasta-   43
sia the Roman at Ta Maurianou from the wealth of Aspar,
who had been executed by Leo Makelles (I, 457–474).[65]
When the blessed one wanted to build the church at Ta Pse-
pha, where mosaic tesserae are also sold, he bought the site
for two thousand gold coins, for the place was abominable, and because of the inscription which was found there,
<which was> written by Saint Gregory the Theologian one
hundred years before, that "this church will be restored to
beauty and majesty, I know this well; this is what the holy
Spirit tells me." For it had previously been a small chapel.
Saint Anastasia had a wooden roof, but Basil covered it with
a golden ceiling.[66]

44 Ὁμοίως καὶ τὴν ἁγίαν Εἰρήνην τὸ Πέραμα ὁ αὐτὸς ὅσιος Μαρκιανὸς ἔκτισεν καὶ ἐτελείωσεν· πρώην γὰρ εἰδωλεῖον ὑπῆρχεν. Καὶ τὸ νοσοκομεῖον τὸ ἐκεῖ ὁ αὐτὸς ἀνήγειρε.

45 Τὸν δὲ ἅγιον Θεόδωρον τὰ Καρβουνάρια ἔκτισεν Ἱλαρίων πατρίκιος ἐν τοῖς χρόνοις τοῦ Λέοντος Μακέλλη.

46 Οἱ δὲ ἅγιοι Τεσσαράκοντα ὑπῆρχον πρότερον πραιτώριον· ὁ δὲ Τιβέριος ὁ Θρᾷξ σὺν τῇ γυναικὶ αὐτοῦ Ἀναστασίᾳ τοὺς δεσμίους ἐξεώσας καὶ τὸν τόπον ἀνακαθάρας καὶ διαμετρήσας καὶ τὴν ὕλην ἐναποθέμενος ἐθεμελίωσεν καὶ ἐξέβαλεν μέχρι πηχῶν τεσσάρων· τελευτήσας δέ, Μαυρίκιος ὁ βασιλεύς, ὁ γαμβρὸς αὐτοῦ εἰς Κωνσταντίναν τὴν θυγατέρα αὐτοῦ, κρατήσας ἀνεπλήρωσεν τὸν ναὸν καὶ ἐνεθρονίασεν αὐτόν.

47 Τὸν δὲ ἅγιον Παῦλον τὸ ὀρφανοτροφεῖον ἀνήγειρεν Ἰουστῖνος καὶ Σοφία· ὡσαύτως καὶ τὸν ὅσιον [Ζωτικὸν τὸ Δεύτερον]· καὶ ἐτύπωσεν ἀναπαύεσθαι τοὺς λωβοὺς ἐκεῖ καὶ σιτηρέσια λαμβάνειν. Παρίστατο δὲ Ζωτικὸς ὁ πρωτοβεστιάριος αὐτοῦ τοῖς κτίσμασιν.

48 [Ἐπὶ Κωνσταντίου τοῦ υἱοῦ τοῦ μεγάλου Κωνσταντίνου Ζωτικὸς πατρίκιος καὶ πρωτοβεστιάριος κτίζει τοῖς ἐν Κωνσταντινουπόλει ἀδελφοῖς κατοικίας, τροφὰς αὐτάρκεις αὐτοῖς ἐπιχορηγήσας καὶ ἄμφια· διὸ καὶ παρὰ τοῦ Κωνσταντίου ἡμιόνοις ἀγρίαις προσδεθεὶς κέντροις πληττομέναις καὶ βιαζομέναις τρέχειν τέλει τοῦ βίου ἐχρήσατο.]

49 Τὰ δὲ Καρπιανοῦ ἀνήγειρεν Καρπιανὸς πατρίκιος ἐν τοῖς χρόνοις Κωνσταντίνου, υἱοῦ Ἡρακλείου, τοῦ Πωγωνάτου.

In a similar way, the same blessed Markianos also built   44
Saint Eirene To Perama and finished it. For it had been a pagan temple before. And he also built the hospital there.

The patrician Hilarion built Saint Theodore of the Char-   45
coal (Ta Karbounaria) in the time of Leo Makelles (I, 457–474).[67]

The Holy Forty <Martyrs> was previously a prison.[68] Ti-   46
berios the Thracian (578–582), together with his wife Anastasia, removed the prisoners from there, cleared the place, measured it out and stored the building materials, laid the foundations and built the walls to a height of four cubits. When he died, the emperor Maurikios (582–602), his son-in-law by his daughter Konstantina, came to power, completed the church and consecrated it.

Justin (II, 565–578) and Sophia built Saint Paul of the Or-   47
phanage, and also the blessed [Zotikos in the Deuteron.][69]
He decreed that the lepers should find repose there and receive their food allowance. Zotikos the *protobestiarios* assisted him with the buildings.[70]

[Under Constantius (II, 337–361), the son of Constantine   48
the Great, the patrician and *protobestiarios* Zotikos built dwellings for the brethren in Constantinople, bestowing upon them sufficient foods and vestments. Because Constantius had him tied to wild mules, which were prodded with sharp sticks and forced to run, he was killed.][71]

Karpianos the patrician built Ta Karpianou in the time of   49
Constantine the Bearded (Constans II, 641–668), the son of Herakleios.[72]

50 Τὰ δὲ Βάσσου ἀνήγειρεν Βάσσος πατρίκιος, ἐπειδὴ ὁ οἶκος αὐτοῦ ἐκεῖ ἦν, ἐν τοῖς χρόνοις Ἰουστινιανοῦ τοῦ κτίτορος τῆς ἁγίας Σοφίας. Εἰς ἔχθραν δὲ ἐλθοῦσα μετ' αὐτοῦ Θεοδώρα ἡ βασίλισσα, ἡ γυνὴ τοῦ Ἰουστινιανοῦ, ἔσφιγξε τὴν κεφαλὴν αὐτοῦ μετὰ κόρδας καὶ ἐξεπήδησαν οἱ ὀφθαλμοὶ αὐτοῦ.

51 Ἡ Ὀξεῖα ὁ ἅγιος Ἀρτέμιος· τὸν δὲ ναὸν τοῦ Προδρόμου ἀνήγειρεν Ἀναστάσιος ὁ Δίκορος ὁ ἀποσελεντιάριος ὁ Δυρραχιώτης. Ὄντος γὰρ αὐτοῦ πρωτοασηκρήτης ἐκεῖσε ᾤκει· μετὰ δὲ τὸ κομισθῆναι τὸ λείψανον τοῦ ἁγίου Ἀρτεμίου ὠνομάσθη ὁ ναὸς οὕτως.

52 Ὁμοίως καὶ τὸν Ἀρχιστράτηγον τοῦ ἁγίου Ἰουλιανοῦ ὁ Δίκορος ἀνήγειρεν, ἐπεί, ὅταν ἦλθεν ἀπὸ Δυρράχιον παῖς καὶ ἐμάνθανεν τὰ γραμματικὰ ἐν Κωνσταντινουπόλει, ἐκεῖσε ᾤκει.

53 Τὸ δὲ λεγόμενον Κονδύλιον ὁ ἅγιος Προκόπιος ἐκλήθη οὕτως· ἔφιππος διερχόμενος ὁ Κωνσταντῖνος ὁ πατὴρ Ἰουστινιανοῦ τοῦ ῥινοκοπημένου, ἐκεῖσε ἐκονδύλισεν ὁ ἵππος αὐτοῦ καὶ ἔπεσεν.

54 Τὰ δὲ καλούμενα Κινθήλια ὁ ἅγιος Ἰωάννης ὁ Πρόδρομος· ἐκεῖσε ἔκαμνον τὰ μικρὰ καρφία τὰ πεταλαρικά, ἅπερ λέγονται κινθήλια.

55 Ὅτι τὸν ναὸν τὸν ὄντα εἰς Κωνσταντιανὰς τῶν ἁγίων Τεσσαράκοντα Ἀναστάσιος καὶ Ἀριάδνη ἀνήγειρεν· μετὰ δὲ τὸ ἐλθεῖν τὸ λείψανον τοῦ ἁγίου πρωτομάρτυρος Στεφάνου ἐκεῖσε ἐτέθη καὶ ἀνήγειρεν ἕτερον μικρὸν ναὸν καὶ ὠνόμασεν τοῦ ἁγίου Στεφάνου.

BOOK 3

The patrician Bassos built Ta Bassou, for his house was 50
there in the time of Justinian (I, 527–565), the builder of Hagia Sophia. When the empress Theodora, the wife of Justinian, became his enemy, she tied a cord tightly around his
neck, and his eyes jumped out.[73]

Saint Artemios He Oxeia.—Anastasios Dikoros (I, 491– 51
518), the former *silentiarios* from Dyrrhachion, built the
church of <Saint John> the Forerunner. When he was *pro-
toasekretis* he lived there, and after the relic of Saint Artemios had been brought there, this is what the church was
called.

In a similar way, Dikoros also built the <church of the> 52
commander in chief (Archangel Michael) of Saint Julian, for
when he came from Dyrrhachion as a child and was studying
in Constantinople, he lived there.

The so-called Kondylion, Saint Prokopios,[74] received its 53
name in this way: when Constantine (IV, 668–685), the father of Justinian the Slit-Nosed, was riding by, his horse
slipped *(ekondylisen)* there and fell.

The so-called Kinthelia, Saint John the Forerunner.— 54
There they made the small nails for horseshoes, which are
also called "running nails" *(kinthelia)*.

Anastasios (491–518) and Ariadne built the church of the 55
Holy Forty <martyrs> which is at the Konstantianai. When
the relic of Saint Stephen the Protomartyr came, it was deposited there, and he built another small church and called
it Saint Stephen.[75]

56   Τὰ δὲ Μεγεθίας Μεγεθία δέσποινα ἀνήγειρεν ἐν τοῖς
χρόνοις Τιβερίου τοῦ Θρᾳκός.

57   Τὸν δὲ ἅγιον Πολύευκτον ἀνήγειρεν Ἰουλιανὴ θυγάτηρ
Οὐαλεντινιανοῦ τοῦ κτίτορος τοῦ ἀγωγοῦ. Ἔκτισεν δὲ
τοῦτον εἰς χρόνους δ' ἥμισυ, τῶν τεχνιτῶν ἀπὸ Ῥώμης
ἐλθόντων· γυναικαδέλφη δὲ ἦν τοῦ μεγάλου Θεοδοσίου.

58   Τὰ Πονολύτου ἐκλήθη, ὅτι πολλαὶ ἰάσεις ἐκεῖσε ἐπετελοῦντο καὶ πόνοι πολλῶν ἐλύοντο.

59   Τὴν ὑπεραγίαν Θεοτόκον τὰ Ἀρεοβίνδου ἀνήγειρεν
Πέτρος μάγιστρος καὶ κουροπαλάτης ὁ ἀδελφὸς Μαυρικίου τοῦ βασιλέως, ἐπεὶ Ἀρεοβίνδου οἶκος ἦν ἐκεῖσε, δι' ὃν
καὶ ἔλαβεν ὁ τόπος τὴν προσηγορίαν, ἐν τοῖς χρόνοις
Ἰουστίνου τοῦ κρατίστου τοῦ Θρᾳκός· καὶ μετὰ ˁβ' χρόνους ἀπ' ἐκείνου τοῦ Ἀρεοβίνδου ἐκτίσθη ἡ ἐκκλησία καὶ
τὸ λοῦμα.

60   Τὴν δὲ ἁγίαν Εὐφημίαν τὰ Ὀλυβρίου ἤρξατο κτίζειν ἡ
θεήλατος Εὐδοξία καὶ ἐξήβαλεν τὸ θεμέλιον ἀπὸ τῆς γῆς
πήχεις δύο. Καὶ ὡς πικρῷ θανάτῳ ἐτελεύτησεν, κατέλιπεν
αὐτὸ ἀτελές. Οἶκος δὲ ἦν ἐκεῖσε Ὀλυβρίου μαγίστρου τοῦ
Ῥωμαίου κἀκεῖνος ἀναπληροῖ τὸν ναὸν διὰ πολυτελῶν καὶ
διὰ ποικίλων μαρμάρων καὶ ἐνεθρονίασεν αὐτὸν καὶ κτήματα δέδωκεν πολλά.

61   Τὰ δὲ Ἀρματίου οἶκος ἦν Ἀρματίου μαγίστρου ἐν τοῖς
χρόνοις Ζήνωνος τοῦ Κωδισαίου τοῦ καὶ προδόσαντος
τὸν στρατὸν τοῦ Βασιλίσκου καὶ ἀναιρεθέντος προτροπῇ
Ζήνωνος εἰς τὸν κοχλίαν τὸν ἀνερχόμενον εἰς τὸ κάθισμα
τοῦ Ἱπποδρομίου.

The lady Megethia built Ta Megethias in the time of Tiberios the Thracian (I, 578–582). 56

Juliana, the daughter of Valentinian (I, 364–375), the builder of the aqueduct, built Saint Polyeuktos. She completed it in four and a half years, with workers coming from Rome. She was the sister of Theodosios the Great's wife.[76] 57

Ta Ponolytou (pain reliever) was so named because many healing cures were performed there, and the pains of many people were relieved. 58

Peter, the *magistros* and *kouropalates* and brother of Emperor Maurikios (582–602), built the most holy Mother of God Ta Areobindou, because the house of Areobindos, from which the place took its name, was there in the time of the most mighty Justin the Thracian (I, 518–527). And the church and the bath were built 92 years after this Areobindos.[77] 59

Eudoxia (d. 462), cursed by God, began to build Saint Euphemia Ta Olybriou, and built the foundations to a height of two cubits above the earth. When she died a bitter death, she left it unfinished. The house of the *magistros* Olybrios the Roman was there, and he completed the church with precious and multicolored marbles, consecrated it, and bestowed much property upon it. 60

Ta Armatiou was the house of the *magistros* Armatios in the time of Zeno the Kodisaios (474–491);[78] he betrayed the army of Basiliskos and was killed on the order of Zeno on the spiral staircase which leads up to the imperial box of the Hippodrome. 61

62 Τοὺς δὲ Κριοὺς τὴν κινστέρναν καὶ τὸ γηροκομεῖον καὶ
τὸ λοῦμα τὸ ὂν εἰς τὰ Ἀρματίου ἔκτισεν Στέφανος παρακοιμώμενος Μαυρικίου τοῦ βασιλέως μετὰ δώδεκα χρόνους.

63 Τὰ δὲ λεγόμενα Πράσινα, διότι ἦν ἐκεῖ σταῦλος τῶν
Πρασίνων, οὕτως ἐκλήθη. Τὸ δὲ γηροκομεῖον ἀνήγειρεν
Μαρκιανὸς μετὰ Πουλχερίας. Ἀρτάβασδος δέ, ὁ τυραννήσας τὸν Καβαλλῖνον καὶ κρατήσας χρόνους τρεῖς καὶ
τυφλωθείς, ἀκίνητα κτήματα καὶ ἱερὰ ἐκεῖσε ἐπεκύρωσεν,
διότι οἶκος ἦν αὐτοῦ. Μετὰ οὖν σπ' ἔτη ἦν ὁ Ἀρτάβασδος
τῆς κτίσεως τοῦ γηροκομείου.

64 Ὅτι τὸ καλούμενον Ζεῦγμα· ὁπόταν ἐκομίσθη τὸ σῶμα
τοῦ πρωτομάρτυρος Στεφάνου, ἐκεῖσε ἐζεύχθησαν μοῦλαι
καὶ ἦραν τὸ σῶμα ἕως Κωνσταντιανάς· καὶ διὰ τοῦτο
ἐκλήθη Ζεῦγμα.

65 Οἱ δὲ ἅγιοι Ἀνάργυροι οἱ ὄντες εἰς τὸ Ζεῦγμα ἐκτίσθησαν παρὰ Πρόκλου πατριάρχου, μαθητοῦ τοῦ Χρυσοστό-
μου, ἐν τοῖς χρόνοις Θεοδοσίου τοῦ μικροῦ.

66 Τὸν δὲ ἅγιον Ἠλίαν τὸ Πετρίν· συνδόσαντες αἱ σχολαὶ
καὶ τὰ τάγματα πολὺ χρυσίον ὑποστρέψαντος Ζήνωνος
τοῦ βασιλέως ἀπὸ Περσίδος, δέδωκεν αὐτὸς συνδρομὴν
μετὰ τῆς Ἀριάδνης· καὶ ἀνήγειραν τὸν μέγαν ναόν, διότι
ἐνεφάνη αὐτῷ ἐν τῷ ταξιδίῳ.

67 Τὴν δὲ ἁγίαν Εὐφημίαν τὴν Πέτραν ἀνήγειρεν Ἀναστάσιος ὁ Δίκορος καὶ Ἀριάδνη.

68 Τὰ δὲ Γηραγάθης τοῦ Πετρίου τὸ γηροκομεῖον πατρικίου θυγάτηρ ἔκτισε τοὔνομα Ἀγάθη, γραῦς ὡραία τῷ
εἴδει σφόδρα· εἶχε δὲ αὐτὸ οἶκον. Ἐκλήθη δὲ Γηραγάθη διὰ

Stephen, the *parakoimomenos* of Emperor Maurikios (582–   62
602), after twelve years built the cistern called the Rams
(Krioi), the home for old people, and the bath which is at Ta
Armatiou.[79]

The so-called Prasina received their name because a sta-   63
ble of the <faction of the> Greens was there. Markianos
(450–457) built the home for old people with Pulcheria. Artabasdos (741–743), who rose up against Kaballinos, reigned
three years and was blinded, bestowed estates and holy objects upon it, for his house was there.[80] Artabasdos was 280
years after the foundation of the home for old people.[81]

The so-called Zeugma.—When the body of the Proto-   64
martyr Stephen was brought <to Constantinople>, mules
were yoked there, and they carried the body as far as the
Konstantianai,[82] and therefore it was called Zeugma (yoke).

The Holy Anargyroi at the Zeugma was built by the pa-   65
triarch Proklos (434–446), the pupil of Chrysostomos, in
the time of Theodosios the Younger (II, 408–450).

Saint Elias To Petrin.—The guards and the regular troops   66
collected much money when Emperor Zeno (474–491) returned from Persia,[83] and he gave them permission together
with Ariadne, and they built the great church, because he
(Elias) had appeared to him (Zeno) during the campaign.

Anastasios Dikoros (491–518) and Ariadne built Saint Eu-   67
phemia the Petra.

The home for old people called Ta Geragathes at the Pe-   68
trion was built by the daughter of a patrician called Agathe,
a very beautiful old woman, for she had it as her house. She

τὸ φυλάξαι αὐτῆς τὴν παρθενίαν χρόνους πολλούς· ταύτην δὲ ἔφθειρεν Κωνσταντῖνος ὁ Κοπρώνυμος δοὺς αὐτῇ πλοῦτον πολύν. Ἱππικοῦ δὲ γενομένου ἔκραζεν ὁ δῆμος, ὅτι "ἡ Ἀγάθη ἐγήρασεν, σὺ δὲ ταύτην ἀνενέωσας." Ἦν δὲ ἐν τῷ κρυπτῷ σεβομένη τὰς ἁγίας εἰκόνας ὡς ὀρθόδοξος. Πληρωθέντος δὲ τοῦ γηροκομείου ὁ θεήλατος Κοπρώνυμος ἀθροίσας τὰς ἁγίας τοῦ Θεοῦ εἰκόνας κατέκαυσεν ἐκεῖσε.

69 Ὁμοίως καὶ εἰς τὸν ἅγιον Ἰουλιανόν, μοναχῶν καθεζομένων ἐκεῖσε ἐντίμων ὄντων καὶ ὁσίων, διὰ τὸ μὴ κοινωνεῖν αὐτοὺς τῆς μυσαρᾶς θρησκείας αὐτοῦ κατέκαυσεν σὺν τῷ ναῷ καὶ αὐτούς· καὶ ἀναλύσας ὁ μόλιβδος τῆς ἐκκλησίας κατῆλθεν ἕως τὸν αἰγιαλὸν τῶν Σοφιῶν. Ἵστατο δὲ ἐκεῖσε πέρδιξ χαλκῆ ἐν καμάρᾳ στηλωθεῖσα παρὰ τοῦ μεγάλου Κωνσταντίνου.

70 Τὰ δὲ Ἀντιόχου οἶκος ἦν Ἀντιόχου πατρικίου καὶ πραιποσίτου καὶ βαιούλου Ἀρκαδίου τοῦ βασιλέως τοῦ πολλὰς ἀρχὰς διανύσαντος ἐν τῇ δόξῃ αὐτοῦ· πλούσιος δὲ σφόδρα γενόμενος πτωχὸς ἐτεθνήκει διὰ τὴν ἀδικίαν, δόλιος ἐπὶ τοῖς πᾶσι φανείς.

71 Ὁ ἅγιος Ἡσαΐας καὶ Λαυρέντιος ἐκτίσθησαν παρὰ Μαρκιανοῦ καὶ Πουλχερίας· τὸ δὲ ἅγιον σῶμα τοῦ προφήτου Ἡσαΐα ἧκεν ἀπὸ Ἰερουσαλήμ.

72 Τὰ Δεξιοκράτου οἶκος ἦν Δεξιοκράτου πατρικίου ἐν τοῖς χρόνοις Θεοδοσίου τοῦ μικροῦ· ἐν ᾧ καὶ ναὸν καὶ γηροκομεῖον ἀνήγειρεν.

73 Τὰ Καριανοῦ τὸν ναὸν καὶ τὸ γηροκομεῖον ἀνήγειρεν Μαυρίκιος ὁ βασιλεὺς σὺν τῶν ἐμβόλων· οἶκος δὲ ἦν ἐκεῖ

was called Geragathe because she had preserved her virginity for many years. Constantine (V, 741–775) Kopronymos corrupted her by giving her much wealth. When a Hippodrome race was being held, the faction cried: "Agathe has aged, but you have made her young again." Being orthodox, she venerated the holy icons in secret. When the home for old people was completed, Constantine Kopronymos, cursed by God, collected the holy icons of God and burned them there.[84]

He also acted in a similar way at Saint Julian, the residence of honorable and blessed monks; since they did not share his abominable belief, he burned them together with the church. And the lead of the church <roof> melted and flowed down to the shore of the Sophiai. A bronze partridge stood there on an arch, which had been set up by Constantine the Great. 69

Ta Antiochou was the house of Antiochos, a patrician, chamberlain and *baioulos* of Emperor Arkadios (395–408), who had held many offices with great distinction. After having become very rich, he died poor because of his injustice, for he had appeared treacherous to all.[85] 70

Saints Isaiah and Laurentios were built by Markianos (450–457) and Pulcheria. The holy body of the prophet Isaiah came from Jerusalem. 71

Ta Dexiokratou was the house of the patrician Dexiokrates in the time of Theodosios the Younger (II, 408–450); there he also built a church and a home for old people. 72

The emperor Maurikios (582–602) built the church and the home for old people Ta Karianou; the house of the pa- 73

Καριανοῦ πατρικίου καὶ ἐξ αὐτοῦ εἴληφεν ὁ τόπος τὴν προσηγορίαν.

74 Τὸν δὲ ναὸν τὸν μέγαν τῶν Βλαχερνῶν Μαρκιανὸς καὶ Πουλχερία ἀνήγειρεν κοσμήσας αὐτὸν διὰ πολυτελῶν μαρμάρων ποικίλων· βλάχνα γὰρ ἦσαν ἐν τῷ τόπῳ καὶ ἐκόπησαν· καὶ εἶθ᾽ οὕτως ἐκτίσθη ὁ ναός. Ἢ ὅτι λακκώδης ὁ τόπος ἐτύγχανεν καὶ ἐκλήθη βλαχέρναι καὶ λακέρναι διὰ τὸ εἶναι πολλὰ ὕδατα.

75 Τὴν δὲ ἁγίαν Σορὸν ἀνήγειρεν Λέων Μακέλλης, διότι ἐν τοῖς χρόνοις αὐτοῦ τῆς Θεοτόκου ἐφάνησαν ἴχνη πολλὰ καὶ θαύματα γεγόνασιν εἰς πλῆθος. Ὁ αὐτὸς δὲ ἔκτισεν καὶ τὸ λοῦμα καὶ ἐπεκύρωσεν κτήματα πολλὰ καὶ σκεύη καὶ κειμήλια χρυσᾶ τε καὶ ἀργυρᾶ. Ἐξώπορτα δὲ ἐτύγχανεν· ἐπὶ δὲ Ἡρακλείου περιεκλείσθησαν γενομένων ἐκεῖσε θαυμάτων καὶ ὀπτασιῶν πολλῶν τῆς ἁγίας Θεοτόκου.

76 Τὸ δὲ Χρυσοβάλανον οἶκος ἦν Νικολάου δομεστίκου τῆς ἀνατολῆς καὶ πατρικίου· καὶ ἀνήγειρεν ναοὺς δύο, τὸν Ἀρχιστράτηγον καὶ τὸν ἅγιον Παντελεήμονα. Χρονίσαντος δὲ ἐν τῷ ταξιδίῳ ἡ σύμβιος αὐτοῦ ἐμοιχᾶτο· εἰσελθὼν δὲ ὁ δομέστικος ἐν τῇ πόλει καὶ μαθὼν τοῦτο καὶ κοιτάσας ἀμφοτέρους μεληδὸν αὐτοὺς κατέκοψεν. Ἔσχατον δὲ εἰς ἔννοιαν ἐλθὼν τοῦ φοβεροῦ κριτηρίου ἀνήγειρεν τοὺς ναούς. Ἐλθὼν δὲ εἰς τέλος τοῦ κτίσματος καὶ ἀδημονῶν διὰ ποσότητα χρυσίου, ὤφθη αὐτῷ κατ᾽ ὄναρ ὁ ἄγγελος λέγων αὐτῷ· "ἄπελθε εἰς τὴν Ἀσπάρου πλησίον καὶ εὑρήσεις βαλάντιον ἔχον χρυσίου λίτρας ἑκατόν." Εὑρὼν δὲ αὐτὸ ἐκέλευσεν οὕτως τὸν τόπον καλεῖσθαι.

trician Karianos was there, and the place received its name from him.[86]

Markianos (450–457) and Pulcheria built the great church 74 of the Blachernai, and decorated it with precious multicolored marbles. For there were ferns *(blachna)* at this place which were cut, and afterward the church was built. Or because the place was full of pits *(lakkodes),* and was called Blachernai and Lakernai because there was much water.[87]

Leo Makelles (I, 457–474) built the Holy Shrine <at 75 Blachernai>, for in his time many signs of the Mother of God appeared, and a great number of miracles happened. He also built the bath and bestowed much property upon it, and many vessels and treasures of gold and silver. It stood outside the walls, but under Herakleios (610–641) they were included <within the walls>, as many miracles and visions of the holy Mother of God had happened there.[88]

The Chrysobalanon was the house of Nikolaos, the *do-* 76 *mestikos* of the east and patrician, and he built two churches, that of the commander in chief (Archangel Michael) and that of Saint Panteleemon. When he stayed away for a long time during a campaign, his wife committed adultery. When the *domestikos* returned to the city, learned about this and himself observed them, he cut them to pieces. But finally he became mindful of the frightful judgment and built the churches. When the construction neared conclusion and he was troubled because of an <insufficient> amount of money,[89] the angel appeared to him in a dream and said, "Go to <the cistern of> Aspar which is nearby, and you will find a purse *(balantion)* with a hundred pounds of gold *(chrysos)*." Having found it, he ordered that the place be given this name.[90]

77 Ἡ δὲ μονὴ τῆς Εὐφροσύνης τὰ Λιβάδια ἐκτίσθη παρὰ Εἰρήνης τῆς Ἀθηναίας μικρὰ καὶ πενιχρά. Ὁ δὲ Μιχαὴλ ὁ υἱὸς Θεοφίλου εἰς ἔχθραν ἐλθὼν μετὰ τῆς μητρὸς αὐτοῦ καὶ τῶν ἀδελφῶν ταύτας κατεβίβασεν ἐκ τοῦ παλατίου καὶ ἐκεῖσε εἰσήγαγεν καὶ μοναχὰς ἐποίησεν πλουτίσας τὴν μονὴν καὶ κτήματα πολλὰ παρασχών. Ἀπὸ δὲ τῆς ἀδελφῆς αὐτοῦ Εὐφροσύνης ἐκλήθη οὕτως.

78 Ὁ δὲ ἅγιος Γρηγόριος τὸ Ξηροκήπιον ἐν τοῖς χρόνοις τοῦ μεγάλου Θεοδοσίου παρὰ πατρικίου τινὸς ἐκτίσθη.

79 Ὅτι εἰς τὴν ἁγίαν Ἄνναν τὸ λεγόμενον Δεύτερον ἐν τῷ κίονι στήλη ἵστατο Ἰουστινιανοῦ τοῦ ῥινοκοπημένου. Τὴν δὲ στήλην κατεβίβασεν Βάρδας Καῖσαρ ὁ θεῖος Μιχαὴλ καὶ ταύτην συνέτριψεν καὶ ἐκλήθη Δεύτερον, διότι ἐξόριστος γέγονεν Ἰουστινιανὸς εἰς Χερσῶνα παρὰ Λεοντίου πατρικίου, ποιήσας ἐκεῖ χρόνους δέκα· φυγῇ δὲ χρησάμενος εἰς τὸν Τέρβελιν τὸν ἀρχηγὸν τῶν Βουλγάρων, ἠγάγετο τοῦ Τερβέλι τὴν θυγατέρα εἰς γυναῖκα τοὔνομα Θεοδώραν. Καὶ δοὺς αὐτῷ λαὸν χιλιάδας ιε', εἰσῆλθεν ἐν τῇ πόλει καὶ μὴ δεχθεὶς ὑπέστρεψεν εἰς τὴν παλαιὰν Πέτραν καὶ εἰσελθὼν εἰς τὸν ἀγωγὸν ἐξέβη εἰς τὸ θεμέλιον τοῦ κίονος ἔσωθεν τῆς πόλεως καὶ ἐκράτησε τῆς πόλεως πάλιν· καὶ ἐκλήθη ὁ τόπος Δεύτερον. Καὶ τότε τὸν ναὸν τῆς ἁγίας Ἄννης ἀνήγειρεν, ὅτι ἔγκυος ἦν ἡ γυνὴ αὐτοῦ καὶ ὤπτάνθη αὐτῇ ἡ ἁγία. Ἀλλὰ καὶ τὸ ὠμόφορον τῆς ἁγίας καὶ τὸ ἅγιον σῶμα ἐπὶ αὐτοῦ εἰσῆλθεν ἐν τῇ πόλει.

80 Ἡ μονὴ τὰ Μητροπολίτου ἐκτίσθη παρὰ Ἰουστινιανοῦ· ἐκλήθη δὲ οὕτως, διότι μητροπολίτου οἶκος ἦν.

81 Τὸν ἅγιον Ῥωμανὸν ἡ ἁγία Ἑλένη ἀνήγειρεν, καὶ τὴν

The monastery of Euphrosyne of the Meadows (Ta Liba-   77
dia) was built by Eirene the Athenian (780–802), as a small
and humble structure. When Michael (III, 842–867), the
son of Theophilos, fell out with his mother and sisters, he
drove them out of the palace, sent them there and made
them nuns, enriching the monastery and granting it much
property. It received its name from his sister Euphrosyne.[91]

Saint Gregory of the Dry Garden (Xerokepion) was built   78
in the time of Theodosios the Great (I, 379–395) by some
patrician.[92]

On the column at Saint Anna called Deuteron stood a   79
statue of Justinian the Slit-Nosed (II, 685–695 and 705–711).
The Caesar Bardas, the uncle of Michael (III, 842–867),
took it down and destroyed it. It was called Deuteron (the
second) because Justinian was exiled to Cherson by the patrician Leontios and spent ten years there. Then he escaped
to Terbelis, the ruler of the Bulgarians, and married Terbelis's daughter, named Theodora.[93] And after he gave him an
army of fifteen thousand men, Justinian approached the
city, but when he was not welcomed, he returned to the Old
Rock, went into the water pipe, and came out inside the city
at the base of the column, and became lord of the city once
more, and the place was called Deuteron. And thereafter he
built the church of Saint Anna, for his wife was pregnant
and the saint appeared to her in a vision. But also the pallium of the saint and her holy body came to the city during
his reign.[94]

The monastery Ta Metropolitou was built by Justinian   80
(II, 685–695 and 705–711). It received its name because it
was the house of a metropolitan.[95]

Saint Helena built Saint Romanos and the Holy Shrine   81

πλησίον αὐτοῦ ἁγίαν Σορὸν καὶ τὸ λείψανον τοῦ προφήτου Δανιὴλ καὶ τοῦ ἁγίου μεγαλομάρτυρος Νικήτα καὶ τῶν λοιπῶν προφητῶν τῶν ἐκεῖσε κειμένων ἐκείνη ἐφανέρωσεν καὶ τέθηκεν ἐκεῖ. Οἱ δὲ ποιηταὶ Ἰωσὴφ καὶ Θεόδωρος ὁ ἀδελφὸς αὐτοῦ ὁ Στουδίτης ἐκεῖσε ἐκαθέζοντο καὶ ἐποίουν τοὺς κανόνας ἐν τοῖς χρόνοις Λέοντος τοῦ Ἀρμενίου. Μετὰ δὲ φ' ἔτη τοῦ κτισθῆναι τὸν αὐτὸν ναὸν ἦσαν Ἰωσὴφ καὶ Θεόδωρος οἱ ποιηταί.

82   Τὴν δὲ μονὴν τὸν ἅγιον Κάρπον καὶ Πάπυλον ἡ ἁγία Ἑλένη ἔκτισεν μετὰ ποικίλων μαρμάρων καὶ κτήματα ἐπεκύρωσεν εἰς μίμησιν τοῦ τάφου τοῦ Χριστοῦ.

83   Τὴν δὲ κινστέρναν τὴν Βώνου Βῶνος μάγιστρος ἔκτισεν τοῦ Ἡρακλείου· καὶ ὁ οἶκος αὐτοῦ ἦν ἐκεῖσε.

84   Τὴν δὲ Μωκισίαν ἔκτισεν Ἀναστάσιος ὁ Δίκορος· ὁπόταν δὲ ἔκτιζεν αὐτήν, λιμὸς ἦν ἐν τῇ πόλει, ὁ μόδιος νόμισμα ἕν· ὠνόμασαν δὲ αὐτὴν οἱ δῆμοι οὕτως διὰ τὸ εἶναι πλησίον τὸν ἅγιον Μώκιον.

85   Τὸν δὲ ἅγιον Λουκᾶν, ἐν ᾧ οἱ τεθνεῶτες θάπτονται, καὶ τοὺς τρικλίνους καὶ τὸν ναὸν τοῦ ἁγίου Λουκᾶ ἔκτισεν Εἰρήνη ἡ Ἀθηναία, ὅπως δωρεὰν θάπτωνται οἱ πένητες· πάνυ γὰρ εὐσεβὴς καὶ φιλάρετος οὖσα πολλὰ γηροκομεῖα καὶ ξενοδοχεῖα καὶ γηροτροφεῖα ἐποίησεν εἰς ἀνάπαυσιν τῶν πενήτων καὶ φόρων βάρη ἐξέκοψεν. Τρία δὲ ἔκτισε κυριώτερα· θάνατον <μὲν ἔκτισεν τὰ ξενο>τάφια,[1] ζωὴν δὲ ἔκτισεν τοὺς τρικλίνους τῆς Λαμίας τοῦ πιστωρείου, ὑγίαν δὲ ἔκτισεν τὸν ξενῶνα τὰ Εἰρήνης καλούμενον.

86   Τὸν δὲ ἅγιον Διομήδην ἔκτισεν ὁ μέγας Κωνσταντῖνος· ὁ δὲ Βασίλειος ὁ βασιλεὺς διὰ τὸ λαβεῖν ἐκεῖσε τὸν

nearby. And she brought to light the bodies of the prophet Daniel, of the holy great martyr Niketas, and the other prophets who are laid to rest there, and deposited them there.[96] The poets Joseph and Theodore, his brother, the Stoudite, resided there and wrote the hymns *(kanones)* in the time of Leo the Armenian (V, 813–820). The poets Joseph and Theodore lived five hundred years after the church was built.[97]

Saint Helena also built the monastery of Saints Karpos   82 and Papylos with multicolored marbles and bestowed property upon it, as an imitation of the grave of Christ.[98]

Bonos, the *magistros* of Herakleios (610–641), built the   83 cistern of Bonos; and his house was there.[99]

Anastasios Dikoros (491–518) built the Mokios cistern.   84 When he built it, there was a famine in the city, and a bushel <of wheat cost> one *nomisma.* The factions gave it this name because it is close to Saint Mokios.

Eirene the Athenian (780–802) built Saint Loukas, where   85 the dead are buried, both the halls and the church of Saint Loukas, as a place for the poor to be buried for free. For being very pious and a lover of virtue, she built many homes for old people, hostels and almshouses where the poor might find a resting place, and reduced the burden of taxes. She built three main <buildings: for death, the foreigners'>[100] cemetery, for life, the halls of the Witch (Lamia)[101] of the bakery, and for health, the hospital called Ta Eirenes.

Constantine the Great built Saint Diomedes. Emperor   86 Basil (I, 867–886), because he had received the prophecy

THE PATRIA

χρησμὸν ἀνήγειρεν μείζονα καὶ ἐκαλλώπισεν καὶ ἐπεκύρωσεν κτήματα πολλά.

87 Τὰ δὲ Στουδίου ἔκτισεν Στούδιος πατρίκιος ἐν τοῖς χρόνοις τοῦ Λέοντος Μακέλλη καὶ κτήματα πολλὰ προσεκύρωσεν καὶ μοναχοὺς χιλίους πεποίηκεν.

88 Τὴν δὲ καλουμένην Αἰμιλιανοῦ πόρταν· <πλησίον> ἦν τοῦ ἁγίου Αἰμιλιανοῦ καὶ ἐκαλεῖτο οὕτως· ὑπῆρχεν δὲ εὐκτήριον μικρόν· ὅτε δὲ ἤχθη τοῦ Μωσέως ἡ ῥάβδος, ἐδέξατο αὐτὴν πεζὸς ὁ μέγας Κωνσταντῖνος καὶ ἔθηκεν ἐκεῖ· καὶ ἀνήγειρεν ἐκεῖσε ναὸν τῆς Θεοτόκου καὶ οὕτως ὠνομάσθη ὁ τόπος Ῥάβδος. Ἀνήγειρεν δὲ καὶ τὸν ἅγιον Αἰμιλιανὸν μέγαν, καὶ εἶθ' οὕτως ἔφερεν τὴν ἁγίαν Ῥάβδον ἐν τῷ παλατίῳ.

89 Ἐν τοῖς χρόνοις τοῦ μεγάλου Θεοδοσίου ἤχθη ἐλέφας μικρὸς ἀπὸ Ἰνδίας καὶ ἐκεῖσε ἔτρεφον αὐτὸν εἰς τὰ οἰκήματα· καὶ ἱππικοῦ γενομένου ἔφερον αὐτόν. Ἐν δὲ τῷ Μιλίῳ ἐρχόμενος, ἔκρουσεν αὐτὸν τραπεζίτης τις μετὰ στυρακίου μετριάζων· μετὰ δὲ χρόνους δέκα ἀνατραφεὶς καὶ πάλιν διερχόμενος ἐν τῷ ἱππικῷ ἐμνήσθη τοῦ δώσαντος αὐτόν· καὶ ἰδὼν αὐτὸν καθεζόμενον καὶ βρυχησάμενος δέδωκεν καὶ ἔσχισεν αὐτὸν μέσον τοῦ Μιλίου.

90 Τὰ δὲ Κλαυδίου οἶκος ἦν Κλαυδίου πατρικίου καὶ κυαίστορος ἐν τοῖς χρόνοις Βασιλίσκου τοῦ βασιλέως· καὶ παλάτια ἀνήγειρεν ἐκεῖσε.

91 Τὸν δὲ λιμένα τὸν Ἐλευθερίου ὁ μέγας Κωνσταντῖνος ἔκτισεν, ὅτε καὶ τὴν πόλιν ἔκτισεν· παρίστατο δὲ εἰς τὸ κτίσμα Ἐλευθέριος πατρίκιος. Ἴστατο δ' εἰς τὸν λιμένα στήλη μαρμάρινος Ἐλευθερίου φέρουσα πτύον καὶ

there, rebuilt it on a larger scale, decorated it and bestowed much property upon it.[102]

The patrician Stoudios built Ta Stoudiou in the time of 87
Leo Makelles (I, 457–474), bestowed much property upon it, and installed a thousand monks there.[103]

The so-called gate of Aimilianos.—It was close to Saint 88
Aimilianos and thus received its name. It was a small chapel. When the rod of Moses was brought, Constantine the Great went on foot to receive it and deposited it there. And he built the <church of the> Mother of God there, and so the place was called the Rod.[104] He also rebuilt Saint Aimilianos on a larger scale, and then transferred the Holy Rod to the palace.

In the time of Theodosios the Great (I, 379–395) a small 89
elephant was brought from India, and was raised there in the houses, and they brought him <to the Hippodrome> when a chariot race was held. When he came to the Milion, a moneychanger hit him in jest with a switch. Ten years later, when he had grown up and passed again on the way to the Hippodrome, he remembered the man who had beaten him. And when he saw him sitting there, he roared and attacked him and tore him apart in the middle of the Milion.[105]

Ta Klaudiou was the house of the patrician and *quaestor* 90
Klaudios in the time of Emperor Basiliskos (474–475), and he built palaces there.

Constantine the Great built the harbor of Eleutherios, 91
when he also built the city. And the patrician Eleutherios assisted him with the construction. A marble statue of Eleutherios stood at the harbor, holding a basket and a shovel.

ἐξακάνθηλον· ὁ δὲ Θεοδόσιος χύσας τὸν χοῦν ἐκεῖ τοῦ κτισθέντος κίονος τοῦ Ταύρου κατέχωσεν τὸν λιμένα.

92 Τὰ δὲ Κανικλείου οἶκος ἦν Θεοκτίστου μαγίστρου καὶ ἐπὶ τοῦ κανικλείου, τοῦ σφαγέντος εἰς τὰ Σκῦλα παρὰ Βάρδα Καίσαρος, τοῦ θείου Μιχαήλ.

93 Τὸν δὲ ἅγιον Παντελεήμονα ἔκτισεν Θεοδώρα Αὐγούστη, ἡ γυνὴ Ἰουστινιανοῦ τοῦ μεγάλου· ὁπόταν δὲ ἦλθεν ἀπὸ Παφλαγονίας, ἐκεῖσε ἔκειτο ἐν τῷ ἐμβόλῳ ὡς πένης καὶ ἔνηθεν ἔρια καὶ ἐπώλει αὐτὰ καὶ οὕτως ἔζη. Μετὰ δὲ τὸ βασιλεῦσαι αὐτὴν ἔκτισεν τὸν ναόν.

94 Τὰ δὲ Ναρσοῦ οἶκος ἦν Ναρσοῦ πατρικίου καὶ πραιποσίτου εὐνούχου ἐν τοῖς χρόνοις Ἰουστίνου καὶ Σοφίας. Τὸν δὲ ξενῶνα καὶ τὸ γηροκομεῖον καὶ τὴν ἐκκλησίαν ἐκεῖνος ἀνήγειρεν μέχρι τοῦ ὀξυβαφείου.

95 Τῶν δὲ ἁγίων Πρόβου, Ταράχου καὶ Ἀνδρονίκου ναὸν ὁ αὐτὸς Ναρσῆς ἀνήγειρεν.

96 Ὅτι τὰ Ἀμαντίου καλούμενα οἶκος ἦν Ἀμαντίου παρακοιμωμένου ἐν τοῖς χρόνοις τοῦ Δικόρου· κἀκεῖνος ἔκτισεν τὸν ἅγιον Θωμᾶν· ἐμπρησθέντος δέ, Λέων ὁ υἱὸς Βασιλείου ἀνεκαίνισεν αὐτόν.

97 Τὰ δὲ Πέτρου οἶκος ἦν Πέτρου πατρικίου ἐπὶ Ἰουστινιανοῦ τοῦ μεγάλου, ὅστις ἀνήγειρεν τὴν ἐκκλησίαν καὶ τὸ γηροκομεῖον.

98 Τὴν μονὴν τοῦ Μαρτινάκη ἀνήγειρεν Μαρτινάκης πατρίκιος ὁ θεῖος τῆς ἁγίας Θεοφανοῦς ἐν τοῖς χρόνοις Βασιλείου καὶ Μιχαήλ.

99 Ὁ δὲ Πρόβος ὁ πατρίκιος ἀνήγειρεν τὸν ναὸν τοῦ Προδρόμου καὶ παλάτια ἔκτισεν ἐκεῖσε θαυμαστὰ πάνυ.

Theodosios (I, 379–395) dumped the earth there when the column of the Tauros was built, and filled up the harbor.[106]

Ta Kanikleiou was the house of the *magistros* and *epi tou*   92 *kanikleiou*[107] Theoktistos who was murdered in the Skyla by the Caesar Bardas, the uncle of Michael (III, 842–867).

The Augusta Theodora, the wife of Justinian the Great   93 (527–565), built Saint Panteleemon. When she came from Paphlagonia, she established herself there in the portico as a poor woman, spun wool, sold it and lived on this. When she became empress, she built the church.[108]

Ta Narsou was the house of the eunuch Narses, patrician   94 and chamberlain in the time of Justin (II, 565–578) and Sophia. He built the hostel, the home for old people and the church there, up to the purple-dyer's workshop.

The same Narses built the church of Saints Probos, Tara-   95 chos and Andronikos.

What is called Ta Amantiou was the house of the cham-   96 berlain Amantios in the time of <Anastasios (I, 491–518)> Dikoros. And he built Saint Thomas. When it burned down, Leo (VI, 886–912), the son of Basil, restored it.

Ta Petrou was the house of the patrician Peter[109] who   97 built the church and the home for old people under Justinian the Great (527–565).

The patrician Martinakes, the uncle of Saint Theophano,   98 built the monastery of Martinakes in the time of Basil (I, 867–886) and Michael (III, 842–867).[110]

The patrician Probos erected the church of the Forerun-   99 ner, and built very wonderful palaces there.

100 Τὰ δὲ λεγόμενα τοῦ Τοξαρᾶ, οἶκος ἦν Τοξαρᾶ μαγκλαβίτου τοῦ ἀνελόντος Μιχαὴλ τὸν βασιλέα εἰς τὸν ἅγιον Μάμαντα.

101 Τὸ Κουρατωρίκιον ἐκτίσθη ἐν τοῖς χρόνοις Βηρίνης τῆς γυναικὸς τοῦ Λεωμακέλλη· καὶ ὁ κουράτωρ ἀνήγειρεν καὶ παρέστηκεν αὐτὸ εἰς ὁμοίωμα τοῦ τάφου τοῦ Κυρίου.

102 Τὰ Διακονίσσης ἔκτισεν Κυριακὸς πατριάρχης ἐν τοῖς χρόνοις Μαυρικίου βασιλέως τοῦ συντέκνου αὐτοῦ· ἐπεκλήθη δὲ οὕτως ὁ τόπος, ὅτι ὁ πατριάρχης διάκονος ὢν ἐκεῖσε ᾤκει· ἀλλὰ καὶ ἡ ἀδελφὴ τοῦ αὐτοῦ πατριάρχου ἐκεῖσε ἦν διακόνισσα.

103 Τὴν δὲ ἁγίαν Ἀναστασίαν τὴν Φαρμακολύτριαν ἀνήγειρεν Ἀναστάσιος ὁ Δίκορος· πρότερον γὰρ ἦν πατρικίου οἶκός τινος Φαρμακᾶ λεγομένου.

104 Τὸ δὲ λεγόμενον Διμακέλιν ἐκλήθη οὕτως, ὅτι ἐκεῖ ὁ Λέων ὁ βασιλεὺς ὁ μέγας κρέατα ἐπώλει· καὶ ἡ γυνὴ αὐτοῦ ἔπλεκε τὰς χόρδας.

105 Τὰ δὲ Φλωρεντίου οἶκος ἦν Φλωρεντίου πατρικίου ἐν τοῖς χρόνοις Ἀρκαδίου βασιλέως· καὶ τελευτῶν ἐποίησεν τὸν οἶκον αὐτοῦ γηροκομεῖον.

106 Τὰ δὲ Ἀνθημίου οἶκος ἦν Ἀνθημίου μαγίστρου ἐν τοῖς χρόνοις Μαρκιανοῦ τοῦ βασιλέως· ὃν καὶ ἔστεψεν ἐν τῇ πόλει δεδωκὼς αὐτῷ τὴν ἐκ τῆς πρώτης αὐτοῦ γυναικὸς θυγατέρα καὶ ἀπέστειλεν εἰς Ῥώμην βασιλέα. Ἐκεῖσε γὰρ καὶ γηροκομεῖον καὶ ναὸν ἀνήγειρεν τὸν αὐτοῦ οἶκον καὶ λοῦμα.

107 Τὰ δὲ λεγομένα τῆς Σπουδῆς τὴν μονήν· Ἄννα ἡ δέσποινα ἡ γυνὴ Λέοντος τοῦ Συρογενοῦς στρεφομένη

186

What is called Tou Toxara was the house of the *mangla-* 100
bites Toxaras who killed the emperor Michael (III, 842–867)
at Saint Mamas.[111]

The Kouratorikion was built in the time of Verina, the 101
wife of Leo Makelles (I, 457–474). And the *kourator* built it
and presented it as an imitation of the tomb of the Lord.[112]

Patriarch Kyriakos built Ta Diakonisses in the time of 102
Emperor Maurikios (582–602) for whose children he had
served as godparent. The place received this name, because
the patriarch had lived there when he was still a deacon. But
the sister of the same patriarch was also a deaconess there.[113]

Anastasios Dikoros (491–518) built Saint Anastasia Who 103
Heals Poisonings (Pharmakolytria). For previously the house
of a patrician called Pharmakas had stood there.[114]

The so-called Dimakellin received its name, because Em- 104
peror Leo the Great (I, 457–474) sold meat there, and his
wife plaited gut strings.[115]

Ta Phlorentiou was the house of the patrician Phloren- 105
tios in the time of Emperor Arkadios (395–408), and when
he died he made his house a home for old people.

Ta Anthemiou was the house of the *magistros* Anthemios 106
in the time of Emperor Markianos (450–457). <Markianos>
crowned him in the city, gave him his daughter from his first
marriage, and sent him to Rome as emperor.[116] For there <in
Constantinople> he made his house and bath a home for old
people and a church.

The monastery called "of Haste."—The lady Anna, the 107
wife of Leo of Syrian origin (III, 717–741), was returning

ἀπὸ Βλαχέρνας, οὖσα ἔγκυος, εἰς τὸν καιρὸν τοῦ τεκεῖν
αὐτὴν εἰς οἶκόν τινος πρωτοσπαθαρίου καταβᾶσα ἔτεκεν·
καὶ ἐποίησεν αὐτὸν τὸν οἶκον μονὴν καὶ ἐπωνόμασεν
Σπουδῆς διὰ τὸ κατεπείγειν αὐτὴν ἐκεῖσε ὁ τοκετὸς καὶ
μὴ φθάσαι εἰς τὸ παλάτιον. Ἡ αὐτὴ δέσποινα ἔκτισεν καὶ
τὰ Ἄννης.

108   Τὰ δὲ Σευήρου· Σευῆρος, πατρίκιος καὶ ἀδελφοποιητὸς
Κώνστα βασιλέως τοῦ ἔγγονος Ἡρακλείου τοῦ ἀναιρεθέντος ἐν τῷ βαλανείῳ εἰς Σικελίαν, ἔκτισεν αὐτὸς τὸ
γηροκομεῖον διότι οἶκος αὐτοῦ ἦν· καὶ ναὸν ἤγειρεν ἡ
γυνὴ αὐτοῦ, διότι μετὰ τὸ σφαγῆναι ἐν Σικελίᾳ τὸν βασιλέα ἐκεῖνος παρέλαβεν τὸν στόλον τὸν Ῥωμαϊκὸν καὶ
ἀνῆλθεν ἕως τὸν Φοίνικα.

109   Τὰ δὲ Γαϊνᾶ οἶκος ἦν Γαϊνᾶ πατρικίου τοῦ τυραννήσαντος εἰς τὰ Θρακῷα μέρη ἐν τοῖς χρόνοις Ἀρκαδίου
καὶ σφαγέντος ἐκεῖσε.

110   Τὰ δὲ Εὐσεβίου Εὐσέβιος πατρίκιος ἔκτισεν ἐν τοῖς
χρόνοις Ἰουστίνου καὶ Σοφίας τῆς Λωβῆς καὶ εὐσεβε-
στάτης.

111   Τὰ δὲ Κύρου τὴν Θεοτόκον ἔκτισεν Κῦρος πατρίκιος
καὶ ἔπαρχος ὁ παριστάμενος τὸ χερσαῖον τεῖχος τὸ κτίσμα
ἐπὶ Θεοδοσίου τοῦ μικροῦ, βάλλοντες φωνὴν οἱ δῆμοι, ὅτι
"Κῦρος εἰς ἄλλο νικήσει καὶ προκόψει." Καὶ φθονηθείς,
ἐποίησεν αὐτὸν ὁ βασιλεὺς μητροπολίτην εἰς Σμύρνην.

112   Τὸ δὲ Χρυσοκάμαρον· ὄπισθεν τοῦ Μυρελαίου ζῴδιον
ἵστατο χρυσοῦν· ἐξ οὗ καὶ ἐκλήθη Χρυσοκάμαρον· παρὰ
δὲ κλεπτῶν ἐν τοῖς χρόνοις Βάρδα Καίσαρος ἐκλάπη.

112a   Εἰς τὸ Χριστοκάμαρον δὲ ἦν ὁ Χριστὸς ἱστορισμένος

from the Blachernai, being pregnant; and when the time of delivery came, she dismounted at the house of a *protospatharios* and gave birth there. And she made the house a monastery and called it "of Haste," for birth pangs had overcome her there and she could not reach the palace in time. The same lady also built Ta Annes.[117]

Ta Seuerou. — Seueros, patrician and spiritual brother of 108 the emperor Constans (II, 641–668), the grandson of Herakleios,[118] who was killed in the bath in Sicily, built it as a home for old people, because it was his house. And his wife built a church there, for after the emperor had been killed in Sicily <Seueros> took over the Roman fleet and returned as far as Phoinix.

Ta Gaïna was the house of the patrician Gaïnas who had 109 rebelled in the region of Thrace in the time of Arkadios (395–408) and was killed there.

The patrician Eusebios built Ta Eusebiou in the time of 110 Justin (II, 565–578) and Sophia the Maimed and most pious.

The patrician and city prefect Kyros built <the church 111 of> the Mother of God at Ta Kyrou. He assisted at the construction of the land walls under Theodosios the Younger (II, 408–450), while the factions shouted, "Kyros will be victorious again and advance." And the emperor became envious and made him metropolitan in Smyrna.[119]

The Chrysokamaron. — Behind the Myrelaion stood a 112 golden statue, for which reason it was called the "golden arch." It was stolen by thieves in the time of Caesar Bardas (d. 866).[120]

In the Christokamaron Christ was depicted near Saint 112a

πλησίον τοῦ ἁγίου Ἀκακίου, ὅπου ἐστὶν τοῦ Μουσελὲ ὁ
οἶκος· καὶ διὰ τοῦτο ἐλέγετο οὕτως.

113 Τὰ δὲ δύο Μυρέλαια· μύρα ἔρρεε καὶ ἰάματα πολλὰ
ἐκεῖσε ἐγένοντο καὶ μέχρι τοῦ νῦν.

114 Τὸ δὲ Ἀνεμοδοῦριν τὸ χαλκοῦν ἐστηλώθη παρὰ
Ἡλιοδώρου τοῦ δυσσεβοῦς ἐν τοῖς χρόνοις Λέοντος τοῦ
Συρογενοῦς, καθώς εἰσιν ἐστηλωμένοι οἱ ιβ' ἄνεμοι. Τὰ δὲ
τέσσαρα χαλκουργεύματα τὰ μεγάλα ἤχθησαν ἀπὸ τοῦ
Δυρραχίου· εἶχεν δὲ αὐτὰ γυνὴ εἰς προῖκα αὐτῆς ἀπὸ ναοῦ
τινος· μετὰ πολλῆς δὲ ἐπιστήμης καὶ ἀστρονομίας τοῦτο
ἐποίησεν.

115 Τὸν δὲ ἅγιον Προκόπιον, ὡς εἴρηται, τὴν Χελῶνα, καὶ
τὸν ἅγιον Μητροφάνην ἔκτισεν ὁ μέγας Κωνσταντῖνος.

116 Τὸν δὲ ἅγιον Ἀκάκιον τὴν Καρέαν ἔκτισεν ὁ ἀδελφὸς
Ναρσῆ πατρικίου ἐν τοῖς χρόνοις Ἰουστίνου καὶ Τιβερίου.

117 Ὁ δὲ ἅγιος Προκόπιος τὰ Βιγλεντίας· εἰς τὸν Ταῦρον
παλάτια ἦσαν κτισθέντα παρὰ τοῦ μεγάλου Ἰουστινιανοῦ
εἰς τὴν Βιγλεντίαν τὴν ἀδελφὴν αὐτοῦ. Ὁ δὲ ναὸς ὑπῆρχεν
τῶν παλατίων. Ὑπὸ δὲ ἐμπρησμοῦ ἀφανισθέντα Ἀντωνῖνα,
ἡ γυνὴ Βελισαρίου τοῦ μαγίστρου, ἥτις ζωστὴ ἦν Θεοδώρας τῆς γυναικὸς Ἰουστινιανοῦ, καὶ μετὰ τὸ χηρεῦσαι αὐτὴν τὴν κατοικίαν ἐποιήσατο μετὰ τῆς Βιγλεντίας· καὶ
συναινέσει αὐτῆς ἀνήγειρεν τὸν ἅγιον Προκόπιον.

118 Τὰ λεγόμενα πορφυροπωλεῖα· τὸ παλαιὸν τὰς πορφύρας ἐκεῖσε ἔβαπτον.

119 Τὸν δὲ ξενῶνα τὰ Σαμψὼν ἔκτισεν ὁ ὅσιος Σαμψὼν
προτροπῇ Ἰουστινιανοῦ τοῦ μεγάλου, διότι ὁ ὅσιος αὐτὸν
ἰάσατο ἐκ τῆς νόσου.

Akakios, where the house of Mosele is, and this is why it received its name.

The two Myrelaia.—Many ointments flowed and healing 113
cures were performed there up to this day.

The bronze Anemodourin[121] was set up by the impious 114
Heliodoros in the time of Leo of Syrian origin (III, 717–
741),[122] just as the twelve winds are set up there. The four
large bronze works were brought from Dyrrhachion. A
woman had them as her dowry from some temple. He made
this with much knowledge of astronomy.

Constantine the Great built Saint Prokopios at the Turtle 115
(Chelone),[123] as has been said,[124] and Saint Metrophanes.

The brother of the patrician Narses built Saint Akakios 116
of the Walnut Tree in the time of Justin (II, 565–578) and Tiberios (I, 578–582).[125]

Saint Prokopios of Biglentia.—Palaces were built at the 117
Tauros by Justinian the Great (I, 527–565) for his sister Biglentia. The church belonged to the palaces. These were destroyed by a fire, and Antonina, the wife of the *magistros*
Belisarios, who was the mistress of the robes of Theodora,
the wife of Justinian, dwelled with Biglentia after she had
become a widow, and with her consent she built Saint Prokopios.[126]

The so-called purple shops.—Formerly the purple gar- 118
ments were dyed there.[127]

The blessed Sampson built the hospital of Sampson on 119
the order of Justinian the Great (I, 527–565), because the
blessed one had cured him of his disease.[128]

120   Τὰ δὲ Εὐβούλου ἐκτίσθησαν παρὰ Εὐβούλου πατρικίου
ἐν τοῖς χρόνοις Ἰουστίνου τοῦ Θρᾳκός, ἐπεὶ οἶκος αὐτοῦ
ἦν.

121   Τὰ δὲ Ἰσιδώρου· ὁ Ἰσίδωρος ἀδελφὸς ἦν τοῦ Εὐβούλου
καὶ ἀνήγειρεν τὸν οἶκον αὐτοῦ γηροκομεῖον καὶ ναόν.

122   Τὸν δὲ ἅγιον Τρύφωνα τὸν ὄντα εἰς τὰ Εὐβούλου
ἀνήγειρεν αὐτὸν Ἰουστινιανὸς ὁ μέγας. Τὸν δὲ ἅγιον
Τρύφωνα τὰ Βασιλίσκου καὶ αὐτὸν ἀνήγειρεν μέγαν ναὸν
πλησίον τοῦ Βασιλίσκου· καὶ ἐποίησεν αὐτὸν κάλλιστον
προσκυρώσας ἐν αὐτῷ κινητὰ καὶ ἀκίνητα κτήματα.

123   Οἱ ἅγιοι Ἀνάργυροι οἱ ὄντες εἰς τὰ Βασιλίσκου ἐκτίσθησαν ὑπὸ Ἰουστίνου καὶ Σοφίας.

124   Τὰ δὲ Βασιλίσκου οἶκος ἦν πρότερον Βασιλίσκου πατρικίου καὶ δρουγγαρίου τῆς βίγλης, τοῦ ἀδελφοῦ Βηρί-
νης· καὶ βασιλεύσας ἐποίησεν τὸν οἶκον αὐτοῦ παλάτια.

125   Τὰ δὲ παλαιὰ παλάτια τῶν Σοφιῶν ἀνήγειρεν Μαυρίκιος
ὁ βασιλεὺς εἰς ὄνομα Ἀναστασίας, τῆς πενθερᾶς αὐτοῦ,
γυναικὸς δὲ Τιβερίου· μετὰ δὲ εἴκοσι ὀκτὼ χρόνους Ἡράκλειος ὁ στρατηγὸς πρὸ τοῦ βασιλεῦσαι αὐτὸν τὴν κατοικίαν ἐκεῖσε ἐποιεῖτο, μετὰ τὸ τεθνάναι τὴν Ἀναστασίαν·
πάνυ γὰρ ἐφίλει τὴν αὐτὴν κατοικίαν. Καὶ ἐκεῖσε ἀπε-
καλύφθη τὸ κράτος τῆς βασιλείας· μετὰ δὲ τὸ βασιλεῦσαι
αὐτὸν ἱστόρησεν τὸ ἑαυτοῦ ὄνομα καὶ τοῦ υἱοῦ αὐτοῦ εἰς
τὰ τείχη.

126   Τὰ δὲ παλάτια τοῦ Βουκολέοντος ἐπάνω τοῦ τείχους
παρεξέβαλεν ὁ μικρὸς Θεοδόσιος· ὁ δὲ Μαρκιανὸς ἐποίησεν τὸν τρίκλινον, καὶ οὗτος καλεῖται Χρυσοτρίκλινος.

Ta Euboulou was built by the patrician Euboulos in the 120
time of Justin the Thracian (I, 518–527), because it was his
house.[129]

Ta Isidorou.—Isidoros was Euboulos's brother, and he 121
converted his house into an old people's home and a church.

Justinian the Great (I, 527–565) built Saint Tryphon which 122
is at Ta Euboulou. He also built a large church of Saint Tryphon at Ta Basiliskou and made it very beautiful and bestowed movable and immovable property upon it.

The Holy Anargyroi at Ta Basiliskou was built by Justin 123
(II, 565–578) and Sophia.

Ta Basiliskou was formerly the house of Basiliskos (474– 124
475), the patrician and commander of the *vigla,* and brother
of Verina; and when he became emperor, he converted his
house into a palace.

The emperor Maurikios (582–602) built the old palaces of 125
Ta Sophias in the name of Anastasia, his mother-in-law, the
wife of Tiberios (I, 578–582). Twenty-eight years later,[130] after the death of Anastasia, the general Herakleios (610–641)
dwelled there before he became emperor, for he loved that
house very much. And his power of rulership was revealed
there. When he had become emperor, he wrote his name
and that of his son on the walls.

Theodosios the Younger (II, 408–450) extended the pal- 126
aces of Boukoleon on top of the wall. Markianos (450–457)
made the hall that is called the Golden Hall.[131]

127 Τὰ δὲ παλάτια τοῦ Ἱππικοῦ καὶ τοῦ Κυαιστορικίου ὁ μέγας Κωνσταντῖνος ἀνήγειρεν.

128 Ἡ δὲ Δάφνη ἐκλήθη διὰ τὸ ἵστασθαι ἐκεῖσε στήλη ὄνομα φέρουσα Δάφνης· ἀπὸ γὰρ τῆς Ῥώμης ἤφεραν αὐτήν· εἰς μαντεῖον γὰρ ἦν ἐκεῖσε· ἀλλὰ καὶ στεφάνους ἀπὸ δάφνης ἐλάμβανον οἱ ἄρχοντες κατὰ τὸν Ἰανουάριον μῆνα.

129 Ὁ δὲ Ἱππόδρομος ἐκλήθη, διότι ἀπὸ τοῦ ἁγίου Κωνσταντίνου ἕως Εἰρήνης τῆς Ἀθηναίας ἐκεῖσε κατ᾽ ἰδίαν ἐπὶ ἄρματος ἔτρεχον οἱ βασιλεῖς.

130 Ὁ δὲ Ἰουστινιανὸς ὁ ῥινότμητος ἔκτισεν τὸν Ἰουστινιανὸν τὸν τρίκλινον καὶ τὸν Λαυσιακόν.

131 Ἡ δὲ Τύχη τῆς πόλεως ἄγαλμα ἦν καὶ ἤχθη ἀπὸ Ῥώμης ἐπὶ τοῦ μεγάλου Κωνσταντίνου· ἵστατο δὲ ἐπάνω τῆς ἁψίδος τοῦ παλατίου. Ὁ δὲ βασιλεὺς Μαυρίκιος συνέτριψεν αὐτήν.

132 Ἐκλήθη δὲ Σιδηρᾶ ἡ Πόρτα· ἐπὶ τοῦ μεγάλου Κωνσταντίνου ὁ μέγας κίων ὁ πορφυροῦς τοῦ Ἀνηλίου τρεῖς χρόνους ἐποίησεν πλωϊζόμενος ἀπὸ Ῥώμης διὰ τὴν ὑπερβολὴν τοῦ μεγέθους αὐτοῦ· καὶ ἐλθὼν εἰς τὰς Σοφίας ἐν τῇ πόρτῃ, θελόντων αὐτὸν ἐκβαλεῖν ἀπὸ τῶν σχιδέων, ἐχώσθη εἰς τὸν αἰγιαλὸν πήχεις τέσσαρεις διὰ τὸ εἶναι χαῦνον καὶ ἀλσώδη τὸν τόπον· μέλλοντες δὲ τοῦτον ἐκσπάσαι οὐκ ἠδύναντο μετὰ ξύλων, ἀλλὰ μετὰ μοχλῶν σιδηρῶν· καὶ διὰ τοῦτο οὕτως ἐκλήθη.

133 Τὸ δὲ Κοντοσκάλιον ἡ πόρτα ἀπὸ Ἀγαλλιανοῦ τουρμάρχου, παρισταμένου ὅτε ἐκτίζετο ὁ λιμήν, ἔλαβε τὸ

BOOK 3

Constantine the Great built the palaces of the Hippo- 127
drome and of the *quaestor*'s office.[132]

The <palace of> Daphne received its name because there 128
was a statue there which bore the name of Daphne (laurel).
They brought it from Rome, for it had served as an oracle
there. But also the magistrates received laurel wreaths in the
month of January.[133]

The Hippodrome[134] received its name, because from 129
Constantine the Great until Eirene the Athenian (780–802)
the emperors privately held chariot races there.

Justinian the Slit-Nosed (II, 685–695 and 705–711) built 130
the Justinian Hall and the Lausiakos.

The city's goddess of Fortune was a statue which had 131
been brought from Rome under Constantine the Great. It
stood on top of the arch of the palace. Emperor Maurikios
(582–602) destroyed it.

How the Iron Gate received its name. — Under Constan- 132
tine the Great the great porphyry column of the Anelios
(Sunless)[135] took three years to be transported by ship from
Rome because of its enormous size. When it arrived at Ta
Sophias at the gate,[136] and they tried to unload it from the
raft, it sank four fathoms deep into the seashore, because
the place was soft and marshy. When they tried to get it out
from there, they could not do this with wooden timbers, but
only with iron bars, and therefore it received this name.

The Kontoskalion gate took its name from Agallianos, 133
the commander of a *tourma,* who helped when the harbor

ὄνομα· ἐκαλεῖτο δὲ ἐκεῖνος Κοντοσκέλης· καὶ διὰ τοῦτο ἐκλήθη οὕτως.

134   Τὰ δὲ καλούμενα Ψαρελαίου Μυρέλαιον ἐκαλεῖτο· ὁ δὲ Καβαλλῖνος διερχόμενος ἠρώτησεν πατρίκιον τὸν Καμουλιανόν, πῶς κέκληται ἡ μονή· καὶ γνωρίσας τῷ βασιλεῖ τὸ ὄνομα τῆς μονῆς, ὁ βασιλεὺς ἐκέλευσε καλεῖσθαι ἔκτοτε τὴν μονὴν τὰ Ψαρελαίου, ἐνυβρίζων τὴν μονήν· καὶ παρευθὺ ἔφυγον οἱ μοναχοί.

135   Ὁ χορτοβολῶν εἰς τὸ Βούκινον ἐκκλησία ὑπῆρχεν τοῦ ἁγίου ἀποστόλου Ἀνδρέου, ἣν ἀνήγειρεν Ἰουστινιανὸς ὁ μέγας ἐκεῖσε βασιλεύων εἰσερχόμενος. Ὁ δὲ Καβαλλῖνος ἐποίησεν αὐτὸν χορτοβολῶνα.

136   Εἰς τὸν Ψωμαθέα ἵστατο εἴδωλον καί τις τῶν εἰδωλολατρῶν ὡς θεὸν αὐτὸ ἐσέβετο· ἔλεγον δὲ αὐτῷ οἱ φιλόχριστοι, ὅτι "τὸ εἴδωλον ὃ σέβεσαι ψευμάτινος θεός ἐστιν." Καὶ ἔλαβεν ὁ τοιοῦτος τόπος τὸ ὄνομα ἐκ τοῦ ψεῦμα θεός [ἢ ἀπὸ τοῦ ὕψωμα θεῖον, διὰ τὸ ἄνωθεν ἵστασθαι τὸν τίμιον σταυρὸν τοῦ κίονος].

137   Ἡ δὲ Πέμπτη Πόρτα ἐκλήθη διὰ τὸ εἶναι κατ' ἀριθμὸν πέμπτην.

138   Ἡ Χαρσίου πόρτα ἐκλήθη ἐκ τοῦ Χαρσίου δευτερεύοντος μέρους Βενέτων [ὅτι αὐτὸς παρίστατο ἐκεῖσε, ὅτε ἐκτίζετο].

139   Ἡ δὲ Ξυλόκερκος· διὰ τὸ εὑρεῖν πολλὰ ὕδατα τοὺς τεχνίτας καὶ πλημμύραν ὑδάτων, εἰς τὸ θεμελιῶσαι ἔρριψαν λίθους καὶ ἐποίησαν παντούρωσιν ξύλων πολλῶν.

140   Ἡ δὲ Πολύανδρος διὰ τὸ ἑνωθῆναι ἐκεῖσε ἀμφότερα

was built. For he was called "the short-shanked" (Konto-skeles), and therefore it received this name.[137]

<The place> called Ta Psarelaiou (of fish oil) was called 134
Myrelaion (perfume oil). But when <Constantine V (741–775)> Kaballinos passed by, he asked the patrician Kamou-lianos what the monastery was called. And when he told the emperor the name of the monastery, he decreed that it henceforth be called Ta Psarelaiou, thus slandering the mon-astery. And the monks fled immediately.[138]

The hay barn at the Boukinon[139] was once a church of the 135
holy apostle Andrew, which Justinian the Great (I, 527–565) built when he had become emperor and entered <the city> there. <Constantine V (741–775)> Kaballinos made a hay barn of it.

At the Psomatheas stood an idol, and one of the idolaters 136
venerated it as a god. The Christ lovers said to him, "The idol you venerate is a false god *(pseumatinos theos)*." And this place received its name from <the words> "false god *(pseuma theos)*" [, or from "divine height *(hypsoma theion),*" because on its top a column stood with the venerable cross.][140]

The Fifth Gate received its name because it was the fifth 137
in number.[141]

The Gate of Charsios received its name from Charsios, 138
the second leader of the Blue faction, [because he assisted there when it was built].[142]

The Xylokerkos <Gate>.—Because the workmen found 139
much water and a great flood of water there, they threw stones into the foundation and made a foundation of a heavy framework of many wood timbers.[143]

The Polyandros <Gate> received its name because both 140

μέρη τῶν δημοτῶν, ὅτε ἔκτιζον τὰ τείχη ἐπὶ τοῦ μικροῦ Θεοδοσίου.

141 Τὰ δὲ Γερμανοῦ Γερμανὸς πατρίκιος ὁ ὢν ἐν τοῖς χρόνοις Οὐαλεντινιανοῦ καὶ Γρατιανοῦ· γέγονεν δὲ στρατηγὸς εἰς Πελοπόννησον καὶ ἀνήγειρεν τὸν οἶκον αὐτοῦ εἰς λοῦμα.

142 Τὴν δὲ Πηγὴν τὴν Θεοτόκον ἔκτισεν Ἰουστινιανὸς ὁ μέγας· ἐξερχόμενος εἰς τὸ κυνηγῆσαι εἰς τὴν Θρᾴκην εἶδεν πλῆθος λαοῦ ἐξερχομένου ἐκ τοῦ ἐκεῖσε ὄντος εὐκτηρίου μικροῦ, ἑνὸς μοναχοῦ καθεζομένου· ἠρώτησεν δὲ ὁ βασιλεύς, τί ἐστιν· ὁ δὲ μάγιστρος Στρατήγιος καὶ φύλαξ τῶν βασιλικῶν χρημάτων εἶπεν αὐτῷ, ὅτι "ἡ πηγὴ τῶν ἰαμάτων ἐστίν." Τότε θαυμάσας ὁ βασιλεὺς ὥρισεν καὶ ἔκτισεν αὐτὴν ἐκ τῆς περιττευούσης ὕλης τῆς Μεγάλης Ἐκκλησίας· ὑπὸ σεισμοῦ δὲ συμπτωθεῖσαν τελείως ἀνήγειρεν αὐτὴν Εἰρήνη ἡ Ἀθηναία σὺν τῷ υἱῷ αὐτῆς Κωνσταντίνῳ· ἐπεὶ πρὸ τῆς Εἰρήνης σξ΄ ἔτη διῆλθον.

143 Ἡ δὲ Ἀχειροποίητος ἐκτίσθη παρὰ τοῦ μεγάλου Κωνσταντίνου εἰς τὸ καθέζεσθαι Ἀβράμιον τὸν μοναχὸν ἐκεῖσε· διὸ καὶ ἐκλήθη Ἀβραμίτης.

144 Τὸ δὲ Ἕβδομον ὁ δρομικὸς ναὸς ἐκτίσθη παρὰ τοῦ μεγάλου Κωνσταντίνου εἰς ὄνομα τοῦ ἁγίου Ἰωάννου τοῦ θεολόγου.

145 Ὁ δὲ στρογγυλόστεγος ὁ ἔχων τὰς κόγχας ὠνομάσθη Πρόδρομος καὶ ἐκτίσθη παρὰ Θεοδοσίου τοῦ μεγάλου, ὅτι ἐν τοῖς χρόνοις αὐτοῦ ἡ ἁγία κεφαλὴ τοῦ Προδρόμου εἰσῆλθεν, καὶ ἐδέξατο αὐτὴν εἰς τὸ Ἕβδομον ὁ βασιλεὺς καὶ ἀπέθετο εἰς τὸν ναὸν τοῦ Θεολόγου μετὰ Νεκταρίου

factions of the partisans united there when they built the walls under Theodosios the Younger (II, 408–450).[144]

Ta Germanou.—The patrician Germanos, who lived in 141 the time of Valentinian (I, 364–375) and Gratian (375–383), became *strategos* of the Peloponnese and converted his house into a bath.[145]

Justinian the Great (I, 527–565) built the Mother of God 142 at the Spring. When he went out to Thrace to hunt, he saw a crowd of people coming out from the small chapel there, where a single monk lived. The emperor asked what this was. Strategios, the *magistros* and keeper of the imperial treasuries, told him, "This is the healing spring." So the emperor marveled at this, and built <the church> from the surplus construction material of the Great Church.[146] After it had collapsed in an earthquake, Eirene the Athenian (780–802) rebuilt it with her son Constantine, when 260 years had passed <from Justinian> to Eirene.[147]

The Acheiropoietos was built by Constantine the Great 143 in order to install the monk Abramios there. Therefore it was also called Abramites.[148]

The basilical church at the Hebdomon was built by Con-144 stantine the Great in the name of Saint John the Theologian.[149]

The <church> with the round roof and the apses was 145 called the Forerunner and was built by Theodosios the Great (I, 379–395), for in his time the holy head of the Forerunner arrived, and the emperor received it at the Hebdomon and deposited it in the church of the Theologian,

πατριάρχου. Ὁ δὲ μάγιστρος Ῥουφῖνος ἔπεισεν τὸν βασιλέα κτίσαι ναὸν τοῦ Προδρόμου εἰς τὸ τεθῆναι τὴν ἁγίαν
αὐτοῦ κάραν.

146   Τὰ δὲ Παυλίνου ἐκτίσθησαν παρὰ Παυλίνου μαγίστρου
καὶ φίλου Θεοδοσίου τοῦ μικροῦ· γνωστὸς γὰρ αὐτῷ
ὑπῆρχεν· ἔστιν δὲ προάστειον αὐτοῦ ὁ τόπος· καὶ ἀνήγειρεν ναὸν τῶν ἁγίων Ἀναργύρων μήπω τελειώσας αὐτόν.
Ἐπὶ δὲ αὐτοῦ εὑρέθη μῆλον ὀπώρας δίκην μοδίου τὸ μέγεθος, ἀπὸ Φρυγίαν κομίσαντος τοῦτό τινος· καὶ ἰδὼν αὐτὸ
ὁ βασιλεὺς καὶ θαυμάσας, ὅτι ἐπὶ τῶν ἡμερῶν αὐτοῦ
εὑρέθη τοιοῦτον, δέδωκεν τῷ κομίσαντι νομίσματα ρ'· τὸ
δὲ μῆλον ἀπέστειλεν Εὐδοκίᾳ τῇ Ἀθηναίᾳ, τῇ Αὐγούστῃ
αὐτοῦ. Ἐκείνη δὲ λαβοῦσα τοῦτο κατεῖχεν καὶ ἐθαύμαζεν
ἐπὶ τῷ μεγέθει καὶ κάλλει τοῦ μήλου· καὶ προσελθὼν τῇ
Αὐγούστῃ Παυλῖνος ὁ μάγιστρος καὶ εὑρὼν παρὰ τῇ δεσποίνῃ τὸ μῆλον ἐθαύμασεν εἰρηκὼς αὐτῇ· "πόθεν εὑρέθη
τὸ ἀγαθόν, δέσποινά μου;" Ἡ δὲ ἔφη, "λάβε τοῦτο," ἐπεὶ
ἠράσθη αὐτοῦ. Ὁ δὲ λαβὼν καὶ μὴ εἰδὼς ὅτι παρὰ τοῦ
βασιλέως ἐδόθη τῇ Αὐγούστῃ, ἔπεμψεν αὐτὸ τῷ βασιλεῖ
ὡς μέγα δῶρον. Ὁ δὲ βασιλεὺς ἰδὼν καὶ γνοὺς ὅτι τὸ ἀπο-
σταλὲν τῇ Αὐγούστῃ μῆλόν ἐστιν, τῇ μὲν Αὐγούστῃ προσκαλεσάμενος ἔφη· "ποῦ ἐστιν τὸ μῆλον ὃ παρέσχον σοι;"
Ἡ δὲ ἔφη· "εἰσελθὼν πρός με Παυλῖνος ὁ μάγιστρος
ἐξῃτήσατο καὶ παρέσχον αὐτῷ." Καὶ αὐτὴν μὲν ἠμύνατο
αὐστηροῖς λόγοις· τὸν δὲ Παυλῖνον προσέταξεν ἀνερχόμενον ἐν τῷ παλατίῳ μελοκοπηθῆναι. Τοῦ δὲ ἀνερχομένου
ὡς πρὸς τὸ Πάνθεον ἔξωθεν εἰς τὸ σκοτεινόν, οὐκ
ἠδυνήθησαν τοῦτον σφάξαι, εἰ μὴ τὰ ὦτα αὐτοῦ ἐξέκοψαν·

together with patriarch Nektarios. The *magistros* Rouphinos convinced the emperor to build a church of the Forerunner in order to place his holy head there.

Ta Paulinou[150] was built by the *magistros* Paulinos, a friend   146 of Theodosios the Younger (II, 408–450), for he was acquainted with him. This place is a country estate, and he built a church of the Holy Anargyroi but had not yet finished it. In his time, an apple was found like a fruit,[151] the size of a bushel, which someone brought from Phrygia. And when the emperor saw it, he was astonished that such a thing had been found in his days, gave the bearer a hundred pieces of gold, and sent the apple to Eudokia the Athenian, his Augusta. When she received it, she held it in her hands and marveled at the size and beauty of the apple. And the *magistros* Paulinos came to the Augusta, saw the apple in the lady's possession, and said to her in amazement, "Where has this beautiful thing been found, my lady?" She said, "Take it," for she was in love with him. He took it, and since he did not know that it had been given to the Augusta by the emperor, he sent it to the emperor as a great gift. When the emperor saw it and realized that it was the apple which had been sent to the Augusta, he summoned her and said to the Augusta, "Where is the apple I gave you?" She said, "The *magistros* Paulinos came to me and asked for it, and I gave it to him." And he reproached her with harsh words, and ordered that Paulinos be cut to pieces when he arrived at the palace. When he had arrived somewhere outside the Pantheon in the dark, they were not able to kill him, but just cut

καὶ εὐθέως ἐνόησεν ὁ Παυλῖνος τὴν ἐπιβουλήν. Τοῦτο δὲ θαῦμα τῶν ἁγίων Ἀναργύρων γέγονεν, ἵνα τελειώσῃ αὐτὸς τὸν ναόν. Ἀκούσας δὲ ὁ βασιλεύς, ὅτι ἠστόχησαν αὐτόν, αἰσχυνθεὶς σφόδρα τὸν Παυλῖνον ἄγνοιαν προεβάλετο μηδὲν εἰδέναι. Τελειώσας δὲ τὸν ναὸν τῶν ἁγίων Ἀναργύρων ἀπεκεφάλισαν αὐτὸν φανερῶς προτροπῇ τοῦ βασιλέως. [Ἡ δὲ δέσποινα ὡς δῆθεν ἀτιμηθεῖσα ἠτήσατο τὸν βασιλέα ἀπελθεῖν εἰς τοὺς ἁγίους τόπους· καὶ συγχωρηθεῖσα ἐξῆλθεν· ἐκεῖσε οὖν γενομένη καὶ εὐαρεστήσασα τῷ Θεῷ ἐν τῷ μέλλειν τελευτᾶν ἐξωμόσατο μὴ συνειδέναι τι μετὰ Παυλίνου.]

147   Τὴν ἁγίαν Σορὸν τὰ Χαλκοπρατεῖα Ἰουστῖνος καὶ Σοφία ἔκτισαν οἱ καὶ τὸν ναὸν ἀνοικοδομήσαντες. Ἐκεῖσε δὲ ἀνεγίνωσκε Μιχαὴλ ὁ Ῥαγγαβὲ ὁ κουροπαλάτης πρὸ τοῦ βασιλεῦσαι καὶ Βάρδας ὁ Καῖσαρ ὁ θεῖος τοῦ Μιχαὴλ καὶ πολλοὶ τῶν μαγίστρων. Ἐκεῖσε δὲ ἀπόκειται ἡ τιμία ζώνη καὶ ἡ ἐσθὴς τῆς ἁγίας Θεοτόκου, τὸ δὲ ἅγιον ὠμοφόριον ἐν Βλαχέρναις.

148   Ἀνήγειρεν δὲ καὶ τὸν ἅγιον Ἰάκωβον ὁ αὐτὸς βασιλεὺς καὶ τέθηκεν ἐν τῇ σορῷ τῶν ἁγίων Νηπίων τὰ λείψανα καὶ τοῦ ἁγίου Συμεὼν τοῦ θεοδόχου καὶ τοῦ προφήτου Ζαχαρίου καὶ τοῦ ἁγίου Ἰακώβου τοῦ ἀδελφοθέου· καὶ ἐν τῇ ἁγίᾳ Σορῷ εὐωνύμως μὲν τοῦ ἁγίου Ἰωάννου Προδρόμου τὰς τρίχας, δεξιὰ δὲ τὰ σώματα πάντα τῶν ἁγίων μυροφόρων γυναικῶν.

149   Ὅτι εἰς τὸ Προσφόριν, καθώς φησιν Ἰωάννης ὁ Ἀντιοχεύς, ὁπόταν ὁ Βύζας ἔκτιζεν τὸ Βυζάντιον, βοῦν ἀπέστειλεν ἀπὸ τοῦ Προσφορίου, καὶ ἐπέρασεν ἐν Χρυσοπόλει·

off his ears. And immediately Paulinos understood the plot. This was a miracle of the Holy Anargyroi so that he could finish the church. When the emperor heard that they had failed to kill him, he was greatly ashamed in front of Paulinos and pretended not to know anything. When he had finished the church of the Holy Anargyroi, they beheaded him, evidently by order of the emperor. [The empress, being truly dishonored, asked the emperor to let her go to the Holy Places, was granted permission, and departed. Having arrived there and having pleased God, she swore, when she was about to die, that she had not done anything in collusion with Paulinos.][152]

Justin (II, 565–578) and Sophia, who had also rebuilt the church, built the Holy Shrine of the Chalkoprateia.[153] The *kouropalates* Michael Rhangabe (I, 811–813) was a reader there before he became emperor, <and so were> the Caesar Bardas, uncle of Michael (III, 842–867), and many of the *magistroi.* There are deposited the worthy girdle and the robe of the holy Mother of God, and the holy pallium is in the Blachernai. 147

The same emperor also built Saint James, and he deposited in the shrine the relics of the Holy Infants, of Saint Symeon who received God in his arms, the prophet Zachariah, and the holy James the brother of God, and in the Holy Shrine on the left the hair of Saint John the Forerunner, on the right all the bodies of the holy perfume-bearing women.[154] 148

At the Prosphorin, as John of Antioch says,[155] when Byzas built Byzantion he sent an ox away from the Prosphorion, and it crossed over to Chrysopolis, and therefore <the 149

καὶ διὰ τοῦτο ἐκλήθη Βοσπόριον. Ἐκεῖσε δὲ ἐπώλουν τοὺς βόας εἰς τὸ σιγματοειδὲς τεῖχος μέχρι τοῦ Κοπρωνύμου· ἐκεῖνος δὲ ὥρισεν εἰς τὸν Ταῦρον πωλεῖν αὐτούς.

150 Εἰς δὲ τὸ Κεντηνάριν τὸν πύργον ὁ μέγας Κωνσταντῖνος κεντηνάριν ἐξωδίασεν· πολὺν γὰρ ἀνήγειρεν αὐτὸν μέγαν. Σεισμοῦ δὲ γενομένου καὶ χαλάσαντος, ἀνηγέρθη παρὰ Θεοφίλου ὡς ὁρᾶται μικρός.

151 Τὸ δὲ παλαιὸν Πετρὶν οἶκος ἦν Πέτρου πατρικίου ἐν τοῖς χρόνοις Ἰουστινιανοῦ τοῦ μεγάλου· ἔλεγον δὲ αὐτὸν Βαρσυνιανὸν τὸν Σύρον τὸν πολλὰς ἀρχὰς διανύσαντα μετὰ δόξης.

152 Τὴν δὲ μονὴν τὰ Ῥωμαίου ἔκτισεν ἐν τοῖς χρόνοις Λεωμακέλλη Αἵμων πατρίκιος Ῥωμαῖος· τότε γὰρ εἰσῆλθεν καὶ ᾤκησεν ἐκεῖ· ἔχει ὅτε ἐκτίσθη χρόνους πεντακοσίους τριάκοντα δύο.

153 Ἡ δὲ μονὴ ἡ καλουμένη τὰ Προκοπίας ἐκτίσθη παρὰ Προκοπίας δεσποίνης, τῆς θυγατρὸς Νικηφόρου τοῦ Σελευκηνοῦ καὶ γυναικὸς Μιχαὴλ Ῥαγγαβὲ τοῦ ἀποκουροπαλάτου. [Ἔκτισε δὲ ἐκεῖσε καὶ παλάτια μικρὰ καὶ περικαλλῆ· διὰ ταῦτα οὖν ἐκλήθησαν Παλατίτζια.]

154 Τὸν δὲ ἅγιον Εὐστάθιον ἔκτισεν Εἰρήνη ἡ εὐσεβεστάτη Αὐγούστη, ἡ Ἀθηναία.

155 Ἡ μονὴ τὰ Ἀρμαμεντάρεας τοῦ ἁγίου Παντελεήμονος πρώην ὑπὸ Μαυρικίου ἀρμαμέντον ἦν· μετὰ δὲ χρόνους σμη' Θεοδώρα ἡ γυνὴ Θεοφίλου μονὴν αὐτὸ ἐποίησεν καὶ κτήματα πολλὰ προσεκύρωσεν.

156 Τὰ δὲ Πικριδίου ἔκτισεν Πικρίδιος κοιτωνίτης ἐν τοῖς χρόνοις Εἰρήνης τῆς Ἀθηναίας.

place> was called Bosporion. There they used to sell cattle at the sigma-shaped[156] wall until <Constantine V (741–775)> Kopronymos, who ordered that they should be sold at the Tauros.

Constantine the Great spent one hundredweight *(kente-* 150 *narion)* <of gold> for the Kentenarin tower, for he made it very large. When an earthquake occurred and it was destroyed, a smaller one was rebuilt by Theophilos (829–842), as can be seen.

The old Petrin was the house of the patrician Peter in 151 the time of Justinian the Great (I, 527–565). They called him Barsynianos the Syrian, who held many honors with distinction.[157]

Haimon, a Roman patrician, built the monastery Ta Rho- 152 maiou in the time of Leo Makelles (I, 457–474).[158] At that time, he came in and dwelled there. 532 years have passed since it was built.[159]

The monastery called Ta Prokopias was built by the lady 153 Prokopia, the daughter of Nikephoros (I, 802–811) from Seleukeia and wife of the former *kouropalates* Michael Rhangabe (I, 811–813). [There she also built small and very beautiful palaces, and therefore they were called Palatitzia.][160]

Eirene, the most pious Augusta, the Athenian (780–802), 154 built Saint Eustathios.

The monastery of Saint Panteleemon Ta Armamentareas 155 was formerly an arsenal under Maurikios (582–602). After 248 years Theodora, the wife of Theophilos (829–842), made it a monastery and bestowed many properties upon it.[161]

The chamberlain Pikridios built Ta Pikridiou in the time 156 of Eirene the Athenian (780–802).

157   Τὸ δὲ Καστέλλιν ἔκτισεν Τιβέριος ὁ πενθερὸς Μαυρικίου διὰ τὸ ἐλθεῖν Χαγάνον τὸν ἄρχοντα Βουλγαρίας
καὶ ἐμπρῆσαι καὶ κατακαῦσαι ἅπαντα τὰ Θρακῷα μέρη
μέχρι τῶν πορτῶν· ἐκαστέλλωσεν δὲ τὸ τεῖχος καὶ ἀπέκλει-
σεν τὰς ναῦς· καὶ ἐκλήθη οὕτως.

158   Τὸν δὲ Ἀνάπλουν ὁ μέγας Κωνσταντῖνος ἀνήγειρεν.

159   Τὸν δὲ ἅγιον Μάμαντα ἀνήγειρεν ὁ Λεωμακέλλης,
διότι ἐνεπυρίζετο ἡ πόλις μῆνας ἕξ· καὶ ἐξελθὼν ὁ Λεωμακέλλης ἔκτισεν ἐκεῖσε παλάτια καὶ ἔμβολον καὶ τὸν ναόν·
καὶ μετὰ τὸ διελθεῖν τὸν ἐμπρησμὸν ἔβρεξεν ἐπ᾽ αὐτὴν
στάκτην, σπιθαμὴν τὸ πάχος· ἔκτισε δὲ καὶ ἱπποδρόμιον
ἐκεῖσε· ἐξ οὗ καὶ Μιχαὴλ ὁ βασιλεὺς ἐκεῖσε ἀνηρέθη παρὰ
Βασιλείου.

160   Τὸν δὲ ἅγιον Ταράσιον λέγουσιν εἶναι προάστειον τοῦ
ἁγίου Ταρασίου τοῦ πατριάρχου· καὶ ἀνέστησεν αὐτὸ μονὴν μετὰ θάνατον.

161   Τὴν δὲ μονὴν τὰ Δαμιανοῦ ἔκτισεν Δαμιανὸς παρακοιμώμενος Σκλάβος ἐν τοῖς χρόνοις Θεοφίλου καὶ Μιχαήλ.

162   Τὸν δὲ ἅγιον Φωκᾶν Βασίλειος ὁ βασιλεὺς κτίζει μετὰ
καὶ τοῦ Φόρου καὶ τῆς Νέας, καὶ τὰ παλάτια τῶν Πηγῶν.

163   Τὸ δὲ Σωσθένιον τὸν Ἀρχιστράτηγον ὁ μέγας Κωνσταντῖνος ἔκτισεν.

164   Τὴν δὲ Χρυσοκέραμον ἔκτισεν Ἰουστῖνος καὶ Σοφία ἡ
Λωβή, ὅταν καὶ τὸ ὀρφανοτροφεῖον τὸν ἅγιον Παῦλον
ἀνήγειρεν καὶ τὸν ὅσιον <Ζωτικὸν> καὶ τὰ Σοφίας τὸν
λιμένα καὶ τὰς Σοφιανάς.

Tiberios (I, 578–582), the father-in-law of Maurikios, built   157
the Kastellin, because Chaganos, the ruler of Bulgaria, came
and torched and burned all the regions of Thrace up to the
gates.[162] He fortified the wall and enclosed the ships within,
and so it received this name.

Constantine the Great built the Anaplous.[163]   158

Leo Makelles (I, 457–474) built <the palace of> Saint Ma-   159
mas, for the city burned for six months. And Leo Makelles
went out and built palaces, a portico and the church there.
And when the conflagration was over, ashes rained on it, a
span thick. He also built a hippodrome there. Furthermore,
the emperor Michael (III, 842–867) was murdered there by
Basil (I, 867–886).

Saint Tarasios, they say, was a country estate of Saint Tara-   160
sios the patriarch (784–806), and he made arrangements to
turn it into a monastery after his death.

The chamberlain Damianos the Slav built the monastery   161
Ta Damianou in the time of Theophilos (829–842) and Michael (III, 842–867).

Emperor Basil (I, 867–886) built Saint Phokas, together   162
with the Forum and the New Church,[164] and the palaces of
Pegai.

Constantine the Great built <the church of> the com-   163
mander in chief <Michael> of the Sosthenion.[165]

Justin (II, 565–578) and Sophia the Maimed built the   164
<church with the> Golden Tiles, when he also erected the
Orphanage of Saint Paul and the blessed <Zotikos>,[166] the
harbor of Ta Sophias and the Sophianai.

165   Τὰ δὲ ζευκτὰ κιόνια· εἶχον ἐκεῖσε τοὺς τιμίους σταυροὺς τοὺς ὄντας νυνὶ εἰς τὴν Βώνου. Ἰουστῖνος δὲ ἐποίησεν τοὺς σταυρούς.

166   Τὰ δὲ Εὐτροπίου ὁ λιμήν, ἐν ᾧ ἀπετμήθη Μαυρίκιος
σὺν γυναικὶ καὶ τέκνοις, ἐποίησεν αὐτὸν λιμένα Εὐτρόπιος
πρωτοσπαθάριος καὶ κυαίστωρ ἐν τοῖς χρόνοις Ζήνωνος
καὶ Ἀναστασίου· ἀνήγειρεν δὲ καὶ τὴν μονήν.

167   Τὰ δὲ Μαλελίας ἀνήγειρεν Λέων πρωτοασηκρήτης,
οὕτω τὸ ἐπίκλην κεκλημένος.

168   Ἡ δὲ Παλαμίδου ἡ λεγομένη· μαρμάρινος στήλη ἐκεῖσε
ἵστατο, ἣν ἀνήγειρεν Θεόφιλος ὁ φιλόσοφος ἐν τοῖς χρόνοις Κωνσταντίνου βασιλέως.

169   Τὰ δὲ τῆς Ἱερείας παλάτια ἐκτίσθησαν παρὰ Ἰουστινιανοῦ τοῦ μεγάλου· ὁ δὲ ἀνεψιὸς αὐτοῦ Ἰουστῖνος καὶ
Σοφία ἐκαλλώπισαν αὐτά· Ἱερεία δὲ ἐκλήθη ὅτι τῆς Ἥρας
ἦν ὁ ναὸς ἐκεῖσε.

170   Τοῦ δὲ Βρύαντος τὰ παλάτια ἔκτισεν Τιβέριος καὶ
Μαυρίκιος· ἐκλήθη δὲ Βρύας ὅτι, μέλλοντος τοῦ ἐσχάτου
βασιλέως ἐξελθεῖν καὶ κατοικῆσαι εἰς Ἱεροσόλυμα, ἐν
αὐτῷ τῷ Βρύαντι θέλει ἀκοῦσαι τὸν βρυγμὸν καὶ τὴν
βοὴν τοῦ κλαυθμοῦ τῆς πόλεως.

171   Ὁμοίως καὶ τοῦ Δαματρὺ τὰ παλάτια ἐκεῖνοι ἔκτισαν·
ἐκεῖσε δέ ἐστιν τὸ πήδημα Κωνσταντίνου βασιλέως τοῦ
τυφλοῦ υἱοῦ Εἰρήνης.

172   Τὰ Φλώρου καὶ τὰ Καλλιστράτου ἔκτισαν δύο ἀδελφοὶ
οὕτως καλούμενοι εἰς οἴκους αὐτῶν· μετὰ δὲ θάνατον
αὐτῶν ἐγένοντο μοναὶ ἐν τοῖς χρόνοις τοῦ μεγάλου Κων-
σταντίνου· ἐξ οὗ καὶ Παῦλος πατριάρχης μετὰ υξη' ἔτη

The Yoked Columns.[167]—There they kept the venerable 165
crosses which are now at <the cistern of> Bonos.[168] Justin
(II, 565–578) made the crosses.

The harbor Ta Eutropiou where Maurikios (582–602) was 166
beheaded with his wife and children.—The *protospatharios*
and *quaestor* Eutropios made this harbor in the time of Zeno
and Anastasios. He also built the monastery.

Ta Malelias was built by Leo the first secretary, who was 167
called by this surname.

The so-called <statue of> Palamides.—There stood a 168
statue of marble which Theophilos the philosopher[169]
erected in the time of Emperor Constantine.

The palaces of Hiereia were built by Justinian the Great 169
(I, 527–565). His nephew Justin (II, 565–578) and Sophia
adorned them. They were called Hiereia because the temple
of Hera was there.[170]

Tiberios (578–582) and Maurikios (582–602) built the pal- 170
aces of Bryas. They were called Bryas because the final emperor, when he is about to leave and dwell in Jerusalem, will
hear at this Bryas the roaring *(brygmos)*, crying, and wailing
of the city.[171]

They <Tiberios and Maurikios> also built the palaces of 171
Damatrys in a similar way. There is the jumping place[172]
of Emperor Constantine (VI, 780–797), the blind son of
Eirene.

Two brothers who were so named built Ta Phlorou and 172
Ta Kallistratou as their houses. After their death they be-
came monasteries in the time of Constantine the Great.[173]
So too when the patriarch Paul (IV, 780–784) knew he would

γνοὺς τὸν θάνατον αὐτοῦ ἐν τοῖς χρόνοις Εἰρήνης παρῃτή-
σατο τὸ πατριαρχεῖον· καὶ κατελθὼν ἐκεῖσε ἐκαθέζετο καὶ
ἡσύχαζεν καὶ τέθνηκεν ἐκεῖσε μετὰ μῆνας δ'.

173   Τὰ δὲ παλάτια τὰ Ἐλευθερίου καὶ τὰ ἐργοδόσια ἔκτισεν
Εἰρήνη δέσποινα καὶ Κωνσταντῖνος ὁ υἱὸς αὐτῆς· ἀπὸ δὲ
τῶν ἐκεῖσε μέχρι τὰ Ἀμαστριανοῦ ἱππόδρομος ἦν, γεγονὼς παρὰ τοῦ μεγάλου Θεοδοσίου. Ἡ δὲ αὐτὴ Εἰρήνη
τοῦτον κατέλυσεν.

174   Τὸ δὲ λεγόμενον μέγα λοετρὸν τὸ πλησίον τοῦ Βοὸς
ἐκτίσθη παρὰ Νικήτα εὐνούχου καὶ γεγονότος ἐπὶ τῆς
τραπέζης ἐν τοῖς χρόνοις Θεοφίλου τοῦ βασιλέως.

175   Ὁ δὲ ἀρχιστράτηγος τὰ Ἀββακερᾶ πλησίον τοῦ Ξηρολόφου ἐκτίσθη παρὰ Λέοντος Μακέλλη· ἐκλήθη δὲ οὕτως,
ὅτι εὑρέθη ἐκεῖσε ἀβάκια παμμεγεθέστατα καὶ ἀξιοθαύμα-
στα.

176   Τὸ Κρύσταλλον δὲ ἐκλήθη ἡ Θεοτόκος οὕτως, ὅτι
ἐκεῖσε διερχόμενος ἔφιππος ὁ Λέων ὁ Μακέλλης ἔπεσεν
κρύσταλλος, χειμῶνος ὄντος, καὶ ἔδωκεν αὐτῷ.

177   Ὅτι τὰ Ἱερίου πέραν· ἱερέως τινὸς ἐσέβετο στήλη τοὔνομα Ἶρος. Λέγεται δὲ Ἱερίου διὰ τὸ μνημεῖα πολλὰ εἶναι
ἐκεῖσε· ἀλλὰ καὶ οἱ πολῖται πάντες ἐκεῖσε ἐθάπτοντο.

178   Τὸν δὲ ἅγιον Γεώργιον ὁ μέγας Κωνσταντῖνος ἀνήγειρεν. Πρῶτον δὲ ὁ ἅγιος Ἀνδρέας ὁ ἀπόστολος ἐκάθι-
σεν ἐκεῖσε καὶ ἐδίδασκεν· εἶθ' οὗτος ἐχειροτόνησεν τὸν
ἅγιον Στάχυν εἰς τὴν ἁγίαν Εἰρήνην τὰ λεγόμενα Γαλάτου·
ἐκλήθη δὲ ἀπὸ Γαλάτου τινὸς οἰκοῦντος ἐκεῖσε.

179   Τὸ Κερατοεμβόλιν· ἦλθεν ὁ ἅγιος Ἀνδρέας πρὸ τοῦ
μεγάλου Κωνσταντίνου ἐπὶ τὸ Βυζάντιον καὶ ἔκτισεν εἰς

die 468 years later in the time of Eirene (780–802),[174] he re-
signed from the patriarchate, went there and established
himself, lived as a monk and died there four months later.

The lady Eirene (780–802) and her son Constantine built   173
the palaces Ta Eleutheriou and the workshops. From there
to Ta Amastrianou was a hippodrome which had been built
by Theodosios the Great (I, 379–395).[175] This same Eirene
had it destroyed.

The so-called large bath near <the Forum of> the Ox was   174
built by the eunuch Niketas who became the official in
charge of banquets in the time of Emperor Theophilos
(829–842).

The <church of the> commander in chief (Archangel Mi-   175
chael) Ta Abbakera near the Xerolophos was built by Leo
Makelles (I, 457–474). It received this name because amazing dice of extraordinary size were found there.[176]

The <church of the> Mother of God was called the Crys-   176
tal because, when Leo Makelles (I, 457–474) was passing by
on horseback in wintertime, an ice crystal fell and hit him.

The statue of a priest (*hiereus*) called Iros was venerated at   177
Hieriou on the other side.[177] It is called Hieriou because
many graves were there, but also all the citizens were buried
there.[178]

Constantine the Great built Saint George. First the apos-   178
tle Andrew resided there and taught,[179] then he ordained
Saint Stachys in Saint Eirene called Ta Galatou. It was
named after a certain Galates who lived there.[180]

The Keratoembolin.[181]—Saint Andrew came to Byzan-   179
tion before Constantine the Great, built <a house> at Ta

τὰ Ἁρματίου καὶ ἐκαθέζετο ἐκεῖσε· ἐποίησεν δὲ σταυρὸν
ἰδιοχείρως λατομήσας αὐτὸν καὶ γλύψας ἔστησεν αὐτὸν
εἰς τὴν ἁγίαν Εἰρήνην τὴν παλαιάν· καὶ εἶθ᾽ οὕτως ἦλθεν
εἰς τὸ Νεώριν, εἰς τὸν ἔμβολον τὸν καλούμενον Κερατο-
εμβόλιν καὶ ἐδίδασκεν· εἴρηται δὲ οὕτως ὁ ἔμβολος, διότι
ἁψίδα χαλκῆ ἦν ἐκεῖσε· καὶ στήλη ἐπάνω ἵστατο ἔχουσα
ἐν τῇ κεφαλῇ κέρατα τέσσαρα· θαῦμα δὲ ἐγένετο ἀεί·
ὅστις εἶχεν ὑπόληψιν εἶναι κερατᾶς, ἐκεῖσε ἀπερχόμενος
καὶ προσεγγίζων τῇ στήλῃ εὐθέως, εἰ ἦν ὡς ὑπελάμβανεν,
ἐγυρίζετο ἐκ τρίτου ἡ στήλη· εἰ δὲ οὐκ ἦν οὗτος ἐνυπόλη-
πτος, ἵστατο σιγῇ καὶ οὕτως διηλέγχοντο οἱ κερατάδες.

180   Λέγεται δὲ Μαναῦρα ὁ τρίκλινος τοῦ μεγάλου Κωνσταντίνου, διότι Ἀναστάσιος ὁ Δίκορος ὁ ἀποσελεντιάριος
τῷ εἰκοστῷ ἑβδόμῳ ἔτει τῆς βασιλείας αὐτοῦ καὶ τῷ
τετάρτῳ μηνί, βροντῶν καὶ ἀστραπῶν πρὸς τὸ παλάτιον
εἰλουμένων, ἀδημονοῦντος καὶ φεύγοντος ἀπὸ τόπου εἰς
τόπον, ἐν ἑνὶ τῶν κοιτωνίσκων αὐτοῦ ἐκεῖσε κατέλαβεν
αὐτὸν ἡ ὀργὴ τοῦ Θεοῦ ἤγουν ἡ ἀστραπὴ καὶ ἡ βροντή·
καὶ ἐκεραυνώθη καὶ ἐγένετο πυρίκαυστος. Ὅτε δὲ ἀπέθνη-
σκεν, ἔβαλεν φωνήν· "ὦ μάνα, ὑπὸ τῆς αὔρας ἀπόλλυμαι."
Τὴν δὲ φωνὴν αὐτοῦ ἤκουσάν τινες τῶν ἀνθρώπων αὐτοῦ
καὶ διὰ τοῦτο οὕτως ἐκάλεσαν τὸν τρίκλινον ἀπὸ τῆς μά-
νας καὶ τῆς αὔρας τοῦ πυρός.

181   Τὸν δὲ Ἀρχιστράτηγον τὸν μικρὸν τῆς Νέας Ἀναστάσιος καὶ Ἀριάδνη ἀνήγειραν.

182   Τὸ δὲ Σίγμα τὴν Θεοτόκον ὁ μέγας Κωνσταντῖνος
ἀνήγειρεν καὶ εἶθ᾽ οὕτως Ἰουστινιανὸς ὁ μέγας· μετὰ δὲ
τκη΄ ἔτη σεισμοῦ φοβεροῦ καὶ ἐξαισίου γεγονότος εἰς τὴν

Armatiou and settled there. He made a cross with his own hands, cutting it from stone and doing the reliefs, and set it up in Saint Eirene the Old. Then he came to the Neorin to the portico called Keratoembolin, and taught. The portico is given this name because a bronze arch was there, and on top of it stood a statue which had four horns on its head. And a miracle always happened there: if someone suspected that he was cuckolded (keratas),[182] he would go there and approach the statue. If it was as he had assumed, the statue immediately turned around three times. If it was not as he suspected, it stood quietly, and in this way the cuckolded men were revealed.

The hall of Constantine the Great is called Manaura because of Anastasios Dikoros (491–518), the former *silentiarios*:[183] when in the twenty-seventh year and fourth month of his reign thunder and lightning struck the palace and he was in great distress and fled from one place to the other, the wrath of God, that is lightning and thunder, reached him in one of his chambers. And he was hit by a lightning bolt and consumed by fire. As he was dying, he cried out, "O mother (mana), I perish by the breeze (aura) <of the fire>." Some of his men heard his voice, and therefore they called the hall this, from the words for mother and the breeze of the fire.   180

Anastasios (491–518) and Ariadne built the small <chapel of the> commander in chief (Michael) at the New Church.   181

Constantine the Great built the <church of the> Mother of God at the Sigma, and thereafter Justinian the Great (I, 527–565). After 328 years[184] a frightful and extraordinary   182

αὐτοκρατορίαν Βασιλείου μετὰ τὸ ἀναιρεθῆναι Μιχαήλ, συνεπτώθη ὁ ναὸς ἐν ἡμέρᾳ Κυριακῇ, μνήμῃ τοῦ ἁγίου Πολυεύκτου, καὶ τοὺς ὄντας ἐκεῖσε πάντας διέφθειρεν· καὶ ἔκτοτε ἐκλήθη σεῖσμα, ἐπεὶ πρῶτον οὐκ ἐκαλεῖτο οὕτως.

183 Τὴν δὲ γυναικείαν μονὴν τὴν καλουμένην Αὐγούστης Ἰουστῖνος ὁ Θρᾷξ ὁ κράτιστος, ὁ θεῖος Ἰουστινιανοῦ τοῦ μεγάλου, ἔκτισεν σὺν τῇ γυναικὶ αὐτοῦ Εὐφημίᾳ, ἐπεὶ καὶ τὸ σῶμα αὐτῆς ἐκεῖσε ἐτέθη.

184 Ἡ Χώρα· τὸ πρῶτον εὐκτήριον ἦν ἡ τοιαύτη μονή. Κρίσπος δὲ ὁ ἔπαρχος καὶ γαμβρὸς τοῦ Φωκᾶ τοῦ Καππά-δοκος περιωρίσθη ἐκεῖσε καὶ ἔκτισεν ταύτην εἰς κάλλος καὶ εἰς μέγεθος ἀποχαρισάμενος ἐκεῖ καὶ κτήματα πολλά. Ἐπεκλήθη δὲ Χώρα, διότι ἐπὶ τοῦ Βύζαντος χωρίον ἦν ἐκεῖσε· ἐπεὶ καὶ τὰ Στουδίου χωρίον ὑπῆρχεν ἔξωθεν τῆς Βύζης.

185 Ἡ δὲ μονὴ τῆς Ξηροκέρκου, ὁ ἅγιος Μάμας, παρὰ τῆς ἀδελφῆς Μαυρικίου ἐκτίσθη· μετὰ γὰρ τὸ ἀποτμηθῆναι τὸν Μαυρίκιον εἰς τὸν Εὐτροπίου λιμένα σὺν τοῖς τέκνοις αὐτοῦ λαβοῦσα τὰ σώματα αὐτῶν κατέθετο ἐκεῖσε ἡ ἀδελφὴ αὐτοῦ· τὴν δὲ γυναῖκα αὐτοῦ καὶ τὰς τρεῖς αὐτοῦ θυγατέρας εἰς τὴν νῦν μονὴν τῆς Νέας Μετανοίας ἐκάθι-σεν πρὸς ὀλίγον. Καὶ εἶθ' οὕτως καὶ αὐτὰς διὰ ξίφους ἀπέκτεινεν ὁ Φωκᾶς. Τὴν δὲ γυναῖκα αὐτοῦ ταφῆς οὐκ ἠξίωσεν, ἀλλ' εἰς τὴν θάλασσαν ἔρριψεν ἀποκεφαλίσας καὶ πᾶσαν αὐτοῦ τὴν συγγένειαν Φωκᾶς ὁ παράνομος ὤλε-σεν.

186 Τὴν δὲ ἁγίαν Εὐφημίαν τὴν μονὴν καὶ τοὺς τάφους

earthquake happened during the reign of Basil (I, 867–886) after the murder of Michael (III, 842–867), and the church collapsed on a Sunday, the memorial day of Saint Polyeuktos, and all those who were there perished. And since then it was called Earthquake (seisma), for before it did not have this name.[185]

Justin the Thracian (I, 518–527), the most powerful, the uncle of Justinian the Great (I, 527–565), built the nunnery called "of the Augusta," together with his wife Euphemia, for her body was also buried there. 183

The Chora:[186] this monastery was at first a chapel. Krispos, the prefect and son-in-law of Phokas the Cappadocian (602–610), was exiled there and built a beautiful and large church, also bestowing much property upon it. It was called Chora, because under Byzas a village (chorion) was there, as also Ta Stoudiou was a village outside <the city of> Byzas.[187] 184

The monastery of Xerokerkos,[188] Saint Mamas, was built by the sister of Maurikios (582–602). After Maurikios had been beheaded at the harbor of Eutropios together with his sons, his sister took their bodies and laid them to rest there.[189] <Phokas> let <Maurikios's> wife and his three daughters reside for a short time in what is today the nunnery of the New Repentance. Then he killed them too by the sword. Phokas the Unlawful did not deem his wife worthy of burial, but threw her into the sea after beheading her, and also killed all his family.[190] 185

Emperor Basil (I, 867–886) built the monastery of Saint 186

τοὺς ὄντας εἰς τὸ Πετρὶν καὶ τὸ λοετρὸν Βασίλειος ὁ βασιλεὺς ἀνήγειρεν καὶ τὰς θυγατέρας αὐτοῦ ἐκεῖσε ἀπέκει-
ρεν.

187 Τὴν ἁγίαν Ζωὴν τὴν οὖσαν εἰς τὴν Μωκισίαν ὁ ὅσιος
Μαρκιανὸς ἀνήγειρεν· ἔνθα καὶ τὸ ἅγιον αὐτῆς σῶμα
κεῖται.

188 Τοὺς ἁγίους Νοταρίους ὁ μέγας Θεοδόσιος ἀνήγειρε
καὶ τὰ σώματα τῶν αὐτῶν ἁγίων ἐκεῖσε ἔθετο.

189 Τὸν δὲ ἅγιον Φίλιππον τὸν ἀπόστολον Ἀναστάσιος ὁ
Δίκορος ἀνήγειρε καὶ κτήματα πολλὰ ἐπεκύρωσεν.

190 Τῶν δὲ ἁγίων Μανουήλ, Σαβὲλ καὶ Ἰσμαὴλ τὸν ναόν·
μετὰ τὸ καυθῆναι αὐτοὺς παρὰ Ἰουλιανοῦ τοῦ παραβάτου
ἐπὶ τὸ χερσαῖον τεῖχος Θεοδόσιος ὁ μέγας τὸν ναὸν ἀνήγειρεν καὶ τὰ σώματα τῶν ἁγίων ἐκεῖ ἔθετο.

191 Τὸν δὲ Πρόδρομον τὴν παλαιὰν πόρταν ὁ μέγας Κωνσταντῖνος ἀνήγειρεν· τὸ δὲ κτίσμα ἡκούμβιζεν εἰς τὸ χερσαῖον τεῖχος.

192 Τὸν δὲ ἅγιον Ἐλευθέριον Βασίλειός τις πατρίκιος ἐν
τοῖς χρόνοις Ἀρκαδίου ἀνήγειρεν.

193 Αἱ μοναὶ τὰ Ἀλεξανδρίας καὶ Γρηγορίας· αἱ δύο μοναὶ
τῆς ἁγίας Δομνίκας ἡ ἐπονομαζομένη τὰ Ἀλεξανδρίας καὶ
ἡ ἄλλη μονὴ ἡ λεγομένη τὰ Γρηγορίας ἐν τοῖς χρόνοις τοῦ
μεγάλου Θεοδοσίου ἐκτίσθησαν. Ἐλθοῦσαι γὰρ ἀπὸ Ῥώμης εὗρον ἄοικον τὸν τόπον καὶ αἰτησάμεναι τὸν αὐτὸν
βασιλέα δέδωκεν αὐταῖς τὸν τόπον καὶ συνδρομὴν καὶ
ἀνήγειραν τὴν μονήν.

193a Ὁ ὅσιος Δῖος ὡσαύτως καὶ αὐτὸς αἰτησάμενος τὸν βασιλέα, δέδωκεν καὶ αὐτῷ τόπον καὶ ἀνήγειρεν τὴν μονήν.

Euphemia, the graves which are at the Petrin, and the bath, and tonsured his daughters there.

The blessed Markianos (450–457) built Saint Zoe which is 187
at the Mokios cistern. There too lies his holy body.[191]

Theodosios the Great built the <church of the> Holy 188
Notaries and deposited the bodies of these saints there.[192]

Anastasios Dikoros (I, 491–518) erected <the church of> 189
Saint Philip the Apostle, and bestowed much property
upon it.

The church of Saints Manuel, Sabel and Ismael.[193]—After 190
they had been burned at the land wall by Julian the Apostate
(361–363), Theodosios the Great (I, 379–395) erected the
church and deposited the saints' bodies there.

Constantine the Great erected <the church of John> the 191
Forerunner at the Old Gate, a building which abutted the
land wall.

A patrician Basil erected Saint Eleutherios in the time of 192
Arkadios (395–408).

The monasteries of Ta Alexandrias and Ta Gregorias.— 193
The two monasteries of Saint Domnika, which are called Ta
Alexandrias and the other monastery Ta Gregorias, were
built in the time of Theodosios the Great (I, 379–395).
When the women came from Rome, they found the place
uninhabited, made petition of the same emperor, and he
gave them the site and <monetary> assistance, and they
erected the monastery.[194]

The blessed Dios also petitioned the emperor in a similar 193a
way, and he gave him a site too, and he built the monastery.

194 Τὸ δὲ καλούμενον Μυροκέρατον ἡ μονὴ ἐκτίσθη ἐν τοῖς χρόνοις Μαυρικίου τοῦ βασιλέως. Φασὶ δὲ πολλοὶ τῶν ἱστορικῶν, ὅτι τὸ κέρας τοῦ ἐλαίου, ὅπερ εἶχεν Σαμουὴλ ὁ προφήτης καὶ ἔχριζεν τοὺς βασιλεῖς, εἰς τὴν αὐτὴν μονὴν ἐκρέματο· καὶ διὰ τοῦτο οὕτως ἐκλήθη.

195 Τοῦ δὲ Ξυλινίτου ἡ μονὴ ἐκτίσθη παρὰ Νικήτα μαγίστρου ἐν τοῖς χρόνοις Λέοντος τοῦ Συρογενοῦς, τοῦ πατρὸς Καβαλλίνου. Ὁ αὐτὸς δὲ Ξυλινίτης ἀπεκεφαλίσθη εἰς τὸν Σφενδόνα παρὰ τοῦ αὐτοῦ Λέοντος δι᾿ ἐπιβουλήν. [Ἔχει δὲ τὸ ὄνομα ἡ μονὴ διὰ τὸ τὰς μοναζούσας χρῆσθαι εἰς ὑπόδησιν τοῖς οὕτω καλουμένοις ξυλίνοις.]

196 Ἡ δὲ μονὴ τὰ Ἰκασίας ἐκτίσθη παρὰ Ἰκασίας τῆς μοναχῆς, εὐπρεποῦς καὶ εὐλαβοῦς καὶ σεβασμίας γυναικός, ὡραίας τῷ εἴδει τῆς τε κανόνας καὶ στίχους ποιησάσης ἐν τοῖς χρόνοις Θεοφίλου καὶ Μιχαὴλ τοῦ υἱοῦ αὐτοῦ.

197 Τὰ δὲ Σμαράγδης σὺν τῷ λοετρῷ ἐκτίσθησαν παρὰ Σμαράγδου πατρικίου καὶ στρατηγοῦ ἐν τοῖς χρόνοις Τιβερίου τοῦ Θρᾳκός, διότι οἶκος αὐτοῦ ἦν ἐκεῖσε.

198 Τὰ δὲ Κουκοροβίου τὴν μονὴν ἔκτισεν ὁ ὅσιος Εὐάρεστος ἐν τοῖς χρόνοις Μιχαὴλ τοῦ Τραυλοῦ τοῦ Ἀμορραίου.

199 Ὁ δὲ ἅγιος Μάρκος πλησίον τοῦ Ταύρου ἐκκλησία ἦν μεγάλη ξυλότρουλος, κτισθεῖσα ὑπὸ Θεοδοσίου τοῦ μεγάλου· καὶ κατενεχθεῖσαν Ῥωμανὸς δεσπότης ὁ γέρων ἀνήγειρεν αὐτήν.

200 Ἀλλὰ καὶ Κωνωπίων ἐστοιχειώθη καὶ ἵστατο ἐστηλωμένος ἐπάνω τῆς ἀψίδος τοῦ Ταύρου τῆς δυτικῆς· χαλκοῦς δὲ ἦν ὁ κώνωψ καὶ μυῖα καὶ κόρις· καὶ ἐξ αὐτῶν τῇ πόλει οὐκ ἐπεφοίτων. Ὁ δὲ Βασίλειος ὁ βασιλεὺς ἔκλασεν αὐτόν.

The monastery called Myrokeraton was built in the time   194
of the emperor Maurikios (582–602). Many historians say
that the horn of oil, which belonged to the prophet Samuel
and which he used to anoint the kings, hung in this same
monastery, and for this reason it received its name.[195]

The monastery of Xylinites was erected by the *magistros*   195
Niketas in the time of Leo of Syrian origin (III, 717–741), the
father of Kaballinos. This Xylinites was beheaded in the
Sphendone by the same Leo because he had made a plot
against him.[196] [The monastery received its name because
the nuns use the so-called wooden clogs *(xylina)* as shoes.][197]

The monastery Ta Ikasias was built by the nun Ikasia, an   196
attractive, pious and venerable woman, of beautiful appearance, who wrote hymns *(kanones)* and verses in the time of
Theophilos (829–842) and his son Michael (III, 842–867).[198]

Ta Smaragdes with the bath was built by the patrician and   197
general Smaragdos in the time of Tiberios the Thracian (I,
578–582), because his house was there.[199]

The blessed Euarestos built the monastery Ta Koukouro-   198
biou in the time of Michael the Stammerer from Amorion
(II, 820–829).[200]

Saint Mark near the Tauros was a big church with a   199
wooden dome, built by Theodosios the Great (I, 379–395).
When it had collapsed, the lord Romanos the Elder (I, 920–
944) restored it.

But also an enchanted couch with mosquito curtains (Ko-   200
nopion) stood on top of the western arch of the Tauros. The
mosquito, the fly, and the bug were made from bronze, and
because of them <these insects> did not affect the city. Emperor Basil (I, 867–886) crushed them.[201]

THE PATRIA

201 Ἡ δὲ καλουμένη Νεκρά· τὰ σώματα τῶν ἀναιρεθέντων
ἐπὶ τοῦ μεγάλου Ἰουστινιανοῦ ἐτέθησαν ἐκεῖ διὰ τὸ μὴ
χωρεῖν ἀλλαχοῦ θάψαι αὐτά. Ἀπέφραξε δὲ τὰ σκάλια ἀπὸ
τοῦ Πρωτοθύρου μέχρι τοῦ Καμελαυκίου· καὶ οὕτως ἐτίθουν τὰ νεκρὰ σώματα. [Ἐστὶ δὲ ἡ λεγομένη Σάπρα.]

202 Ἡ δὲ στήλη ἡ ἱσταμένη εἰς τὴν φιάλην τοῦ Ἱπποδρομίου εἰς τὸ στυράκιν ἡ χαλκῆ καὶ γυναικοειδὴς Εἰρήνης
ἐστὶν τῆς Ἀθηναίας, ἣν ἀνήγειρεν Κωνσταντῖνος ὁ υἱὸς
αὐτῆς εἰς θεραπείαν αὐτῆς.

203 Τὰ δὲ κτίσματα τὰ εὐμεγεθέστατα τὰ εἰς τὸν ἅγιον
Σέργιον οἶκος ἦν τοῦ μεγάλου Ἰουστινιανοῦ ὄντος αὐτοῦ
πατρικίου.

204 Τὰ Πατρικίας ἡ Θεοτόκος ἡ οὖσα ὄπισθεν τῆς ἁγίας
Σοφίας πρὸς ἀνατολάς· οἱ βασιλεῖς διερχόμενοι ἐπὶ προελεύσεως μετὰ τῶν δεσποινῶν, ὁπόταν ἤθελον ἀπελθεῖν
εἰς τὴν ἁγίαν Σοφίαν, ἐν αὐτῷ τῷ τόπῳ ἵσταντο. Οἶκος δὲ
ἦν κτισθεὶς παρὰ τοῦ μεγάλου Κωνσταντίνου. Αἱ δὲ πα-
τρικίαι αἱ ζωσταὶ καὶ οἱ πατρίκιοι ἐκεῖσε προσήρχοντο καὶ
ἤλλασσον τὸν βασιλέα καὶ τὴν βασίλισσαν μετὰ καὶ τῶν
πραιποσίτων.

205 Τὰ δὲ Βασιλίδου οἶκος ἦν πατρικίου Βασιλίδου καὶ κυαίστορος τοῦ μεγάλου Ἰουστινιανοῦ.

206 Αἱ δὲ πύλαι αἱ χαλκαῖ αἱ ἱστάμεναι εἰς τὴν Τρικύμβαλον
τοῦ Τζυκανιστηρίου παρὰ Βασιλείου τοῦ βασιλέως ἐπήρθησαν ἀπὸ τῶν ἐμβόλων τοῦ Φόρου ἐκ τὰ Χαλινάρια·
ἐστάθησαν δὲ παρὰ τοῦ μεγάλου Κωνσταντίνου ἄντικρυς
τοῦ Σινάτου· κτίσας δὲ τὴν Νέαν ὁ Βασίλειος ταύτας
ἀνελάβετο.

The so-called Nekra: the bodies of those killed under Justinian the Great (I, 527–565) were put there because there was no room elsewhere to bury them.[202] He walled up the stairways from the Protothyron to the Kamelaukion, and so they put the dead bodies there. [This is the so-called Sapra.][203] 201

The bronze female statue on the small column of the fountain in the Hippodrome is Eirene the Athenian (780–802), a statue which Constantine (VI, 780–797) her son set up to gain her favor.[204] 202

The huge buildings at Saint Sergios were the residence of Justinian the Great (I, 527–565), when he was still a patrician. 203

The <church of the> Mother of God Ta Patrikias which is behind Hagia Sophia toward the east: as the emperors passed by in procession with their ladies when they wished to go to Hagia Sophia, they would stop at this place. It was a house built by Constantine the Great. The girded female patricians and the patricians would come there together with the chamberlains to help the emperors and empresses to change their robes. 204

Ta Basilidou was the house of the patrician Basilides, the *quaestor* of Justinian the Great (I, 527–565).[205] 205

The bronze doors which stand at the Trikymbalon of the Tzykanisterion were removed by Emperor Basil (I, 867–886) from the porticoes of the Forum, from <the place called> Chalinaria.[206] They had been set up by Constantine the Great across from the Senate. Basil (I, 867–886) removed them when he built the New Church. 206

207   Ἡ μονὴ τὰ Δαλμάτου ἐκτίσθη παρὰ Δαλμάτου πατρικίου, ἀνεψιοῦ τοῦ μεγάλου Κωνσταντίνου· ἐξ οὗ καὶ
Ἀψίμαρος ὁ Τιβέριος βασιλεύς, ὅτε ἀνῆλθε μετὰ χελαν-
δίων καὶ ἐκράτησε τῆς βασιλείας, τὸν βασιλέα Λεόντιον
περιορίσας ῥινοκοπηθέντα ἐν τῇ αὐτῇ μονῇ ἐφρούρει.

208   Τὸν δὲ ἅγιον Γεώργιον τὸν ἐν Καλχηδόνι Σέργιος ὁ
πατριάρχης ἔκτισεν [ὁμοίως καὶ τὰ Μαρνακίου τὴν Θεοτό-
κον]· ἐν ᾧ καὶ τὸ βέβηλον αὐτοῦ σῶμα ἐκεῖσε κεῖται.
Ὁμοίως καὶ τὰ εὐκτήρια πάντα τῆς ἁγίας Σοφίας τὰ ἐν
τοῖς κατηχουμένοις ἔκτισεν δοὺς ἐκεῖ σκεύη χρυσᾶ καὶ ἀργυρᾶ πολλὰ καὶ πορφύρας διαχρύσους ἐκ βύσσου καὶ κειμήλια εἰς πλῆθος.

209   Τὸν δὲ ἅγιον Στέφανον εἰς τὸ Σίγμα πλησίον ὁ μέγας
Κωνσταντῖνος ἀνήγειρεν. Ὁ δὲ Λέων ὁ βασιλεὺς ἀνήγειρεν αὐτὴν μικράν, καὶ τὴν ὕλην πᾶσαν τῶν χρυσῶν ψηφίδων καὶ τῶν πολυποικίλων λίθων καὶ κιόνων ἀπέθετο εἰς
τοὺς ἁγίους Ἀποστόλους καὶ ναὸν ἀνήγειρεν τοὺς ἁγίους
Πάντας [διὰ τὴν τῆς γυναικὸς αὐτοῦ θαυματουργίαν καὶ
ἁγιότητα, τῆς πρώτης λέγω Θεοφανοῦς τῆς ἁγίας καὶ
θαυματουργοῦ βασιλίδος]. Ἐκεῖσε δὲ κεῖται ὁ ὅσιος Ἰσά-
κιος.

210   Τὸν ἅγιον Μητροφάνην ὁ μέγας Κωνσταντῖνος ἀνήγειρεν. Ἡ ἁγία Τριὰς ἡ οὖσα εἰς τὸ Ἐξακιόνιν, νῦν δὲ οἱ
ἅγιοι Ἀπόστολοι ὀνομαζομένη, ἀνήγειρεν αὐτὴν ὁ μέγας
Κωνσταντῖνος· συμπτωθεῖσαν δὲ ὁ μέγας Ἰουστινιανὸς
ἀνήγειρεν.

211   Ὅτι τὰ Ἴλλου ὁ Πρόδρομος πηγὴ τυγχάνει ἐκεῖσε· καὶ
ἐφώλευεν δράκων παμμεγεθέστατος ἐκεῖσε· ἦν δὲ καὶ

The monastery Ta Dalmatou was built by the patrician 207
Dalmatos, the nephew of Constantine the Great.[207] Therefore also the emperor Apsimaros Tiberios (II, 698–705),
when he arrived with large ships and seized the throne, exiled the emperor Leontios (695–698) with his nose slit and
kept him under guard in this same monastery.

The patriarch Sergios (610–638) built Saint George in 208
Chalkedon [and in a similar way also the Mother of God Ta
Marnakiou];[208] here also his accursed body lies. In a similar
way, he also built all the chapels in the galleries of Hagia Sophia, bestowing many gold and silver vessels on them, as
well as purple textiles from linen woven with gold, and a
great number of precious objects.

Constantine the Great erected Saint Stephen near the 209
Sigma.[209] Emperor Leo (VI, 886–912) rebuilt it on a small
scale, and stored all the materials—the golden mosaic cubes,
the multicolored <marble> stones and the columns—at the
Holy Apostles, and built a church, that of All Saints [be-
cause of the wonderworking and holiness of his wife, I mean
the first Theophano, the holy and miracle working empress.][210] There also lies the blessed Isaakios.

Constantine the Great erected Saint Metrophanes. Con- 210
stantine the Great erected the Holy Trinity which is at the
Exakionin, which is now called the Holy Apostles. When it
collapsed, Justinian the Great (I, 527–565) restored it.

The Forerunner Ta Illou.—A spring is there, and a huge 211
dragon dwelled in it, for it also was an imperial treasury. And

ταμεῖον βασιλικόν. Καὶ πολλοὺς ὁ δράκων ἤσθιεν· ὁ δὲ ἅγιος Ὑπάτιος ἐκεῖσε παραγενόμενος μετὰ τῆς ῥάβδου αὐτοῦ ἐχούσης κάτω ἧλον σιδηροῦν σφραγίσας καὶ κρούσας τὸν δράκοντα ἐξέψυξε· καὶ λαβὼν αὐτὸν μέσον τοῦ Φόρου προέθηκε νεκρὸν καὶ ἔκαυσεν αὐτόν. Καὶ διὰ τοῦτο ὠνομάζετο ὁ τόπος οὕτως, καὶ ἀπὸ Ἴλλου μαγίστρου τυραννήσαντος καὶ ἐκεῖ οἰκοῦντος.

212   Τὴν ἁγίαν Θεοφανὼ ἔξωθεν τῆς παλαιᾶς κόγχης τῶν μνημοθεσίων, ἀνήγειρεν αὐτὴν Κωνσταντῖνος ὁ υἱὸς Λέοντος ὁ Πορφυρογέννητος· [ἥτις κατέκειτο εἰς τοὺς ἁγίους Ἀποστόλους, ἥτις μέχρι τῆς σήμερον ἀναπηγάζει κρουνοὺς θαυμάτων μεγίστων ἐν τῇ γυναικείᾳ μονῇ τῆς εἰς ὄνομα τιμωμένης τοῦ μεγάλου καὶ ἁγίου Κωνσταντίνου.]

213   Τὴν δὲ Χαλκῆν τὸν Σωτῆρα ἀνήγειρεν Ῥωμανὸς ὁ γέρων ὑπὸ στυρακίων δύο μικρὸν πάνυ, ὥς ἐστιν ὁρώμενον τὸ θυσιαστήριον, ποιήσας καὶ δώδεκα κληρικούς. Ὁ δὲ Ἰωάννης ὁ Τζιμισκὴς ἐπλάτυνεν καὶ ἀνήγειρεν αὐτὸν καὶ καλλωπίσας ἐκ χρυσοῦ καὶ ἀργύρου πολλοῦ, ποιήσας καὶ κληρικοὺς ν' καὶ ῥόγας ἀπὸ νομισμάτων λ'· τὰ δὲ ἱερὰ στέμματα καὶ σκῆπτρα καὶ δίσκους καὶ λυχνίας χρυσᾶς τε καὶ ἀργυρᾶς καὶ ἐσθῆτας χρυσᾶς καὶ ἄμφια βασιλικὰ ἰδιόκτητα αὐτοῦ ἐχαρίσατο καὶ ἀκίνητα κτήματα προσεκύρωσε πλεῖστα· κἀκεῖσε ἀπέθετο ἅπερ αὐτὸς ἀπὸ τοῦ ἰδίου ταξιδίου ἔφερεν, τήν τε τιμίαν Σταύρωσιν, τὴν ἁγίαν εἰκόνα τῆς Βηρυτοῦ καὶ τὰ ἅγια σανδάλια τοῦ Χριστοῦ καὶ Θεοῦ ἡμῶν ἐν ποικίλοις χρυσοῖς καὶ διαλίθοις κιβωρίοις. Καὶ τὸ ἑαυτοῦ μνῆμα ἐκεῖσε ἐποίησε καὶ ἐτέθη ἐκεῖ.

the dragon ate many people. Saint Hypatios came there with his staff which had an iron nail on its lower end. He made the sign of the cross, struck the dragon, and it died. And he took it to the middle of the Forum, displayed its corpse and burned it.[211] And therefore the place had this name, and because of the *magistros* Illos, the rebel who lived there.

Constantine Porphyrogennetos (VII, 944–959), the son of Leo (VI, 886–912), built <the church of> Saint Theophano outside the old apse of the <imperial> mausoleum.[212] [She was laid to rest in the Holy Apostles, and to this day she produces streams of very great miracles in the nunnery which is honored by the name of the Great and Holy Constantine.][213]   212

Romanos the Elder (I, 920–944) erected the <church of the> Savior of the Chalke on a very small scale, resting it on two columns, as the sanctuary can still be seen, and he also installed twelve clerics there.[214] John Tzimiskes (I, 969–976) enlarged it, rebuilt it, and decorated it with much gold and silver, also installing fifty clerics and providing an annual allowance of thirty gold coins. He donated the holy crowns, scepters and plates, the gold and silver candlesticks, the golden robes and imperial garments from his own possessions, and bestowed much immovable property upon it. And there he deposited what he had himself brought back from his expedition, namely the worthy <icon of the> Crucifixion, the holy image of Beirut, the holy sandals of Christ our God, in multicolored reliquaries of gold and precious stones. And he made his own grave there and was buried there.   213

214 Τῶν δὲ Βλαχερνῶν τὸ ἅγιον λοῦμα ὁ νέος Βασίλειος ὁ εὐσχήμων καὶ καλοπράγμων καὶ συμπαθής, ὁ υἱὸς βασιλέως Ῥωμανοῦ τοῦ Νέου, τοῦ πορφυρογεννήτου, παρέλυσεν καὶ ἀνήγειρεν αὐτὸ νεωστὶ καλλωπίσας κρεῖττον καὶ βέλτιον παρ' ὃ ἦν· καὶ ἐξ ἀργύρου πολλοῦ καὶ χρυσίου εἰκόνισεν καὶ κατεκόσμησεν αὐτό.

215 Κτίζων δὲ τὴν πόλιν ὁ ἅγιος Κωνσταντῖνος, ὄντος τοῦ τόπου πετρώδους καὶ μέλλοντος αὐτὸν ἐξισοῦν πρὸς τὸ κτίσαι τούς τε ἐμβόλους καὶ τὸ ἐξάερον, κόπτοντες οἱ λιθοξόοι καὶ λατόμοι τὰς κορυφὰς τῶν πετρῶν κατεκύλιον τοὺς λίθους τοὺς κειμένους ἔξω τῶν τειχῶν, οὓς μὲν ἀπὸ τῆς Βαρβάρας μέχρι τοῦ παλατίου καὶ τῶν Σοφιῶν καὶ τῶν Ἐλευθερίου μέχρι τῆς Χρυσείας· ἔσωθεν δὲ τῶν αὐτῶν λίθων ἔπηξε τὰ τείχη εἰς διαστήριξιν τοῦ τείχους, ὅπως ἡ κυμαινομένη θάλασσα εἰς τὰς πέτρας κρούουσα γαληνιᾷ.

Basil the Younger (II, 976–1025), the handsome and com- 214
passionate benefactor, the son of Emperor Romanos the
Younger (II, 959–963), the Porphyrogennetos, dismantled
the Holy Bath of the Blachernai and rebuilt it again, decorating it in a better and finer manner than before. And he
made icons of much silver and gold and decorated it.

When Saint Constantine built the city, the site was rocky, 215
and as he wished to make it level in order to build the porticoes and the courtyards, the stonecutters and masons cut
off the tops of the rocks and rolled down those stones which
lie outside the walls, from <Saint> Barbara to the palace,
and from the Sophiai and Ta Eleutheriou to the Golden
Gate. Within these stones, he set up the <foundation> walls
for supporting the walls, so that the billowing sea might
strike against the stones and be calmed.[215]

BOOK FOUR

Διήγησις περὶ τῆς οἰκοδομῆς τοῦ ναοῦ τῆς
Μεγάλης τοῦ Θεοῦ Ἐκκλησίας τῆς
ἐπονομαζομένης ἁγίας Σοφίας

Ἐστὶν δὲ ἡ οἰκοδομὴ τῆς αὐτῆς ἐκκλησίας
ἐν Κωνσταντινουπόλει οὕτως·

Ἡ Μεγάλη Ἐκκλησία ἡ ἁγία Σοφία, πρῶτον μὲν
ἀνήγειρεν αὐτὴν ὁ μέγας Κωνσταντῖνος δρομικήν, ὁμοίαν
τοῦ ἁγίου Ἀγαθονίκου καὶ τοῦ ἁγίου Ἀκακίου. Καὶ
πληρώσας αὐτὴν στήλας ἔστησε πολλάς. Διήρκεσε δὲ τὸ
κτίσμα ἐκεῖνο χρόνους οδ'. Ἐν δὲ τοῖς χρόνοις Θεοδοσίου
τοῦ μεγάλου εἰς τὴν δευτέραν σύνοδον τὴν ἐν Κωνσταντινουπόλει γενομένην στασιάσαντες οἱ Ἀρειανοὶ κατέφλε-
ξαν τὴν στέγην τῆς αὐτῆς Μεγάλης Ἐκκλησίας, ὄντος
πατριάρχου Νεκταρίου τοῦ ἁγιωτάτου ἐν τῇ ἁγίᾳ Εἰρήνῃ
τῇ παλαιᾷ καθεζομένου, ἣν καὶ αὐτὴν ἀνήγειρεν ὁ μέγας
Κωνσταντῖνος. Διῆλθον δὲ χρόνοι δύο καὶ ἵστατο ἀσκεπής.
Προστάξας δὲ Θεοδόσιος ὁ βασιλεὺς Ῥουφῖνον τὸν μάγιστρον αὐτοῦ καὶ ἐστέγασεν αὐτὴν διὰ κυλινδρικῶν καμά-
ρων. Μετὰ δὲ ρλβ' χρόνους τοῦ Θεοδοσίου, ση' ἐτῶν
διελθόντων ἀπὸ τοῦ μεγάλου Κωνσταντίνου, εἰς τὸν πέμπτον χρόνον τῆς βασιλείας Ἰουστινιανοῦ τοῦ μεγάλου
μετὰ τὸ γενέσθαι τὴν σφαγὴν ἐν τῷ Ἱππικῷ (λε' χιλιάδων
ἐκεῖσε ἀναιρεθέντων διὰ τὸ ἀναγορευθῆναι ὑπὸ τῶν δύο

Narrative about the Construction of the Temple of the Great Church of God which Is Called Hagia Sophia

This is <the story of> the construction
of that same church in Constantinople:

Constantine the Great (306–337) was the first to build the Great Church Hagia Sophia,[1] on a basilical plan similar to Saint Agathonikos and Saint Akakios.[2] And when he had completed it, he set up many statues.[3] This building lasted for seventy-four years.[4] In the time of Theodosios the Great (I, 379–395), at the Second Council which was held in Constantinople (381), the Arians caused a riot and burned the roof of this same Great Church, when the most holy Nektarios (381–397) was patriarch and held his see in old Saint Eirene, which Constantine the Great had also built. Two years passed, and it remained without a roof. Then, Emperor Theodosios gave an order to his *magistros* Rouphinos, and had it roofed with barrel vaults.[5] 132 years after Theodosios, when 208 years had passed since Constantine the Great, in the fifth year of the reign of Justinian the Great (I, 527–565),[6] after the massacre had happened in the Hippodrome—thirty-five thousand were killed there, because the

δημοτικῶν μερῶν Ὑπάτιον πατρίκιον καὶ δήμαρχον μέρους Βενέτων)—ἐν τῷ πέμπτῳ ἔτει τῆς βασιλείας αὐτοῦ
τοῦ Ἰουστινιανοῦ ἐνέπνευσεν ὁ Θεὸς εἰς τὴν διάνοιαν
αὐτοῦ τοῦ οἰκοδομῆσαι ναόν, οἷος οὐκ ἐκτίσθη ἀπὸ τοῦ
Ἀδάμ.

2   Ἔγραψε δὲ καὶ τοῖς στρατηγοῖς καὶ σατράπαις καὶ κρι-
ταῖς καὶ φορολόγοις τοῖς ὑπὸ τῶν θεμάτων ἅπασιν ἐρευνᾶν
πάντας αὐτούς, ὅπως εὕρωσι κίονάς τε καὶ συστεμάτια
στήθεά τε καὶ ἀβάκια καὶ καγκελλοθυρίδια καὶ τὴν λοιπὴν
ὕλην τὴν ἀνήκουσαν εἰς τὸ ἀνεγεῖραι ναόν. Πάντες δὲ οἱ
παρ' αὐτοῦ ὁρισθέντες ἀπὸ εἰδωλικῶν ναῶν καὶ ἀπὸ παλαιῶν λουτρῶν τε καὶ οἴκων ἔπεμπον τῷ βασιλεῖ Ἰουστινιανῷ μετὰ σχιδέων ἀπὸ πάντων τῶν θεμάτων ἀνατολῆς
τε καὶ δύσεως, βορέα τε καὶ νότου καὶ ἐκ πάντων τῶν νήσων. Καὶ τοὺς μὲν ὀκτὼ κίονας τοὺς Ῥωμαίους, καθὼς
φησιν ὁ Πλούταρχος πρωτασηκρήτης καὶ ἐπιστολογράφος
Ἰουστινιανοῦ, μετὰ σχιδέας ἀπέστειλε χήρα γυνὴ ἀπὸ
Ῥώμης, ὀνόματι Μαρκία· εἶχε δὲ αὐτοὺς εἰς προῖκα αὐτῆς.
Ἵσταντο δὲ εἰς Ῥώμην εἰς τὸν ναὸν Ἡλίου τὸν κτισθέντα
παρὰ Αὐρηλιανοῦ βασιλέως Ῥώμης τοῦ προδώσαντος
ἑαυτὸν Πέρσαις. Ἡ δὲ προειρημένη Μαρκία ἔγραψε τῷ
βασιλεῖ οὕτως· ὅτι "ἀποστέλλω κίονας ἰσομήκους, ἰσοπλά-
τους, ἰσοστάθμους ὑπὲρ ψυχικῆς σωτηρίας μου." Τοὺς δὲ
ὀκτὼ πρασίνους κίονας τοὺς ἀξιοθαυμάστους ἐκόμισε
Κωνσταντῖνος στρατηγὸς ἀπὸ Ἐφέσου λελατομημένους
ἀμφοτέρους. Τοὺς δὲ λοιποὺς κίονας τοὺς μὲν ἀπὸ Κυζίκου, τοὺς δὲ ἀπὸ Τρωάδος, ἄλλους ἐκ τῶν Κυκλάδων
νήσων οἱ ἄρχοντες τῷ βασιλεῖ ἀπέστειλαν· καὶ λοιπὴν
ἱκανὴν ὕλην ἀπετίθουν. Ἀπεσωρεύθη δὲ πᾶσα ἡ ὕλη διὰ

two circus factions had proclaimed as emperor Hypatios, the patrician and faction leader of the Blues — so in the fifth year of his reign God inspired him to build a church such as had never been built since Adam's time.

He also wrote to all his generals, satraps, judges and the tax officials of the themes[7] that they all should search for columns, revetments, parapets, slabs, chancel barriers and doors and all the other materials which are needed to build a church. All those who had received his order sent <materials>, from pagan temples and from old baths and houses, to the emperor Justinian by rafts, from all themes of the east and west, north and south, and from all islands.[8] And, as Ploutarchos, the first secretary and letter writer of Justinian, relates, the eight Roman columns were sent from Rome by a widow named Markia, who had them as her dowry.[9] They stood in Rome in the temple of Helios which was built by the emperor Aurelian of Rome, who had surrendered to the Persians.[10] The aforementioned Markia wrote to the emperor thus: "I send you columns of equal length, equal diameter and equal weight for the salvation of my soul." The general Constantine brought the eight wondrous green columns from Ephesos, all having been quarried there.[11] Of the remaining columns, the noblemen sent some to the emperor from Kyzikos, others from the Troas, others from the Cycladic islands, and stored a large amount of other material. And these were all kept for seven and a half years. In the

χρόνων ἑπτὰ ἥμισυ. Τῷ δὲ δωδεκάτῳ ἔτει τῆς βασιλείας Ἰουστινιανὸς τὸν προειρημένον ναὸν τὸν παρὰ τοῦ μεγάλου βασιλέως κτισθέντα Κωνσταντίνου ἐκ θεμελίων κατέστρεψε. Τὴν δὲ ὕλην ἰδίως ἀπέθετο· οὐδὲ γὰρ χρείαν αὐτῆς εἶχε διὰ τὸ πολλὴν καὶ ἄπειρον ὕλην ἑτοιμάσαι.

3   Ἤρξατο δὲ ὠνεῖσθαι οἰκήματα τῶν ἐκεῖσε οἰκούντων· καὶ πρῶτον μὲν χήρας τινὸς γυναικός, ὀνόματι Ἄννης, οἰκήματα· καὶ ἀπετιμήθησαν νομίσματα πε'. Ἐκείνης δὲ μὴ βουλομένης ταῦτα διαπωλῆσαι τῷ βασιλεῖ ἔλεγεν· ὅτι "μέχρι πεντήκοντα λιτρῶν ἐάν μοι παρέχεις, οὐ δίδω σοι αὐτά." Καὶ ὁ βασιλεὺς τῶν μεγιστάνων αὐτοῦ πολλοὺς ἀποστείλας εἰς ἱκεσίαν τῆς γυναικός, οὐδὲν ἤνυον. Παραγενόμενος τοίνυν ὁ βασιλεὺς εἰς ἱκεσίαν τῆς γυναικὸς ἐδέετο αὐτῆς περὶ τῶν οἰκημάτων. Ἡ δὲ θεασαμένη τὸν βασιλέα προσέπεσε τοῖς ποσὶν αὐτοῦ δεομένη τὸν βασιλέα καὶ λέγουσα ὅτι "τιμὴν μὲν οὐκ ὀφείλω λαβεῖν εἰς τὰ οἰκήματα· τὸν δὲ ναὸν ὃν βούλει κτίσαι, αἰτοῦμαί σοι, ἵνα ἔχω καὶ ἐγὼ <κοινωνίαν εἰς αὐτὸν καὶ ἔχω> ἐν ἡμέρᾳ κρίσεως μισθὸν καὶ ταφῶ εἰς τὰ οἰκήματα πλησίον." Ὁ δὲ βασιλεὺς ὑπέσχετο αὐτῇ ταφῆναι ἐκεῖσε μετὰ τὸ τελειωθῆναι τὸν ναόν, ὡς ἴδιον κτῆμα δοῦσα, καὶ μνημονεύεσθαι διηνεκῶς. Ἔστιν δὲ ὁ τόπος τῶν οἰκημάτων αὐτῆς τὸ σκευοφυλακεῖον ὅλον.

4   Τὸ δὲ ὀνομαζόμενον ἅγιον Φρέαρ καὶ τὸ θυσιαστήριον ὅλον καὶ ὁ τόπος τοῦ ἄμβωνος καὶ ἕως τὴν μέσην τοῦ ναοῦ ὑπῆρχεν οἶκος Ἀντιόχου εὐνούχου ὀστιαρίου καὶ ἀπετιμήθη λίτρας λη'. Τοῦ δὲ δυσχεραίνοντος μὴ πρᾶσαι τὸν ἴδιον οἶκον τῷ βασιλεῖ, φιλοδίκαιος ὢν ὁ βασιλεὺς καὶ μισοπόνηρος πρὸς τὸ μὴ θέλειν τινὰ ἀδικῆσαι ἠθύμει

twelfth year of his reign,[12] Justinian destroyed the aforementioned church, which had been built by Constantine the Great, from its foundations. He stored its materials separately, as he had no need of them because such a large and vast amount of materials had been prepared.

He began to buy the houses of the people living there,[13] and first of all the houses of a widow called Anna, and they were worth eighty-five pieces of gold. She did not want to sell them to the emperor and said, "Even if you offer me fifty pounds, I will not give them to you." And although the emperor sent many of his grandees to supplicate the woman, they achieved nothing. So the emperor himself came to supplicate the woman and asked her for the houses. When she saw the emperor, she fell down at his feet, beseeched the emperor, and said, "I do not need to receive compensation for the houses. Build the church you want, I beg of you, so that I may <have my share in it, and>[14] have my reward on the day of the Judgment, and be buried near these houses." The emperor promised that she would be buried there after the church was completed, as she had given away her own property, and that she would be remembered forever. The site of her houses comprises the whole area of the treasury.[15]

The so-called Holy Well and the entire presbytery, and the site of the ambo and beyond as far as the middle of the nave was the house of a eunuch and doorkeeper Antiochos,[16] and was worth thirty-eight pounds. When he had qualms about selling his house to the emperor, the emperor, who loved justice and hated evil, was unwilling to do injustice to anybody, and became dispirited as he did not know what to

ἀδημονῶν, τὸ τί ἂν πράξοι. Στρατήγιος δὲ μάγιστρος, ὁ τῶν βασιλικῶν χρημάτων φύλαξ, ὁ τοῦ βασιλέως ἀδελφοποιητός, ὑπισχνεῖται τῷ βασιλεῖ διοικῆσαι τοῦτο διά τινος μηχανῆς. Ὁ δὲ ῥηθεὶς Ἀντίοχος ὀστιάριος φιλοϊππόδρομος ὤν, ἱππικοῦ ἀγομένου ὁ μάγιστρος Στρατήγιος καθεῖρξεν τὸν εὐνοῦχον ἐν τῇ φρουρᾷ. Τῇ δὲ ἡμέρᾳ τοῦ ἱππικοῦ ἤρξατο στριγγίζειν ἐκ τῆς εἰρκτῆς· "θεάσωμαι τὸ ἱπποδρόμιον καὶ τὸ θέλημα τοῦ βασιλέως ποιήσω." Ἤγαγον δὲ αὐτὸν ἐν τῷ Στάματι τοῦ καθίσματος, ἐν ᾧ ἐκαθέζετο ὁ βασιλεὺς ἐν τῷ ἱπποδρομίῳ, καὶ ἐκεῖσε ἐποίησε τὴν διάπρασιν ὑπογράψαντος ἐκεῖσε τοῦ κυαίστορος καὶ τῆς συγκλήτου πάσης πρὸ τοῦ τοὺς ἵππους γυμνάσαι. Τύπος δὲ ἦν ἐκ παλαιοῦ, ἡνίκα ἀνήρχετο ὁ βασιλεὺς ἐν τῷ καθίσματι, παρευθὺς ἔτρεχον οἱ ἡνιοχευτικοὶ ἵπποι· διότι δὲ ἤργησαν εἰς τὴν πρᾶσιν τῶν οἰκημάτων τοῦ εὐνούχου, μέχρι τῆς σήμερον ἀργῶς ἐξέρχονται τὰ ἡνιοχευτικὰ ἅρματα τῶν ἵππων.

5 Τὸ δὲ δεξιὸν μέρος τοῦ γυναικίτου ὅλον καὶ ἕως τοῦ κίονος τοῦ ἁγίου Βασιλείου καὶ ἐκ τοῦ ναοῦ μέρος τι ὑπῆρχον οἰκήματα Χαρίτωνος εὐνούχου τὸ ἐπίκλην Χηνοπούλου, ἃ καὶ ἐξωνίσθησαν μετ᾽ εὐχαριστίας. Τὸ δὲ ἀριστερὸν μέρος τοῦ γυναικίτου καὶ ἕως τοῦ κίονος τοῦ ἁγίου Γρηγορίου τοῦ θαυματουργοῦ ὑπῆρχον οἰκήματα Ξενοφῶντός τινος τῇ τέχνῃ βασιλισκαρίου· ὃς θέλων ἐξωνισθῆναι τὰ οἰκήματα αὐτοῦ ἠτήσατο τῷ βασιλεῖ μὴ μόνον τίμημα διπλοῦν λαβεῖν εἰς τὰς σκηνὰς αὐτοῦ, ἀλλ᾽ ἵνα ποιήσῃ τοῦτον ἐν τῷ ἀγομένῳ ἱππικῷ, ἐν ᾧ ἐπιτελεῖται, τιμᾶσθαι καὶ προσκυνεῖσθαι παρὰ τῶν τεσσάρων ἡνιόχων.

do. The *magistros* Strategios, the keeper of the imperial treasures, the spiritual brother of the emperor,[17] promised the
emperor to arrange this by some trick. The aforesaid door-
keeper Antiochos was a great lover of Hippodrome games,
and while a race was being held the *magistros* Strategios put
the eunuch into prison. On the day of the race, Antiochos
began to scream from the prison, "Let me see the Hippodrome games, and I will do the will of the emperor." They
brought him to the Stama before the imperial loge where
the emperor used to sit during the games, and there he made
the sale, with the *quaestor* and all the senate subscribing before the horses started their race. It was an old custom that,
as soon as the emperor went up to the loge, the chariot
teams started to race. But because they were delayed by the
selling of the eunuch's houses, up to this day the racing chariots of the horses go out slowly.

The whole right side of the women's section as far as the 5
column of Saint Basil[18] and a portion of the nave were the
houses of the eunuch Chariton, surnamed Chenopoulos,[19]
which were sold gratefully. The left part of the women's
section as far as the column of Saint Gregory the Wonderworker was the houses of a certain Xenophon who was a
basiliskarios by profession.[20] When he wanted to sell his
houses, he asked the emperor not only to give him double
the price for his abode, but also to let him be honored and
venerated by the four charioteers when the Hippodrome

Τοῦ δὲ βασιλέως προστάξαντος τοῦτο, πρὸς γέλωτα πεποίηκεν εἰς τὸ διηνεκές, ἵνα τυπωθῇ εἰς τοὺς ἀεὶ χρόνους,
ἐν τῇ ἡμέρᾳ τοῦ ἀγομένου ἱππικοῦ καθέζεσθαι τοῦτον ἐν
τοῖς καγκέλλοις μέσον καὶ τὰ ὀπίσθια αὐτοῦ προσκυνεῖσθαι παρὰ τῶν ἡνιόχων πρὸς γέλωτα πρὸ τοῦ ἀναβῆναι
αὐτοὺς ἐπὶ τῶν ἁρμάτων· καὶ τοῦτο διήρκεσε μέχρι τῆς
σήμερον· ὃς καλεῖται ἄρχων τῶν καταχθονίων· ἀμφιέννυται
δὲ χλαμύδα λευκὴν μετὰ βύσσου ἠμφιεσμένην. Τὸ δὲ ἐπί-
πεδον τοῦ ναοῦ καὶ οἱ τέσσαρες νάρθηκες καὶ ὁ λουτὴρ
καὶ τὰ πέριξ αὐτοῦ ὑπῆρχον οἰκήματα Μαμιανοῦ πατρικίου
Σελευκίας· ἅπερ ἀπετιμήθησαν λίτρας Ϟ· καὶ μετὰ πολλῆς
περιχαρίας δέδωκεν αὐτὰ τῷ βασιλεῖ.

6   Ὁ δὲ βασιλεὺς Ἰουστινιανὸς τὸν τόπον καταμετρήσας
καὶ εὑρὼν στεφαναίαν πέτραν ἀπό τε τοῦ θυσιαστηρίου
καὶ μέχρι τῆς κάτω ἁψίδος ἐθεμελίωσεν αὐτὴν γύροθεν τὰ
βάθρα τοῦ μεγάλου τρούλου· ἀπὸ δὲ τῆς ἁψίδος μέχρι τοῦ
ἐξωτάτου νάρθηκος εἰς τὸν χαῦνον καὶ ἀλσώδη τόπον ἐθεμελίωσεν. Ἀρξάμενος δὲ τὸ θεμέλιον κτίζειν προσεκαλέσατο
Εὐτύχιον πατριάρχην καὶ ἐποίησεν εὐχὴν περὶ συστάσεως
ἐκκλησίας· τότε ὁ βασιλεὺς Ἰουστινιανὸς λαβὼν ἰδίαις
χερσὶ τὸ ἄσβεστον μετὰ τοῦ ὀστράκου καὶ εὐχαριστῶν τῷ
Θεῷ ἔβαλεν ἐπὶ τῶν θεμελίων πρὸ πάντων. Πρὸ δὲ τοῦ
ἄρξασθαι κτίζειν τὸν ναὸν προέκτισεν εὐκτήριον χρυσόρο-
φον καὶ περικαλλὲς κυκλικὸν μετὰ λίθων πολυτίμων· ὅπερ
ὠνόμασε τοῦ ἁγίου Ἰωάννου τοῦ Προδρόμου (ὅπερ ἐστὶ
πλησίον τοῦ ὡρολογείου τὸ καλούμενον βαπτιστήριον),
ἵνα ἐκεῖσε παραμένῃ μετὰ τῶν ἀρχόντων αὐτοῦ, πολλάκις
δὲ καὶ ἐσθίῃ. Τότε γὰρ καὶ τὰ διαβατικὰ ἀπὸ τοῦ παλατίου

games are being held. The emperor gave these instructions, but made him a perpetual object of ridicule, for he ordered that <his statue> should be set up in perpetuity, on the day when the Hippodrome games were performed, in the middle of the starting boxes, and that his backside should be mockingly reverenced by the charioteers before mounting their chariots. This has lasted to this day, and he is called the ruler of the underworld.[21] He wears a white mantle made of linen. The floor of the nave, the four narthexes,[22] the fountain and its surroundings were the houses of the patrician Mamianos from Seleukeia.[23] They were worth ninety pounds, and he gave them to the emperor very gladly.

Emperor Justinian measured the site, and when he found 6 bedrock from the presbytery as far as the lower arch, he laid the foundations of the great dome all around it. From the arch to the outermost narthex he laid the foundations in a soft and marshy place. When he began to build the foundations, he invited the patriarch Eutychios,[24] and he said a prayer for the construction of a church. Then, Emperor Justinian took lime with crushed brick in his own hands, thanked God, and was the first of all to put it on the foundations. Before he began to build the church, he built a very beautiful round chapel with a golden roof and with precious stones, which he named that of John the Forerunner, which is the so-called baptistery near the clock house, so that he could stay there with his grandees, and also eat there often.[25]

μέχρι τῆς Μεγάλης Ἐκκλησίας ἔκτισεν, ἵνα διέρχεται καθ᾽ ἑκάστην συνεχῶς καὶ μὴ ὁρᾶσθαι παρά τινος πρὸς τὸ παρίστασθαι ἐν τῇ οἰκοδομῇ τοῦ ναοῦ.

7 Ὑπῆρχον δὲ τεχνῖται μαΐστορες ἑκατόν, ἔχοντες ἕκαστος αὐτῶν ἀνὰ ἑκατὸν ἀνδρῶν, ὁμοῦ γινόμενοι χιλιάδες δέκα. Καὶ οἱ μὲν πεντήκοντα μαΐστορες μετὰ τοῦ λαοῦ αὐτῶν τὸ δεξιὸν μέρος ᾠκοδόμουν, οἱ δὲ ἕτεροι πεντήκοντα ὁμοίως τὸ εὐώνυμον μέρος ᾠκοδόμουν διὰ τὸ εἰς ἔριν καὶ σπουδὴν ταχέως κτίζεσθαι τὸ ἔργον.

8 Τὸ δὲ σχῆμα τοῦ ναοῦ ἄγγελος Κυρίου ἔδειξε κατ᾽ ὄναρ τῷ βασιλεῖ. Ὑπῆρχε δὲ ὁ πρωτοοικοδόμος <Ἰγνάτιος> μηχανικὸς καὶ λίαν φρονήσεως ἀντεχόμενος καὶ εἰς τὸ ἐγεῖραι ναοὺς ἐπιτήδειος. Εἰς τοὺς κακάβους δὲ ὀπτεῖτο ἡ κριθή· καὶ τὸν χυλὸν αὐτῆς ἐμίγνυον τῷ ἀσβέστῳ σὺν τῷ ὀστράκῳ ἀντὶ ὕδατος· ὁ δὲ αὐτῆς χυλὸς ὑπάρχει γλίσχρος καὶ μιξώδης καὶ κολλητικός. Ὁμοίως καὶ τὸν φλοῦν τῶν δένδρων τῶν πτελεῶν κατατέμνοντες ἐνέβαλον τοῖς κακάβοις μετὰ τῆς κριθῆς· καὶ ἐποίησαν μάζας τετραγώνους ἐχούσας ἀνὰ πηχῶν πεντήκοντα τὸ μῆκος καὶ πεντήκοντα τὸ πλάτος καὶ εἴκοσι τὸ πάχος· καὶ ἐτίθουν εἰς τοὺς θεμελίους καὶ οὔτε θερμὸν τοῦτο ἐτίθουν οὔτε πάλιν ψυχρόν, ἀλλὰ χλιαρὸν διὰ τὸ εἶναι κολλητικόν· καὶ ἐπάνω τῆς μάζης ἐτίθουν λίθους εὐμεγέθεις ἰσομήκους καὶ ἰσοπλάτους· καὶ ἦν ἰδεῖν τότε αὐτοὺς κρατεῖν οἷάπερ σίδηρον.

9 Δύο δὲ πηχῶν τοῦ θεμελίου ὑψωθέντος ἐκ τῆς γῆς, ὥς φησιν ὁ προειρημένος <Στρατήγιος ὁ τοῦ βασιλέως ἀδελφο>ποιητὸς ὁ καὶ ἀπογράφων τὴν ἔξοδον, ἐξωδιάσθησαν χρυσοῦ κεντηνάρια υνβʹ. Μιλιαρίσια γὰρ ἀργυρᾶ καθ᾽

At that time, he also built the passages from the palace to the Great Church, so that he could pass there daily and visit the church during its construction without being seen by anyone.

There were a hundred master craftsmen, and each of them had a hundred men, so that all together there were ten thousand. Fifty masters with their crews were building the right-hand side, and the other fifty were likewise building the left-hand side, so that the work would proceed quickly, in competition and haste. 7

An angel of the Lord showed the emperor in a dream the outline of the church. The master builder was the engineer <Ignatios>,[26] a man full of great wisdom and experienced in the building of churches. Barley was cooked in cauldrons, and they mixed the decoction with lime and crushed brick instead of with water, for this decoction is sticky, good for mixing and as an adhesive. They also cut elm bark into pieces and threw it in the cauldrons together with the barley.[27] They made square barley cakes, fifty cubits long, fifty cubits wide and twenty cubits thick, and placed them in the foundations, neither too hot nor too cold, but lukewarm because that way it would be adhesive. And on top of the cakes they placed big stones, of equal length and width, and they could be seen to hold like iron. 8

When the foundation had been raised two cubits above the ground—as the aforementioned <Strategios, the emperor's spiritual brother>, who kept account of the expenses, stated—452 hundredweights of gold had already been spent. 9

ἑκάστην ἐκομίζοντο ἐκ τοῦ παλατίου καὶ ἐτίθοντο εἰς τὸ
ὡρολογεῖον καὶ ὅσοι ἀνεβίβαζον λίθους, ἐλάμβανον καθ᾽
ἑκάστην ἡμέραν ἀνὰ ἀργυροῦ ἑνός, διὰ τὸ μὴ ἀκηδιάσαι
τινὰ ἐξ αὐτῶν ἢ βλασφημῆσαι. Εἷς δὲ τῶν βασταζόντων
λίθους ἀγανακτήσας καὶ στενάξας εἰς γῆν κατηνέχθη καὶ
συνετρίβη. Τὴν δὲ ἔξοδον ἐποίει ὁ προρρηθεὶς Στρατήγιος,
ὁ φύλαξ τῶν βασιλικῶν χρημάτων, ὁ καὶ ὑπάρχων πνευ-
ματικὸς ἀδελφὸς τοῦ βασιλέως Ἰουστινιανοῦ. Τῶν δὲ πινσῶν ὑψωθέντων καὶ τῶν κιόνων τῶν μεγάλων τῶν τε
Ῥωμαίων καὶ τῶν πρασίνων σταθέντων, ὁ βασιλεὺς τὸ
δειλινὸν οὐκ ἐκάθευδεν, ἀλλ᾽ εἶχε πολλὴν τὴν ἐπιμέλειάν
τε καὶ σπουδὴν εἰς τὸ ὁρᾶν τούς τε λιθοξόους καὶ λατόμους
καὶ τεκτονικοὺς καὶ πάντας τοὺς οἰκοδόμους· μετὰ καὶ
Τρωΐλου κουβικουλαρίου τούτους ὁρῶν σπουδὴν αὐτοῖς
ἐπηγγείλατο· καὶ διὰ τοῦτο ἔξωθεν τοῦ μισθοῦ αὐτῶν τῶν
ἐργατῶν τῇ ἑβδομάδι ἅπαξ ἢ δὶς εὐεργέτει τούτους, ποτὲ
μὲν ἀπὸ νομίσματος ἑνός, ἄλλοτε δὲ καὶ πλεῖον. Πορευό-
μενος δὲ ὁ βασιλεὺς ἠμφιέννυτο ὀθόνην λευκὴν καὶ ψιλὴν
καὶ σουδάριον ἀμυδρὸν ἐν τῇ κεφαλῇ αὐτοῦ, ἐν δὲ τῇ χειρὶ
ῥάβδον πτενὴν κατεῖχεν.

10   Ἀνεγείραντες δὲ τὰς ἁψίδας τῶν τε ὑπερῴων εὐωνύμων
τε καὶ δεξιῶν καὶ ταύτας στεγάσαντες σκαφικὰς¹ ἁψίδας,
ὡρίσθη ἀγαγεῖν μιλιαρίσια ἐκ τοῦ παλατίου τῷ κρατοῦντι
ἡμέρᾳ Σαββάτου· ἦν γὰρ ὥρα τρίτη τῆς ἡμέρας καὶ προσέταξεν ὁ Στρατήγιος τοῦ ἐξελθεῖν τοὺς ἐργάτας καὶ τεχνίτας εἰς τὸ ἄριστον· κατερχόμενος δὲ καὶ ὁ προρρηθεὶς
Ἰγνάτιος, ὁ πρῶτος τῶν οἰκοδόμων, ὁ μηχανικός, κατέλιπεν
τὸν υἱὸν αὐτοῦ ἄνωθεν, ἐν ᾧ ἔκτιζον δεξιὸν μέρος ἄνωθεν

Every day silver coins were brought from the palace and placed at the clock house,[28] and those who carried up the stones received one silver piece per day so they would not lose heart or curse. One of the stone carriers became vexed and groaned, fell down to the ground, and was crushed. The aforementioned Strategios, the keeper of the imperial money, who was also the spiritual brother of the emperor Justinian, paid the expenses. When the piers had been raised and both the great Roman[29] and the green columns had been set up, the emperor did not sleep in the afternoon, but showed much care and zeal in observing the stone carvers, masons, carpenters, and other builders, and overseeing them with the chamberlain Troilos[30] he admonished them to work quickly. And therefore, in addition to their wages, he gave a bonus to the workers once or twice a week, sometimes a *nomisma* each, sometimes even more. When the emperor made his rounds, he was dressed in white and simple linen and had an unobtrusive headdress on his head, and in his hand held a thin rod.

When they had set up the arches of the left-hand and right-hand galleries and roofed them with bowl-shaped vaults,[31] it was decreed that on Saturday silver pieces should be brought to the emperor from the palace. For it was the third hour of the day, and Strategios ordered that the workers and craftsmen should go out for breakfast. When the aforementioned Ignatios, the chief of the builders, the engineer, also went down, he left his son up above, where they

10

THE PATRIA

τῶν ὑπερῴων, εἰς τὸ ὁρᾶν τὰ πρὸς οἰκοδομὴν ἐργαλεῖα
ἅπαντα. Ὁ δὲ παῖς ἦν ὡσεὶ χρόνων δεκατεσσάρων. Καθεζομένου οὖν τοῦ παιδὸς ἐφάνη αὐτῷ εὐνοῦχος λαμπρὰν
ἐσθῆτα ἠμφιεσμένος, ὡραῖος τῷ εἴδει, ὡς δῆθεν ἐκ τοῦ
παλατίου πεμφθείς, καὶ λέγει τῷ παιδαρίῳ· "τίνος χάριν τὸ
ἔργον οὐκ ἐκπληροῦσι τοῦ Θεοῦ οἱ κάμνοντες ταχέως,
ἀλλὰ καταλιπόντες αὐτὸ ἀπῆλθον ἐσθίειν;" Ὁ δὲ παῖς
λέγει ὅτι "κύριέ μου, ταχέως παραγένωνται." Ἐκείνου δὲ
πάλιν εἰπόντος, "πορευθεὶς λάλησον αὐτοῖς· σπεύδω γὰρ
τοῦ ταχέως τελειωθῆναι τὸ ἔργον," τοῦ δὲ παιδὸς φήσαντος
αὐτῷ μὴ ἀπελθεῖν διὰ τὸ μή πως ἀπολεσθῶσι τὰ ἐργαλεῖα
ἅπαντα, ἔφη ὁ εὐνοῦχος· "Ἄπελθε ἐν σπουδῇ καὶ φώνησον
αὐτοῖς τοῦ ταχέως ἐλθεῖν καὶ ἐγὼ ὀμνύω σοι, τέκνον,
οὕτως· μὰ τὴν ἁγίαν Σοφίαν, ἥτις ἐστὶ Λόγος Θεοῦ, τὴν νῦν
κτιζομένην, οὐχ ὑποχωρῶ τῶν ὧδε—ἐνταῦθα γὰρ ἐτάχθην
καὶ δουλεύειν καὶ φυλάττειν παρὰ τοῦ Λόγου τοῦ Θεοῦ—,
ἕως ὅτου καὶ ὑποστρέψεις." Ταῦτα ἀκούσας ὁ παῖς δρο-
μαῖος ἐπορεύθη καταλιπὼν ἐν τῷ ὑπερῴῳ κτίσματι τὸν
ἄγγελον Κυρίου φυλάττειν. Ὡς δὲ κατῆλθεν ὁ παῖς, εὑρὼν
τὸν πατέρα αὐτοῦ τὸν πρωτοκτίστην μετὰ καὶ τῶν λοιπῶν
ἐξηγήσατο πάντα· καὶ ὁ πατὴρ λαβὼν τὸν παῖδα ἤγαγεν
ἐπὶ τὸ ἄριστον τοῦ βασιλέως· ἐκεῖσε γὰρ ἦν ὁ βασιλεὺς
ἐσθίων ἐπὶ τὸ εὐκτήριον τοῦ ἁγίου Ἰωάννου τοῦ Προδρόμου ἐν τῷ ὡρολογείῳ. Ὁ δὲ βασιλεὺς ἀκούσας τὰ ῥήματα
τοῦ παιδὸς προσεκαλέσατο πάντας τοὺς εὐνούχους καὶ
ὑπεδείκνυεν ἕνα ἕκαστον αὐτῶν τῷ παιδαρίῳ λέγων· "μήτι
οὗτός ἐστιν;" Ὁ δὲ παῖς βοήσας μήτινα εἶναι ἐξ αὐτῶν τῆς
θεωρίας ἐκείνου τοῦ εὐνούχου ὃν ἐν τῷ ναῷ ἐθεάσατο—

244

were building the right side over the galleries, to keep an eye
on all the construction tools. The boy was about fourteen
years old. When the boy sat down, a eunuch appeared to
him clad in a shining robe, and with a beautiful face, as if he
had been sent from the palace, and said to the boy, "Why do
the workers not complete the work of God quickly, but have
abandoned it and gone away to eat?" The boy said, "My lord,
they will be back soon." When he said again, "Go and talk to
them, for I am anxious for the work to be finished quickly,"
and the boy told him that he would not leave lest all the
tools disappear, the eunuch said, "Go quickly and summon
them to come quickly, and I swear to you thus, my child: by
the Holy Wisdom, the Word of God, which is now being
built, I will not leave here—for I have been assigned to this
place by the Word of God to work and to keep watch—, until you return." When the boy heard this, he ran off, leaving
the angel of the Lord to keep watch over the building site
for the gallery. When the boy came down, he found his father, the master builder, together with the others and explained everything. And his father took him to the emper-
or's breakfast, for the emperor was eating there in the
chapel of Saint John the Forerunner at the clock house. The
emperor heard the boy's words and summoned all the eunuchs, and showed the boy each of them, saying, "Isn't it
this one?" When the boy declared that none of them looked
like the eunuch he had seen in the church, the emperor un-

ἔγνω τότε ὁ βασιλεύς, ὅτι ἄγγελος Κυρίου ἐστὶν καὶ τὸ
ῥῆμα γνώριμόν ἐστιν καὶ ὁ ὅρκος αὐτοῦ· εἰπόντος δὲ τοῦ
παιδός, ὅτι λευκοφόρος ἐτύγχανε καὶ αἱ παρειαὶ αὐτοῦ
πῦρ ἀπέπεμπον καὶ ἐνηλλαγμένη ἦν ἡ πρόσοψις αὐτοῦ,
μεγάλως ἐδόξασε τὸν Θεὸν ὁ βασιλεύς, λέγων ὅτι "εὐδοκεῖ
ὁ Θεὸς εἰς τὸ ἔργον τοῦτο," καὶ ὅτι "ἔφεσις πολλή μοι
ὑπῆρχε, πῶς δὴ καλέσω τὸν ναόν·" καὶ ἔκτοτε ἔλαβε τὴν
προσηγορίαν ὁ ναὸς "ἁγία Σοφία," ὁ Λόγος τοῦ Θεοῦ
ἑρμηνευόμενος. Καὶ σκοπήσας ὁ βασιλεὺς εἶπεν οὕτως·
"μὴ ἐάσαι τὸν παῖδα ὑποστρέψαι εἰς τὴν οἰκοδομήν, ἵνα εἰς
τὸ διηνεκὲς φυλάττῃ ὁ ἄγγελος, καθὼς εἶπεν ἐν ὅρκῳ.
Ἐὰν γὰρ ὁ παῖς ὑποστρέψῃ καὶ εὑρεθῇ ἐν τῷ κτίσματι, καὶ
ὁ ἄγγελος Κυρίου ὑποχωρήσει." Βουλευσαμένου δὲ τοῦ
βασιλέως τοὺς κρείττονας τῆς συγκλήτου καὶ ἱερατικοὺς
ποιμένας, εἶπον αὐτῷ μὴ ἀποστεῖλαι τὸν παῖδα εἰς τὴν
οἰκοδομὴν κατὰ τὸν ὅρκον τοῦ ἀγγέλου, ὅπως ἐκ Θεοῦ
φυλάξει τὸν ναὸν ἕως τέλους κόσμου. Ὁ δὲ βασιλεὺς
πλουτίσας τὸν παῖδα καὶ ἀξιώμασι δοξάσας, ἀπέστειλε
μετὰ βουλῆς τοῦ πατρὸς αὐτοῦ ἐν ἐξορίᾳ εἰς τὰς Κυκλάδας
νήσους. Ἐγένετο δὲ τὸ ῥῆμα πρὸς τὸν παῖδα τοῦ ἀγγέλου,
ὅπως ἐκ Θεοῦ φυλάξει τὸν ναόν, φήσαντος εἰς τὸ δεξιὸν
μέρος τοῦ πινσοῦ τῆς ἄνω ἀψίδος τῆς ἀνερχομένης ἐπὶ τὸν
τροῦλον.

11   Φθασάντων δὲ τῶν οἰκοδόμων εἰς τὰ δεύτερα ὑπερῷα
καὶ ἐγειράντων τοὺς ἐπάνω κίονας καὶ τὰς καμάρας καὶ
σκεπασάντων τὰ πέριξ, ἠθύμει ὁ βασιλεὺς διὰ τὸ μὴ ἔχειν
χρυσίου ποσότητα. Ἱσταμένου οὖν αὐτοῦ εἰς τὰ ὑπερῷα
τῶν κτισμάτων μέλλοντος ἐγεῖραι τὸν τροῦλον κατὰ
<ἔκ>την ὥραν[2] τοῦ Σαββάτου, ὡς ἤδη βαθέου ἀρίστου,

246

derstood that he was an angel of the Lord, and that his word and oath were true. When the boy said that the eunuch was dressed in white and his cheeks sent out fire and his face was completely transformed, the emperor praised God greatly and said, "God is pleased with this work," and "I was in great anxiety as to what name I should give the church," and since then the church received the name "Holy Wisdom," which is understood to be the Word of God.[32] And having considered the matter, the emperor said, "The boy is not to return to the construction site, so that the angel may be forever on guard, as he has sworn. For if the boy returns and is found in the building, then the angel of the Lord will leave." The emperor consulted with the leaders of the Senate and the priestly bishops, and they told him not to send the boy to the building, as, according to the angel's oath, he is to protect the church on God's behalf until the end of the world. The emperor made the boy rich and elevated him to high ranks, and, with his father's consent, sent him into exile to the Cycladic islands. The angel's declaration to the boy, that he would protect the church on behalf of God, was made on the right side of the pier for the upper arch that reaches up to the dome.

When the builders had reached the second gallery and 11 had erected the upper columns and the vaults,[33] and roofed everything all round, the emperor was discouraged because he did not have enough gold. As he was standing in the building's galleries during a very late breakfast time at the sixth hour of Saturday, wanting to build the dome, the em-

ἀδημονοῦντος τοῦ βασιλέως, ἐφάνη αὐτῷ εὐνοῦχος λευκοφόρος εἰρηκὼς αὐτῷ· "τί λυπῆσαι, δέσποτα, περὶ χρημάτων;
πρόσταξον ἐξελθεῖν αὔριον ταχὺ ἐκ τῶν μεγιστάνων σου
καὶ κομίσω σοι χρυσίου χάραγμα ὅσον ἂν βούλῃ." Τῇ δὲ
ἐπαύριον ἐλθὼν ὁ εὐνοῦχος καὶ εὑρὼν τὸν βασιλέα ὅτι
ἐπορεύετο ἐπὶ τὸ ὁρᾶν τὰ κτίσματα, δέδωκεν ὁ βασιλεὺς
τόν τε Στρατήγιον καὶ Βασιλίδην τὸν κυαίστορα καὶ Θεόδωρον πατρίκιον τὸ ἐπίκλην Κολοκύνθην τὸν καὶ ἔπαρχον
καὶ ὑπηρέτας μέχρι τῶν πεντήκοντα καὶ ἡμιόνους εἴκοσι
μετὰ εἴκοσι βουλγιδίων ζυγῶν· τούτους λαβὼν ὁ εὐνοῦχος
ἐξῆλθεν τῆς Χρυσῆς πόρτης. Καὶ ἐλθόντες εἰς τὸ Τριβουνάλιον ἐφάνησαν μὲν τοῖς ἀποσταλεῖσι παλάτια κτιστὰ
θαυμαστά· ἐκ τῶν ἵππων δὲ καταβάντες ἀνεβίβασεν αὐτοὺς ὁ εὐνοῦχος εἰς κλίμακα θαυμαστήν· καὶ ἐκβαλὼν
κλεῖδα λαμπρὰν χαλκῆν ἤνοιξεν κουβούκλιον· καὶ ὥς
φησιν Στρατήγιος ὁ μάγιστρος, ἦν τὸ ἔδαφος ἐστρωμένον
καὶ πεπληρωμένον χρυσίου χαράγματος. Καὶ λαβὼν
πτύον ὁ εὐνοῦχος ἔβαλεν ἐφ᾽ ἕνα ἕκαστον βουλγίδιον
κεντηνάρια χρυσοῦ τέσσαρα, ὁμοῦ κεντηνάρια ὀγδο-
ήκοντα· καὶ δοὺς αὐτοῖς ἀπέστειλεν εἰς τὸν βασιλέα. Καὶ
κλειδώσας ἔμπροσθεν αὐτῶν τὸ κουβούκλιον, ἐν ᾧ ἦν τὸ
χάραγμα, ἔφη αὐτοῖς· "ὑμεῖς κομίσατε ταῦτα τῷ βασιλεῖ
εἰς τὸ κατακενῶσαι εἰς τὴν οἰκοδομὴν τοῦ ναοῦ." Ὁ δὲ
εὐνοῦχος κατελείφθη ἐκεῖσε. Καὶ ἐλθόντες ἤγαγον τῷ
βασιλεῖ τὸ χρυσίον, καὶ ἐκπλαγεὶς ὁ βασιλεὺς ἔφη αὐτοῖς·
"ἐν ποίῳ τόπῳ ἀπέλθατε καὶ τίς ἦν ὁ εὐνοῦχος;" Καὶ
ἀνήγγειλαν αὐτῷ πάντα, τόν τε τόπον τῶν οἰκημάτων
αὐτοῦ καὶ ὅτι χρυσίον εἶχεν κεχυμένον ἐπὶ τὸ κουβούκλιον

peror was at a loss, and a eunuch in white dress appeared
to him and said, "Why are you so aggrieved, my lord, about
the money? Order one of your grandees tomorrow to go out
quickly, and I will bring you as many gold coins as you want."
The next day, the eunuch came and found the emperor as
he went out to supervise the construction, and the emperor gave Strategios, the *quaestor* Basilides,[34] and the patrician Theodore surnamed the Pumpkin, who was also the
prefect,[35] as many as fifty servants and twenty mules with
twenty saddle bags. The eunuch took them and went out of
the Golden Gate. And when they had arrived at the Tribunal,[36] wonderfully built palaces appeared to those who
had been sent out. When they had dismounted from their
horses, the eunuch led them up a wonderful staircase, and
producing a shiny bronze key, he opened a chamber. And, as
Strategios the *magistros* says, the floor was covered and filled
with minted gold. And the eunuch took a shovel and put
four hundredweights of gold into each leather bag, all together eighty hundredweights. And after giving this, he sent
them back to the emperor. And after locking in their presence the chamber which held the gold coins, he said to
them: "Bring this to the emperor so that he may spend it on
the construction of the church." They left the eunuch behind. And they came and brought the gold to the emperor,
and the emperor was astonished and said to them, "Where
did you go, and who was the eunuch?" And they told him
everything, the location of his houses, and that a great
amount of gold was spread out in his chamber. The emperor

αὐτοῦ εἰς πλῆθος πολύ. Καραδοκῶν δὲ ὁ βασιλεὺς τὸν
εὐνοῦχον ἐλθεῖν εἰς αὐτὸν καὶ ὡς οὐ παρεγένετο, ἀπέστειλεν ὁ βασιλεὺς τὸν ἀκόλουθον αὐτοῦ εἰς τὸν εὐνοῦχον·
καὶ εὑρὼν τὸν τόπον, ἐν ᾧ ἐθεάσατο τὰ παλάτια, ὅλον
ἄοικον καὶ ὑποστρέψας ἐγνώρισεν τῷ βασιλεῖ πάντα.
Ἐκπλαγεὶς δὲ καὶ γνοὺς εἶπεν ὅτι "ἀληθῶς τοῦτο τοῦ
Θεοῦ θαῦμα γέγονεν, ἵνα γνῶμεν," καὶ μεγάλως ἐδόξασε
τὸν Θεόν.

12   Ἐν δὲ τῷ μέλλειν τὸ ἅγιον θυσιαστήριον τελειῶσαι καὶ
διὰ τῶν στοῶν φωταγωγῆσαι τῶν διὰ τῶν ὑελίων ὄντων
προσέταξε τὸν μηχανικόν, ἵνα γένηται ὁ μύαξ μονοκάμαρος·
καὶ πάλιν μεταμεληθεὶς προσέταξεν γενέσθαι δίφωτον
μετὰ δύο ἀψίδων διὰ τὸ μὴ δέξασθαι βάρος, ὅτι ἐκεῖσε
κριώματα οὐκ ἔθεντο, ὥσπερ ἐν τῷ νάρθηκι καὶ ἐπὶ τὰς
πλευρὰς τοῦ ναοῦ. Τῶν δὲ λοιπῶν τεχνιτῶν ἀντιλεγόντων,
ὡς μία καμάρα φωτίζει τὸ θυσιαστήριον, καὶ ἀδημονοῦντος
τοῦ πρωτοοικοδόμου τὸ τί ἂν ποιήσει, ὅτι ποτὲ μὲν λέγει
ὁ βασιλεὺς μίαν ἀψίδα γενέσθαι, ἄλλοτε δὲ δύο, καὶ ἑστῶ-
τος αὐτοῦ ἐκεῖσε καὶ ἀκηδιῶντος, ἡμέρᾳ δ' ὥρᾳ ε' ἐφάνη
αὐτῷ ἄγγελος Κυρίου ἐν ὁμοιώματι Ἰουστινιανοῦ μετὰ
βασιλικῆς ἐσθῆτος καὶ ἐρυθρῶν πεδίλων καί φησι τῷ
τεχνίτῃ· "θέλω ἵνα μοι ποιήσῃς τρίφωτον τὸν μύακα καὶ
διὰ τριῶν στοῶν εἰς ὄνομα Πατρὸς καὶ Υἱοῦ καὶ ἁγίου
Πνεύματος." Παρευθὺ δὲ ἀφανὴς ἐγεγόνει καὶ καταπλα-
γεὶς ὁ μαΐστωρ παρεγένετο πρὸς τὸ παλάτιον καὶ ἀντέλεγε
τῷ βασιλεῖ αὐστηρῶς ὅτι "σύ, βασιλεῦ, λόγον ἕνα οὐκ
ἔχεις· μέχρι τῆς ἄρτι ἐβόας ποιεῖν με μίαν στοάν, ἄλλοτε
δὲ δύο ἐν τῷ θυσιαστηρίῳ, καὶ ὅταν ἐτελείωσα τὸ ἔργον,

expected the eunuch would come to him, but as he did not come, the emperor sent his attendant to the eunuch. And when he found the place where he had seen the palaces completely uninhabited, he returned and told the emperor everything. He was astonished and understood, and said, "Truly, what has happened here was a miracle of God, so that we may understand," and praised God greatly.

When the holy presbytery was about to be completed 12 and to be lit by galleries with glazed windows, he instructed the engineer that the apse should have a single vault; but then he changed his mind and ordered that it should have two openings and two arches to reduce the weight, for they had not set up a centering there, just as in the narthex and the aisles of the church.[37] But since the other craftsmen objected, saying that one vault would light the presbytery, the master builder was troubled about what he should do, since at one time the emperor said that there should be one arch, and at other times that there should be two. And as he stood there in distress, an angel of the Lord appeared to him on a Wednesday at the fifth hour in the guise of Justinian, with imperial vestments and red boots, and said to the craftsman, "I want you to make the apse for me with three lights by means of three galleries, in the name of the Father, the Son and the Holy Spirit." Immediately he disappeared; the master builder was astonished and went to the palace, and reproached the emperor with harsh words, saying, "You, emperor, do not speak with one tongue. Until recently, you told me to make one gallery in the presbytery, another time two, and when I finished the work, you came to me and said, 'Il-

παρέστης μοι λέγων ὅτι 'ἐν τρισὶ καμάραις φώτισον τὸ
θυσιαστήριον διὰ τὴν τῆς Τριάδος πίστιν.'" Ὡς δὲ ἐγνώρισεν ὁ βασιλεὺς ὅτι τῇ αὐτῇ ἡμέρᾳ καὶ ὥρᾳ ἐκ τοῦ
παλατίου αὐτοῦ οὐκ ἐξῆλθε, ἀκριβῶς ἐπέγνω ὅτι "ἄγγελος
Κυρίου ἦν ὁ λαλήσας σοι, καὶ ὡς εἶπέν σοι, οὕτως καὶ
ποίησον."

13   Πάντες δὲ οἱ πινσοὶ ἔξωθεν καὶ ἔσωθεν ὑπὸ σιδηρῶν
μοχλῶν κρατοῦνται ἐγχυλιασμένοι πρὸς τὸ ἀλλήλους
κρατεῖν καὶ εἶναι ἀμετακινήτους. Ἡ δὲ ἔμπλασις αὐτῶν
πάντων τῶν πινσῶν μετὰ ἐλαίου καὶ ἀσβέστου· καὶ οὕτως
ἐπάνω ἀνέστησεν τὰς ποικίλας ὀρθομαρμαρώσεις.

14   Ἀπέστειλε δὲ ὁ βασιλεὺς Τρώϊλον κουβικουλάριον καὶ
Θεόδωρον ἔπαρχον καὶ Βασιλίδην κυαίστορα ἐν τῇ Ῥόδῳ
νήσῳ καὶ ἔκαμνον ἐκεῖ μετὰ τῆς πηλοῦ βήσαλα ἰσόσταθμα
καὶ ἰσόμηκα παμμεγέθη σφραγίζοντα οὕτως· ὁ Θεὸς ἐν
μέσῳ αὐτῆς καὶ οὐ σαλευθήσεται· βοηθήσει αὐτῇ ὁ Θεὸς τὸ
πρὸς πρωῒ πρωΐ. Καὶ διαμετροῦντες αὐτῶν τὴν ποσότητα
ἀπέστελλον τῷ βασιλεῖ. Ὁ δὲ σταθμὸς τῶν δώδεκα
βησάλων ἐκείνων ἡμετέρων βησάλων ἐστὶ σταθμὸς ἑνὸς
διὰ τὸ εἶναι τὴν πηλὸν ἐκείνην ἐλαφρὰν πάνυ καὶ
σπογγοειδῆ καὶ κοῦφον καὶ λευκόχροιον. Διὸ ὁ λόγος
ἰδιωτικὸς ἐμφέρεται ὅτι κισσηρίου ἐστὶν ὁ τροῦλος· ἀλλ'
οὐκ ἔστιν μέν, ἐλαφρὸν δὲ ὑπάρχει. Μετ' αὐτῶν δὲ
ἀνοικοδομήσαντες τὰς τέσσαρας μεγίστας ἀψίδας καὶ
ἀρξάμενοι κυλίειν τὸν τροῦλον ἕως δώδεκα βησάλων ἐτίθουν καὶ ἀναμεταξὺ τῶν δώδεκα βησάλων ἐποίουν οἱ
ἱερεῖς εὐχὴν περὶ συστάσεως ἐκκλησίας· καὶ ἐποίουν οἱ
κτίσται κατὰ δώδεκα βήσαλα ὀπήν, ἐμβάλλοντες ταῖς
ὀπαῖς τίμια καὶ ἅγια λείψανα διαφόρων ἁγίων, ἕως οὗ

luminate the presbytery with three vaults because of our belief in the Trinity.'" As the emperor realized that he had not
left his palace at this day and hour, he understood well that
"the one who talked to you was an angel of the Lord, so do as
he told you."

All the piers outside and inside are held by iron tie-rods ₁₃
set in cast lead, so that they hold together and do not move.
The plaster of all the piers was of oil mixed with lime, and
upon it he set up the multicolored marble revetments.

The emperor sent Troilos the chamberlain, Theodore the ₁₄
prefect and Basilides the *quaestor* to the island of Rhodes,
and there they made enormous bricks of clay, of equal
weight and size which they stamped as follows: *God is within
her, and she shall not be shaken. God shall help her at break of day.*[38]
And, after counting their number, they sent them to the emperor. The weight of twelve such bricks is the same as that
of one of our bricks because that clay is very light, spongy,
delicate, and white in color. Therefore a popular story is told
that the dome is made of pumice, but this is not the case,
just that it is light. With these <bricks> they built the four
huge arches, and when they started to vault the dome, they
laid up to twelve courses of bricks, and between each twelve
the priests said a prayer for the construction of the church.
And every twelve bricks the builders made a hole and inserted sacred and holy relics of different saints in the holes

ἐτελείωσαν τὸν τροῦλον· ἦν δὲ νεωτερικὸς ὄρθιος ἱστάμενος.

15 Καὶ εἶθ' οὕτως πληρώσαντες τὰς τερπνὰς καὶ περικαλλεῖς ὀρθομαρμαρώσεις, κατεχρύσωσε τάς τε ζεύξεις τῶν ὀρθομαρμαρώσεων καὶ τὰς κεφαλὰς τῶν κιονίων καὶ τὰ λακαρικὰ καὶ τοὺς κοσμήτας τῶν ὑπερῴων τῶν τε διορόφων καὶ τριορόφων. Ἐχρύσωσε δὲ πάντα ἐκ χρυσίου καθαροῦ ὑπερτελείου, τὸ σύμπαχον³ τοῦ χρυσώματος δακτύλων δύο· τοὺς δὲ ὀρόφους πάντας ἀπό τε τῶν ὑπερῴων καὶ τῶν ἐκ πλαγίου καὶ τοῦ ναοῦ καὶ τῶν πέριξ καὶ τῶν τεσσάρων ναρθήκων κατεχρύσωσε [τὰ ὄροφα] ἐξ ὑελίνου χρυσοῦ λαμπροτάτου καὶ μέχρι τῶν πέριξ προαυλίων. [Κατεχρύσωσε τά τε ὑπερῷα καὶ τοὺς κίονας καὶ τὰς ὀρθομαρμαρώσεις.] Τὸ δὲ ἔδαφος τοῦ ναοῦ κατεκόσμησε διὰ ποικίλων καὶ πολυτελῶν μαρμάρων· καὶ στιλπνώσας κατέθηκε καταστρώσας αὐτά· τὰ δὲ πλάγια τὰ ἔξω καὶ τὰ πέριξ κατέστρωσε διὰ λευκῶν λίθων πολυτίμων μεγίστων.

16 Τὸ δὲ ἅγιον θυσιαστήριον ἐξ ἀργύρου λαμπροῦ· τά τε στήθεα καὶ κίονας ἀργύρῳ πάντα περιέκλεισε σὺν τοῖς πυλεῶσιν αὐτῶν, πάντα ἀργυρᾶ καὶ χρυσέμβαφα. Τραπέζας δὲ ἀργυρᾶς τέσσαρας τῷ ἁγίῳ θυσιαστηρίῳ ἔστησεν ἐπὶ τοὺς κίονας καὶ αὐτοὺς κατεχρύσωσε. Τὰς δὲ βάσεις τὰς ἑπτὰ τῶν ἱερέων ἐν αἷς καθέζονται, σὺν τοῦ ἀρχιερέως θρόνου καὶ τῶν τεσσάρων κιόνων τῶν ἀργυρέων κατεχρύσωσε, στήσας ἑκατέρῳ μέρει ἀνὰ δύο ἐν τῷ εἰσπορεύεσθαι ἐν τῷ εἰλήματι τῷ καλουμένῳ κυκλίῳ, ὅπερ ἐστὶν ὑποκάτω τῶν βαθμίδων· τοῦτο ἅγια ἁγίων προσηγόρευσε. Ἔστησε

until they finished the dome. And it stood in a novel upright fashion.

And afterward, when they had finished the delightful and 15 most beautiful marble revetments, he gilded the joints of the revetments, the column capitals, the carvings,[39] and the cornices of the second and third galleries.[40] He gilded all with perfectly pure gold, with a gilding two fingers thick. And as for the entire ceiling of the galleries, the lateral parts, the nave and all around, and of the four narthexes, he gilded [the ceiling] with gleaming gold glass,[41] all the way to the surrounding forecourts. [He also gilded the galleries, the columns and the revetments.][42] He decorated the pavement of the church with various precious marbles that he polished and laid down, thus making the floor. He paved the outer lateral sides and the surrounding areas with very big, precious slabs of white marble.

The holy presbytery was of shining silver. He sheathed 16 the parapets and columns completely in silver together with their doors, all of silver and plated with gold. He set up four silver tables on the columns in the holy presbytery, and gilded them too. He also gilded the seven steps on which the priests sit, together with the bishop's throne and the four silver columns, setting up two of them on each side at the entrance to the tunnel called the circle, which is underneath the steps;[43] this he called the Holy of Holies. Also he set up

δὲ κίονας εὐμεγέθεις καὶ αὐτοὺς ἀργυροχρύσους σὺν τοῦ κιβουρίου καὶ τῶν κρίνων. Τὸ δὲ κιβούριον ἀργυροέγκαυστον ἐποίησεν. Ἐπάνω δὲ τοῦ κιβουρίου ἔστησε σφαῖραν ὁλόχρυσον ἔχουσαν σταθμὸν χρυσοῦ λίτρας ριη΄ καὶ κρίνα χρυσᾶ στήσανα λίτρας Ϛ΄· καὶ ἐπάνω αὐτῶν σταυρὸν χρυσοῦν μετὰ λίθων πολυτελῶν καὶ δυσπορίστων, ὅστις σταυρὸς εἷλκε σταθμὸν χρυσίου λίτρας ο΄.

17   Ἐποίησε δὲ μηχανὴν τοιαύτην· βουλόμενος γὰρ κρείττονα τὴν ἁγίαν τράπεζαν καὶ πολυτελεστέραν ποιῆσαι ὑπὲρ χρυσίου προσεκαλέσατο ἐπιστήμονας πολλοὺς εἰρηκὼς αὐτοῖς τοῦτο. Οἱ δὲ ἔφησαν αὐτῷ· "εἰς χωνευτήριον ἐμβάλωμεν χρυσόν, ἄργυρον, λίθους τιμίους καὶ παντοίους καὶ μαργαρίτας καὶ ζάμβυκας, χαλκόν, ἤλεκτρον, μόλιβδον, σίδηρον, κασσίτερον, ὕελον καὶ λοιπὴν πᾶσαν μεταλλικὴν ὕλην·" καὶ τρίψαντες ἀμφότερα αὐτῶν εἰς ὅλμους καὶ δήσαντες, ἐπὶ τὸ χωνευτήριον ἔχυσαν. Καὶ ἀναμαξάμενον τὸ πῦρ, ἀνέλαβον ταῦτα οἱ τεχνῖται ἐκ τοῦ πυρὸς καὶ ἔχυσαν εἰς τύπον· καὶ ἐγένετο χυτὴ πάμμιγος ἡ ἁγία τράπεζα ἀτίμητος· καὶ εἶθ᾽ οὕτως ἔστησεν αὐτήν· ὑποκάτω δὲ αὐτῆς ἔστησε κίονας καὶ αὐτοὺς ὁλοχρύσους μετὰ λίθων πολυτελῶν καὶ χυμεύσεως, καὶ τὴν πέριξ κλίμακα, ἐν ᾗ ἵστανται οἱ ἱερεῖς εἰς τὸ ἀσπάσασθαι τὴν ἁγίαν τράπεζαν, καὶ αὐτὴν ὁλοάργυρον. Τὴν δὲ θάλασσαν τῆς ἁγίας τραπέζης ἐξ ἀτιμήτων λίθων πεποίηκε καὶ κατεχρύσωσεν αὐτήν. Τίς γὰρ θεάσηται τὸ εἶδος τῆς ἁγίας τραπέζης καὶ οὐκ ἐκπλαγείη; ἢ τίς δυνήσηται κατανοῆσαι ταύτην διὰ τὸ πολλὰς χροιὰς καὶ στιλπνότητας ἐναλλάσσειν, ὡς ὁρᾶσθαι τὸ ταύτης εἶδός ποτε μὲν χρυσίζον, ἐν ἄλλῳ δὲ τόπῳ

big silver-gilt columns together with the ciborium and the lilies. The ciborium he made of silver and niello. On top of the ciborium he set up a globe of pure gold, which weighed 118 pounds, and golden lilies that weighed six pounds, and above them a golden cross with precious and rare stones, which cross, being of gold, weighed seventy pounds.

He also made the following contrivance. Wishing to make the holy altar table better and more precious than gold, he consulted many wise men and told them so. They said to him. "Let us throw gold, silver, various precious stones, pearls and mother of pearl, bronze, electrum, lead, iron, tin, glass and every other metallic material into a melting furnace." Having crushed and bound all of these in mortars, they poured them into the melting furnace. And when the fire had kneaded these together, the craftsmen took them out of the fire and poured them into a casting mold. And so the altar table was cast, made up of all materials and priceless. And then he set it up in this manner, and placed columns of pure gold under it with precious stones and enamels; and he made the surrounding stairs, on which the priests stand when they kiss the holy altar table, also of pure silver. He made the liturgical basin *(thalassa)*[44] of the altar table of priceless stones and gilded it. So who can behold the beauty of the holy altar table and not be amazed? Or who can comprehend it as its many colors and brilliances change, so that it appears sometimes as gold, in other places as silver,

ἀργυρίζον, εἰς ἄλλο σαμφειρίζον, ἐξαστράπτον καὶ ἁπλῶς
εἰπεῖν ἀποστέλλον οβ' χροιὰς κατὰ τὰς φύσεις τῶν τε
λίθων καὶ μαργαρίτων καὶ πάντων τῶν μετάλλων;

18   Ἐποίησε δὲ καὶ πυλεῶνας, κάτωθεν καὶ ἄνωθεν [ἐξ ἐλε-
φαντίνων μεγάλων γλυπτῶν κεχρυσωμένων]⁴ τὸν ἀριθμὸν
τξε'. Ἐν δὲ τῇ εἰσόδῳ τῇ πρώτῃ τοῦ λουτῆρος ἐποίησε
πυλεῶνας ἠλέκτρους καὶ ἐν τῷ νάρθηκι ἠλέκτρους πύλας
ἐμμέτρους. Ἐν δὲ τῷ δευτέρῳ νάρθηκι ἐποίησεν ἐλεφαν-
τίνους πύλας <τρεῖς κατὰ τὸ ἀριστερὸν μέρος καὶ τρεῖς
κατὰ τὸ δεξιόν· μέσον δὲ αὐτῶν ἔστησε>⁵ καὶ πυλεῶνας
τρεῖς, δύο ἐμμέτρους καὶ μέσον τῶν δύο μεγίστην ἀργυ-
ρέαν χρυσέμβαφον, τὰς πάσας πύλας καταχρυσώσας· ἔσωθεν δὲ τῶν τριῶν πυλῶν ἀντὶ ξύλων κοινῶν ἔβαλεν ἐκ τῶν
τῆς κιβωτοῦ ξύλων.

19   Βουλόμενος δὲ καὶ τὸν πάτον ὁλοάργυρον ποιῆσαι, οὐ
συνεβούλευσαν αὐτῷ διὰ τὸ εἰς τὰ ἔσχατα πένητας ἁρπάσαι
αὐτά. Οἱ δὲ αὐτὸν ἀναπείσαντες ἦσαν Ἀθηναῖοι φιλόσοφοι
καὶ ἀστρολόγοι, Μαξιμιανὸς καὶ Ἱερόθεος καὶ Σύμβουλος,
λέγοντες ὅτι ἐν ταῖς ἐσχάταις ἡμέραις βασιλεῖαι ἀμυδραὶ
ἐλεύσονται καὶ ταῦτα ἀφέλωνται· καὶ ἐκ τῆς βουλῆς αὐτῶν
ἔασε τοῦτο.

20   Καθ' ἑκάστην δὲ ἡμέραν ἔβαλλεν ὁ βασιλεὺς εἰς τὸν
χοῦν χιλιάδας δύο μιλιαρίσια· καὶ ὅτε ἐπλήρουν τὸ ἔργον
οἱ τεχνῖται τῇ ἑσπέρᾳ, ἐσκύλευον τὸν χοῦν καὶ εὕρισκον
τὰ μιλιαρίσια. Τοῦτο δὲ εἰς χαρὰν τοῦ λαοῦ ὁ βασιλεὺς
ἐποίησε καὶ εἰς προθυμίαν.—Καὶ ἡ μὲν ὕλη ἀπεσωρεύθη,
καθὼς προεῖπον, εἰς χρόνους ἑπτὰ ἥμισυ καὶ ἀπετέθη. Ὁ
δὲ ναὸς ἐκτίζετο καὶ ἐτελειώθη παρὰ τῶν προειρημένων

elsewhere gleaming with sapphire—radiating and, in a word, sending out seventy-two colors according to the nature of the stones, pearls and all the metals?

He also made doorways below and above [from big gilded ivory reliefs][45] to the number of 365. At the first entrance of the atrium he made doorways of electrum, and the same number of doors in the narthex, also of electrum. In the second narthex he made three ivory doors <on the left side and three on the right, and in the middle he also set up>[46] three doorways, two matching ones and between the two a very large one of gilded silver, and gilded all the doors. Inside these three doors he placed wood from the Ark instead of ordinary wood.[47]

When he also wanted to make the whole floor of pure silver, they dissuaded him because the poor would steal it in the end. Those who convinced him were philosophers and astrologers from Athens, Maximianos, Hierotheos and Symboulos,[48] saying that in the last days weak reigns would come and this silver would be taken away, and on their advice he refrained from doing it.

Every day the emperor mixed two thousand silver pieces into the sand. And in the evening, when their work was finished, the workers used to search the sand for the silver pieces. The emperor did this for the enjoyment of the work crews and to keep them in good spirits.[49] And as I have said before, the material was stored and set aside for seven and a half years. The church was then built with care and much

ἀνδρῶν δέκα χιλιάδων μετὰ ἐπιμελείας καὶ πολλῆς σπουδῆς εἰς χρόνους ἐννέα παρὰ μῆνας δύο, ὁμοῦ χρόνοι ις' καὶ
μῆνες δ'.

21   Τὸν δὲ ἄμβωνα ἐποίησε σὺν τῆς σωλέας μετὰ σαρδο-
νύχων, ἐντιθέμενος καὶ πολυτίμους λίθους σὺν κιόνων
ὁλοχρύσων καὶ κρύων καὶ ἰασπίων καὶ σαμφείρων· καὶ
χρυσίον πολὺ ἐνέδυσε τὰ ἐπάνω τῆς σωλέας. Εἶχε δὲ τροῦλον χρυσοῦν μετὰ μαργαριταρίων καὶ λυχνιταρίων καὶ
σμαράγδων. Ὁ δὲ σταυρὸς τοῦ ἄμβωνος ἔστενε χρυσοῦ
λίτρας ρ'· εἶχε δὲ καὶ σειστὰ καὶ λυχνίτας σὺν μαργαριταρίων
ἀπιδωτῶν· ὁλόχρυσα δὲ πετάσια ἀντὶ στηθέων εἶχεν ἄνω
ὁ ἄμβων.

22   Τὸ δὲ στομίδιον αὐτὸ τοῦ φρέατος ἤχθη ἀπὸ Σαμα-
ρείας· τούτου χάριν ἐκλήθη ἅγιον Φρέαρ, ὅτι ἐν αὐτῷ
ὡμίλησε τῇ Σαμαρίτιδι ὁ Χριστός. Αἱ δὲ τέσσαρες σάλπιγγες αἱ χαλκαῖ, ἃς ἔστησεν ἐν τῷ Φρέατι τῷ ἁγίῳ, ἀπὸ
Ἱεριχὼ ἐκόμισεν αὐτάς, ἃς εἶχον τότε οἱ ἄγγελοι † εἰς
μίμησιν, ὅτε ἔπεσον τὰ τείχη Ἱεριχώ. Ὁ δὲ τίμιος σταυρὸς
ὁ ἱστάμενος σήμερον ἐν τῷ σκευοφυλακείῳ τὸ μέτρον ἐστὶ
τῆς ἡλικίας τοῦ Κυρίου ἡμῶν Ἰησοῦ Χριστοῦ· ὃς ἀκριβῶς
ἐμετρήθη παρὰ πιστῶν καὶ ἀξιολόγων ἀνδρῶν ἐν
Ἱερουσαλήμ. Καὶ διὰ τοῦτο ἐνέδυσεν αὐτὸν ἄργυρον καὶ
λίθους παντοίους καὶ κατεχρύσωσεν αὐτόν· καὶ μέχρι τῆς
σήμερον ἰάσεις ποιεῖ νοσημάτων καὶ δαίμονας ἐλαύνει. Ἕν
δὲ ἕκαστον κιόνιον τῶν ἄνω καὶ τῶν κάτω ἅγιον λείψανον
ἔχει ἐνθρονιασμένον.

23   Ἐποίησε δὲ καὶ σκεύη ὁλόχρυσα, τῶν δώδεκα ἑορτῶν
ἄλλα καὶ ἄλλα, ἀπό τε εὐαγγελίων ἱερῶν, χερνιβοξέστων,

zeal by the aforementioned ten thousand men and completed within nine years minus two months, all together sixteen years and four months.[50]

He made the ambo and its *solea*[51] of sardonyx, providing ²¹
it with precious stones, columns of pure gold, crystal, jasper and sapphire; and he revetted the upper part of the *solea* with much gold. <The ambo> had a golden dome with pearls, rubies and emeralds. The golden cross of the ambo weighed one hundred pounds; it also had pendants of rubies and pear-shaped pearls. Instead of parapets, the ambo had a canopy of pure gold on top.

The wellhead of the well was brought from Samaria, for ²²
which reason it was called the Holy Well, for Christ had spoken to the Samaritan woman there. He brought the four bronze trumpets, which he displayed at this Holy Well, from Jericho, imitations of those[52] which the angels had when the walls of Jericho fell. The venerable cross which stands today in the treasury is the measure of the height of our Lord Jesus Christ, who was measured exactly by pious and worthy men in Jerusalem.[53] And therefore he covered it with silver and stones of all kinds and gilded it. And up to this day it heals diseases and drives away demons. Every single column of those above and below has a holy relic enshrined in it.

He also made vessels of pure gold, those for the twelve ²³
feasts[54] and others, consisting of holy Gospel books,[55] ba-

ὀρκιολίων, δισκοποτηρίων, δίσκων· ἐποίησε δὲ πάντα ὁλόχρυσα διὰ λίθων καὶ μαργάρων· ὁ δὲ ἀριθμὸς τῶν ἱερῶν
σκευῶν χιλιὰς α'. Ἐνδυτὰς διὰ λίθων χρυσᾶς σωληνωτὰς
τ', στέμματα ρ', ἵνα ἔχωσι ἐν μιᾷ ἑκάστῃ ἑορτῇ ἴδια· ποτη-
ροκαλύμματα, δισκοκαλύμματα ὁλόχρυσα διὰ μαργαριταρίων καὶ λίθων ἀτιμήτων χιλιάδα α'· εὐαγγέλια, ἔχοντα
<σταθμὸν> ἀνὰ κεντηναρίων δύο, εἴκοσι καὶ τέσσαρα·
θυμιατήρια ὁλόχρυσα λς' διὰ λίθων, λυχνίας χρυσᾶς τ',
ἐχούσας σταθμὸν ἀνὰ λιτρῶν μ', πολυκάνδηλα καὶ βοτρύ-
δια τοῦ νάρθηκος καὶ τοῦ ἄμβωνος καὶ τοῦ βήματος
ὁλόχρυσα σὺν τῶν δύο γυναικίτων χιλιάδας ἕξ. Ἐπεκύρωσε
δὲ καὶ κτήματα τξε' ἀπὸ Αἰγύπτου καὶ Ἰνδίας καὶ πάσης
ἑῴας καὶ δύσεως ὑπάρχοντα εἰς διοίκησιν τοῦ ναοῦ· ἐκτυ-
πώσας μίαν ἑκάστην ἑορτὴν δίδοσθαι ἔλαιον μέτρα χιλιάδα
μίαν καὶ οἴνου μέτρα τ', ἄρτους τῆς προθέσεως χιλίους.
Ὁμοίως καὶ τὰς ἐφημέρους ἐξέθετο κληρώσας ἱερεῖς τε καὶ
ἕως ἐσχάτου τῶν ὑπουργούντων τῷ ναῷ χιλιάδα μίαν,
ᾀδούσας ρ', μεριζομένας εἰς δύο ἑβδομάδας. Δέδωκε δὲ τῷ
κλήρῳ κέλλας εἰς τὰ πέριξ κατὰ τὴν τάξιν αὐτῶν καὶ ταῖς
ᾀδούσαις σκηνώματα, δύο ἀσκητήρια.

24   Σταυροὺς δὲ ἐποίησε πέντε στένοντας χρυσοῦ ἀνὰ κεντηνάριον ἕν, καλλωπίσας αὐτοὺς ἀπὸ παντοίων λίθων
πολυτελῶν ὡς διατιμᾶσθαι τούτους κεντηνάρια η'· καὶ
μανουάλια δύο ὁλόχρυσα διὰ λίθων σὺν μεγίστοις μαργα-
ριταρίοις, ἃ καὶ ἀπετιμήθησαν χρυσοῦ κεντηνάρια ε'· καὶ
ἕτερα μανουάλια β' ὁλόκρυα γλυπτὰ παμμεγέθη· τοὺς δὲ
πόδας αὐτῶν ὁλοχρύσους τιμωμένους χρυσοῦ κεντηνάριον
ἕν. Καὶ ἐποίησε φατλία διάχρυσα διὰ λίθων τέσσαρα

sins, pitchers, sets of chalices and patens, and patens: he made all these of pure gold with stones and pearls, and the number of holy vessels was one thousand; three hundred golden pleated altar covers with precious stones and one hundred crowns[56] so that they should have a different one for every single feast day; one thousand chalice covers and paten covers of pure gold with pearls and priceless stones; twenty-four Gospel books, <weighing> two hundredweights each; thirty-six censers of pure gold with precious stones; three hundred golden lamps weighing forty pounds each, six thousand candelabra and lamps in the form of a grapevine of pure gold for the narthex, the ambo, the sanctuary, and for the two women's galleries. He also bestowed 365 estates spread from Egypt to India and in all the east and west, to be administered by the church. He decreed that one thousand measures of oil be given at every feast day, and three hundred measures of wine, and one thousand loaves for the offering. In a similar way, he also fixed for the daily services in the church, from the priests down to the last servant, one thousand <people>, and one hundred female singers, divided into two weeks.[57] He gave the clerics dwellings in the vicinity according to their rank, and two convents as domiciles for the female singers.

He made five crosses of gold, weighing one hundred- 24 weight each, decorating them with various costly stones so that they were valued at eight hundredweights each; and two candle stands of pure gold with precious stones and huge pearls which have been valued at five hundredweights of gold; and another two very large candle stands of carved crystal, with feet of pure gold, each worth one hundredweight of gold. He also made four golden candlesticks with

τιμώμενα κεντηνάριον ἕν, ἵνα ἵστανται ἐπάνω τῶν χρυσῶν
καὶ κρύων μανουαλίων. Ἕτερα δὲ εὐμεγέθη ἐποίησεν μανουάλια ὁλοάργυρα ν' καὶ ἀνδρόμηκα ὁλοάργυρα σ' τοῦ
ἵστασθαι εἰς τὸ θυσιαστήριον.

25   Εἰς δὲ τὸν ἄμβωνα ἐξωδίασε χρόνου πάκτον, ὅπερ ἐλάμ-
βανεν ἐκ τῆς Αἰγύπτου μόνης, κεντηνάρια τξε'. Ταῦτα εἰς
τὸν ἄμβωνα ἐξωδίασεν σὺν τῆς σωλέας· πάκτα γὰρ ἐλάμβανε μέχρι χίλια κεντηνάρια· ὁ γὰρ μέγας Κωνσταντῖνος
ἐτύπωσεν <πάκτα λαμβάνειν> ἀπὸ Σαρβάρου Περσῶν
βασιλέως καὶ ἑτέρων πολλῶν. Ὁ δὲ ναὸς ὅλος σὺν τῶν ἔξω
καὶ τῶν πέριξ ἔχει ἔξοδον χωρὶς τῶν ἱερῶν σκευῶν καὶ τῶν
λοιπῶν εἰδῶν καὶ τῶν κατὰ δωρεὰν προσελθόντων ἀπὸ
πάσης τῆς βασιλείας χρυσοῦ χάραγμα ὁμοῦ κεντηνάρια
,γσ'.

26   Ὁ δὲ Ἰουστινιανὸς μόνος ἤρξατο καὶ μόνος ἐτελείωσε
τὸν ναὸν μηδενὸς ἑτέρου συνδρομὴν ποιήσαντος ἢ οἱανδή-
ποτε οἰκοδομήν. Θαῦμα δὲ ἦν ἰδέσθαι ἐν τῷ κάλλει καὶ τῇ
ποικιλίᾳ τοῦ ναοῦ· ὅτι πάντοθεν ἔκ τε χρυσοῦ καὶ ἀργύρου
ἐξήστραπτεν. Καὶ εἰς τὸ ἔδαφος θαῦμα ἦν τοῖς εἰσιοῦσι ἐν
τῇ πολυποικιλίᾳ τῶν μαρμάρων δίκην θαλάσσης ὁρᾶσθαι
καὶ ποταμοῦ ἀεὶ ῥέοντα ὕδατα. Τὰς γὰρ τέσσαρας φίνας
τοῦ ναοῦ ὠνόμασε τοὺς τέσσαρας ποταμοὺς τοὺς ἐξερχο-
μένους ἐκ τοῦ παραδείσου καὶ ἔδωκεν νόμον κατὰ τὰς
ἁμαρτίας ἵστασθαι ἐν αὐτοῖς ἕνα ἕκαστον ἀφοριζομένους.—
Ἐποίησε δὲ καὶ εἰς τὴν φιάλην γύροθεν στοὰς φρεατίας
ιβ' καὶ λέοντας λιθίνους ἐρεύγεσθαι τὸ ὕδωρ εἰς ἀπόνιψιν
τοῦ κοινοῦ λαοῦ. Ἐν δὲ τῇ δεξιᾷ πλευρᾷ τοῦ δεξιοῦ γυναικίτου ἐποίησε θάλασσαν μέχρι σπιθαμῆς, ἵνα ἀνέρχεται τὸ

precious stones, each worth one hundredweight, to be placed upon the golden and crystal candle stands; and another fifty large candle stands of pure silver and two hundred, also of silver, the height of a man, to stand in the sanctuary.[58]

He spent a year's tributes from Egypt, that is 365 hundredweights, on the ambo; this is what he expended on the ambo and the *solea,* for he received up to one thousand hundredweights of tribute. For Constantine the Great had fixed that <tributes should be received> from the Persian king Sarbaros and many others.[59] The entire church, together with its outer parts and surroundings, represents an expense, without the holy vessels, other furnishings and objects donated from all parts of the empire, of all together 3,200 hundredweights of minted gold.   25

Justinian began the church alone and finished it alone without anyone else helping or building for him. It was wonderful to see the beauty and variety of the church, for it shone all around with gold and silver. And the floor, too, was a wonder for those who entered, for by the great variety of its marbles it appeared like the sea or the constantly flowing waters of a river. He called the four strips in the nave the four rivers that flow out of paradise,[60] and made a law that all excommunicated persons should stand upon them according to their sins. —He also made twelve waterspouts and stone lions around the fountain house spouting water for the ablutions of the common people. On the right-hand side of the women's section on the right[61] he made a pool   26

ὕδωρ, καὶ κλίμακα μίαν, ὅπως ἄνω τῆς θαλάσσης διέρχον-
ται οἱ ἱερεῖς. Ἔστησε δὲ κατὰ πρόσωπον δεξαμενὴν ὀμβρι-
αίαν ναμάτων καὶ ἔγλυψε λέοντας δώδεκα, παρδάλεις δώδεκα, δορκάδας δώδεκα, ἀετοὺς καὶ λαγωοὺς καὶ μόσχους
καὶ κορώνας καὶ αὐτοὺς ἀνὰ δώδεκα· καὶ ἐκ τῶν φαρύγγων
αὐτῶν ἐμεῖσθαι τὸ ὕδωρ διὰ μηχανημάτων εἰς τὸ τοὺς
ἱερεῖς νίπτεσθαι μόνον. Ἐκάλεσε δὲ τὸν τόπον Λεοντάριον·
καὶ μητατώριον, ὅπερ ἐκεῖσε ἀνήγειρεν κοιτῶνα ὡραῖον
διάχρυσον, ἵνα πορευομένου αὐτοῦ ἐν τῷ ναῷ ἐκεῖσε καθ-
εύδῃ. Τὴν δὲ ὡραιότητα καὶ τὴν ὑπερβολὴν τοῦ κάλλους
τοῦ κεχρυσωμένου καὶ διηργυρωμένου ναοῦ ἀπὸ ὀρόφους
ἕως ἐδάφους τίς διηγήσεται;

27   Ὅμως τελειώσας τὸν ναὸν καὶ τὰ ἱερὰ ἀναθήματα τῇ
κβ΄ τοῦ Δεκεμβρίου μηνὸς εἰσῆλθεν ἀπὸ τοῦ παλατίου
μετὰ προελεύσεως ἕως τῶν πυλῶν τοῦ Αὐγουστίωνος τῶν
ἐξερχομένων[6] εἰς τὸ ὡρολογεῖον, καθεζόμενος ἐφ᾽ ἅρματος
τετραΐππου καὶ ἔθυσε βόας ,α, πρόβατα ,ς καὶ ἐλάφους χ΄
καὶ σύας ,α, ὄρνεις καὶ ἀλεκτρυόνας ἀνὰ δέκα χιλιάδας.
Καὶ δέδωκε πένησι καὶ τοῖς δεομένοις σίτου μόδια τρισμύ-
ρια· ταῦτα δέδωκε τοῖς πένησιν τῇ ἡμέρᾳ ἐκείνῃ μέχρι
ὡρῶν γ΄, καὶ τότε εἰσώδευσεν ὁ βασιλεὺς Ἰουστινιανὸς
μετὰ τοῦ σταυροῦ καὶ τοῦ πατριάρχου Εὐτυχίου. Καὶ
ἀποδράσας ταῖς χερσὶ τοῦ πατριάρχου ἀπὸ τῶν βασιλικῶν
πυλῶν ἔδραμε μόνος μέχρι τοῦ ἄμβωνος καὶ ἐκτείνας τὰς
χεῖρας αὐτοῦ εἶπε· "Δόξα τῷ Θεῷ τῷ καταξιώσαντί με τοιοῦτον ἔργον ἀποτελέσαι· ἐνίκησά σε, Σολομών." Καὶ μετὰ
τὸ εἰσοδεῦσαι ἐποίησεν ὑπατείαν καὶ δέδωκε κεντηνάρια
τρία τῷ λαῷ Στρατηγίου μαγίστρου ταῦτα χύνοντος εἰς

in which the water was one span deep, and a walkway, so that the priests could walk over the pool. Facing the pool he set up a cistern of rainwater, and he carved twelve lions, twelve leopards, twelve deer, eagles and hares, calves and crows, twelve each. Out of their throats water was spouted by means of a device for the ablution of the priests alone. He called this place "the Little Lion," and constructed the changing room there,[62] a beautiful chamber covered with gold, so that, whenever he went to the church, he could rest there. Who can relate the loveliness and the excessive beauty of this church, gilded and sheathed with silver from ceiling to floor?

After the completion of the church and the holy offer- 27 ings, on the 22nd of December he came in from the palace in a procession up to the doors of the Augoustion which lead out to the clock house, sitting on a chariot drawn by four horses, and offered one thousand oxen, six thousand sheep, six hundred deer and one thousand boars, and ten thousand each of chickens and roosters.[63] And he gave thirty thousand bushels of grain to the poor and those in need. He distributed these to the poor on that day for three hours, and then the emperor Justinian entered with the cross and the patriarch Eutychios. And releasing the hands of the patriarch, he rushed on his own from the imperial gates to the ambo, stretched out his hands and said, "Glory be to God who deemed me worthy to accomplish such a work. I have defeated you, Solomon!"[64] And after entering, he made a consular offering and gave three hundredweights <of coins> to the people, with the *magistros* Strategios pouring them

τὸ ἔδαφος· καὶ τῇ ἐπαύριον ἐποίησε τὰ ἀνοίξια τοῦ ναοῦ, τοσαῦτα καὶ πλείονα ὁλοκαυτώματα θύσας, καὶ μέχρι τῶν ἁγίων Θεοφανίων δι' ἡμερῶν πεντεκαίδεκα κλητορεύων πάντας καὶ ῥογεύων καὶ εὐχαριστῶν τῷ Κυρίῳ. Οὕτως ἐτελείωσε τὸ ἐφετὸν ἔργον αὐτοῦ.

28   Διήρκεσε δὲ ὁ νεωτερικὸς τροῦλος ὁ ὑπὸ τοῦ μεγάλου Ἰουστινιανοῦ κτισθεὶς καὶ ὁ ἄμβων ὁ πολυτίμητος καὶ πολύολβος καὶ πολυθαύμαστος σὺν τῆς σωλέας καὶ τοῦ ποικίλου πάτου τοῦ ναοῦ χρόνους ιζ'. Μετὰ δὲ τὸν θάνατον τοῦ Ἰουστινιανοῦ ἐκράτησεν Ἰουστῖνος ὁ ἀνεψιὸς αὐτοῦ τῆς βασιλείας καὶ εἰς τὸν δεύτερον χρόνον αὐτοῦ ἡμέρᾳ ε', ὥρᾳ ἕκτῃ τῆς ἡμέρας, ἐγένετο πεσεῖν τὸν τροῦλον καὶ συντρίψαι τὸν ἀξιοθαύμαστον ἄμβωνα καὶ τὴν σωλέαν, τούς τε σαρδονύχους καὶ σαμφείρους καὶ ζάμβυκας καὶ μαργαρίτας σὺν τῶν χρυσῶν στηθέων καὶ κρύων καὶ κιόνων ὁλοαργύρων, καὶ τὸν πολύτιμον πάτον· αἱ δὲ τέσσαρες ἁψίδες καὶ οἱ κίονες καὶ τὰ λοιπὰ κτίσματα ἔμειναν ἀσάλευτα. Ὁ δὲ αὐτὸς βασιλεὺς προσκαλεσάμενος τὸν ζῶντα καὶ καμόντα ἐκεῖσε μηχανικὸν ἐπυνθάνετο παρ' αὐτοῦ, τί τὸ συμβὰν εἰς τὸ χαλάσαι τὸν τροῦλον. Ὁ δέ, φησίν, εἶπεν "ὅτι ὁ θεῖός σου σπεύσας ἐπῆρεν τοὺς ἀντινύκτας τοὺς ὄντας ἐν τῷ τρούλῳ ξυλίνους καὶ ταχέως ἐμουσείωσεν αὐτόν, καὶ ὅτι ὑψηλὸν ἐποίησεν αὐτὸν πρὸς τὸ πανταχῇ ὁρᾶσθαι καὶ ὅτι τὰς σκαλώσεις κόπτοντες οἱ τεχνῖται ἔρριπτον, καὶ ἐκ τοῦ βάρους ἐσπαράσσοντο τὰ θεμέλια καὶ ἔλαβε † πέψιν ὁ τροῦλος." Ἔφησαν δὲ οἱ τεχνῖται τῷ βασιλεῖ καὶ εἶπον αὐτῷ ταῦτα· "εἰ κελεύεις, δέσποτα, ἵνα γένηται ὁ τροῦλος ἐπίπεδος κυμβαλικός,

out on the floor. And on the following day he inaugurated the church, sacrificing again the same number and more of burned offerings, and until the holy Epiphany he offered hospitality to all for fifteen days, distributing money and thanking the Lord. And so he accomplished his desired goal.

The innovative dome built by Justinian the Great, the 28 precious ambo worthy of all blessing and admiration, together with the *solea* and the variegated floor of the church, lasted seventeen years. After Justinian's death, his nephew Justin (II, 565–578) held power, and in his second year, on a Thursday at the sixth hour of the day, it happened that the dome collapsed[65] and crushed the wondrous ambo and the *solea,* with all their sardonyx, sapphires, mother of pearl and pearls, together with the parapets of gold and crystal, the columns of pure silver and the precious pavement. The four arches, the columns, and the remaining structure, however, remained unshaken. So the same emperor called in the engineer who was still alive and had worked there, and asked him what had happened that the dome was destroyed. And he said, "your uncle removed the wooden supports[66] that were in the dome too hastily and covered it with mosaic too quickly, and made it too high so that it would be seen from everywhere. Also, when the workmen cut down the scaffolding, they threw it down, and from its weight the foundations were shattered, and so the dome became unstable." The craftsmen also spoke to the emperor and told him this: "If you order, lord, that the dome be made flat like a cymbal,

ἀπόστειλον ἐν νήσῳ τῇ Ῥόδῳ, καθὼς καὶ ὁ θεῖός σου
ἐποίησεν, καὶ ἐκ τοῦ αὐτοῦ πηλοῦ καὶ τῆς αὐτῆς σφραγίδος
ἰσόσταθμα βήσαλα τοῦ πρώτου μέτρου ἃς ἀγάγωσι." Καὶ
προσέταξεν ὁ βασιλεύς, καὶ ἤγαγον τὰ βήσαλα ἀπὸ τῆς
Ῥόδου καθὼς καὶ τὸ πρότερον· οὕτως τοίνυν καὶ πάλιν
ἐκαμαρώθη ὁ τροῦλος· κόψαντες ἐκ τοῦ προτέρου ὕψους
τοῦ τρούλου ὀργυιὰς εʹ, ποιήσαντες αὐτὸν τυμπανικόν,
πτοούμενοι, ἵνα μὴ τάχιον πάλιν καταπέσῃ, ἐάσαντες τὰ
ξύλα καὶ τοὺς κριοὺς τῶν ἀντινύκτων χρόνον ἕνα, ἕως οὗ
ἔγνωσαν ποιῆσαι πῆξιν τὸν τροῦλον. Τὸν δὲ ἄμβωνα καὶ
τὴν σωλέαν μὴ δυνάμενος ποιῆσαι τοιοῦτον πολυέξοδον
καὶ πολύτιμον, ἐποίησεν αὐτὸν οὐδαμινὸν διὰ λίθων καὶ
κιόνων ἀργυροενδύτων καὶ στηθέων ἀργυρῶν καὶ βήλων
καὶ περιφερίων ἀργυρῶν μετὰ καὶ τῆς σωλέας. Τροῦλον
δὲ τοῦ ἄμβωνος οὐκ ἠθέλησε ποιῆσαι, ὡς εἶπεν, διὰ τὴν
πολλὴν ἔξοδον. Εἰς δὲ τὸν πάτον οὐκ ἠδύνατο εὑρεῖν τοι-
αῦτα πολυποίκιλα καὶ μέγιστα ἀβάκια, καὶ ἀποστείλας
Μανασσῆ πατρίκιον καὶ πραιπόσιτον ἐν Προκοννήσῳ
ἔπρισεν ἐκεῖ τὰ μάρμαρα εἰς ὁμοιότητα τῆς γῆς, τὰ δὲ
πράσινα εἰς ὁμοιότητα τῶν ποταμῶν τῶν ἐμβαινόντων ἐν
τῇ θαλάσσῃ.

29   Ὅταν δὲ ἔκοψαν τὰς σκαλώσεις τοῦ τρούλου καὶ ἤθελον καταβιβάζειν τὰ ξύλα, ἐγέμισαν τὴν ἐκκλησίαν ὕδωρ
μέχρι πηχῶν πέντε καὶ ἔρριπτον τὰ ξύλα καὶ ἀπεθύμαινον
εἰς τὸ ὕδωρ καὶ οὐκ ἐσπαράσσοντο οἱ θεμέλιοι. Καὶ εἶθ’
οὕτως ἐτελείωσεν αὐτόν· καὶ τούτου χάριν λέγουσί τινες,
ὅτι Ἰουστῖνος ἔκτισεν, ἀλλὰ ψεύδονται οἱ ταῦτα λέγοντες.

30   Ἔχει δὲ ὁ ναὸς ἀφ’ οὗ ἐκτίσθη χρόνους υνηʹ ἕως τῆς

send to the island of Rhodes, as also your uncle did, and let them bring bricks of the original size, made of the same clay, bearing the same stamp, and of the same weight." The emperor gave the order, and they brought the bricks from Rhodes as before, and so the dome was vaulted again. They reduced its former height by five fathoms,[67] making it like a drum, for they feared that it might soon collapse again, and they left the timbers and supports of the centering in place for a year until they were sure that the dome had set. Being unable to make the ambo and the *solea* as lavish and precious as before, he made it cheaply of stones and columns covered with silver, with the parapets, curtains and other surfaces also of silver, together with the *solea*. He did not want to make a dome for the ambo, as he said, because of the great expense. For the floor he could not find such variegated slabs of great size, and so he sent Manasses, patrician and chamberlain,[68] to Prokonnesos, who cut slabs there that resemble the earth, while the green ones resemble the rivers that flow into the sea.

When they removed the scaffolding of the dome and 29
wanted to take the timbers down, they filled the church with water to a depth of five cubits and threw the timbers down and these floated in the water, and the foundations were not shattered.[69] So the church was completed, and therefore some people say that Justin built it, but those who say this are mistaken.

458 years[70] have passed from the building of the church 30

THE PATRIA

σήμερον. Πλησίον δὲ τοῦ ναοῦ ἔστησε τὴν στήλην αὐτοῦ εὐχαριστῶν τῷ Θεῷ καὶ δεικνύων τοῖς πολίταις ὅτι "ἐγώ εἰμι ὁ κτίτωρ."

31   Τὸν δὲ εἰρημένον μαΐστορα τῆς Μεγάλης Ἐκκλησίας τὸν Ἰγνάτιον, διότι ἠγαπᾶτο παρὰ πάντων διὰ τὰ θαυμαστὰ ἔργα ἃ ἐποίησε, φοβηθεὶς ὁ βασιλεύς, μή ποτε εὐφημισθῇ καὶ ἀναγορευθῇ ὑπὸ τῶν δύο δημοτικῶν μερῶν, μὴ θέλων τοῦτον ἀποκτεῖναι καθὼς πολλοὶ συνεβούλευον αὐτῷ, καὶ ἀθυμῶν συνῄνεσαν αὐτῷ ἐκ δευτέρου, ἵνα κτιζομένης παρ' αὐτοῦ τῆς στήλης τοῦ Αὐγουστίωνος ἐάσας αὐτὸν ἐκεῖσε ἄρωσι τὰς σκαλώσεις, ὅπως ὑπὸ τοῦ λιμοῦ τελευτήσῃ· ὃ καὶ ἐποίησε. Καὶ γνοὺς ὁ Ἰγνάτιος μετὰ τὸ τελειῶσαι καὶ στῆσαι τὴν ἔφιππον στήλην τοῦ βασιλέως ὅτι εἰάθη ἐκεῖσε καὶ ὀδυρόμενος ὀψίας ἤδη γενομένης εὗρεν ἐπιτήδευμα ἄριστον. Εὗρε δὲ καὶ σχοινίον λεπτάριον εἰς τὸ περσίκιον αὐτοῦ ἔχον ὀργυιὰς ε', καὶ τὴν μάχαιραν αὐτοῦ ἐκβαλὼν ἔκοψεν εἰς λεπτὰ τὸ ἱμάτιον αὐτοῦ καὶ τὸ ὑποκαμισοβράκιον καὶ τὸ σφικτούριον αὐτοῦ καὶ τὸ φακιόλιον, καὶ συνέδησεν αὐτὰ καὶ ἔκλωσε καὶ ἐδοκίμασεν, εἰ φθάνουσιν ἕως κάτω. Εὑρὼν δὲ οὕτως, ἐλθούσης τῆς γυναικὸς αὐτοῦ μετὰ κλαυθμοῦ πολλοῦ καὶ ὀδυρμοῦ, ἐφώνησεν αὐτῇ κοιμωμένων πάντων τῶν τῆς πόλεως (νὺξ γὰρ ἦν βαθεῖα) ὅτι "ἐγὼ μὲν ὧδε κατελείφθην ἀποθανεῖν, σὺ δὲ ὕπαγε καὶ κρυφίως ἀγόρασον παχὺ σχοινίον κατὰ τὸ μῆκος τοῦ κίονος καὶ ἄλειψον αὐτὸ ὑγρόπισσον καὶ πάλιν ἐλθὲ μεσούσης τῆς νυκτός." Καὶ καταλαβοῦσα τῇ ἐπιούσῃ νυκτί, καὶ χαλάσας ἐκεῖνος ἅπερ εἶχεν, καὶ δήσασα ἡ γυνὴ τὸ σχοινίον, ἔσυρεν ἐκεῖνος ἐπάνω καὶ προσέδησεν εἰς τὸν

272

to this day. Near the church he set up his statue, thanking God and saying to the people, "I am the founder."[71]

Since the aforementioned master of the Great Church, 31 Ignatios, was loved by everybody because of the wonderful works he had created, the emperor feared that he might be acclaimed and proclaimed as emperor by the two circus factions. He did not want to kill him, as many had advised him to do, and when he was despondent, they suggested to him again that, when the column of the Augoustion had been built by him, Justinian should leave him there <on top of the column> while they removed the scaffolding, so that he would die from hunger, and this he did. When Ignatios had finished it and set up the statue of the emperor on horseback, he realized that he had been left behind there, and after some lamentation, when it had already become evening, he had a splendid idea. He found in his bag a thin rope, five fathoms long, pulled out his knife, and cut his garment and undershirt and pants, his belt and headgear into thin strips, tied and knotted them together, and tested to see whether they would reach down to the ground. When he had just found out that <this was the case>, his wife came with great moaning and wailing, and he called out to her, while all the people of the city were sleeping (for it was late at night), saying, "I have been left here to die, but you should go and secretly buy a thick rope as long as the column, rub it with liquid pitch, and come again in the middle of the night." She came the following night and he let down what he had, she bound the rope to it, and he pulled it up. Above, he fixed it

πόδα τοῦ ἵππου καὶ κρατῶν αὐτὸ κατέβη ὑγιής. Ἐποίησε δὲ τοῦτο, ἵνα κολλᾶται τὸ σχοινίον ἐκ τοῦ ὑγροπίσσου εἰς τὰς χεῖρας αὐτοῦ, ὅπως μὴ συρεὶς ἀθρόως πεσὼν συντριβῇ καὶ ἵνα τὸ σχοινίον καυθήσεται ὑπὸ τοῦ πυρὸς μετὰ τὸ καταβῆναι αὐτόν. Καὶ οὕτως λαβὼν τήν τε γυναῖκα αὐτοῦ καὶ τοὺς παῖδας νυκτὸς κατέλαβε τὴν Ἀδριανούπολιν, μετασχηματισθεὶς μοναχὸς ἕως τρεῖς χρόνους, λεγόντων πάντων ὅτι ἀπέθανεν ἐπάνω τοῦ κίονος. Μετὰ δὲ ταῦτα ἐλθὼν ἐν Κωνσταντινουπόλει ἔστη εἰς τὰ Λαύσου. Διερχομένου δὲ τότε τοῦ βασιλέως εἰς προέλευσιν τῶν ἁγίων Ἀποστόλων ὑπήντησεν αὐτῷ ἐκεῖσε αἰτῶν λόγον συμπαθείας τοῦ μὴ φονευθῆναι. Καὶ γνωρίσας τοῦτον ὁ βασιλεὺς ἐθαύμασε καὶ πᾶσα ἡ σύγκλητος αὐτοῦ. Προεβάλλετο δὲ ὁ βασιλεὺς ἄγνοιαν τοῦ γενομένου ἐπὶ τὸν Ἰγνάτιον καὶ πολλὰ δῶρα δοὺς αὐτῷ ἀπέλυσεν ἐν εἰρήνῃ εἰπών· "Ἰδέ, ὃν θέλει ὁ Θεὸς ζῆν, χίλιοι οὐκ ἀποκτείνουσιν." Καὶ ἔκτοτε ἔζησεν ἐν εἰρήνῃ πολλῇ.

Ἕως ὧδε τὸ πέρας τῶν κατὰ τὴν Μεγάλην Ἐκκλησίαν.

32 Περὶ τοῦ ναοῦ τῶν ἁγίων Ἀποστόλων. — Τοὺς δὲ ἁγίους Ἀποστόλους τοὺς μεγάλους, καθὼς προείρηται, εὗρε δρομικὴν ἐκκλησίαν ξυλότρουλον, κτισθεῖσαν παρὰ τοῦ μεγάλου Κωνσταντίνου καὶ Ἑλένης τῶν βασιλέων. Ἡ δὲ Θεοδώρα ἡ γυνὴ τοῦ μεγάλου Ἰουστινιανοῦ πολλὴν σπουδὴν θεμένη διὰ τὸ διέρχεσθαι κάτωθεν τὸν ποταμὸν Λύκον, ἀνεγείρασα θεμελίους παμμεγέθεις καὶ λίθους μεγίστους ἔκτισε τὸν ναόν. Τὰ δὲ σκάριφα καὶ τὸ σχῆμα ἀπῆρε τοῦ ἁγίου Ἰωάννου τοῦ Θεολόγου ἀπὸ Ἐφέσου. Τὴν δὲ ὕλην

to the horse's leg, held on to it, and descended safely. He did this so that the rope would stick to his hands as a result of the liquid pitch, and he would not suddenly fall down when dangling and be smashed, and so that the rope could be burned by fire after he had descended. So he took his wife and children, reached Adrianople by night, and disguised himself as a monk for three years while everyone said he had died on top of the column. Thereafter he came to Constantinople and stayed at Ta Lausou.[72] Once, when the emperor went by on a procession to the Holy Apostles, he met him there, and asked him for forgiveness, so that he would not be killed. When the emperor recognized him, he was astonished with all his senate. The emperor feigned ignorance of what had happened to Ignatios, gave him many gifts, and dismissed him in peace, saying, "Look, whom God wants to live, a thousand people will not kill." And from that time he lived in great peace.[73]

Here is the end of <the report about> the Great Church.

On the church of the Holy Apostles.[74]—<Justinian> 32 found the great Holy Apostles, as said before, as a basilical church with a wooden dome, built by the emperors Constantine the Great and Helena. Theodora, the wife of Justinian the Great, made a great effort, because the river Lykos[75] passed underneath, and erecting huge foundations and very big stones, she built the church. The plan and design she took from <the church of> Saint John the Theologian at Ephesos.[76] She took all of the material from Hagia

THE PATRIA

ἄπασαν ἔλαβεν ἀπὸ τῆς ἁγίας Σοφίας μετὰ τὸ τελειωθῆναι αὐτὴν καὶ τὰ εὐκτήρια αὐτῆς· ἀφ' ὅτου γὰρ ἤρξατο κτίζεσθαι ἡ ἁγία Σοφία, μετὰ τέσσαρα ἔτη ἤρξατο καὶ αὐτὸς κτίζεσθαι ὁ ναός. Ἐλθόντος δὲ εἰς τὸ μουσειωθῆναι ἔλειψε τῇ δεσποίνῃ χρυσίου ποσότης. Καὶ ἀδημονούσης ἐπὶ τούτῳ τῆς Αὐγούστης κατ' ὄναρ ἐφάνησαν οἱ ἅγιοι ἀπόστολοι λέγοντες αὐτῇ· "μὴ λυποῦ περὶ χαράγματος χρυσίου, μηδὲ Ἰουστινιανῷ τῷ ἀνδρί σου ἐπιζητήσῃς νομίσματα· ἀλλ' ἀπελθοῦσα ἔξω τῆς πόρτης Δεξιοκράτους εἰς τὸν αἰγιαλὸν εὑρήσεις δώδεκα κεράμια γέμοντα χρυσίου κεχωσμένα." Ἡ δὲ Αὐγούστα ἀποστείλασα εὗρεν αὐτὰ ἔχοντα ἓν ἕκαστον αὐτῶν ἐπιγραφὴν τὰ ὀνόματα τῶν ἁγίων ἀποστόλων. Καὶ λαβοῦσα ταῦτα ἐδόξασε τὸν Θεόν, ἐξωδίασεν δὲ αὐτὰ εἰς τὸν ναόν. Καὶ πολλὰ κτήματα καὶ ἀναθήματα καὶ σκεύη χρυσᾶ καὶ ἀργυρᾶ προσεκύρωσε. Τελειώσασα δὲ τὸν ναὸν ἔμελλεν κρεμάσαι τὰς χαλκᾶς ἁλύσεις καὶ τὰς λυχνίας, ὅπως ἐνθρονιάσῃ καὶ ἐγκαινίσῃ αὐτόν. Γνοὺς δὲ ὁ βασιλεὺς Ἰουστινιανὸς ἐφθόνησεν, ἵνα μὴ προλάβῃ καὶ ἐγκαινισθῇ πρὸ τῆς ἁγίας Σοφίας, καὶ παρήγγειλε πανταχοῦ τῆς πόλεως, ἵνα μὴ ποιήσωσιν ἁλύσεις καὶ κρεμάσωσιν ἐκεῖσε. Ἡ δὲ βασίλισσα ἐποίησεν ἀπὸ μετάξης πλεκτὰ σχοινία πίστει καὶ μόχθῳ καὶ κρεμάσασα τὰς πολυφώτους ἀργυρᾶς λυχνίας ἐνεκαίνισε καὶ ἐνεθρόνιασε τὸν ναὸν προλαβοῦσα τὴν Μεγάλην Ἐκκλησίαν. Τὰ δὲ λείψανα τὰ κείμενα κάτωθεν τῆς ἁγίας τραπέζης τῶν ἁγίων ἀποστόλων παρὰ Κωνσταντίου βασιλέως ἤχθησαν, υἱοῦ τοῦ μεγάλου βασιλέως Κωνσταντίνου, διὰ τοῦ ἁγίου μεγαλομάρτυρος Ἀρτεμίου.

Sophia, after it had been finished with its chapels. Four years after the construction of Hagia Sophia had started, the building of this church began. When it had reached the point where it should be decorated with mosaics, the empress lacked the necessary sum of money. And when the Augusta was aggrieved about this, the holy apostles appeared to her in a dream, saying to her, "Do not worry about the gold coins, nor ask your husband Justinian for money, but go out through the Dexiokrates gate to the shore,[77] and you will find twelve buried pots, full of gold." The Augusta sent there and found them, each one with the name of one of the holy apostles. She took them, praised God, and spent them on the church. And she bestowed many properties, offerings, and gold and silver vessels upon it. When she had finished the church, she wanted to hang up the bronze chains and candelabra in order to dedicate and inaugurate it. When the emperor Justinian heard this, he became jealous, fearing she might anticipate him, and that <the church> might be inaugurated before Hagia Sophia. So he gave the order throughout the whole city that no chains should be made and hung up there. But the empress made plaited ropes from silk with faith and toil, hung up the silver candelabra, and inaugurated and dedicated the church, prior to the Great Church. The relics of the holy apostles which lie below the holy altar were brought under the emperor Constantius (337–361), the son of Emperor Constantine the Great, by the holy and great martyr Artemios.[78] The presby-

Τὸ δὲ βῆμα, καθώς ἐστι μέσον, οὕτως καὶ γέγονε παρὰ τῆς Αὐγούστης Θεοδώρας. Τὸ δὲ μνημοθέσιον τῆς ἁγίας Θεοφανοῦς ὁ μέγας Κωνσταντῖνος ἐποίησε· τὸ δὲ ἔξωθεν μνημοθέσιον τῶν τε αἱρετικῶν καὶ ὀρθοδόξων ὁ μέγας Ἰουστινιανὸς ἐποίησε καὶ διὰ μουσείων ἐκαλλώπισεν αὐτό, καὶ ἐκεῖσε ἐτάφη· ὡσαύτως καὶ ἡ γυνὴ αὐτοῦ Θεοδώρα ἡ κτίσασα τοὺς ἁγίους Ἀποστόλους. Τὸ δὲ μουσεῖον ἐκεῖνο καὶ τὰ μάρμαρα ἀπῆρε Βασίλειος ὁ βασιλεύς, ὅτε ᾠκοδόμησε τὴν Νέαν καὶ τὸν Φόρον.

33   Ὁ δὲ ἅγιος Λάζαρος ἐκτίσθη παρὰ Λέοντος υἱοῦ Βασιλείου· καὶ κτήματα πολλὰ ἐκεῖσε ἀπεχαρίσατο. Ἔφερε δὲ ἀπὸ τῆς Κύπρου καὶ τὰ ἅγια λείψανα τοῦ ἁγίου Λαζάρου καὶ ἀπὸ Βηθανίας τῆς ἁγίας Μαρίας τῆς μυροφόρου καὶ ἐκεῖσε ἀποτίθεται αὐτά.

34   Ὅτι τοῦ Τζαούτζη ἡ μονὴ ἐν τοῖς χρόνοις τοῦ αὐτοῦ βασιλέως ἐκτίσθη παρὰ τῆς γυναικὸς Στυλιανοῦ βασιλεοπάτορος τοῦ Τζαούτζη· καὶ κτήματα πολλὰ ἐκεῖσε ἀπεχαρίσατο.

35   Τοῦ δὲ Λιβὸς ἡ μονὴ ἐν τοῖς χρόνοις Ῥωμανοῦ τοῦ γέροντος καὶ τοῦ πορφυρογεννήτου Κωνσταντίνου υἱοῦ Λέοντος ἀνηγέρθη παρὰ πατρικίου τοῦ Λιβὸς τοῦ γεγονότος δρουγγαρίου τῶν πλωίμων, ποιήσαντος ἐκεῖ καὶ ξενῶνα.

tery, which is in the middle,[79] was also made in this way by the Augusta Theodora. Constantine the Great made the mausoleum of Saint Theophano;[80] Justinian made the outer mausoleum of the heretics and the orthodox[81] and decorated it with mosaics, and was buried there, as was his wife Theodora, the builder of the Holy Apostles. Emperor Basil (I, 867–886) took the mosaic and the marbles away when he built the New Church and the <church of the Mother of God of the> Forum.[82]

Saint Lazaros was built by Leo (VI, 886–912), the son 33 of Basil, and he bestowed much property upon it. He also brought the holy relics of Saint Lazaros from Cyprus and of Saint Mary the Perfume-bearer from Bethany, and deposited them there.

The monastery of Tzaoutzes was built in the time of the 34 same emperor by the wife of Stylianos Tzaoutzes, the *basileopator*,[83] and she bestowed much property upon it.

The monastery of Lips was built in the time of Romanos 35 the Elder (I, 920–944) and Constantine Porphyrogennetos (VII, 944–959), the son of Leo, by the patrician Lips, a *droungarios* of the fleet, who also built a hospital there.

Note on the Text

The *Patria* of Constantinople has come down to us in more than sixty manuscripts. The most recent editor of the text, Theodor Preger, grouped these manuscripts into the two main classes A and B, some free versions with a shortened and occasionally rearranged text, and the topographical versions C and M.[1]

Class A consists of seventeen manuscripts dating from the fourteenth to sixteenth centuries, class B of one complete and twenty-two incomplete manuscripts (in which about half of the text is missing between 1.59 and 3.66), all from the sixteenth century. The topographical version of the *Patria* is represented by a family of seven manuscripts from the fourteenth to sixteenth centuries, called C, and the single twelfth-century codex M.

The only complete manuscript of class B also contains a fourteenth-century treatise on the court offices and ceremonies of Constantinople,[2] whose traditional attribution to a certain Georgios Kodinos was extended by the first edition (George Dousa, Heidelberg 1596) to the *Patria,* which thus became known in modern scholarship as "Pseudo-Codinus" and is sometimes still cited under this name.

The *Patria,* as a nonliterary text, was not copied by the manuscript writers in a strictly canonized form; it was often

amplified or shortened, sometimes even rephrased. An "original" version of the text can therefore not be reconstructed, and the reader should always be aware that Preger's edition is rather a synthesis of the tradition, which tries to offer the complete material in a reasonable arrangement.

The Greek text is that of Preger's edition; the few necessary corrections are listed below in the Notes to the Text. A few typographical errors in the Preger edition have been corrected tacitly. As a courtesy to the Greekless reader, notes on material in square brackets are included in the Notes to the Translation.

NOTES

1 See Preger, "Beiträge," and *Scriptores,* vol. 2, iii–xxiv.

2 On which see now Ruth Macrides, Joseph Munitiz, and Dimiter Angelov, eds., *Pseudo-Kodinos. The Constantinopolitan Court Offices and Ceremonies* (Farnham, 2013).

Notes to the Text

Sigla

<...> = Lacuna, with or without amendment by editor or translator

[. . .] = Passages preserved in older versions of the text or in single manuscripts

[[. . .]] = A misplaced addition within an additional passage preserved only by certain manuscripts

{. . .} = Deletions by the editor or translator

† = Obelization, indicating corrupted text passages

Book 1

1   *The rendering of the Roman name Severus in Greek as* Σευῆρος *or* Σεβῆρος *is inconsistent in Preger's edition and has been unified here to* Σευῆρος.

2   *I have removed the obelisk marks (†) in the Preger edition around the phrase* † τοῖς θείοις τῶν βασιλέων ἀπεδόθη †.

3   *After* εἰσῆλθον *I have removed the* <αὐτὸς καὶ> *of the Preger edition.*

4   *After* Μακεδόνων *I have removed the* † *of the Preger edition.*

5   *The word* μυδρῶνες *of Preger's edition is not attested and must be emended to* μ' ὑδρῶνες.

BOOK 2

1   *I have removed the † of the Preger edition, obelizing* Καὶ σκεδάννυται.
2   *Preger does not indicate a lacuna here, but two others later in the text of this chapter.*
3   *Read* ἱπτάμενον *for* ἱστάμενον, *as in Parastaseis, chap. 38.*
4   *I have removed the † of the Preger edition, obelizing* ἐμπόδιον.
5   *Read* στηθαίων *(balustrades) for* στηθέων *(breasts).*
6   *Read perhaps* ὑπὸ Τιβερίου = *by Tiberios.*

BOOK 3

1   *Instead of* θάνατον <μὲν ἔκτισε τὰ ξενο>τάφια, *Preger supplied:* <εἰς> θάνατον, <ζωήν, ὑγείαν· καὶ εἰς θάνατον μὲν ἔκτισε τὰ ξενο>τάφια.

BOOK 4

1   *Read* σκαφικὰς *with manuscripts P V Z for Preger's* κεφαλικὰς ἀψίδας; *see n. 4.31 of the translation.*
2   *Here Preger emended* κατὰ τὴν ὥραν *(at the time) to* κατὰ ἕκτην ὥραν *(at the sixth hour).*
3   *Read* σύμπαχον *for Preger's* σύμ<παν> πάχος.
4   *Excluded by Preger.*
5   *Emendation by Preger in the apparatus to his edition.*
6   *Read* τῶν ἐξερχομένων *for* τοῦ ἐξερχομένου.

Notes to the Translation

BOOK I

1   Up to chap. 36, this book is a literal quote from Hesychios; see p. xii above.

2   The two first chapters of Hesychios's text are omitted by the *Patria,* but they have been included here for the sake of completeness. The beginning of chap. 1 is quoted in 1.42 below.

3   In the following sections, Hesychios apparently draws from a common source with the *Anaplous Bosporou,* a description of both shores of the Golden Horn and the Bosporos, written by Dionysios of Byzantion, probably in the third century CE.

4   The last two verses are also quoted by Dionysios, chap. 23.

5   Cf. Dionysios of Byzantion, chaps. 24 and 25.

6   Ibid., chap. 24.

7   Ibid., chap. 7.

8   Bosporos is actually a Thracian name that predates the Greek settlement, but it was explained by the Greeks, from the words *bous* and *poros,* as "ox-ford."

9   Semestre is otherwise known only from Dionysios of Byzantion, chap. 24, where she is called Semystra.

10   Dionysios of Byzantion, chap. 24, explains the name Keroessa (= the horned) by the fact that she had two horns on her forehead, being born to Io after her transformation into a cow. Actually, the name "horn" for the bay to the north of the peninsula of Byzantion is suggested by its shape, and the name Keroessa is derived from it.

11   According to Hesiod's *Theogony,* Kronos swallowed all his chil-

dren immediately after birth. His sister and wife, Rhea, hid the infant Zeus in a cave on a mountain in Crete, where the nymph Amaltheia, turned into a goat, nursed him. When Kronos found the cave and tried to put his head into it, the goat jumped up and attacked him; she lost one of her horns, which became later known as the cornucopia.

12   Bizye, a small town in Thrace, lies ca. 120 kilometers to the northwest of Byzantion. From the surrounding area, a great aqueduct—perhaps the longest in antiquity—supplied Constantinople from the times of Theodosios I (379–395). The connection to Byzas is established here by a paretymology based on phonetic similarity. The name Byzas, which can be understood in Greek as "with a broad chest," is actually derived from the Thracian word *Byzantion,* not the other way round, as suggested by ancient Greek writers.

13   Unknown from other sources, but probably derived from Melia, the nymph of the ash tree, who was Inachos's wife and the mother of Io.

14   Chrysopolis means "golden city." For the name, two competing explanations are given by ancient sources, either that Chrysopolis was the place where the Persians collected the tributes paid by the Greek cities, or that it was the burial site of the priest Chryses, the father of Chryseis, who was taken prisoner by Agamemnon during the Trojan War. The story told here is a variant of the second version, while a variant of the first version, though with Alexander the Great as its hero, is told below in 2.59.

15   The same story is told in 3.38 and evidently connected there to the part of the pre-Constantinian city wall which descended from the Forum of Constantine to the harbor of Sophia, on which see below, 3.37.

16   On which see below, 2.41.

17   Probably at the place of the later Milion or Golden Milestone, on which see below, 2.29.

18   On which see below, 1.51 and 3.2. This is the only mention of a Christian building in Hesychios's text and therefore possibly a later interpolation.

19   Not mentioned elsewhere; on Hekate, see also below, 1.25.

20   On the altar of Semestre, see above, chaps. 1 and 6.

21   The bath of Achilles near the Strategion square is mentioned again below, 1.52.

22   Sykai is the old name of the region later called Pera or Galata, opposite Constantinople across the Golden Horn, and actually means "the fig trees."

23   Amphiaraos was a hero from Argos in Greece and one of the Seven Against Thebes. His altar in this region is unknown to other sources, but Dionysios of Byzantion, chap. 34, mentions here a holy grove of Schoinikles, allegedly Amphiaraos's charioteer, whose cult had been brought to Byzantion by Greek emigrants from Megara.

24   Haimos is the ancient name of the Balkan mountains. He appears again as a barbarian king in 3.35 and possibly inspired also the figure of the Roman patrician Haimon in 3.152.

25   Eponymous founder of the Odrysians, an ancient people in Thrace.

26   Phidaleia was, according to legend, the daughter of a local king called Barbyses. The oldest source in which her name appears is Dionysios of Byzantion, chap. 59, who mentions a white rock on the western bank of the Bosporos halfway to the Black Sea that was believed to be her grave. For another mention of Phidaleia in the *Patria* see below, 2.86.

27   See above, 1.6 and 1.7. Strombos was thus a half brother of Byzas. He appears as Stroibos in a similar story in the *Ethnika,* a work of Hesychios's contemporary Stephanos of Byzantion.

28   Unknown from other sources.

29   Here three etymologies are offered, of which the second and third are based on a certain phonetical similarity. The word must actually be connected to the Greek *chalkos* = copper.

30   A well-known story usually told about the colonists from Megara.

31   On the Anaplous, see 3.158 below.

32   Apollonios of Tyana, a pagan philosopher, actually lived in the second century CE; see also below, 2.79 and 2.103.

33   Leo is known from other sources as a student of Plato or Aris-

totle from Athens, and as the author of a seven-book history of the siege.

34   In 340/39 BCE.

35   The name Tymbosyne is unknown from other sources. Stephanos Byzantios notes in his *Ethnika*, s. v. Bosporos, that this word was pronounced by the locals as Phosphoros (bringer of light), and he claims that according to older patriographers Byzantion was saved from Philip's attack because Hekate, the torchbearing goddess of magic, caused torches to appear at night.

36   Chares was actually the commander of a grain fleet that was captured by Philip during the siege of Byzantion.

37   On the Asian shore near Chalkedon. The story is also found in Dionysios of Byzantion, chap. 110, with the name of Chares's wife or concubine, but without the poem which is also transmitted by the Greek Anthology VII 169 and other later sources.

38   See chap. 4 above.

39   That is, a member of the Athenian *phyle* (tribe) bearing this name.

40   Protomachos is otherwise unknown. The Milion (on which see below, 2.29) was built only after the foundation of Constantinople, but, according to tradition, it replaced a temple of Rhea (chap. 13 above), which may be the place intended here.

41   Unknown from other sources and possibly derived from the Roman general Timasios in the time of Theodosios I (379–395). A man called Timasios appears also as the father of Pescennius Niger in the *Patria*'s addition to Hesychios; see 1.37 below.

42   The "Ephesian harbor" is also mentioned by Dionysios of Byzantion, chap. 79, and is located on the European shore of the Bosporos near the exit to the Black Sea.

43   See chap. 1 above.

44   This is the so-called Hieron, a place on the Asiatic side of the Bosporos, which was regarded as the point where the Black Sea begins. Jason's sanctuary is also mentioned by Polybios 4.39.6.

45   Unknown to other sources.

46   Kalliades is otherwise unknown. The inscription is also in the Greek Anthology XVI 66, probably copied from Hesychios.

47   On which see above, chap. 13.

48   The siege of Byzantion lasted until 195 or 196, well after Niger's
       death in 193.

49   On these events, see the accounts in Dion Kassios 75.10–14, and
       Herodian 3.6.9.

50   This well-known Byzantine legend is historically incorrect, for
       the rebuilding of Byzantion took place only long after Severus's
       death. In the *Patria* and Byzantine tradition, the alleged activi-
       ties of Severus were regarded as a symbolic prefiguration of
       Constantine's refoundation.

51   The famous Baths of Zeuxippos were burned in the Nika Riot
       of 532 and subsequently restored. Zeuxippos is attested several
       times in antiquity as a personal name and explained here first by
       an imaginative paretymology as Zeus Hippios (Zeus of the
       horses), then more accurately as "the one who harnesses the
       horses." To give more weight to the latter, one of the twelve
       Deeds of Hercules, which actually took place at Abdera in
       Thrace, was transferred to Byzantion.

52   That is, having a grove or temple of the Dioskouroi, the holy
       twin brothers Castor and Pollux in the ancient Greek religion.

53   The circuits in horse races were counted by removing egg-
       shaped bowls from rods near both ends of the *spina* (the barrier
       in the middle of the Hippodrome) on which they had been
       stacked.

54   Here ends the literal quotation from Hesychios. The conclud-
       ing chapters of his text, which describe Constantine's founda-
       tion very briefly (39–42 in the original numbering), are inserted
       later as 43–46, and then quoted again, heavily paraphrased and
       interpolated, as 61–71.

55   Unclear calculation, perhaps from the Jewish king Manasses
       696 BCE to Augustus, not Severus, in 31 BCE, with a mistake of
       ten years. Byzantine chronicles, such as that of George Synkel-
       los, date the foundation of Byzantion to the reign of Manasses
       (696–642 BCE) without indicating the exact year 660 BCE. Au-
       gustus is not mentioned in the text of Hesychios, but this time
       calculation, which is probably, like the others, an addition of the

tenth-century redactor, suggests he used a chronological table, which contained also his name.

56   The name of Niger's father, Annius Fuscus, is mentioned only by the notoriously unreliable *Historia Augusta,* but it was certainly not Timasios. On Timasios, see above, n. 41.

57   Stories featuring pagan philosophers from Rome or Athens are a stock feature of the patriographical literature on Constantinople; see 2.82 and 3.37 below.

58   See chap. 35 above.

59   This bath cannot be identified. Median fire may here refer to crude oil.

60   A remote reminiscence of the alleged temple of the Dioskouroi, mentioned in chap. 35 above.

61   The curved southeastern part of the Hippodrome.

62   Correctly calculated from the beginning of Augustus's reign, 31 BCE to 330 CE.

63   Quoted from Hesychios, chap. 1.

64   Hesychios, chap. 39.

65   No trace of these walls survives. The Troadesian porticoes, probably named after their columns of marble from the Troas (in northwestern Asia Minor), flanked the main street from the city center to the main gate in the southwest.

66   Note the deliberately vague expression which may refer either to pagan or to Christian sanctuaries. For later Christian additions to Hesychios's text, see below, 1.48–50.

67   Also mentioned in Sokrates's *Church History* 1.16, where it is claimed that Constantine's decree, which made his city equal in rank to Rome and gave it the name "New Rome," was affixed to a column in the Strategion.

68   Hesychios, chap. 40.

69   The statue of Helena is mentioned also by John Malalas 13.8. On the August(a)ion, see 2.15 below.

70   A similar remark also in Zosimos, *New History* 2.31.

71   This chapter and chap. 46 = Hesychios, chap. 41.

72   On Constantine's column, see 2.45 below.

73   Addition of manuscript B.

74 One of these Senate houses lay to the north of the Forum, on which see below, 2.44 and 94; the other is probably identical to the so-called Magnaura, on which see below, 3.180.

75 These "reeds" were fossilized stem pieces of crinoids used as token coins for the acquisition of subsidized bread.

76 Here the text of Hesychios is "completed" by the mention of churches built by Constantine. In contrast to chaps. 49 and 50, which are quoted from Books 2 and 3 of the *Patria,* this short notice may belong to an earlier Christianized version of Hesychios's text; see above, p. xii and n. 18.

77 Quoted from 2.96, and thus indirectly from *Parastaseis,* chap. 11.

78 Quoted from 3.1, as a complement to chap. 48.

79 Here begins the second part of Book 1, see p. xii above.

80 Quoted from 3.2.

81 Here a pre-Constantinian city wall is invented which includes a much smaller area than the actual one which ran near the Forum, by explaining a number of arched doorways at churches and public squares as former city gates. For Eugenios, see 3.21 below; for the Strategion, 2.59 (the bath of Achilles is not mentioned elsewhere in the *Patria*); for Ourbikios, 3.22; for the Chalkoprateia, 3.32; for the Milion, 2.29; for Tzykalareia, 2.104; for the Mangana, 3.8; and for the Arkadianai, 2.27.

82 No building used as a reference point for the description of the Constantinian land wall has survived, so that its exact line is still disputed. Note also that the sea walls, which were not built before 438/39, are attributed here to Constantine.

83 For Eugenios, see 3.21 below; the church of Saint Antonios lay near the church of Laurentios (on which see 3.71 below), but it is not mentioned later in the *Patria.*

84 For the Topoi, see 2.27 and 3.26; for the Mother of God of the Rod, see 3.88; for the Exakionion, 2.54; for the old gate of the Forerunner, 3.191; for the monasteries of Dios and Ikasia, 3.193a and 196; for the cistern of Bonos, 3.83; for the church of Manuel, Sabel and Ismael, 3.190.

85 Calculation probably quoted from 2.54.

86 Here, the foundation of Constantinople is dated to the twelfth

year of Constantine's reign (the correct year of the Byzantine era, however, would be 5825), as also in chaps. 58 and 59.

87 These dates correspond to November 26, 328, and May 11, 330, of our era. The second of these calculations is entirely correct, the first almost correct, except for the rarely used number of Olympiads (correctly 277). While the inauguration date is well attested, no date for the beginning of the construction of the walls is given by any other source. The last phrase has been transposed to this place from the beginning of the following paragraph.

88 Addition in manuscript groups A and B.

89 This chapter is a paraphrase of Hesychios, chap. 42. The Stama is the rectangular place below the imperial box of the Hippodrome.

90 The legendary group of twelve noblemen, who came from Rome with Constantine (see 1.63 and 67 below), is complemented here by a second group of twelve "helpers" partially drawn from a fourth-century source about the time *after* Constantine: For Euphratas see 1.65 below; for Ourbikios, 3.22; for Olybrios, 3.60; for Isidoros, 2.65 and 3.121; Eustorgios may be identified with the fourth-century rhetor and historian from Cappadocia; Michael must be connected to the otherwise unknown "gate of the *protobestiarios* Michael," mentioned by sources describing Constantine Doukas's revolt in 913, on which see below, n. 1.101; Honoresios is probably identical with Honoratos, the first prefect of Constantinople in 361; Eutychianos and Eutropios were actually historians who took part in Julian's failed expedition against Persia in 363; Eleusios is perhaps the person attested as bishop of Kyzikos in 359; Troilos the rhetor a well-known figure in Constantinople around 400. Of all the persons called Hesychios in the fourth to sixth centuries, the tenth-century author of this text can have thought only of Hesychios of Miletos, the author of the original *Patria* of Byzantion.

91 Here, most buildings on the upper terraces of the Great Palace are listed, including a number of post-fourth-century construc-

tions such as the church of Saint Stephen (built after 439) and the Sigma (built under Theophilos, 829–842).

92   On which see also 2.85 and n. 2.116 below.

93   Expanded version of 1.40.

94   Expanded version of 1.41.

95   The statue described here was apparently a satyr; on its identification with Bellerophon, see below, 2.47.

96   From here to chap. 67 the text is an expanded version of 1.44, and therefore originally going back to Hesychios, chap. 42.

97   For Addas and Protasios, see 3.36 and 23; for Probos, 3.99; for Rhodanos and Salloustios, n. 3.35; and for Euboulos, 3.122. All senators on this list, with the exception of Skombros (mackerel), can be identified with historical personages living in Constantinople between ca. 360 and 395.

98   A war with Persia did not take place in Constantine's time.

99   A *kentenarion* was one hundred Roman pounds.

100 On the war against the Persians and the legendary personage Euphratas, see the Introduction, p. xiii.

101 The name Agrikolaos, which appears in the Life of Saint Basil the Younger as a disrespectful nickname for patriarch Nikolaos IV Mystikos (907–907, 912–925), and the mention of Toubakes and Iberitzes in 1.71 below suggest that the names of the supposed later owners are taken from a source describing the unsuccessful revolt of Constantine Doukas in 913, in which both these individuals took part.

102 From here to chap. 71, the text is, in its substance, an expanded version of chap. 45, originally going back to Hesychios, chap. 41.

103 For the Tzykanisterion and the Mangana, see 3.29 and 3.8 below; for the Akropolis, see chap. 51 above, and for Eugenios, 3.21 below.

104 The Daphne is the old main building of the Great Palace, which is otherwise not mentioned in the *Patria;* for the palace of Sophia see 3.37 below; for the church of the Rod, 3.88.

105 For these see 2.28, 29, 45, 47, 53, and 54 below.

106 These cities, reconquered from the Bulgarians by Emperor John Tzimiskes in 971, did not yet, with the exception of Konstantia

(Constanţa), exist in Constantine's time. The Bulgarians are often called Scythians in classicizing Byzantine sources.

107 John Toubakes, a partisan of the successful party in the 913 revolt, may well have succeeded Gregoras Iberitzes as the owner of his house, for Iberitzes, the father-in-law of Constantine Doukas, lost this house, which other sources locate on the Akropolis, after the end of the revolt. The identification of it with the old palace of Constantius (which was actually a bath, see n. 2.116 below) is therefore definitely wrong.

108 This chapter is a later addition without relation to the preceding text. The date is not 413, the fifth year of Theodosios II, but rather 438/39, the fifth year of the patriarch Proklos, to which the introduction of the *Trisagion* is dated by other sources.

109 A dyophysitic, but iconoclastic Armenian sect, which does not appear in other sources before the eleventh century.

110 This is the place usually called Hebdomon, on which see below, 3.144 and 145.

111 On which see below, 2.58. The new Theodosian land walls were actually finished in 413.

BOOK 2

1 Chaps. 1–15 are excerpts about words beginning with *a* (alpha) from the sixth-century author John Lydos, with chaps. 2–14 being a series on statues *(agalmata)*, on which see p. xiii above. Only the last of these excerpts, that about the Augoustion in chap. 15, actually refers to Constantinople, but it is probably the reason why the complete series was inserted here.

2 The parts of the text included in angle brackets are actually missing in the *Patria* but were supplied by the editor Preger from John Lydos's original.

3 Nikanor was actually not Seleukos's son, but a Macedonian ruler in Mesopotamia, who was defeated by him in 310 BCE.

4 Here, as already in John Lydos, the public square Augoustaion or Augoustion is apparently confused with the courtyard in

front of a reception hall of the Great Palace, the Augousteus, where the statue of Helena stood.

5   Cf. *Parastaseis,* chap. 16; a shortened doublet to 2.102 below.
6   On which see also 4.31 below.
7   See chap. 2.15 above.
8   Addition of the topographical version C. The report about the Vandalic war goes back to Prokopios, while the story of Belisarios's blinding appears here for the first time. On Ta Lausou, see 2.36 below.
9   Cf. *Parastaseis,* chap. 16.
10   The Greek word κοχλίαι means "spiral staircase" but is probably used here for smaller columns with a spiral relief decoration, without staircases inside.
11   *Parastaseis,* chap. 20. The Forum of Arkadios or of Theodosios on the "dry hill." No monument in this fantastic description is mentioned by any other source; on the role of Severus as an alleged pre-Constantinian, pagan refounder of the city, see above, p. xii with n. 17.
12   *Parastaseis,* chap. 71. This is certainly not a genuine quotation from the lost *Church History* of the fifth-century author John Diakrinomenos.
13   From *Parastaseis,* chap. 23.
14   *Parastaseis,* chap. 22. The suburb of Saint Mamas lay to the north of Constantinople at present-day Beşiktaş. The Basiliskos mentioned here can surely be identified with the usurper in 475 CE (on whom see 3.26 below), although his descent from the emperor Numerianus and his paganism are, of course, legendary. The "second year of his reign" is rather Zeno's second reign after his victory over Basiliskos.
15   *Parastaseis,* chap. 25.
16   On this church, see 3.115 below.
17   *Parastaseis,* chap. 26. Platon and his fate are unknown to other sources and probably a product of the author's imagination.
18   *Parastaseis,* chap. 28. The Kynegion was an arena for animal fights on the acropolis of old Byzantion, later used for executions of

criminals. Theodore the Lector was, like John Diakrinomenos in chap. 19, actually a late-antique church historian, who is transposed here into the early eighth century.

19   The Artotyrianos Topos (the "bread-and-cheese" place) is probably identical to the Artopoleia described in 2.46 below.

20   *Parastaseis,* chap. 29.

21   *Parastaseis,* chap. 30. On the church and the actual circumstances of its foundation, see 3.60 below.

22   *Parastaseis,* chap. 32. The actual name Topoi (places), which is found in the *Parastaseis,* is missing from the *Patria.* As Ariadne survived Zeno, he cannot have had a second wife. On the church of the Archangel, see 3.24 below.

23   This chapter collects a number of dispersed entries in the *Parastaseis* about the decoration of the Chalke gate, adding also some new material.

24   *Parastaseis,* chap. 33.

25   Ibid., chap. 80.

26   Ibid., chaps. 44a, 78.

27   Ibid., chap. 44a.

28   Ibid., chap. 77.

29   Ibid., chap. 34. The Tyche, the semipagan town goddess of Constantinople, was added to this entry by an intermediate source, the so-called *Anonymus Treu.* Note that the subsequent addition of the *Patria* shows a completely different concept of the Tyche.

30   Ibid., chap. 35. On Arabia, see also 3.37 below.

31   *Parastaseis,* chap. 67. The actual name of this place must have been "the petitions" *(pittakia),* as it appears later in the story added by the *Patria.* Leo's sister is not a historical figure, but she may be inspired by Euphemia, daughter of Emperor Markianos (450–457) and wife of the western emperor Anthemius (467–472).

32   Ibid., chap. 36.

33   Ibid., chap. 73.

34   Heavily abbreviated excerpt from *Parastaseis,* chap. 74.

35   The following entry is apparently an abbreviated excerpt from an unknown source: the complete story appears only in two late

manuscripts of the *Patria,* but probably not in exactly the same form as in the lost source. It tells about Phokas's visit to Maurikios as the emissary of the army, his maltreatment by the emperor, and his dramatic flight.

36 Preger does not indicate a lacuna here, but two others later in the text.

37 Lausos is not dated here in the time of Constantine the Great, so the allusion to the story of the twelve senators who came with him from Rome is somewhat surprising. See 1.63 above, and 67, where the house of Lausos is not mentioned.

38 From *Parastaseis,* chap. 35a.

39 Literally, "a statue of colors," i.e., a fresco. The entry may go back to a version of the *Parastaseis* that was more complete than the one preserved, for in this text Philippikos seems to play an important role; see, for example, 2.24 above.

40 Of the series of seven "spectacles" described in chaps. 37–43 of the *Parastaseis,* six are excerpted here as 2.41–43, 46, 52, 53.

41 From *Parastaseis,* chap. 37. On the interpretation of this allegorical story, see now Anderson, "Classified Knowledge." Julian was consul in 322 and served from 326 to 329 as city prefect of Rome.

42 From *Parastaseis,* chap. 38. Byzas is the legendary founder of Byzantion, Azotios another fictitious figure. On the birthday of Constantinople and its celebration, see also chaps. 2.49 and 87 below.

43 From *Parastaseis,* chap. 39, where it is listed as spectacle no. 3.

44 Ibid., chap. 59. Kallistratos is unknown from other sources, and the whole story probably a doublet to the story about the city prefect Kyros in 3.111.

45 The claim that the Palladion, a wooden statue from Troy that had been brought to Rome by Aeneas, was buried under the Forum by Constantine, appears first in the sixth century but is unknown to the *Parastaseis.* The mention of "many other miraculous objects" refers to an originally competing legend about the deposition of Christian relics, which is present here above in 2.20.

46 In a similar way, a non-Christian and a Christian legend about

the statue on the porphyry column in the Forum are combined here. The last phrase is quoted from 1.45 and goes back to Pseudo-Hesychios, chap. 41.

47   Artopoleia means "the bakeries." The text describes the relief decoration of the so-called Anemodoulion (Anemodourin), a four-sided arch at this place, on which see also 3.114 below.

48   Excluded by Preger, though probably added by the same redactor who inserted also the following chap. 46a.

49   From *Parastaseis,* chap. 40, where the Artopoleia are listed as spectacle no. 4.

50   The vault of the "bread-and-cheese" place is without doubt identical to the four-sided arch of the Artopoleia.

51   The Forum of Theodosios I.

52   From *Parastaseis,* chap. 66.

53   Remains of a gate with sets of quadruple columns instead of pillars have actually been found in the Tauros region near the bath of Bayezid. The "threshing floor" mentioned before, probably a circular plaza in the vicinity, is unknown from other sources.

54   This remark identifies the statue with the one mentioned in 1.64, which is, however, described in an entirely different way.

55   The report about the destruction of the statue in 1204 by Niketas Choniates (ed. van Dieten 1975, 643.16–32, 649.1–21) is apparently based on this description in the *Patria* or a similar text.

56   From *Parastaseis,* chap. 70. The story refers, despite the different number of persons, to the porphyry statues of two pairs of embracing emperors, which actually represented the emperors of the first Tetrarchy (293–305) and are now at San Marco in Venice. Philadelphion means "the place of brotherly love."

57   Ibid., chap. 56.

58   Anelios (Sunless) is a pun on the old designation of the statue as Anthelios ("Anti-Sun," in the sense of "second sun" or "competing sun") and may refer to the loss of the statue's gilding in later times.

59   John Diakrinomenos is the author of a now-lost church history from the early sixth century.

60　　From *Parastaseis,* chap. 56. This semi-Christian foundation cere-
　　　mony is most probably a later invention.

61　　Ibid., chap. 58. This monumental cross probably did not predate
　　　the reign of Theodosios I (379–395).

62　　Here and at the end of the chapter the author misunderstands
　　　the Latin word *horreion* (granary) as *horologion* (clock). The La-
　　　mia was a granary nearby on the south coast of Constantinople.

63　　From *Parastaseis,* chap. 12; for another excerpt from the same
　　　text, see below, 2.97.

64　　The phrase is corrupted, for Lykos (Wolf) is actually the name
　　　of the river itself which passes nearby.

65　　From *Parastaseis,* chap. 41, listed there as spectacle no. 5.

66　　These are obviously the same as the statues of Zeus and Hera-
　　　kles mentioned before, which are reinterpreted in an attempt to
　　　explain the mysterious name Amastrianon, or rather Ta Amas-
　　　trianou, which means "of the man from Amastris," a town in
　　　Paphlagonia.

67　　From *Parastaseis,* chap. 42, listed there as spectacle no. 6. A vari-
　　　ant of the well-known legend about a furnace in the shape of an
　　　ox used for executions, which was originally connected to
　　　Phalaris, tyrant of Agrigentum in the sixth century BCE, and to
　　　the oriental cult of Baal.

68　　Calculated from Constantine's twelfth year, 317 (see p. xii
　　　above), to 449/50 in which the walls of Constantinople were
　　　heavily damaged by an earthquake.

69　　A paretymology which explains (H)exakionion (with six col-
　　　umns, probably referring to the main gate of the Constantinian
　　　wall) as Exokionion (a column outside).

70　　This fantastic story plays with the paretymology of Tetrapylon
　　　(with four gates) as Tetrabelon (with four curtains) and origi-
　　　nally was told about the Tetrapylon on the Mese, i.e., the Arto-
　　　poleia (2.46) or Anemodourin (3.114), not the other one here,
　　　near the Exakionion and the Sigma.

71　　Calculated from Constantine's twelfth year, 317 (see p. xii
　　　above), to the beginning of Zeno's second reign, in 477.

72　　A courtyard in the shape of the Greek letter sigma (C), origi-

nally a part of the palace of Helena, which is not mentioned by the *Patria*.

73 Tzoumas was Chrysaphios's surname, not a title.

74 Magdalas and Eulampios are not historical figures, while the name Charisios alludes to the gate of Charisios, whose eponym is actually unknown. See also below, 3.138.

75 Polyandros (many men) alludes to *polyandron* (graveyard), while *koliandron* means "coriander." See also below, 3.140.

76 Unknown.

77 From *Parastaseis,* chap. 69, where the name Strategion ("the general's place" or "parade ground") is applied to a tripod (on which see 2.61 below), while here it designates a statue.

78 Calculated from 334 BCE, when Alexander crossed the Hellespont—not the Bosporos as claimed here—to Asia Minor, to Constantine's twelfth year, 317 (see p. xii above). Chrysopolis means "golden city."

79 The city prefect Proklos of Constantinople in the time of Theodosios I (379–395), mentioned in the bilingual inscription of the obelisk base in the Hippodrome, is apparently confused here with the homonymous Neoplatonic philosopher from Athens who actually lived in the time of Theodosios II.

80 Probably the group of statues (?) that, according to the *Parastaseis* and *Patria,* had previously stood at Hagia Sophia; see 2.96 below.

81 See 3.24 below.

82 No other sources mention a statue of Leo I (457–474) on a separate part of this square called the "small Strategion." Strategios is a personal name; see, for example, 4.4 below, for a historical person in the 6th century.

83 A doublet in 3.37 below.

84 This harbor and its founder are attested only by the *Patria* here and in the doublet 3.91, in contrast to the well-known palace of Eleutherios, on which see 3.173 below.

85 The courtyard actually belonged to the church of the Forty Martyrs, on which see 3.46 below, and the cross was set up by Herakleios in 612. For the "vale of tears," see Psalm 83(84):6.

86　The original legend about this house, as contained in the Chronicle of Symeon Logothetes, claims that it was first built by Isidoros, a patrician who had come from Rome with Constantine the Great, served later as a brothel, and was turned into a hospital by Leo III (717–741) and into a nunnery by the widow of Constantine VI, who had lived there after his blinding in 797, before Theophilos made it a hospital again. The very short summary of this story in the *Patria* was expanded again by the topographical version C, with the sentence included here in brackets. Isidoros is mentioned by the *Patria* in 1.58 among the supporters of Constantine during the construction of the city, but not in the list of senators and their buildings in 1.63 and 67. On his church, see 3.121 below.

87　The following story has no historical background, and a sister-in-law of Justin II is unknown. On the bath of the Blachernai, see 3.75 below.

88　From *Parastaseis,* chap. 53. A church of the Mother of God can hardly have been built in Constantine's time, while a church bearing the name of Saint Thekla is well attested at this place from other sources. On the etymology of the word *kontaria,* see 3.35 below.

89　Allusions to the alleged wall of Byzantion described in 1.52, and to the story about the flight of Phokas, 2.35 above.

90　From *Parastaseis,* chap. 54. The name means "<property> of Biglentios," but is derived here from *bigla* (Latin *vigilia* = guard). The actual eponym was Biglentia, on whom see 3.117 below.

91　From *Parastaseis,* chap. 72.

92　Ibid., chap. 74.

93　Ibid., chap. 87. The cistern was actually built in 421, probably by Aetios, city prefect in 419.

94　Ibid., chap. 88.

95　Addition of the topographical version C.

96　The eunuch Basil, illegitimate son of Romanos I (920–944), served under Constantine VII Porphyrogennetos (944–959) and later emperors as *parakoimomenos* and *proedros* (president).

97　Bonos, the defender of Constantinople in 626 against the Avars,

may actually have been of western origin, as his Latin name suggests, but most probably did not come "from Rome." The cistern is also mentioned in 1.53 as a point of reference in the description of the Constantinian land walls. It is probable that it was actually open, not covered as claimed by the *Patria,* and it may in fact be identical to the cistern of Aspar. A shorter doublet is in 3.83 below.

98   From *Parastaseis,* chaps. 60, 74.

99   The origin of this list is unclear, but the mention of Cyprus and Crete, which were reconquered in 965 and 961, respectively, suggests that it was compiled shortly thereafter, as the list in 2.73.

100   From *Parastaseis,* chap. 79.

101   Ibid., chap. 84. These are probably the horses now at San Marco in Venice.

102   Ibid., chap. 19.

103   Ibid., chap. 61.

104   The text added by the *Patria* actually refers to a bronze group of Scylla with Odysseus and his ship, which is also known from other sources.

105   Herodion should probably be identified with the historian Herodian who lived in the third century CE; cf. 2.99.

106   From *Parastaseis,* chap. 61.

107   Ibid., chap. 62.

108   On Apollonios, see n. 1.32.

109   This entry apparently belongs to the series of excerpts concerning the letter *a* from John Lydos, see chaps. 1–15 above.

110   Probably from the same intermediate source, though not from Lydos.

111   This episode is found some lines later in the original context of the *Parastaseis,* and therefore appears here twice.

112   From *Parastaseis,* chap. 64. On the meaning of this story, see p. x above. The lacuna in Pelops's last statement is assumed after Cameron and Herrin, *Constantinople,* p. 145.

113   Ibid., chap. 65.

114   The name of the Nabataean God Dushara is rendered here as Theosares, thus explaining it as *theos Ares* = the God Ares; the

excerpt, which appears also in the Suda, θ 302, may therefore be from the same series of excerpts belonging to the letter *a* as before, on which see 2.1–15, 80, and 81 above.

115 *Parastaseis,* chap. 85.

116 The bath mentioned here in the *Parastaseis* is actually called Konstantianai, i.e., the bath of Constantius; the *Patria* ascribes it to Constantine and wrongly identifies it in the added text with the big bath near the Oikonomion in the Great Palace, mentioned above in 1.60. The Tzykanisterion is the polo ground in the Great Palace.

117 *Parastaseis,* chap. 4. The "ground-level gate" cannot be identified. Phidaleia is the legendary wife of King Byzas; see 1.32 above. Saint Sabas, the founder of several monasteries in Palestine, visited Constantinople in 512/13 and in 531.

118 *Parastaseis,* chap. 5. The text is lost in the *Parastaseis* from here to the middle of *Patria,* 2.91 below. It is difficult to identify abridgements and additions of the *Patria* in this part, but the parallel case of 2.29 above suggests that the last sentence of this chap. 87 did not belong to the original text of the *Parastaseis.*

119 Lost in *Parastaseis.*

120 Lost in *Parastaseis.* Ligyrios is also mentioned in *Parastaseis,* chap. 64, and dated to the reign of Leo I (457–474), but he is omitted in the excerpt of the *Patria,* 2.82 above.

121 Lost in *Parastaseis.* The story blames the "followers of Eutyches," i.e., the Monophysites of the mid-fifth century, for the Persian attacks on Chalkedon in 609 and 616/17, while the relic of Saint Euphemia was not transferred to Constantinople before 681. Neither Akatos nor Perittios can be identified with historical persons.

122 Beginning lost in *Parastaseis.* The "hollow place" may have been a crypt-like subterranean space or grave near the church, or the so-called cistern of Saint Mokios.

123 *Parastaseis,* chap. 6, probably from the same source as the preceding chapter.

124 Ibid., chap. 7. The story about Constantine's murder of his wife Fausta and his son Crispus is attached here to an unknown place called the "Smyrnion" (perfume market?) near the Octagon and

the church of Saint Theodore, on which see 3.30 below. The other five alleged victims of his cruelty are more or less legendary founders of buildings in Constantinople; see 1.35 with n. 51 (Zeuxippos), 2.33 (Severus), 2.63 and 3.91 (Eleutherios), 2.67 (Biglentios), 3.61 (Armatios).

125   *Parastaseis,* chap. 8. The second statue was actually not of Aphrodite, but of Amphitrite, a sea goddess of Greek mythology.

126   Ibid., chap. 9. On the Christian relics under the Forum of Constantine, see above, n. 2.45.

127   *Parastaseis,* chap. 11. As the last sentence suggests, this is actually a list of statues in Constantinople, of which it is claimed that they originally stood at one place, Hagia Sophia. Of these, the Zodiac is mentioned by the *Life* of Euthymios (patriarch 905–912) in the Hippodrome, the South Pole in 2.61 above, at the Tzykanisterion.

128   In the source of this chapter, the *Parastaseis,* the general is called Manaim and thus bears the name of a Jewish king (Menahem, 745–738 BCE), who is not mentioned by any other source outside the context of the Old Testament. The archaizing name "Scythians" may refer to any people attacking the empire from the north of the Balkan peninsula, but the following mention of Emperor Valentinian perhaps connects the episode to the latter's Sarmatian wars in 374/75.

129   This sentence, although restored to the text of the *Parastaseis* by Preger, is probably a later addition, as Krateros may be identified with either Theodore or Andreas Krateros, both high officials in ninth-century Constantinople.

130   *Parastaseis,* chap. 12; another excerpt from the same text at 2.51 above. Here a fantastic story is attached to an ancient work of art, apparently a monumental votive relief depicting two Roman military standards with hands as emblems, and an altar for burnt offerings with flames visible on its top, which was taken for a heaped bushel.

131   Ibid., chap. 12.

132   Ibid., chap. 13. On the Artopoleia, see 2.46 above.

133   *Parastaseis,* chap. 14. A story about the malevolence of pagan statues, similar to the one in 2.24 above.

134   *Parastaseis.* chap. 15. At the beginning, understand "the Forum
... contains twelve statues," etc. The phrase "in our time" probably refers to the age of Constantine V (741–775). On the palace
of Saint Mamas, see 3.159 below.

135   *Parastaseis,* chap. 16, a longer doublet to 2.16 above.

136   *Parastaseis,* chap. 17. The Forum was built on an ancient necropolis, so that the discovery of an ancient casket with bones and an
inscription on it, though not inside a hollow bronze statue, is a
plausible event. The mention of Aphrodite refers to the statue
in front of the Senate, on which see above, 2.94 with note; by
removing her name from the inscription and changing the order
of the last three words, it becomes hexametric.

137   *Parastaseis,* chap. 18. The statue is also mentioned in 2.40 above.

138   The Tzykalareia (Potteries), apparently a door-like structure located somewhere on the eastern coast of Constantinople below
the Great Palace, are also mentioned with their plaited columns
in 1.52, but nowhere else.

139   *Parastaseis,* chap. 19, a doublet to 2.76 above.

140   Ibid., chap. 20, a doublet to 2.19 above. The remark that it
"lasted until Constantine Kopronymos" probably refers to the
destruction of the statue of Arkadios (395–408) by an earthquake in 740.

141   Ibid., chap. 10. Note that Paul became bishop of Constantinople only after Constantine's death, in 337, and icons of
the Mother of God are not otherwise attested before the
sixth century. The mention of Ankyrianos may be a reference
to Saint Neilos of Ankyra, as Anastasios appears in the *Parastaseis* as an intermediate source transmitting Neilos's works and
may actually have been the author of a florilegium quoting
him.

142   Ibid., chap. 2. No other source supports the claim that the first
seven patriarchs of Constantinople, from Anatolios (451–458) to
Timotheos I (511–518), had their residence in this church.

143   Read perhaps ὑπὸ Τιβερίου = by Tiberios.

144   *Parastaseis,* chap. 3b, where the acclamation has the text "Leo
and Constantine are victorious." This suggests that the Leo intended here is actually Leo III with his son and coemperor

Constantine V, not Leo the Great (I, 457–474) as assumed by the *Patria,* and the entry refers to the repairs after the earthquake of 740.

145 Ibid., chap. 3.

146 Ibid., chap. 1. That the church of Saint Mokios replaced an ancient pagan temple is also claimed by other sources, among them 3.3 of the *Patria.* However, the location of it in a Christian necropolis, outside of Constantine's walls and far away from ancient Byzantion, rather suggests that this is a legend elicited by the ample use of antique spolia.

Appendix to Book 2

1 Two manuscripts of the *Patria,* called A and J by the editor Preger, also contain the following eight chapters, which have nothing to do with the remaining text, but present an example of the widespread genre of the "synopses of councils," here with a short text of limited and rather confused content.

2 Pope Silvester (314–335) actually played no role in the theological controversies of his time and did not attend the Council of Nicaea. His mention here, as that of Popes Damasus at the Second, Leo at the Fifth, and Agathon at the Sixth Council, indicates that he was acknowledged, according to the concepts of precedence in later times, as the highest ranking bishop of his age.

3 Christianity was adopted as the state religion by the Georgian kingdom of Iberia already in 327, while the missionary travels of Theophilos the Indian took place only under Emperor Constantius (337–361).

4 The *chrysargyron,* or in Latin *collatio lustralis,* was a tax on traders that was actually introduced by Constantine, and not abolished by him.

5 The church of Saint Euphemia at the Petrion; see 3.67 below.

6 On the Hebdomon, see 3.144 and 145 below, where the church of Samuel is not mentioned.

7 Nestorios, patriarch of Constantinople from 428 to 431, had ar-

gued theologically against the rising cult of the Virgin Mary and
was deposed at this council.

8   The condemnation of Dioskoros's Monophysite theology at
    this council held in Chalkedon, an Asian suburb of Constanti-
    nople, caused the lasting separation of the eastern churches
    from the "orthodoxy" of Rome and Constantinople.

9   The doctrine of Origenes and his followers Euagrios and Didy-
    mos was already condemned, at the instigation of Emperor Jus-
    tinian, shortly before the council. The council was in fact con-
    cerned with the so-called Three Chapters, the teachings of the
    fifth-century theologians Ibas of Edessa, Theodoret of Kyrrhos,
    and Theodore of Mopsuestia.

10 Tiberios was actually Constantine's brother. Herakleios and Ti-
    berios had both been crowned as coemperors with Constantine
    but were deposed and mutilated by him shortly after the coun-
    cil.

11 This is a description of Monotheletism, which had been the of-
    ficial doctrine of the Byzantine Church since 638.

12 Makarios, patriarch of Antioch, was deposed at the council; his
    alleged pupil Isidoros is not mentioned in other sources.

13 The Seventh Council actually established the cult of icons in
    the eastern church. The Theodosios mentioned here is the
    bishop Theodosios of Amorion, who recanted, together with
    others, his former iconoclastic teachings at the beginning of the
    first session.

14 This synod, which was held after the end of the second phase of
    Iconoclasm, without the participation of the western church,
    restored the cult of images and is usually not counted as an Ecu-
    menical Council.

Book 3

1   Summary attribution of old churches to Constantine and Hel-
    ena; see also 1.48–50 above.

2   See 1.51 and 2.110 above.

3   Unclear calculation; perhaps read 139 for 169 years. The date

would then be between Constantine's twelfth year, 317 (see p. xii above), and Markianos's death, in 457, with a mistake of one year.

4   See 2.110 above.

5   The following story gives a fantastic but charming explanation for the name of the monastery called Gastria, which indeed means "bowls, flowerpots." The actual reason for this name is unknown.

6   On the Psomatheas, see 3.136 below.

7   On which see 3.90 below.

8   See 1.70 above, and 3.69 below.

9   Unknown from other sources; the name suggests a round place. The beginning is quoted from 2.47.

10 The legend about the humble origins of Theodosios I (379–395) and his general Rouphinos (Rufinus) has no historical basis and is, like the similar story about Leo I below in 3.104, probably modeled on the legendary origins of Basil I; on which see below, n. 3.102.

11 The church was actually installed in the former main hall of the palace of Antiochos, on which see 3.70 below, after the Sixth Council of Constantinople in 681.

12 Calculated from Constantine's twelfth year, 317 (see p. xii above), to 759, and from there to 796. The "invention" and return of the relics in 796 is known also from other sources, while their alleged desecration in 759 is not.

13 A similar legend, but without topographical indications, appears first in Philostorgios, bk. 1, frag. 9. The mention of the Forum indicates that the entry is the work of the last redactor, who imagined a pre-Constantinian wall of Byzantion.

14 Calculated from Constantine's twelfth year, 317 (see p. xii above), to 600; Phokas came to power two years later, in 602.

15 Markia reappears as a widow from Rome in the *Diegesis;* see 4.2.

16 Actually, the Chalke was first built under the emperor Anastasios in 491.

17 Calculated from Constantine's death, in 337, to 628, the historical date of Anastasios's death.

18   On this church, see 3.115 below.

19   The church of Saint Akakios at the Heptaskalon (the "seven piers") near the Golden Horn is first attested in 359 and still existed in the fourteenth century.

20   Mesomphalon ("middle navel") is actually the correct name, referring to a monument that indicated the symbolical center of the city, while Mesolophon (between the hills) is a playful paretymology.

21   The famous icon of Christ on the Chalke gate, which was probably installed as late as 692 under Emperor Justinian II, is here dated back to Constantine's time.

22   Calculated from Constantine's twelfth year, 317 (see p. xii above), to 726, when the image of Christ on the Chalke was allegedly destroyed.

23   The redactor of the *Patria* apparently identifies the founder of this church with the usurper Eugenios in the time of Theodosios I (392–394), who actually apostatized from the Christian faith during his revolt and was never in Constantinople.

24   That is, not the legendary eunuch Ourbikios mentioned in 1.58 and 70, but the historical, uncastrated (hence "bearded") author of a strategic manual.

25   Calculated from 317 to the beginning of Anastasios's reign in 491.

26   In 1.63. Protasios may be the governor of Syria attested there in the years after 360.

27   Calculated from 317 to 569, the year for which Justin's buildings are usually mentioned by the chronicles.

28   The correct name Ta Tzerou points to a foundation by a person surnamed Tzeros (dried mackerel), perhaps the sixth-century general Theodore Tziros, and not by an infertile *(steiros)* woman as claimed here. One of these churches is probably the church of Saint Michael called elsewhere "of the Senator," while the other, that of Saint Gabriel, may have been added only by Basil I.

29   Calculated from the beginning of Leo's reign, in 457, to the Nika Riot, in 532, and from there to the earthquake of 869.

30   On which see 3.200 below.

31   The attribution to Emperor Arkadios (395–408) may simply be
      due to the nearby Arkadianai bath. The foundation of the Arka-
      diakoi is dated by other sources to the year 400.

32   The "steps known as Topoi" are also mentioned, without the
      subsequently attached story, in 2.27 above, in an entry taken
      from the *Parastaseis.*

33   On Armatios, see also 3.61 below.

34   This monastery acquired its great importance only after the *Pa-
      tria* was written. The name Hodegoi (guides) supposedly refers
      to the people who led the blind to the miraculous spring.

35   The following anecdote, which is actually told not about Mi-
      chael III himself but about his father Theophilos, tries to ex-
      plain the epithet of the church, which may go back to a ship
      model suspended there as a votive gift. It combines a well-
      known story, dated in the chronicles to the time of Emperor
      Valentinian and the year 364, about the widow Berenike, a
      chamberlain called Rhodanos, and a prefect Salloustios, in
      which only the names have been changed, with a mention of the
      so-called Vegetable Race, the celebration of the city's birthday
      on May 11, during which, among other things, vegetables and
      cakes were thrown into the crowd, as were fish from a small ship
      that was brought into the Hippodrome on a carriage.

36   "Marble house" *(apo marmarou oikos)* is apparently another at-
      tempt to explain the name Ta Maurianou, on which see 3.42 be-
      low.

37   The polo ground of the palace, first mentioned in Theodosios's
      own time as *lusorium.*

38   Addition of the topographical version C.

39   The important New Church and the Mother of God on the Fo-
      rum, both founded by Basil I, are mentioned by the *Patria* only
      here and in 3.162 below. On Ta Steirou, see 3.24 above; on Saint
      Diomedes, 3.86 below.

40   Calculated from the last year of Theodosios II, 449/50, to the
      beginning of Maurikios's (582–602) reign in 582. In the following

story, the actual discovery of the money is missing due to excessive abridgment.

41   Apparently an octagon with an ambulatory, set into a rectangular structure with four outer porticoes.

42   Calculated from the beginning of Constantine's sole rule in 312—that is, before Constantinople was even founded—to 726.

43   The supposed assassination of orthodox monks by the Iconoclasts in 726 is also reported by various other sources, but never located in the Octagon.

44   Calculated from Constantine's twelfth year, 317 (see p. xii above), to the last year of Theodosios II, 449/50. Most sources from the ninth century on attribute this church to his sister Pulcheria.

45   The following story combines elements from Illos's insurrection in 484 with those of an Isaurian rebellion after Zeno's death, in 491.

46   Two competing etymologies for the place-name, supported by fictitious authorities. Actually, the house of Emperor Nikephoros Phokas's family lay in this area.

47   Executions on the *furca* (fork) were performed by fixing the delinquent's head in the crotch of a huge wooden fork.

48   Probably quoted from 2.66, with the name of King Haimos added, on whom see 1.15 above; on Byzas see 1.3 above.

49   Addas is identified here with the *magister militum* Addaios in the late fourth century, who appears also in the list of Constantine's senators (see 1.63), but must actually be the prefect of Constantinople executed on the orders of Justin II in 567.

50   Historically erroneous addition of the topographical manuscript E; on the church of Saint Thomas, see chap. 96.

51   See n. 1.57 above.

52   Addition of the topographical manuscript E.

53   Doublet to 2.62.

54   Added by the topographical version C from the original entry 2.62.

55   Calculated as in 3.23 above.

56   Elaborate version of 1.11 above. The place-name Boukinon or Bykanon is attested for the last time in 1203.

57   In reality there were two churches with a common narthex and adjoining each other, one of Saints Sergios and Bacchos, and the other of the apostles Peter and Paul. The massacre in the Hippodrome occurred during the Nika Riot, in 532.

58   Actually, the harbor was first built under the emperor Julian.

59   Anastasios's accession actually fell in the year 6000 of the Byzantine era.

60   See 3.213 below.

61   This is the sixth-century bath of Dagisthaios, which was out of use by the early ninth century at the latest.

62   Unclear calculation, probably starting from Constantine's twelfth year, 317 (see p. xii above).

63   For a similar legend, see 3.107 below.

64   Another attempt, in addition to the one at the end of 3.28 above, to explain the name Ta Maurianou, which, of course, goes back to a person called Maurianos.

65   Aspar was, in fact, executed in 471, long after the restoration of the church by Markianos (450–457). The actual foundation goes back to Saint Gregory the Theologian, i.e., of Nazianzos.

66   An elegant way to describe the rebuilding of a large late-antique basilica as a much smaller, but vaulted cross-in-square church.

67   Hilarion should probably be identified with Hilarianos, a high court official attested in the last years of Leo's reign.

68   That is, it replaced an old prison.

69   Erroneous addition of the topographical manuscript E: the person intended is certainly Sampson, on whom see 3.119 below.

70   This sentence refers to Zotikos's alleged role in the foundation of Constantinople, on which see also 3.48; Zotikos "of most pious memory" is first mentioned in a law from 472, but cannot be dated more exactly, and the title *protobestiarios* given to him here is anachronistic.

71   Addition of manuscript H.

72   Ta Karpianou is first mentioned for the year 602 in the chroni-

cle of Theophanes, but not in its source, Theophylaktos Simo-
kates.

73   Bassos is attested in Justinian's time. He features also in Prokopios's *Anekdota,* where, however, Theodora has a man called
Theodore tortured in this manner, while a man called Bassianos
is simply executed.

74   Probably identical to the church at the Turtle (Chelone), on
which see 3.115 below.

75   The relics of Saint Stephen were actually deposited in a church
of the Forty Martyrs which later took Stephen's name; see also
3.64 below.

76   Confusion of the actual founder Iouliane Anikia (d. 527), daughter of the western Roman emperor Olybrios (see 3.60 below),
with Galla, daughter of Valentinian and second wife of Theodosios, and also another Iouliane, wife of an Olybrios in Theodosios's time. The actual builder of the aqueduct was Valentinian's
brother Valens (364–378); see 2.69.

77   Calculated from the consulate of Areobindos in 506 to 598, a
date for the church mentioned also by other sources.

78   See also above, 3.26.

79   That is, in the twelfth year of Maurikios (582–602), 594.

80   A contradiction: a building that had already served as a home
for old people for 280 years cannot be a private residence later.

81   Unclear calculation, perhaps from the Council of Chalkedon
held under Markianos (450–457) and Pulcheria in 451 to Artabasdos's seizure of power in 741, with a mistake of ten years.

82   See also 3.55 above.

83   I.e., from his flight to the east during the civil war against Basiliskos in 474–475, on which see 3.26 above.

84   From a series of anti-iconoclastic anecdotes about Constantine
V; see also 3.9 above, and 68, 134, 135 below. The supposed acclamation is a parody of the well-known acclamation for the prefect Kyros, on which see below, 3.111.

85   The main hall of this palace was later converted into a church of
Saint Euphemia, on which see 3.9 above.

86   The chronicle of Theophanes mentions the "Carian portico"

built by Maurikios (582–602) in 588 in a way which suggests that the name was actually derived from a wall revetment of Carian marble, not from a person called Karianos.

87 Note that the subsequent major restorations under Justin I and II are not mentioned. The third etymology alludes to the robe of the Mother of God, the *lacerna* in Latin, which was kept in the chapel of the Holy Shrine (see 3.75).

88 Actually, after the Avar siege in 626, during which the church had also been occupied for some time. On the bath, see also 3.214 below.

89 Miraculous discoveries of money for building a church are a frequent motif in Constantinopolitan folklore; see, for example, 4.11 and 32.

90 Chrysobalanon is actually a fruit (golden acorn), but the story told here fits the more usual name Chrysobalanton (purse of gold), under which the monastery appears in the Vita of its legendary abbess Eirene.

91 Euphrosyne, the actual founder of this monastery, was Eirene's granddaughter and the second wife of Theophilos's father, Michael II, not the sister of Theophilos's son Michael III. The story confuses Euphrosyne's retirement into her monastery in 829 with the detention of Michael III's mother, Theodora, and his sisters in 859 at Ta Karianou (3.73 above).

92 The "dry garden" is perhaps the cistern of Aspar, which must have been out of operation after the destruction of the water supply line in 626. On the cistern, see 2.71 above.

93 Actually, Justinian first fled to the Khazars and married the khan's sister before returning to Constantinople in 705 with the help of the Bulgarians under their khan Terbelis.

94 The name Deuteron, for which a satisfactory explanation has not yet been found, is already attested in the time of Justinian I, under whom the church of Saint Anna was also built.

95 According to the chronicle of Theophanes, the church "of the metropolitan" in the Great Palace area was dismantled under Justinian II and rebuilt near the Petrion (on which see 3.151 below).

96   The church of Saint Romanos is not mentioned by any other
      source before 518.

97   Unclear calculation, probably starting from Constantine's
      twelfth year, 317 (see p. xii above). The remark rather refers to
      the Stoudios monastery, where Joseph and Theodore actually
      lived; see 3.87 below.

98   That is, as a rotunda with an ambulatory. The church, of which
      the substructure still exists, was certainly built long after Hele-
      na's death.

99   Doublet of 2.72.

100   Corrupted text, restored by Preger from manuscripts G H.

101   A granary, probably named after a relief or sculpture on its fa-
      cade.

102   The church is not mentioned before 518 and therefore can
      hardly have been built by Constantine. According to tradition,
      Basil I slept on the steps before the gate when he first arrived in
      Constantinople, and a divine voice exhorted the abbot to invite
      the future emperor inside.

103   This number must refer to a time when the Stoudios monastery
      had become the head of a large network of monasteries near
      Constantinople and include all monks living in them.

104   A completely legendary entry. On the church of the Mother
      of God, see also 1.53, 1.68, and 1.73 above. Aimilianos was ac-
      tually martyred after Constantine's lifetime, under Julian (361–
      363).

105   This story is probably attached to the same statue of an ele-
      phant as that in 2.41.

106   Doublet to 2.63.

107   The "secretary of the ink pot." The Skyla are the access gates to
      the Great Palace from the covered hippodrome, on which see
      3.129 below.

108   Conflation of Theodora, wife of Justinian I, who came from
      humble origins in Constantinople, and Theodora, wife of
      Theophilos and mother of Michael III, who originated from an
      aristocratic family in Paphlagonia. The old Homonoia church
      took Panteleemon's name before the lifetime of either of them,

so the historical core, if it exists at all, can consist only in a restoration of this church by the first Theodora.

109 Probably to be identified with Peter Barsymios; see 3.151 below.

110 Martinakes became a monk and converted his house into a monastery already in 837, so he can hardly have been an uncle of the empress Theophano (d. 897).

111 On Saint Mamas see 3.159 below. The *manglabitai* were a corps of the imperial bodyguard.

112 That is, as a rotunda with an ambulatory, similar to the church of Karpos and Papylos, on which see 3.82 above. Nothing is said about the identity of this *kourator.*

113 A desperate attempt to reconcile the surname "of the deaconess" with the information taken from a chronicle (such as that of Theophanes, where the church is dated to 598).

114 Pharmakas is a fictitious person whose name is drawn from the saint's surname Pharmakolytria, i.e., the one "who heals poisonings" or "who cures wounds."

115 Although the name Dimakellin is used in the title here, the following story gives a paretymology of the more usual form Leomakelli(o)n, which probably means "people's market," but is explained here as the place where Leo I and his wife Verina supposedly worked before he became emperor. Leo's surname Makelles (the Butcher) appears only long after his death and is presumably already derived from the Leomakelli(o)n.

116 Anthemios was not sent to Rome until 467 by Emperor Leo I, ten years after Markianos's death.

117 The epithet Tes Spoudes means, in reality, not "of Haste," but "of (religious) Zeal." Also, Anna was not Leo III's wife, but his daughter. The parallel to the stories on the Diegesteas and Deuteron in 3.41 and 79 above suggest that the church was dedicated to Saint Anna and that this is the reason why an empress was introduced into the story.

118 A person called Seueros (Severus) in this time is unknown to other sources, while the toponym Seueriana is attested in Constantinople already in the fifth century. Phoinix (modern Finike) is the place in Lycia where Constans suffered a disastrous naval

defeat at the hands of the Arabs in 655, and has nothing to do
with his assassination in 668.

119   Rather in Kotyaeion in Phrygia, as stated by the chronicles,
where the acclamation is "Constantine built it (the wall), Kyros
made it new."

120   The "golden arch" may have been a remnant of the huge fifth-
century palace of Arkadia (?), into whose ruins the Myrelaion
monastery had been built, on which see 3.134 below. The existence of a golden statue is probably a product of the author's
imagination.

121   The tetrapylon of the so-called Artopoleia (on which see 2.46
above), named after the weather vane at its summit, the Anemodourin or Anemodoulion ("servant of the winds").

122   The magician Heliodoros is the hero of the Life of Bishop Leo
of Catania, a ninth-century "hagiographical novel" with a fantastic plot set in the reign of Leo III the Syrian.

123   The Chelone can be located in the region where Dionysios of
Byzantion, in his *Anaplous* of the Bosporos (second century
CE?), mentions a place called the Skironian Rocks, an obvious
allusion to the legend of a giant named Skiron who threw way-
farers from a rock near Corinth, thus feeding them to a gigantic
turtle that lived on the shore below.

124   In 3.18.

125   Probably to be distinguished from the Akakios church at the
Heptaskalon, on which see 3.18 above.

126   No other source gives any information about the life of Antonina after the death of her husband in 565.

127   Perhaps identical with the purple workshops mentioned in 3.94
above.

128   Sampson actually lived long before Justinian's time, probably in
the fourth century.

129   Euboulos and Isidoros in the following chapter were not·broth-
ers, but they successively held the office of the praetorian
prefect of the Illyricum in the 430s, long before the reign of
Justin I.

130   Nothing is known from other sources about Herakleios's life in

Constantinople before his revolt, which started from Carthage in 608.

131   According to all other sources, the Boukoleon palace was built under Theophilos, and the Golden Hall under Justin II.

132   That is, the old parts of the Great Palace.

133   Two alternative etymologies, the latter going back to John Lydos's *De mensibus*.

134   The "covered hippodrome," a courtyard inside the Great Palace which was actually unsuitable for chariot races.

135   See 2.49 above.

136   Both the harbor and the gate were built long after Constantine's time.

137   Agallianos fell before Constantinople as the leader of a rebel fleet in 726, but probably has nothing to do with the construction of the Kontoskalion harbor. The surname attached to him here is a playful etymology of the harbor's name, which simply means "with short piers."

138   Actually, this monastery was built by Romanos Lekapenos, about 150 years after Constantine V. Theodore Kamoulianos appears in the sources only during the reign of his grandson Constantine VI.

139   See 3.38 above.

140   Addition of manuscript H. Both etymologies are, of course, fantastic, since the more usual form of the name, Psamathia, simply means "the sands."

141   Beginning of a series of entries on the gates of the land walls. This gate was not the fifth in number, but rather lay at or on the road to an unknown place called To Pempton (the Fifth).

142   Addition of manuscripts B H. Char(i)sios was the founder of a monastery near the gate, which was most probably built *after* the land walls; see also above, 2.58. Note that he is called a member of the Green faction in 1.58.

143   Xylokerkos actually means "wooden circus," with the Latin word *circus* as the second part. The marshy terrain must have been more to the north where the Lykos river crosses the wall.

144   Excerpted from 2.58 above.

145 Germanos is probably the fourth-century *consularis* who may have also served as *proconsul* of Achaia, with both his title and place of employment updated to the middle Byzantine terminology.

146 As the church first appears in a source in 536, it was actually built in the first years of Justinian's reign, before Hagia Sophia was finished. On the alleged role of Strategios as Justinian's friend and close counselor, see below, 4.4.

147 Probably calculated from 537, the year in which Hagia Sophia was completed, to Eirene's accession in 797.

148 Abramios actually lived in the mid-fifth century.

149 The Hebdomon was a great military camp to the west of Constantinople at present-day Bakırköy. Both churches, that of John the Evangelist and that of John the Baptist in the next entry, already existed in the late fourth century, but the octagonal church described here is the second building from Justinian's time.

150 The building, a monastery of Saints Kosmas and Damianos (the Anargyroi), was actually founded by a noble lady called Paulina in the 470s and is therefore usually called Ta Paulines. The name is slightly changed here to accommodate the well-known anecdote about the *magistros* Paulinos and the empress Eudokia, which first appears in the chronicle of John Malalas.

151 I.e., big as a pumpkin (?).

152 Addition of manuscript H.

153 See 3.32 above.

154 This entry has a close parallel in the description of Constantinople by the anonymous Englishman from the late 11th century.

155 Fictitious quote; on Byzas see n. 1.12 above.

156 That is, half-round.

157 Correctly Barsymios.

158 There is no such historical person, but perhaps this is a variant of King Haimos in 1.15 and 3.35 above.

159 Calculated from Leo's accession in 457 until "today," that is 989/90; see p. xii above.

160   Addition of the topographical manuscript E.

161   Probably calculated from Maurikios's (582–602) accession in 582 to 830, a date not mentioned elsewhere for this monastery.

162   Confusion between Tiberios I (578–582) and II (Apsimaros, 698–705). Chaganos is the title, not the name, of the ruler of the Avars whose attacks began in Tiberios I's reign; the Bulgarians appeared on former Byzantine territory only one hundred years later, around 680.

163   I.e., the church of Saint Michael on the European side of the Bosporos in modern Arnavutköy.

164   On the church of the Forum and the New Church, see 3.29a above.

165   That is, a church of the archangel Michael.

166   Added from manuscript B; on Zotikos, see 3.47 and 48 above.

167   Later called the Double Column (Diplokionion), probably the last remnant of the already destroyed palace of Saint Mamas, on which see 3.159 above.

168   On the cistern and palace of Bonos, see 2.72 and 3.83 above.

169   Probably Theophilos the Indian, a missionary in southern Arabia and Ethiopia in the mid-fourth century.

170   On the etymology, see also 3.177 below.

171   The name Bryas actually means "owl." The paretymology as "roaring" *(brygmos)* connects the place to an idea of Byzantine apocalypticism that the last emperor before the coming of the Antichrist will leave Constantinople for Jerusalem and see the city sinking into the sea.

172   No explanation has been found for this expression.

173   ·Neither monastery is attested before the late seventh century.

174   Calculated from Constantine's twelfth year, 317 (see above, p. xii), to 784/85, the actual date of Paul's death.

175   Not attested by other sources.

176   Pun on the word *abbakia* (dice); the actual meaning must be *abba Kyrou,* "of the abbas (father) Kyros." This church and the following one are known only from the *Patria.*

177   That is, of the Golden Horn. All three etymologies offered are subsequent constructions, for *hierion* means "animal for sacri-

fice." See also the following note for an additional etymology of
a similar place-name.

178 Another paretymology alluding to the word *heroön,* that is
"monument for a hero," or later simply "grave."

179 See next chapter.

180 This etymology must be essentially correct, as the name
Galata(s) for this suburb appears only long after the older form
Ta Galatou.

181 The Keratoembolin, meaning "horn-shaped portico," must
have been a curved portico along the bay of the Neorion harbor.
On Ta Armatiou, see 3.61–62; on Saint Eirene, see 3.1; on the
Neori(o)n, see 2.68.

182 Literally, "horned."

183 The following anecdote is reported by chronicles from the sixth
century on, but Anastasios's death is not situated in the Magnaura, and the pun on the words *mana* and *aura* is missing. The
actual name "Magnaura" is derived from either Latin *magna aula*
or *magna aurea,* the "great hall" or "great golden (hall)."

184 Calculated probably from the Nika Riot, in 532, to the earthquake of 869/70, so the number should be corrected to 338. The
church, being dedicated to the Mother of God, can hardly have
been older than the mid-fifth century.

185 A play on the words *sigma* (a semicircular plaza) and *seisma*
(earthquake). On other examples of *sigma* in Constantinople,
see 1.60, 2.45, 2.57, 3.149.

186 The following story about the general Priskos exiled in the
Chora monastery is a very short excerpt from one of the chronicles where Priskos is called Krispos. The topographical version
C expands the story again with an insertion that is taken from
the same chronicle.

187 "Under Byzas" meaning "before Constantine." The actual meaning of Chora here is "field" rather than "village."

188 That is, "dry circus," a variant of Xylokerkos, the "wooden circus," on which see 3.139 above.

189 This monastery was founded, according to other sources, in the
mid-sixth century by a eunuch called Pharasmanes. If the *Patria*

ascribes it to an unnamed sister of the emperor Maurikios (582–602), this may be explained by the fact that although his body had been thrown into the sea after his execution in 602, his grave was later shown in the Mamas monastery.

190   The monastery of the New Repentance is otherwise only mentioned as the place where Herakleios's fiancée Eudokia was detained by Phokas in 610, and no other source claims that the bodies of Maurikios's (582–602) wife and daughters were also thrown into the sea.

191   Or perhaps emend to "her holy body." Markianos (on whom see 3.43 above) was buried, according to his Life, in a Prodromos church near the Mokios cistern (on which see 3.84 above), which has here taken the name of an otherwise unknown Saint Zoe.

192   The church of the holy notaries Markianos and Martyrios was actually built in the time of Theodosios II.

193   This church and that of Saint John "at the Old Gate" are also mentioned in 1.53 to define the course of the Constantinian land walls.

194   A completely garbled entry: Saint Domnika came, according to her Life, from Rome to Constantinople via Alexandria and founded her monastery. The monastery Ta Gregorias is not mentioned in this text.

195   The monastery is unknown to other sources. Samuel's horn of oil is mentioned only once among the relics in the Great Palace, by Anthony of Novgorod in the year 1200.

196   Confusion of two persons called Nikephoros Xylinites: the one mentioned here was executed after a failed revolt in 719, while the actual founder of the monastery became a monk in 875 and was later treasurer of Hagia Sophia.

197   Addition of manuscript H.

198   Note that the famous, but probably unhistorical story about the bride show of Theophilos, where Kassia/Ikasia was first chosen and then rejected after her bold response to the emperor, is not mentioned here.

199   A parallel to 3.146 above: as no information was available about

the founder, a lady called Smaragde, the redactor changed the name to the male form and identified the person with Smaragdos, the first exarch of Italy in 585–589.

200   This monastery was actually founded in the time of Michael II's grandson Michael III.

201   See 3.24 above.

202   The name actually refers to a gate of the western long side of the Hippodrome and existed already before the Nika Riot, in 532, to which the text alludes here. The *Patria* does not mention a gate, and the two points mentioned to describe its location actually lie on the eastern long side near the imperial box.

203   Addition of the topographical manuscript E.

204   Clearly a later reinterpretation of an antique statue.

205   The chapel of Saint Nikolaos at the southeastern corner of Hagia Sophia, which was certainly not converted from a residential house.

206   The Trikymbalon (the "three cymbals") is mentioned only once outside the *Patria*; the Chalinaria (the "bridles") never.

207   The monastery was named for its second abbot Dalmatos, who directed it from 406 to 438 and bears no relation to the homonymous nephew of Constantine the Great (d. 339).

208   Addition of family A, and the topographical versions. The correct name is Ta Marinakiou, after a person called Marinakes.

209   The actual founder was Aurelianos, consul in 400. Isaakios, founder of the monastery later called Ta Dalmatou (on which see 3.207 above), was buried in the church in 408.

210   Addition of the topographical manuscript E. On the church of Saint Theophano, see 3.212 below.

211   In the Life of Hypatios of Gangra, the episode with the dragon is dated to the time of Constantine the Great's son Constantius II, without reference to a concrete place. On the church of Illos, see 3.33 above.

212   The church was actually built for the burial of Theophano (d. 897) by her husband Leo VI but soon renamed the church of All Saints, and her body was transferred to the Church of the Apostles.

213   Addition of the topographical manuscript E.

214   This first building phase of the famous Chalke chapel is known only by the *Patria,* in contrast to the enlargement by John Tzimiskes.

215   The last phrase after the words "for supporting" actually belongs to the preceding sentence.

Book 4

1   Hagia Sophia was built not by Constantine the Great but by his son Constantius II, and it was inaugurated only in 360.

2   I.e., as a three-aisled basilica with a wooden ceiling; see also above, 3.1. For the church of Saint Agathonikos, see above, 2.107; for that of Saint Akakios, 3.18.

3   For these statues, see above, 2.96.

4   Calculated either from the inauguration of Constantinople, in 330, to the historically correct date of the fire in 404, or from the foundation of the city in 324 to 398; see n. 6 below. The fire actually took place after Theodosios I's death in 395, and the Second Council in 381, so the emperor mentioned here is Theodosios II (408–450), under whom the restored church was completed in 414.

5   It is usually assumed that the church was completely rebuilt at this time, but with a timber roof, as in the preceding phase.

6   Calculated either from 398 to the Nika Riot, in 532, when the Theodosian church was destroyed, or from 406 — two years after the fire, as stated in the text — to the inauguration of Justinian's church, in 537. Note that no connection is established between the Nika Riot and the destruction of the old Hagia Sophia.

7   The gradual replacement of the Roman provinces by military districts *(themata)* began only in the late seventh century, long after Justinian's time.

8   Cf. Psalm 106 (107):3.

9   Not historical persons. The title "first secretary" *(protasekretis)* did not yet exist in Justinian's time, while Markia appears also in

3.14 as a widow from Constantinople. The origin of these columns from Rome is a legend based on the designation of porphyry as "Roman stone"; see below, n. 29.

10   Aurelian (270–275) is probably confused here with Valerian (253–260), who was taken prisoner by the Persians and died in captivity.

11   Constantine is not a historical person. The big columns of greenstone on the ground level actually came from quarries in Thessaly.

12   A date chosen for symbolical reasons. In fact, the church was rebuilt within five years immediately after its destruction in 532.

13   After this point, the existence of a church before the age of Justinian is ignored throughout the text.—The widow Anna is not a historical person.

14   Supplied by Preger from two manuscripts, but not necessary for an understandable text.

15   The treasury (*skeuophylakion*), a domed rotunda, which predates Justinian's church, still stands today to the northeast of Hagia Sophia.

16   Probably an allusion to the well-known patrician Antiochos in the time of Theodosios II, on whom see 3.70 above.

17   Strategios, an Egyptian landowner, was head of the imperial finances (*comes sacrarum largitionum*) from 533 to 538. There is no reason to believe that he was actually Justinian's spiritual brother.

18   The column of Saint Basil obviously took its name from the mosaic that depicted him in the southern tympanum over the galleries, in the second niche from the east. The tympanum was rebuilt after the earthquake of 869, but its mosaics were probably executed much later: among the saints depicted is the patriarch Ignatios, who was in office at the time of the earthquake and died in 878, and whose cult as a saint began only after Photios's final deposition in 886.

19   This surname (meaning "son of a goose") is hardly imaginable in the sixth century.

20   Xenophon is not a historical person, and the meaning of the

word *basiliskarios* in this context is unknown. The column of Saint Gregory the Wonderworker had received its name in the same way as that of Saint Basil; the mosaic of Gregory was in the third niche of the northern tympanum from the west.

21 A statue in the starting boxes of the Hippodrome, which for some reason had been set up with its back to the spectators, may have actually existed, while this story and the person of Xenophon must have been attached to it later.

22 Hagia Sophia has two narthexes, so the third and fourth (mentioned also in 4.15) are presumably the two wings of the atrium.

23 Not a historical person.

24 In fact, the patriarch at this time was Menas (536–552); Eutychios was in office later in Justinian's reign, and a second time long after his death (552–565, 577–582).

25 The original baptistery of Hagia Sophia lay to the north of the main building. A later baptistery survives as a mausoleum to the south. The clock house *(horologion)* is at the southwest corner of Hagia Sophia.

26 The name actually first appears in 4.10. The real architects of Hagia Sophia, mentioned by the historian Prokopios, were Anthemios of Tralles and Isidoros of Miletos. Ignatios appears only in the *Diegesis;* see also below, n. 73.

27 Extracts of barley and elm tree bark have a slimy consistency and were also in pharmaceutical use.

28 These silver coins, the *miliarisia,* were struck between the early eighth and late eleventh centuries mainly for ceremonial distributions at coronations and processions.

29 Porphyry, though imported in the Roman era from Egypt in large quantities, was usually called "Roman stone" in Byzantine texts because of the imperial symbolism associated with it and because most of the porphyry used had actually been brought to the east from Rome and Italy.

30 Not a historical person.

31 The expression σκαφικὰς ἀψίδας (not κεφαλικὰς ἀψίδας) clearly refers to the domical groin vaults over the aisles.

32 "Wisdom" (Sophia) appears as a popular name for the Great Church already in the fifth century, while "Holy Wisdom" (Hagia Sophia) is only attested after Justinian's time.

33 As the upper row of columns is said to stand on a "second gallery," it is clear that this expression refers to the present single gallery of the building.

34 Basilides, member of the commission responsible for forming the *Corpus Iuris Civilis,* served as *quaestor* of the Sacred Palace from 532 to 534.

35 Mentioned in Prokopios's *Anekdota,* 9.37–42, as Theodotos Kolokynthios.

36 In the Hebdomon, on which see 3.144 and 145 above.

37 The passage is difficult to understand because of the unclear terminology used in the Greek text. There is no obvious connection between the number of windows and the absence of centering. The vertical wall of the apse is actually lit by two rows of three windows each.

38 Cf. Psalm 45 (46):5.

39 The term *lakarika* is derived from Latin *laquearia* = coffered ceiling.

40 The "third gallery" is apparently the level of the big tympana under the northern and southern arches of the dome.

41 I.e., with gold mosaic.

42 Deleted by Preger.

43 A semi-circular tunnel of this kind under the *synthronon* (a semi-circular bench for the clergy in the apse of a church) may still be seen at Saint Eirene, Constantinople, and elsewhere.

44 The *thalassa* was a liturgical basin, probably on a stand, for ritual ablutions.

45 Excluded by Preger.

46 The text in angled brackets is Preger's emendation in the apparatus of his edition.

47 This chapter is missing from the version in the *Patria.*

48 Unknown from other sources. Philosophers from Athens or Thebes are stock characters of patriographical literature; they

appear also, for example, in 2.82 and 3.37 above. Hierotheos is the name of the legendary first bishop of Athens, who was allegedly ordained by Saint Paul himself.

49   Mutilated fragment of a well-known building legend (which appears later also, for example, as a proposal made during the construction of Florence Cathedral in the early fifteenth century): in order to save the expense for the centering, a church is filled with sand mixed with money, which the citizens are allowed to remove, keeping the money, after its completion. Another building legend is told in 4.29.

50   In fact, the church was built in the five years between 532 and 537. The calculation here leads us, if starting from 532, to 548, and if starting from 537 (see nn. 4.2 and 4.6 above), to 553.

51   A passage from the presbytery to the ambo, raised by a step and with parapets on either side.

52   The text has "which the angels had as imitations," which is hardly understandable. The passage must mean that the trumpets were not actual relics.

53   This cross probably contained parts of the relic of the True Cross, which was brought to Constantinople from Apameia in Syria in 568, thus only after Justinian's death.

54   The Twelve Feasts are the Annunciation, Nativity, Circumcision, Presentation in the Temple, Baptism, Transfiguration, Raising of Lazarus, Entry into Jerusalem, Crucifixion, Resurrection, Ascension, and Pentecost. Their codification in this canonical form happened, however, only in the eleventh/twelfth century.

55   The mention of Gospel books appears to be out of place here.

56   Votive crowns for suspension.

57   The number of clerics and other staff of the Great Church was actually limited to 525 by Justinian's Novella 3. The presence of female singers in churches was still usual when Justinian's Great Church was built, but not in later times.

58   This chapter is missing from the version in the *Patria*.

59   For Constantine's legendary expedition against Persia, see also

the story in 1.63–65 above, where 365 hundredweights are the tribute paid by the Persians on this occasion.

60   These strips of marble in the pavement are called *phina* (from Latin *finis*), a word denoting any kind of boundary line. For the four rivers of Paradise, see Genesis 2:10–14.

61   This must refer not to the right-hand gallery, which was actually reserved for the emperor and his family, but to a structure on ground level in the south aisle below it.

62   The emperor's changing room *(mutatorium)* lay in the eastern bay of the south aisle.

63   An animal sacrifice at the inauguration of a Christian church is entirely inconceivable and can be understood only as an allusion to the mention of such sacrifices at the inauguration of Solomon's temple (3 Kings 8:5).

64   Probably an allusion to the church of Saint Polyeuktos (on which see above, 3.57), which had been built shortly before Hagia Sophia on the same measurements as Solomon's temple in Jerusalem.

65   The dome actually collapsed in 558, according to the chronicle of Theophanes on Tuesday, May 7, when Justinian was still emperor, not in Justin's second year, 566. Note that May 7 was a Thursday only in 554, seventeen years after the actual inauguration, in 537.

66   The word *antinyktas* is not attested elsewhere.

67   In fact, the dome was heightened by more than three fathoms.

68   Not a historical person, but perhaps an allusion to the well-known chamberlain Narses in Justinian's time.

69   Another building legend, technically as impossible as the one in 4.20 above.

70   The *Patria* additions to the *Diegesis* begin here. If the date is calculated from the Nika Riot, in 532, this gives the year 989/90 as the date for these additions.

71   On this statue on horseback, which stood on a high column in the Augoustion courtyard to the south of Hagia Sophia, see above, 2.17.

72   On Ta Lausou, see above, 2.17 and 36.

73   An allusion to the following story is also contained in the report
      of the Arab traveler Harun ibn-Yahya from about 912, but with
      Stylianos as the architect's name. The name Stylianos is not at-
      tested before the ninth century; it means "stylite" but is appar-
      ently understood here as "the builder of the *stylos* (column)." It
      cannot be determined which name, Ignatios or Stylianos, is
      older in the context of this story.

74   The following chapter forms a shorter pendant to the long story
      of Justinian and "his" church in the *Diegesis* by making the Holy
      Apostles Theodora's church. In reality, the church was inaugu-
      rated only in 550, two years after her death, in 548.

75   Actually, the river Lykos flowed at a distance of about one thou-
      sand meters south of the Holy Apostles.

76   The Church of the Apostles, of which nothing remains today,
      was cruciform in plan and had five domes, one in the center and
      one on each arm. The Church of Saint John the Theologian (i.e.,
      the Evangelist) in Ephesos was a copy of the Church of the
      Apostles rather than the other way round; it had an additional
      sixth dome on the longer western arm of the cross and was
      probably built on a smaller scale.

77   Below the church on the shore of the Golden Horn; see above,
      3.72. For a pendant to this story in the *Diegesis,* see 4.11 above.

78   Artemios, a former governor of Egypt, was accused and exe-
      cuted under the emperor Julian (361–363) for cruelties during his
      time in office. As Julian had been the last pagan emperor who
      persecuted the Christians, however, Artemios was later re-
      garded as a saint and was credited with the translation of the
      relics of Saints Andrew, Luke, and Timothy to Constantinople
      earlier in his career.

79   That is, under the central dome.

80   Theophano (d. 896), the first wife of Leo VI, was first buried in
      her own mortuary church but later transferred to Constantine's
      mausoleum at the Holy Apostles; see above, 3.212.

81   Justinian and his successors, including the iconoclastic emper-

ors from Leo III (717–741) to Theophilos (829–842), were buried in this mausoleum.

82   On which see above, 3.29a and 162.

83   Stylianos Tzaoutzes (d. 899), the third father-in-law of Leo VI, was the first to receive the title *basileopator* (the emperor's father).

Glossary of Offices, Titles,
and Technical Terms

asekretis: a secretary or notary of the imperial chancery (from Latin *a secretis*).

baioulos: a preceptor or mentor of a prince (from Latin *baiulus*).

basileopator: "father of the emperor"; honorary title created in 891? by Leo VI for his father-in-law, Stylianos Tzaoutzes (d. 899), and later also used by Romanos I Lekapenos in 919/20.

caesar: in the late Roman and early Byzantine era, a title designating the heir apparent; later, when the heir apparent was usually crowned as coemperor, generally used for second- and third-born sons and other close relatives.

chartoularios: an administrative official with fiscal and administrative duties (from *chartes* = papyrus, document).

consularis: originally the title of a former consul; later also used for provincial governors and other officials.

domestikos: originally the commander of the *Scholai*, a corps of professional soldiers under direct imperial command created in the eighth century. The position evolved into a high command of the imperial field armies and was split in the tenth century between eastern and western fields of responsibility.

droungarios: originally the leader of a *droungos* (one thousand men) in the army; later the commander of the fleet at Constantinople.

exkoubitor: member of the *Exkoubitores,* a corps of bodyguards founded by Leo I in ca. 460 (from Latin *excubitor*).

hebdomarios: an official on weekly duty.

hikanatissa: the wife of a *hikanatos* (member of a military corps attested in the ninth and tenth centuries), or the wife of a man from the Hikanatos family.

illoustrios: the highest title of senators in the late Roman and early Byzantine Empires (from Latin *illustris*).

kourator: the manager of an imperial domain.

kouropalates: a high-ranking court dignity (from Latin *cura palatii*) in the sixth to tenth centuries, mainly conferred on members of the imperial family and foreign princes.

logistes: an imperial inspector of accounts.

magistros: a high-ranking title derived from the Latin *magister officiorum* (the "master of the offices") of the early Byzantine period, but not connected to a public office any more.

manglabites: a member of the *Manglabitai,* a corps of bodyguards first appearing in the ninth century, named after their cudgels *(manglabion).*

nomisma: Greek name of the *solidus,* the Roman gold coin that was struck from the fourth to the tenth centuries with unaltered weight and purity at a rate of 72 to a Roman pound, thus weighing about 4.5 grams.

parakoimomenos: literally, "who sleeps beside (the emperor's chamber)"; in the ninth and tenth centuries the highest court position, usually reserved for eunuchs. Although the title is not safely attested before the eighth century, it was often anachronistically used for prominent eunuchs at the imperial court since the reign of Constantine I, begin-

ning with the legendary *parakoimomenos* Euphratas (mentioned here in 1.58 and 65).

praipositos: chamberlain; in the early Byzantine period the highest-ranking eunuch serving the emperor (from Latin *praepositus sacri cubiculi* = head of the sacred bedchamber); in the middle Byzantine period his functions were taken over by the *parakoimomenos.*

protasekretis: the "first *asekretis,*" or head of the imperial chancery.

protobestiarios: the "first *bestiarios*" (Latin *vestiarius*), or head of the imperial wardrobe, a high Byzantine court position, mostly reserved for eunuchs.

protospatharios: originally the head of the *spatharioi,* a corps of imperial bodyguards; the *protospatharios* became a high court dignity from the eighth century onward and was granted to provincial governors and senior generals; see *Oxford Dictionary of Byzantium* 3:1748.

quaestor: a high-ranking court official who supervised financial affairs.

silentiarios: the master of ceremonies at the imperial court, responsible for order and silence (*silentium,* in Latin) during audiences in the early Byzantine period; later transformed into a purely honorific dignity.

strategos: In antiquity the highest official in a Greek or Roman city; in the Byzantine period, the governor or commander of a *thema* (military districts that virtually replaced the Roman provinces from the late seventh century on).

tourma: a military unit (Latin *turma*), and also a subdivision of a *thema.*

tourmarches: the commander of a *tourma.*

vigla: the "guard" (from Latin *vigilia*); an elite unit of the Byzantine army created in the late eighth century, responsible for the safety of the emperor in the palace and on campaign.

Bibliography

EDITIONS AND TRANSLATIONS

Berger, Albrecht, *Untersuchungen zu den Patria Konstantinupoleos.* Ποικίλα Βυζαντινά, 8. Bonn, 1988. Includes an annotated German translation of Books 1 (from chap. 51), 2, and 3 of the *Patria.*

Cameron, Averil, and Judith Herrin. *Constantinople in the Early Eighth Century. The Parastaseis Syntomoi Chronikai. Introduction, Translation and Commentary.* Columbia Studies in the Classical Tradition 10. Leiden, 1984. Includes Greek text based on Preger and English translation.

Mango, Cyril, ed. and tr. *The Art of the Byzantine Empire 312–1453. Sources and Documents.* Englewood Cliffs, N.J., 1972, pp. 96–102. Partial English translation of *Diegesis* (Book 4).

Preger, Theodor, ed. *Scriptores originum constantinopolitanarum.* Leipzig, 1901–1907. Edition of Greek text with full critical apparatus. Vol. 1 contains Hesychios, the *Parastaseis,* and the *Diegesis;* vol. 2, the *Patria* as translated here, plus additional chapters of Books 1 and 4.

Vitti, Evangelia, ed. *Die Erzählung über den Bau der Hagia Sophia in Konstantinopel. Kritische Edition mehrerer Versionen.* Bochumer Studien zur neugriechischen und byzantinischen Philologie 8. Amsterdam, 1986.

SECONDARY LITERATURE

Anderson, Benjamin. "Classified Knowledge: The Epistemology of Statuary in the Parastaseis Syntomoi Chronikai." *Byzantine and Modern Greek Studies* 35 (2011): 1–19.

Berger, Albrecht. "Regionen und Straßen im frühen Konstantinopel." *Istanbuler Mitteilungen* 47 (1997): 349–414.

Ciggaar, Krijne. "Une description de Constantinople traduite par un pèlerin anglais." *Revue des études byzantines* 24 (1976): 211–67.

Dagron, Gilbert. *Constantinople imaginaire. Études sur le recueil des Patria.* Bibliothèque byzantine, Études 8. Paris, 1984. Includes an annotated French translation of the *Diegesis* (Book 4).

Ehrhard, Marcelle. "Le livre du pèlerin d'Antoine de Novgorod." *Romania* 63 (1932): 44–65.

Halkin, François. "Une nouvelle vie de Constantin dans un légendier de Patmos." *Analecta Bollandiana* 77 (1959): 63–107.

James, Liz. "'Pray Not to Fall into Temptation and Be on Your Guard': Pagan Statues in Christian Constantinople." *Gesta* 35 (1996): 12–20.

Kaldellis, Anthony. "Hesychios of Miletos." *Brill's New Jacoby:* http://referenceworks.brillonline.com/entries/brill-s-new-jacoby/hesychios-of-miletos-390-a390. Includes Greek text and English translation.

——. "The Works and Days of Hesychios the Illoustrios of Miletos." *Greek, Roman, and Byzantine Studies* 45 (2005): 381–403.

Maas, Michael. *John Lydus and the Roman Past: Antiquarianism and Politics in the Age of Justinian.* London, 1992.

Majeska, George P. *Russian Travelers to Constantinople in the Fourteenth and Fifteenth Centuries.* Dumbarton Oaks Studies 19. Washington, D.C., 1984.

Mango, Cyril. "Byzantine Writers on the Fabric of Hagia Sophia." In *Hagia Sophia from the age of Justinian to the Present,* edited by Robert Mark and Ahmet S. Çakmak, 41–56. Cambridge, 1992.

Preger, Theodor, "Beiträge zur Textgeschichte der Πάτρια Κωνσταντινουπόλεως." *Programm des kgl. Maximilians-Gymnasiums 1894/95.* Munich, 1895.

——. "Die Erzählung vom Bau der Hagia Sophia." *Byzantinische Zeitschrift* 10 (1901): 455–76.

Opitz, Hans Georg. "Die Vita Constantini des Codex Añgelicus 22." *Byzantion* 22 (1934): 535–93.

Scheer, Tanja. *Mythische Vorväter.* Munich, 1993.

Seeck, Otto, ed. *Notitia dignitatum.* Berlin, 1876.

Index

church of, at Ta Olybriou, 2.26,
3.60; church of, at Petra, 3.67;
monastery of, at Petri(o)n,
App2.2, 3.186
Euphemia (sister of Leo I), 2.3
Euphemia (wife of Justin I), 2.26,
3.183
Euphratas (*parakoimomenos*), 1.58,
1.65
Euphrosyne (sister of Michael III),
3.77
Eusebios (patrician), 3.110
Eustathios, Saint, church of, 3.154
Eustorgios, 1.58
Eutropios (*protospatharios* and
quaestor), 3.166
Eutropios (sophist), 1.58
Eutropios, harbor of, 3.166, 3.185
Eutyches (archimandrite and her-
etic), 2.89a, App2.4
Eutychianos (chief of chancellery),
1.58
Eutychios (patriarch of Constanti-
nople, 552–565, 577–582), App2.5,
4.6, 4.27
Eve, statue of, 2.87
Exakioni(o)n, 1.53, 1.68, 1.73, 2.54,
2.56, 3.10, 3.210
Exkoubita (in the Great Palace),
1.59

Famine, statue of, 2.87
Fausta (wife of Constantine the
Great), 2.93
Fifth Gate, 3.317
Firmillianus, 2.76, 2.104a

Forty Martyrs, Saints, church of,
3.46; at the Konstantianai, 3.55
Forum of Constantine, 1.44, 1.68,
2.16, 2.18, 2.20, 2.43, 2.49, 2.100,
2.102, 2.102a, 2.103, 3.10–12,
3.206, 3.211; porphyry column,
2.45, 2.106, 3.132
Furnaces (bath), 1.39

Gainas (patrician), 3.109
Galates, 3.178
Galen (doctor and philosopher),
2.46
Galen (*quaestor*), 2.96
Gallery (in the Hippodrome), 2.76,
2.104a
Gallienus (Roman emperor, 260–
268), 2.66
Gallos (caesar, d. 354), 2.28
Gastria (monastery), 3.4
Gauls, Gaul, 1.41, 2.48
Gelimer (Vandal king), 2.17
Genikon, 1.60
George, Saint, church of: in
Chalkedon, 3.208; at Ta Galatou,
3.178; at Ta Sphorakiou, 3.30
Geragathe, 3.68
Geranion (in the Great Palace),
1.60
Germanos (patrician), 3.141
Golden Gate, 1.73, 2.35, 2.58, 2.58a,
3.215, 4.11
Golden Hall (in the Great Palace),
3.126
Golden Tiles (church), 3.164
Gorgon, 2.3, 2.28, 2.46, 2.85